New Hampshire Name Changes 1923-1947

Richard P. Roberts

HERITAGE BOOKS
2006

HERITAGE BOOKS
AN IMPRINT OF HERITAGE BOOKS, INC.

Books, CDs, and more—Worldwide

For our listing of thousands of titles see our website
at
www.HeritageBooks.com

Published 2006 by
HERITAGE BOOKS, INC.
Publishing Division
65 East Main Street
Westminster, Maryland 21157-5026

Copyright © 2005 Richard P. Roberts

All rights reserved. No part of this book may be reproduced or transmitted in any form or by any means, electronic or mechanical, including photocopying, recording or by any information storage and retrieval system without written permission from the author, except for the inclusion of brief quotations in a review.

International Standard Book Number: 978-0-7884-3270-2

INTRODUCTION

This book is a sequel to the New Hampshire Name Changes, 1768-1923 published by Heritage Books, Inc. in 1996. That work covered many name changes made by Acts of the General Court, probate courts and superior courts during the years indicated and includes members of many of the earliest families of the state.

The information contained in this book is taken from the compiled lists of name changes that were published in the various session laws of the General Court. The contents of those lists were provided pursuant to statute and printed with those session laws in the sections indicated in the footnotes. After 1947, the requirement of publication apparently was repealed.

Many of the name changes reflected in the following pages demonstrate the demographic changes in the state's population and the influx of immigrants from various other nations. Many of the others simply are the product of a divorce or an adoption. In either case, the compilation of these name changes should provide a useful tool for genealogists seeking a missing link or breaking through the proverbial brick wall.

Bear in mind that the massive number of names in the lists lends itself to typographical and other errors, particularly since these lists had probably been transcribed and retranscribed two or three times before now. The risk is particularly great in connection with the names of some of the European immigrants whose names were Anglicized after their arrival.

TABLE OF CONTENTS

Introduction   1

<u>Name Changes</u>
1923-1925   5
1925-1927   14
1927-1929   23
1929-1931   32
1931-1933   41
1933-1935   50
1935-1937   60
1937-1939   70
1939-1941   82
1941-1943   97
1943-1945   120
1945-1947   141

Index of Surnames   165

January 1923 - January 1925[1/]

Name changes made by the probate courts:

Rockingham County - Isaac Leonard Peal to Leonard Elkins Pearl; John Francis Kubiak to Donald Lawrence Lapoint; Charlotte Lucretia Gladding to Charlotte Lucretia Massey; Vivan M. Butcher to Vivian M. Stone; Bernard Arnold Robertson to Bernard Arnold Lexner; Walter Michael Radigan to Walter Michael Roach; Louise E. Meeks to Louise Edith Wyman; Murray Nelson to Nelson Peneault; Esther Eleanor Theg to Esther Eleanor MacDonald; Thelma Irene Richards to Ann Shelton; Frances Stack to Frances Shirley Longley; Bernice Connors to Ethel Shirley Tremblay; Charles Moore to Ralph Marc DesRosiers; Mary Lenora Monroe to Mary Lenora Gallacher; Dora Pearl Nichols to Dora Pearl Tibbetts; Mabel J. Odiorne to Mabel J. Trecartin; Robert Whitney Wilson to Robert Whitney Tuck; Loren Bailey McLachlan to Loren Bailey; Doris Jones to Doris Smith; Mary E. Varrell to Mary E. Belcher; Margaret M. Greenwood to Margaret M. Gilman; Francis Edward Fournier to Francis Edward Lemay; Edith Adams to Edith Adams Baine; Frances P. Tucker to Frances Johnson Peirce; Leon Eugene Hardy to Leon Eugene Abbott; Lillian Elizabeth Whittier to Elizabeth Frances Kimball; Stella Bilat to Josephine Stella Pilarczyk

Strafford County - Vasileke Papageorge to Vasileke Baras (adpt.); Eva Marion Moody to Eva Marion Pearson (adpt.); Hugh MacNeil to Herbert Edwin MacNeil; Rose Spinney to Rose Audrey Roxbee (adpt.); Sarah E. Webber to Maida S. Webber; Kriakos Georgion to Kyriakos Theodore Chigres; Louis Napoleon Emond to Louis Napoleon Emmons; Ruth Feris to Ruth Hurd; Frances Pauline Rouckey to Arlene Frances O'Leary (adpt.); Ronald T. Marsh to Forrest Linwood Marsh; Robert Freeman Hall to Robert Freeman Rowe (adpt.); May Myrh to Vemba May Braudis (adpt.); "Son of Annie Cleary" to Charles Henry Jewell (adpt.); Vivian G. Gregoire to Vivian G. Bickford

Belknap County - Lillian I. Joudry to Lillian Joudry Rollins (adpt.); Arthur L. Brown to Arthur L. Fogg (adpt.); Eunice S. Young to Eunice S. McIntyre; Charles Edward Dennis to Charles Smith Marsh (adpt.); Mary

---

[1/]   Chapter 269, 1925 N. H. Public Laws

1923-1925

Dennis to Mary Alice Dennis (adpt.); Norma Trowridge to Norma Bowlby (adpt.); Ruth Louise LaCourse to Ruth Louise Gilpatric (adpt.); Alice Lillian Thomas to Alice Lillian Pierce; Eunice Austin Thomas to Eunice Austin Pierce; Henry Trembly diMercier to Henry Trembly; Winnie I. Starr to Winnie I. Sherburne; Almon Kelly to William Albert Kelley; Frederick Landry to Frederick Nelson Seaver (adpt.); Clifton A. Smith to Clifton A. Ferguson (adpt.); Thelma A. Aston to Thelma A. Seeley; John Joseph Cummings to John Joseph McDonough (adpt.); Sidney Milton Balch to Sidney Milton Wooldridge (adpt.); Rex F. Cotton to Reginald F. Cotton; Roger Sanders to Roger Cone (adpt.); Bernice Mae Huckins to Bernice Mae Hoadley (adpt.); Dorothy Vigina Wells to Dorothy Vigina Wells (adpt.); Maude E. Dame to Maude E. Sleeper; Thelma D. Place to Thelma D. Place (adpt.); Charles L. Place to Charles L. Place (adpt.); Emery Fountain to Emery Fountain (adpt.)

Carroll County - Robert Vernon Gilman to Robert Vernon Woodward; Mabel Idella Clough to Mabel Idella Tilton; Mary Ruth Martin to Mary Elsie Ruth Duke; Lyndolph Tracy Keefe to Lyndolph Tracy Bowen; Lillian Mary Gouin to Lillian Mary Melanson; Dorothy Hill to Dorothy Sawyer Rogers

Merrimack County - Stanislaw Jermuziah to Stanley Young; Inez N. Calley Ladd to Inez N. Calley; Edward Albert Pichette to Edward Albert Pickett; Louis Emile Pichette to Louis Emile Pickett; Royce Day to Royce Day Kelley; Agnes L. Carder Martin to Agnes L. Horwood Martin; Catherine E. Mead to Catherine E. Morse; Bertha E. Sanborn to Bertha E. Emerson; Charles Francis Pichette to Charles Francis Pickett; Dorothy I. Kelley to Dorothy I. Ford; Addie A. Hamblett to Addie A. Calvert; Frederick Joseph Guymond to Frederick Joseph Bedell; Margaret Jane Kerslake to Margaret Jane Grant; Emilien Pichette to Emilien Pickett; Mary M. Pichette to Mary M. Pickett

Hillsborough County - Paul Gerald Hatzigogas to Paul Gerald Gogas; Ernest James Hatzigogas to Ernest James Gogas; Bertha Lane Currie to Bertha Lane; Ernest F. Floberg to Ernest F. Magnuson; Mary Knopel to Mary Anna Pfeiffer; Agnes Melina Grant to Agnes Melina Wyman; Attilio Santucci to Frank Wilson; Dora L. Wellman to Dora L. Merrill; Verona F. Allen to Verona F. Burnham; Mildred E. Brown to Mildred E. Loveren; Rose Cohen to Roslyn Kahn; Robert Leon Cohen to Robert

1923-1925

Leon Kahn; Sarah Cohen to Sarah Kahn; Benjamin Louis Cohen to Benjamin Louis Kahn; Charles John Johnson to Costas John Prutsalis; Arthur John Johnston to Arthur John Prutsalis; Bridget McCabe to Beatrice McCabe; James Quackenbush to Henry LaPlante; Walter C. Padelinetti to Walter C. Padell; Harold E. Heacock to Harold E. Johnson; Mary A. Huntoon to Mary A. Thompson; Adele Chocquette to Adele Beaudet; Martha E. Merrill to Martha E. Currier; Marie Caroline Clement to Winifred Caroline Clement; Lauretta Marie Dionne to Lauretta Marie Cote; Beatrice Orvin to Beatrice Wallace; Alberta M. Laroche to Alberta M. Bean; Saheed William to Saheed William Dahar; Thomas Francis Mazza to Anthony Thomas Francis Mazza; O. Veronica Roberts to O. Veronica Demers; Marie L. Boisclair to Lottie L. Cassidy; David Beard to Lawrence Quentin Goodhue; Louisa Coletti to Elizabeth Bell Rollins; Thelma Lambi also known as Thelma Gauthrie to Thelma Madeline Maynard; Ruth Evelyn Madison to Florence Ruth Bickford; Irene Meyer to Barbara Louise Greenhalgh; Stanislawa Kolano to Stanislawa Bednarz; Jennie E. Thompson to Fannie Elisabeth Mitchell; Mary Jane Meiklen to Jean Bellavance; Georges Perrault to Georges Tousignant; Frank Malonay to Frank Nelson Daley; Louise Althea Delaney to Louise Althea Hebert; Cora E. Anderson to Beryle Elizabeth Dubois; Robert Milton Hood to Robert Milton Dion; Florence Margaret Morton to Margaret Morton Haselton; Edouard Beaudoin to Edouard Lareau; Mary Elizabeth Flanders to Mary Elizabeth Osborne; Flora Margaret Flanders to Flora Margaret Osborne; Margaret Ellen Bennett to Margaret Ellen Newman; Thomas F. Fitzgerald to John Francis Gowans; William Richard to William Richard Racette; William Bunton to Herman Francis Cronshaw; Bertha Esther Clement to Bertha Esther Burpee; Mildred Moran to Marie Frances McCarty; Margaret Helen Leistner to Margaret Helen Merrill; Ruth G. Parker to Ruth Parker Carlton; Geraldine Lorraine Jacques to Geraldine Lorraine O'Brien; Robert Wallace to Robert Wallace Nesbit; Phyllis Arba Peaslee to Phyllis Arba Perham; Geraldine Henrietta Peaslee to Geraldine Henrietta Perham; Idella A. Lonergan to Idella A. Totton; Richard Donald Paradie to Richard Donald Ireland; Marcell Robinson Pecker to Marcell Robinson Pecker Parker; Felix Couture to Felix Laliberte; Louise Gardner Downing to Louise Gardner Sturtevant; Charles Beard to Westley G. Rollins, Jr.; Raymond MacGillivray to William F. Devine; Alphee Toupin to Alphee Delisle; Elphege Toupin to Elphege Toupin Duval; Alice Toupin to Alice Toupin Duval; Russell

1923-1925

Derby to Robert Atherton Randall; Mary Alice Robin to Mary Alice Lillian Roberge; Robert Goulet to John Augustus McCarty; Rodney Belliveau to Rodney Belliveau White; Virginia Hamm to Magela Bellerose; Lionel Huffman to Earnest Winslow Porter; Arthur Elmer Lyon to Arthur Lyon Clement; Jeanne D'Arc Bellemore to Jeanne D'Arc Rioux; Edward James Perkins to Robert Martin Wheatley; Verna May Badger to Verna May Fox; Bernice Arlin Dow to Mary Lillian Duperron; Florence Marion Wood to Florence Wood Rolland; Pauline Palm to Pauline Tufts; Joseph Stanislas Aryell to Gerald Joseph Stanislas Caron; Mary Rita Burke to Mary Rita Smith; Barbara Louise Carter to Barbara Louise Farrell; Francis D. Charpentier to Roger A. Roy; Muriel Johnson to Muriel Eva Merrill; Herbert Speney to Dickian Michael Bakaian; Francis Smith to Thomas T. Clair; Frances Constine to Beatrice Chevrette; Ruth E. Thompson to Ruth E. Hatch; Avonia M. Goethnee to Avonia M. Rogers; Vela Georgianna Arell to Georgianna Gartner; Illie Brandt to Marguerite Schunemann; Murial May Duke to Murial May Emroy; Charles Francis Stone to Charles Francis Wheeler

<u>Cheshire County</u> - Sybil Emeline Pillsbury to Sybil Emeline Sawyer; Edgar Junior Manuel to John Badger Leitch; Minnie Evans Manuel to Ruth Ann Leitch; Irene Isabel Ingell Baker to Irene Isabel Ingell; Louis Noel Lavender to Louis Noel Fosburgh; Beatrice Marie Slack to Bernice Elizabeth Anderson; Bernice Elizabeth Anderson to Bernice Elizabeth Maxwell; Ferdinand Desoto Coffin to Ferdinand Desoto Kenney; Maxwell V. Burpee to Maxwell Burpee Lambert; Ethel Mae Frederick to Ethel Mae Kenney; Beulah Pomeroy to Delia Alice Armstrong; Virginia Willard to Virginia Hardy; Ruth Lena Ingram to Ruth Lena Goodrich; Ruth Shackette to Ruth Clark; Martha E. Fairbanks to Martha E. Rich; Harold Lloyd Weeks to Harold Francis Pasno; ----- Collins to Franklin Shedd Austin; Forest Everett Jaquith to Forest Everett Burbee; Vivian Orrie Worcester to Vivian Orrie Buswell; Jasper Brown Wheeler to Jasper Wheeler Hunt; George Edward Sawtelle to George Frank Sawtelle; Harold Loyd MacLean to Harold Loyd Nason; Dorothy June Leahy to Dorothy June Wetherbee; Lauretta Turcotte to Laurette Boufford; Ernesto Amato Solari to Ernesto Amato Oliver; Robert O. Roundy to Robert William Paddock; Aramildo Portia Colburn to Aramilda Portia Johnson; Albert Dustin to Walter Cyrus Bunker

1923-1925

Sullivan County - Earlena Frances Densmore to Earlena Densmore Wright; Frances Geraldine Page to Frances Geraldine Costello; Orrin Calvin Doolittle to Orrin Calvin Whitney; Robert Eugene Clement to Robert Eugene Hayward; Shirley Davis to Ruth Libby; Dorothy Emma Carley to Dorothy Belle Cook; Phyllis E. Lewis to Phyllis E. Johnson; Ada G. Johnson to Ada G. Colby; Arthur Warren Guyer to Arthur Warren Barrows; Evelyn Aurore Guyer to Evelyn Aurore Barrows; Rose Emma Guyer to Rose Emma Barrows; Eileen Margaret Guyer to Eileen Margaret Barrows; Theresa Guyer to Theresa Barrows; Herbert Gardner Bemis to Herbert Milton Swan; Vernon Franklin Kingsbury to Theodore Vernon Thompson; Ruth Elder to Ruth MacAdams; Gorden Elder to Gordon MacAdams; Jacob N. Shulinsky to Jacob M. Shulins; Richard Johnson to Richard Osborne

Grafton County - Howard Avery to Howard Avery Stickney; Paul Boyan to Paul Jobin; Josephine Annabelle Calef to Josephine Annabelle Chamberlin; Lydia E. Cossar to Mildred Eliza Ham; Hazel V. Chamberlin to Hazel V. Tatro; Malcom George Campbell to Malcom George Lucia; Madelene M. Day to Madelene M. Day; Helen Beatrice Downing to Helen Beatrice Russell; Mary Guyette to Mary M. Wilcox; Mona A. Gitchell to Mona A. Palmer; Mary Helen Hill to Mary Helen Teel; Verna M. Homan to Verna M. Record; Pauline E. Harper to Pauline E. Johnson; Luella Holt to Luella MacDonald; Stanislaus Carl Kuszewski to Carl Stanley Smith; Clara Bertha Kuszewski to Clara Bertha Smith; Clara E. Ledoux to Clara Margaret Elizabeth Gray; Stella G. Lindsay to Stella G. Stuart; James Madison Magoon to James Madison Jackson; Francis L. Murphy to James Hutchinson Wallace; Flora N. Nash to Flora N. Sleeper; Gertrude F. Neil to Barbara Louise Dearth; Harold Porter to Harold Porter Jewell; Edwin Leroy Predue to Edwin Leroy Fisher; Dorothy Pearl Place to Dorothy Pearl Young; Martha Flanders Page to Martha Flanders; Ellen B. Quigley to Ellen A. Barker; Louis Stolovsky to Louis Stahl; Nathan Stolovaky to Nathan Stahl; Robert Thomas Smith to Robert Thomas Turner; Della E. Sargent to Della E. Smith; Gertrude Tucker to Gertrude Marguerite Merrill; Muriel L. Thibedeau to Muriel L. Carroll; Walter Tuzik to Walter McManus; Earl Delbert Thomas to Earl Delbert Harvey

Coos County - Edward Hills to Edward Hills Gray; Dean W. Gadwah to Dean W. Smith; Maude E. Ricker to Maude E. McGettrick; Lula Ann

1923-1925

Dunn to Lula Ann Briggs; Alice Rose Lalerle to Alice Rose Berube; Albion Albertus Alden to Albion Alden Perkins; Clifford Lyman Palmer to Clifford Lyman Annis; Austin Robert Simpson to Austin Robert Carr; Louise Lupiers to Louise Buckley; Audrey Elizabeth Kane to Audrey Elizabeth Cole; Alfred L. Lebelle to Alfred L. Schoff; Kenneth Parsons to Robert Edwin Tyrrell; Lawrence Elwin Cantin to Lawrence Elwin Wilson; Ronald Hermann to Joseph Colin Pushee; Cecil Alvah Dale to Alvah Dale; Ila S. Brown to Ila Schoff; Thomas Edward Hanes to Thomas Edward Dorman; Octave Deslauriers to Philip Carpenter; Jessie Constantine to Jessie Gessner; Lottie E. Boutwell to Lottie E. Spaulding

Name changes made by the superior court in divorce proceedings:

Rockingham County - Nellie E. Fogg to Nellie E. Seymore; Mable P. Peck to Mabel P. Webster; Helen N. B. Emery to Helen N. Brooks; Flora L. Krieger to Flora L. Bretschneider; Gertrude J. Young to Gertrude Frances Johnson; Pearl Higgins to Pearl Osgood; Bernice I. Charron alias Sharron to Bernice I. Buzzelle; Sarah L. Chase to Sarah L. Eaton; Eva Belle Loftus to Eva Belle Jenkins; Dora J. Harness to Dora Jordan; Margaret A. Shuttleworth to Margaret A. Howe; Helen M. Redlon to Helen M. Oliver; Melissa Berthiaume to Melissa T. Cook; Beatrice E. Burnett to Beatrice E. Macia; Grace R. Steele to Grace Ruany Williamson; Maud Dynkowski to Maud Wilcox; Ethel Holmgren to Ethel B. Watt; Mary Simon to Mary Anton; Waldyslaw Polchlopek to Walter Polchlopek (sic); Eva M. McGarr to Eva Maynard; Florence L. Day to Florence Louise Emerson; Phyllis V. Barclay to Phyllis V. Worden; Ethel M. Prescott to Ethel M. Johnson; Margaret Hale to Margaret Pickering; Mary Emma Glover to Mary Emma Sanborn; Bessie B. Osgood to Bessie Belle Ham; Anne P. Ramesdell to Anne P. Wallace; Agnes M. Chapman to Agnes M. Cornish; Katherine J. Smart to Katherine J. Mack

Strafford County - Esther M. Weeks to Esther M. Jenness; Hazel E. Abraham to Hazel E. Williams; Mabel E. Gotts to Mabel E. Thompson; Flora May Hayes to Flora May Shattuck; Edna F. Allen to Edna F. Hurd; Anna Isabel Ruel to Anna Isabel Roxbee; Sarah E. Coskoran to Sarah E. Brean; Rosa E. Foss to Rosa E. Herbert; Teresa E. Babb to

1923-1925

Teresa E. Pratt; Mabel E. Churchill to Mabel E. Joy; Doris Wallace to Doris Desmarais; Edna J. Murray to Edna J. Dearborn; Josephine Colell to Josephine Harb; Agnes E. Corson to Agnes E. Rogers; Mary Ellen McCarthy to Mary Ellen Sullivan; Catherine Carras to Catherine Rossiter; Florence Etta Gilman to Florence Etta Rollins; Maggie McMillan to Maggie McRae; Elsie M. Thompson to Elsie M. Dennett; Margaret Britton to Margaret Spellman

Belknap County - Elizabeth A. Horne to Elizabeth A. Bouley; Mildred Francis Davis to Mildred Francis Roberts; Rena E. Landry to Rena E. Bartlett

Carroll County - Edith S. Jacobs to Edith S. Caverly; Lottie F. Dearborne to Lottie F. Irish; Bernice F. Whitfield to Bernice F. Lane; Ella G. Watson to Ella G. Merrill

Merrimack County - Frances E. Hodgdon to Frances E. Willcox; Doris L. Clifford to Doris L. Cota; Ruth A. Sargent to Ruth A. Bucklin; Gladys M. Bingham to Gladys M. Stewart; Myra F. Kennedy to Myra F. Collins; Doris L. Carkin to Doris L. Clough; Emma Alice Arbour to Emma Alice Magee; Grace A. Pethick to Grace A. Cole; Leona C. Sisk to Leona C. Huntoon; Frances G. Brazier to Frances G. Sefton; Elsie Viola Bishop to Elsie Viola Parsons; Nora Gillespie Kelly to Nora Gillespie; Rose A. Roy to Rose A. Dorval

Hillsborough County - Lelia May Heyl to Lelia May Hayes; Emma McMillan Tergis to Emma McMillan; Etterlelar A. Pelletier; to Etterlelar A. Fitch; Angie F. Duncan to Angie F. Barker; Jane Dinwoodie Fitzgerald to Jane Dinwoodie; Esther Roberts to Esther Reardon; Yvonne Pelletier to Yvonne Lessard; Annie Graff to Annie Newton; Ella C. Ayer to Ella C. Stacy; Rose Poehlman to Rose Gelinas; Stella Richmond to Stella M. Boardman; Evelyn E. Harrison to Evelyn E. Johnson; Catherine E. Johnston to Catherine E. Whitlock; Rosalia Swietuk to Rosalia Melenkwich; Dorothy MacD. Rausch to Dorothy Florence MacDonald; Agnes P. Kendall to Agnes Pauline Donah; Ella S. Webber to Ella S. Jones; Bertha M. George to Bertha E. Magee; Madeline E. Reed to Madeline Perkins; Ethelyn Rice Chase to Ethelyn Alfreda Rice; Jessie Paton Crosby to Jessie Paton; Adeline Bourassa to Adeline Barrett; Evangelia A. Kaperonis to Evangelia T. Caldara;

1923-1925

Florida Lambert Chabot to Florida Lambert; Margaret S. Kelliher to Margaret S. Keefe; Hazel M. Cheney to Hazel M. Maker; Etta Bailey to Etta Morison; Florence Elizabeth Gerry to Florence Elizabeth Bruce; Eva A. Foss to Eva A. Ouellette; Marguerite A. Clark to Marguerite A. Greene; Rose Lavoie to Rose Lefebvre; Agnes M. LaMountain to Agnes M. McCann; Hazel E. Knight to Hazel E. Roy; Lillian Estelle Thompson to Lillian E. Moir; Madeline L. McSweeney to Madeline L. Carlson; Brunislawa Chiesinski to Brunislawa Futyra; Harriet B. Perkins to Harriet B. Morse; Rose B. Lapointe to Rose B. Lamy; C. Pearl Devoll to C. Pearl Maxwell; Marie Moulaert to Marie DeVlaminck; Delia P. Faucher to Delia P. Bennett; Thelma G. Soper to Thelma G. Conery; Bernice Merlin to Bernice Young

Cheshire County - Wilma G. Blanchard to Wilma G. Damon; Leda Orlene Peroskas to Leda Orlene Hurley; G. Madeleine Crossley to G. Madeleine Quinn; Hazel K. Holbrook to Hazel K. Eastwood; Beatrice L. Oliver to Beatrice L. Jordan; Ivy E. Aptt to Ivy E. Ashcroft; Celia M. Mansfield to Celia M. Roy; Hattie E. Bean to Hattie Emma Kimball; Doris N. Gates to Doris M. Cole; Charlotte E. Ells to Charlotte E. Larner; Anna M. Blair to Anna M. Gannon; Erma O. Patno to Erma I. Olmstead; Esther Brannock to Esther Royce

Sullivan County - Marguerite W. George to Marguerite W. Putnam; Georgia E. Weyant to Georgia Empey; Eliza Touchette to Eliza Boucher; Eva L. Dunbar to Eva L. Melendy; Helen Baxter Hanson to Helen Baxter Thrasher; Eva A. Lambert to Eva A. Simano

Grafton County - Helen Griffin Gober to Helen Griffin; Marie A. Bednard to Marie Lachat; Elizabeth H. Witt to Elizabeth H. Devino; Dorothy A. Smith to Dorothy A. Miller; Mary A. Morton to Mary A. Pride; Elsie E. Delaney to Elsie E. Proctor; Florence B. Chalmers to Florence B. Wells; Margaret H. Greene to Margaret H. Webb; Betsy Kinne to Betsy Johnson; Mary Rebecca Everet to Mary Rebecca Crabb; Mary E. Batchelder to Mary B. Tippett; Exilda Mikowski to Exilda Sanville; Jessie M. Perkins to Jessie M. Davis; Elizabeth P. Marden to Elizabeth M. Pickering; Bulah C. Marsh to Bulah C. Cutting; Bertha E. Kimball to Bertha E. Braynard; Eva M. Marcotte to Eva M. Dunham; Rosilda E. Emerson to Rosilda E. Gagnon; Nora S. Emerson to Nora S. Spooner; Ferne E. Smith to Ferne E. Thomas; Elizabeth I. Clement to Elizabeth

1923-1925

I. Barker; Ella D. Barnhart to Ella Pierce; Edna A. Ayers to Edna A. Bradford; Elsie L. Giguere to Elsie L. Watson

Coos County - Jennie M. Proof to Jennie M. Spinney; Alica L. Towle to Alica L. Gordon; Pearle Lillian Tripp to Pearl Lillian Campbell

January 1925 - January 1927[2/]

Name changes made by the probate courts:

Rockingham County - John P. Currier to John P. Wheeler; Margaret E. Currier to Margaret E. Wheeler; Dorothy C. Stickeny to Dorothy Carter; Vera O. Wade to Vera O. Eastman; Roy Herbert Perkins to Roy Herbert Cutting; Theodore Politopoulos to Theodore N. Pullos; Jemeely Peter Sarkise to Jemeely Peter Hashim; Peter Sarkise to Peter Sarkise Hashim; Abbie E. Cate to Abbie E. Hartford; Joseph W. Kalinsky to Joseph W. Kalens; Ellen F. McDonough to Ellen F. Wilson; George Carl Brassard to George Carl Price; Perley C. Osborn to Perley C. Warden; Sadie M. Olson to Sadie M. Levesque; Jeannette E. Zimmerman to Jeannette E. Saylor; Frank Demarski to Frank Herman Schultz; Lillian Mary Demarski to Lillian Mary Schultz; Frederick Edward Ham to Frederick Edward Pike; John Sidebottom to John Joseph Burkhardt; William Edgar Strickland to William Edgar Welch; Marion R. Corthell to Marion Corthell Brown; Albert Sumner Eastman to Robert Deane Eastman; Lester William Newell to Lester William White; Flora M. Noyes to Flora May Gleason; Burton Jenness Caswell to Junior Caswell Bartlett; Muriel Arlene Caswell to Muriel Arlene Bartlett; Barbara May Hussey to Barbara May Duke; Mary Pratt to Mary Waterhouse; Mary Edith Rice to Mary Edith Pike; Octavia Durette to Octavia Beaudet; William Powers to Miles Herbert Maltby, Jr.; Arthur M. Coleman to Arthur Coleman Sherburne; Ralph E. Goad to Ralph E. Huddell; Norma A. Goad to Norma A. Huddell; Joseph Ovide Chapdelaine to Joseph Ovide Belanger; Lillian Adeline Manning to Ruby May Otis

Strafford County - Vivian G. Gregoire to Vivian G. Bickford; Helen Palardy to Beulah Ellen Locke; Harold Franklin Dorr to Harold Franklin Roberts; Peter Pappas to Peter Adamopoulos; Rita Millette to Bettey W. Nutter; Sadie Helen Brown to Helen Louise Scott; Russell Theodore Ham to Theodore Russell Therrien; Mescal Louise Shupe to Mescal Louise Robinson; James Warrington Bryson to James Rowland Bryson; Barbara Palm to Barbara Ruth Nason; Mathias Christopoulos to Mathias Brown; Katherine Christopoulos to Katherine Brown; Bernice Brown to Bernice Bassett; Lester Gordon Stickney to Lester

---

2/   Chapter 203, 1927 N. H. Public Laws

1925-1927

to Mathias Brown; Katherine Christopoulos to Katherine Brown; Bernice Brown to Bernice Bassett; Lester Gordon Stickney to Lester Irving Piper; Rachel Louise Rowe to Rachel Martha Shaw; Dora Andreanopoulos to Dora Papageorge; Florence O. Perkins to Martha Florence Osborne; Mary E. Burley to Mary E. Sterling; Eugene Driscoll to Eugene McIntire; Marylon Arlena Harrell to Marylon Arlena Twombly

Belknap County - Ola M. London to Ola M. Ash; Ernest Grant to Robert Stuart Foster (adpt.); Kenneth Grant to Kenneth James Foster (adpt.); Meredith Everett Chase to Frederick James Terrill (adpt.); Florence L. Baxter to Florence Baxter Rowe; Nellie May Lessard to Nellie May Skinner; William H. Haskell to Edward William Fogg (adpt.); Norma Bowlby to Norma Trowbridge (adpt.); Christine Louise Coffin to Christine Louise Sanborn (adpt.); Bernice Delphia Therrian to Bernice Delphia Eryou; Howard Robert MacIntosh to Howard Robert Lyman (adpt.); Eleanor Bailey to Eleanor B. Shepard; Robert Densmore to Robert Densmore Smith (adpt.); John Turgeon to Lionel Corno (adpt.); Ethel F. King to Ethel King Cross; Willard Aulcott Snow to Willard Auclott Jessup (adpt.); Guennlyn Weeks Smith to Guennlyn Simpson (adpt.); Charlotte May Ford to Charlotte May McLane (adpt.); Dorene Evelyn Chase to Dorene Evelyn Batchelder (adpt.); Charlie Nicholas Peter to George Nicholas Peter; Joan Eastman to Dorothy Joan Fields (adpt.)

Carroll County - Frances Avery to Frances Thurston; Filene M. Eastman to Filene M. Moody; ----- Warner to Arline Ruth Bodge; Olive Margary Stetson to Olive Margary Merrill

Merrimack County - Alvin Bachelder Edmunds to Alvin Craig Edmunds; Peter John to Peter Kreshpani; John Gunnion to Melvin Heartz; Florence M. Corriveau to Florence M. Leroux; Marion Baratelli to Marion Baratelli Lancisi; Sylvia Dennerly to Lillian Brown; Doris L. Mozroll to Doris L. Currier; Addie Maria Dearborn to Dorothy Adelaide Dearborn; Zelma Cleola Smith to Zelma Cleola Baillie; Eva Mae Haines to Evelyn Mae Haines; Mildred L. Randall to Jean Laska Randall; James Pano Anastas to Gure Pano; Ella Augusta Holmes to Helen Eastman Holmes; Laura Kathleen Johnson to Laura Kathleen Porter; Clara I. Brown to Clara I. Tuttle; Carrie V. Osgood to Carrie V. Willard; Esther S. Nelson to Esther S. Eastman; Dorothy Fay Woods to Dorothy

1925-1927

Fay Fosberg; Catherine Quimby to Catherine Quimby Taylor; Eugene Guevin to Joseph Wilfred Robert Raymond; Charlotte Mary Lashua to Charlotte Mary Daniell; Delina Duvernay to Mary Dorothy Delina Raymond; Gertrude M. Sanborn to Evelyn M. Vadney; Hazel Ellen Sanborn to Hazel Ellen Lessard; Phylis Mae Prince to Phylis Mae Cross; Constance Louise Hazelton to Constance Louise Hill; Henry M. Bessette, Jr. to Henry Thorp Corson; Helen Irene Black to Agnes Irene Cheney; Florence Elizabeth Clarke to Florence Elizabeth Grant; Kathleen Mackay to Sarah Elizabeth Weed; Irene Mary Foskett to Irene Foskett Fowler; Constance Riel to Constance Riel Poliquin; William Place to John Brenton Bare; Donald Robert Bird to Duane Bruce Rockwell; Hazel Lillian Madeline Tibbetts to Hazel Lillian Madeline McClintock; Margaret Fitzgerald to Sherlie Burt Brown; James Edward Venette to Paul Parker Metcalf; Joseph Raymond Bonin to Raymond Ordway; Ralph George Nokes to Ralph George Gallagher; ----- Knowlton to Fay Knowlton; Roger Donald Knapp to Robert Daniel Caverly; Rose Labrecque to Laura Frances Murphy

<u>Hillsborough County</u> - Robert E. Chagnon to Robert E. Cleary; Phyllis May Dunbar to Muriel Hazel Goodwin; William Dewey to William M. Stratton; Phrosene Siomas to Phrosene Bitos; Henry Armond to Henry Armond Belisle; Lillian Bunton to Lillian Whitehead; Demetrius Hatzigoga to Demetrius Arthur Koutsonikas; George Crosby to Robert Charles Larmy; Joseph Arthur to Joseph Arthur Cronin; William H. Connor to William H. Northrup; Paul Cross Kidder to Paul Cross; Muriel Anne Hodgman to Harriet Florence Ames; Lillian Gertrude Morton to Lillian Morton Haselton; Agnes Rose to Agnes Rose Juneau; Pauline M. Russell to Pauline L. Fontaine; Mary P. Fortin to Mary H. Sheldon; Paul Schellinger to Paul David Cochran; Marguerite Therese Soucy to Theresa Fournier; Gloria Mitchell to Gloria Belisle; George Alfred Leavitt to George Alfred DeMontigny; Paul Eugene Leavitt to Paul Eugene DeMontigny; Glenna Juanita Haselton to Barbara Helen Patch; Beulah A. Staples to Elaine Boulton; Harry Ferguson to Barr Smith; Efthemios A. Kassraras to Efthemios A. Adamopoulos; Beatrice Owens to Beatrice Owens Menter; Lawrence E. Avery to Lawrence Avery Hawkins; Lillian Gabriel to Lillian Gabriel Moritts; June Maden Estes to June Maden Carrier; John Leslie Estes to John Leslie Carrier; Emma Blanchard to Emma Woodard; Fred G. Scott to Edward Frederick Schroeder; Everett William Lyon to Everett William Linscott;

1925-1927

Ralph Warren to Ralph Warren Strong; Robert Daniel Peach to Robert Daniel Atkinson; Paul Gerard Gogas to Paul Gerard Fletcher; Ernest James Gogas to Ernest James Fletcher; Ethel Grace Gordon to Marie Caroline Prud'homme; Ruth Joyce Fisher to Ruth Joyce Seaver; Eileen Goodwin to Rosalie Laflotte; Dorothy Belle Peach to Dorothy Belle Duncan; William Frank Peach to Arthur William Duncan; Dorothy E. Grant to Dorothy Grant Young; Edward Albert Smith to Edward Albert Hock; Constance Ide to Constance Brailey; Bernice Hardy to Bernice Elizabeth Greene; David J. Humphrey to Arthur Lemuel Whitney; Marie Margaret Duffy to Marie Margaret Farrell; Alfred Couture to Alfred Miller; Evelyn May Griffith to Evelyn Mabel Aldridge; Vernon Howard Chase to Vernon Howard Baker; Josephine Merrill to Josephine Stratton; John F. Pratt to John F. Sheehan; Louise Rhoades to Louise Ellingworth; Joseph Eugene Landry to Joseph Eugene Boisvert; John Kubiszyn to John Joseph Kerby; Leith Darwin Manning to Leith Darwin Gerrish; Edith Soulakiotis to Edith Otis; George Soulakiotis to George Otis; Alexander John Simon to Alexander Simon Malouf; Helen G. Atherton to Helen F. Greeley; Oliva Boisvert to Oliver J. Boisvert; Bridget A. Shea to Bridget A. Blake; Hazel May Dowling to Hazel May Little; Bessie Lue Cottrell to Bessie Lue Cleveland; Darila Basil Dupuis to Fred Dupuis; Luella M. Flagg to Doris M. Flagg; Iva F. Lenz to Iva F. Jennings; Dionysios D. Grimoutes to Daniel D. Grimes; Paraskeve Manouras to Paraskeve Coustas; Gertrude Frances Marsh to Gertrude Frances Towne; Clara Belle Eaton to Clara Belle Rowell; Margaret E. Hamblett to Margaret E. Davis; Charles Irving Harvey to Charles Irving Pentland; Dikran Harry Manissadjian to Dicran Harry Manis; Margaret Swart to Margaret Beason Swart; Elizabeth McQuesten to Elizabeth Swart McQuesten; William Lebel to William Cameron; Albert Starrett to Thomas Robert Starrett; Toivo Edward Liimatainen to Toivo Edward Layman; Kalle Liimatainen to Charles Layman; Michael Akstulewiz to Michael Akstull; Edward P. York to Ollo P. York

<u>Cheshire County</u> - Harold Lloyd Hayes to Harold Francis Peterson; Catherine Orr Bixby to Catherine Orr Sweeney; Jennie L. Bowen to Jennie L. Wheeler; Llewellyn Harrington to Llewellyn LaPage; Alice May Watson to Alice May Barker; Roger Gilman Wheeler to John Wilson Wheeler; Melvin Bernard Tyo to Wallace Elwin Tyo; Dorothy Louise Shufelt to Dorothy Louise Johnson; Amos Fontaine Eola to Arthur Amos Parttinaa; Christine Parker Clark to Christine Gladys

1925-1927

Parker; Addie E. Church to Addie E. Chadwick; James Hayward Batchelder to Peter Hayward Batchelder; Luigi Barbarossa to Luigi Barbarossa Quintillio; Tulio Barbarossa to Tulio Barbarossa Quintillio; Palmina Barbarossa to Palmina Barbarossa Quintillio; Angelo Barbarossa to Angelo Barbarossa Quintillio; Della Louise Heard to Della Louise Crafts; Harold W. Brown to Fred A. Prescott; Hillgard June MacLean to Harriet June Prescott; Charles Henry Jelley to Charles Henry Curtis; Ruth Murray to Ruth Harris; Florence Lillian Richardson to Gladys Lillian Lewis; Ilene Erva Merrill to Ilene Erva Pasno; Beatrice Eliza Stone to Beatrice Eliza Wixson; Nellie M. Blazo to Nellie M. Cunningham; Irene Campbell to Lillian Irene Rollinson; Ethel Gertrude Holcomb to Josephine Helen Holcomb; Horace Joseph Holcomb to Joseph Horace Holcomb; Francis Temple Tweedy James to Alexander Robertson James; Elsie Shelley to Elsie M. McCoy

<u>Sullivan County</u> - Richard Arthur Gordan to Richard Arthur Howe; Priscilla Hope Aldworth to Idella Marie Martin; Hilda M. Roys to Hilda M. Wallace; George Louis Hamel to George Louis Franco; Martha Miller to Martha Miller Zeriadki; Ernest C. Gonyea to Raymond Edmund Lamare

<u>Grafton County</u> - Clarence Rodney Ashford to Clarence Rodney Daniels; Alice F. Banfill to Alice F. Fellows; Mary B. Belford to Mary B. Cordon; Alfa May Brackett to Alfa Brackett Guyer; Preston Clark to Gordon Benjamin Willis; Lorraine E. Dimick to Lyle Elizabeth Welch; Ella M. Dodge to Ella M. Silver; Sylvia Eunice Dillon to Sylvia Eunice Dustin; Raymond Edmund Fillion to Raymond Edmund Fillion; Maxine Fournier to Maxine Fournier; Marjorie V. Howland to Marjorie V. Paro; Bertha G. King to Bertha G. Smith; Nina Berl LaBelle to Nina Bell Killam; Sylvia Marcroft to Sylvia Warner; Raymond C. Paige to Raymond C. Williams; Robert Arthur Paige to Robert Arthur Williams; Emile Paquett to Joseph P. Paquett; Helen M. Valia to Helen Marr Sulloway; Roderick Pike Whiting to Roderick William Ewen; Una Marion Abbott to Una Marion Abbott; Eva Brown to Eva Elizabeth O'Connor; Richard A. Burpee to Richard A. Bowles; Ethel May Brown to Grace Elizabeth Casteels; Patricia C. Gilpatric to Patricia C. Jenness; Donald R. Jordan to Donald R. Jordon; Reginald Chase Leach to Reginald Chase Corey; Norma Mitton to Norma Mitton Flodin; Claudia Mitton to Claudia Mitton Flodin; Theresa Parent to Theresa

1925-1927

Parent; Curtis Wright to Curtis Wickersham Wright; Violet Wright to Violet Bundy

Coos County - John Walter Hynes to Walter John Hynes; Albert Lidstone to Albert Powers; Mary Louise Chapman to Rachel Louise Barbour; Stewart Albert Hamilton to Raymond Perreault; Frances May Gall to Frances May Hayes; Ellen Florence Thomas to Ellen Florence McCarthy; Emile Richard to Richard Lambert; Joseph Leopold Levesque to Thomas Leopold Levesque; Kedah G. Small to Kedah G. Evans; Dorothy R. Dutton to Dorothy R. Cotnoir; Victor Demers to Victor Miller; Marion Boyce to Marion Mansfield; Child of Dorothy L. Hale to Helen Ruth Carter; Frances Violet Bryan to Frances Violet Noyes; Barbara Warfield to Barbara Willis; Poisson Antonia to Antonia Dussault; David Haynes to David Haynes Crockett; George L. Knapp to George L. Hilliard; John Warren Crowley to John Warren Halloway; Bertha R. Keough to Bertha R. Trask; Theresa Boisvert to Pauline Hamel; John Henry Roberts to John Powell; Bernard Lynaugh to Bernard Wilson

Name changes made by the superior court in divorce proceedings:

Rockingham County - Victoria M. Morris to Victoria M. Moody; Mildred G. Goodrich to Julia A. Davidson; Mary A. Houde to Mary A. Ryan; Florence E. Blair to Florence E. Hartford; Eva M. Johnson to Eva M. Erickson; Gladys I. Chase to Gladys I. Hoolock; Alice Enire to Alice M. Robbins; Louise D. Henderson to Louise D. Annis; Bernice M. Horton to Bernice M. Mason; Frances E. DeVeau Pevear to Frances E. DeVeau; Nellie G. Robinson to Nellie G. Ross; Jennie E. Gove to Jennie E. Gordan; Frances Louise Carr O'Connor to Frances Louise Carr; Ethel M. Hamblett to Ethel M. Ray; Annie M. Hall to Annie M. Hersey; Elizabeth H. Stevens to Elizabeth H.Severance; Stella Biancki to Stella Lougee; Gladys T. Kimball to Gladys T. Coleman; Annie T. Nudd to Annie T. Coleman; Marion Cooley to Marion Tibbets; Ora J. St. Clair to Ora Spinney; Jessie J. Simonelli to Jessie J. Cole; Marion J. Hepworth to Marion J. George; Constance Williford to Constance Whittier

1925-1927

Strafford County - Jennie M. Walton to Jennie May Foss; Avis L. Morrill to Avis L. Shumway; Marie E. Stanley to Marie E. St. Peter; Ruth A. Babbitt to Ruth Elizabeth Allen; Florence C. Marcotte to Florence C. Mulligan; Alice M. Canney to Alice M. Brownell

Belknap County - Hattie E. Hayward to Hattie E. Ingram; Agnes H. Buffington to Agnes H. Coburn; Leranda A. Adams to Leranda A. Fox; Bertha G. Olsen to Bertha G. Bacon; Nellie M. Roberts Gleason to Nellie M. Roberts; Velzora F. Brooks to Velzora F. Wallett; Catherine M. Amazeen to Catherine T. Clough

Carroll County - Priscilla E. Thompson to Priscilla E. Willey; Hattie B. Reed to Hattie B. Estes; Charlotte H. Ames to Charlotte Hoag

Merrimack County - Marie S. Parshley to Marie S. Houle; Elsie Viola Bishop to Elsie Viola Parsons; Nora Gillespie Kelly to Nora Gillespie; Rose A. Roy to Rose A. Dorval; Eva M. Cloutier to Eva M. Leblanc; Maude Helen G. Lucier to Maud Helen Goodwin; Eliza M. Stevens to Eliza M. Sweet; Mildred F. Hayes to Mildred Irene Flint; Alice G. Madison to Alice G. Allen; Mary M. Seaward to Mary M. Sanders; Lottie A. Howes to Lottie A. Farnsworth; LaVerne H. Wallace to LaVerne H. Frary; Hattie M. Cummings to Hattie M. Rundlett; Arabella P. Mayhew to Arabella P. Dow; Annie M. Brockway to Annie M. Colby; Rachel B. French to Rachel Buchanan; Cyrena B. Clement to Cyrena B. Woodward; Martha Jones to Bertha Messer; Clara H. Smith to Clara Piper; Rose B. Brill to Rose B. Robertson; Minnie C. McGrath to Minnie Crane

Hillsborough County - Cornelia St. Germaine to Cornelia Hall; Marion Ardelle King Fitch to Marion Ardelle King; Florence M. Farrar to Florence M. Murdough; Ottilie B. McNally to Ottilie Bryer Drew; Rowena E. Wade to Rowena E. Werden; Anna Majkowski to Anna Saida; Annie K. Sansoucie to Annie Katherine Holt; Geanula Kukurabas to Geanula Thaoharis; Ethel I. Swett to Ethel I. Brown; Doris M. Beauregard to Doris M. Campbell; Anna Misiak to Anna Lula; Mary Cecchini to Mary Bruno; Mattie Whitcher to Mattie Fox; Frances C. King to Frances A. S. Crowell; Annie Sapurka to Annie Klara Schirnack; Marguerite Blake to Marguerite Chandler; Doris May Myhaver to Doris May Warren; Mathilda Keko to Mathilda Bussiere; Mary Lariviere to Mary Lepage;

1925-1927

Irene A. LeBlanc to Irene A. Galipeau; Marjory E. Wolahan to Marjory E. Drew; Lida B. Dion to Lida B. Reed; Anna Dubois to Anna Paquette; Erma Luccille McCabe to Erma Luccille Baker; Mildred H. Miner to Mildred Smith; Harriet M. Wood to Harriet M. Shaw; Lillian Marion Mahoney to Lillian Marion McGowan; Ola A. Preston to Ola A. Stafford; Mabel B. Thomas to Mabel B. Westcott; Lena Grassi to Lena Ouellette; Winona P. Larose to Winona Prescott; Abbie E. Murphy to Abbie E. Wiggin; Grace J. G. Warren to Grace J. G. Moir; Lillian Dubey Burdette to Lillian Mary Dubey; Marie H. Racette to Marie Helene Perrault; Bernice F. Dane to Bernice F. Lintott; Marie Debusschere Meersman to Marie Debusschere

Cheshire County - Clara M. Brady to Clara M. Chase; Mary Robinson to Mary Marcotte; Josephine M. Duval to Josephine M. LaBier; Edna Tenney to Edna Butler; Ella M. Tourtellott to Ella M. Lincoln; Christabel C. Whittemore to Christabel C. Higgins; Alice Zecha to Alice Whitcher; Calista Ellor to Calista Cloutier; Rena Gerard to Rena Bushey; Lillian W. Kibbie to Lillian W. Whitney

Sullivan County - Vina Allen Willis to Vina Allen; Irene Frances Grant to Irene Frances Straw; Ruth Esther Davio to Ruth Esther Prue; Dorothy Ellen Hatch to Dorothy Ellen Chamberlain; Ruth Dorothy Phelps to Ruth Dorothy Hunt; Anna E. Miller to Anna E. Chase; Florence Beatrice Smith to Florence Beatrice Morris; Hazel Edith Jones to Hazel Edith Dougherty; Laurel Vane Smith to Laurel Vane Hopkins; Juliet Marie Nichols to Juliet Marie Patten; Minnie Silverman to Minnie Blacker; Ellen Jennie Rayno to Ellen Jennie Pinard; Marion L. Craig to Marion L. Davis; Sadie Elizabeth McElreavy to Sadie Elizabeth Guyette; Elizabeth C. Buzzell to Elizabeth C. Gallup; Sybil F. Swain to Sybil F. Marshall

Grafton County - Madge Lahaye to Madge Talbot; Ruth Marion Parker to Ruth Marion Allen; Vivan F. Gardner to Vivian F. Plant; Madeline A. Tupper to Madeline A. Hernon; Mabel C. Farrell to Mabel C. Harper; Mamie B. Sears to Mamie B. Burnor; Lucile Woodward to Lucile Church; Lillian M. McCarthy to Lillian M. Hanson; Grace C. French to Grace C. Fox; Rachel Byron Gould to Rachel Maud Byron; Nellie F. Paige to Nellie F. Chapman; Lora Belle Fredette to Lora Belle Knapp; Ivis L. MacLean to Ivis L. McLeod; Nellie J. Simpson to Nellie J. Wright;

1925-1927

Anna M. Hill to Anna M. Way; Charlotte M. Johnson to Charlotte M. Mather

Coos County - Harriett E. Stone to Harriett E. Ball; Mary A. Richards to Mary A. Hovey; Lilla E. Owen to Lilla E. Frizzell; Doris Sanborn to Doris Belanger; Helen Jane Caird to Helen Jane Daley; Vivian C. G. Fortier to Vivian C. G. Hall; Ruth M. Prowell to Ruth M. Trainer; Margaret Delena Lavoie to Margaret Delena Cutler; Mary E. Day to Mary E. Stahl; Pearl Bushnell to Pearl Dickey; Gladys Goldie Springer to Gladys Goldie Scalion; Inez E. Iacoboni to Inez N. Eaton; Mertie Henderson to Mertie Eastman

January 1927 to January 1929[3/]

Name changes made by the probate courts:

Rockingham County - Charles Sanderson to Kenneth William Morrison; Evelyn Pickard to Evelyn Lillian Downs; Margaret E. Arps to Margaret E. Mates; Gladys Blidberg to Bonnie Hunt Irvin; Elwin Stanley Fellows to Elwin Stanley Pingree; Floyd William Allen to Floyd William Brown; Kenneth McBride to Kenneth Griffin; Philip Earl Kelly to Philip Earl Thomas; Elizabeth M. Chapman to Elizabeth M. Tytus; Arthur Guerin to David LeRoy Guerin; Rosimund Georgia Foster to Roma Georgia Leacock; Lorette Jeane Denault to Lorette Jeanne Butler; Barbara H. Fitts to Barbara Helen Butler; Raymond Albert to Raymond Albert Cook; Ira Metcalf Redman to Ira Metcalf Holmes; Gertibell Holt to Muriel Ruth Bryan; Pauline Burnham to Pauline B. Philbrick; James Everett Chenevert to James Everett Bunker; Gertrude Geraldine Levia to Gertrude Geraldine Jacobs; William Sidney LeVine to William Sidney Chandler; John Bliss LeVine to John Bliss Chandler; George Emerson McCartney, Jr. to George Robert Hall; Gertrude Reed Haggerty to Gertrude Reed; Carlyle Wilson Haggerty to Carlyle Wilson Reed; William A. Herbert to William A. Kreger; Virginia Frances Downes to Virginia Frances Nelson

Strafford County - Charles Sumner Bryant to Harlan Moore Bryant; Rose L. Dolliver to Rossa Nell Lowe; Jessie E. Locke to J. Elizabeth Williams; Walter R. Spinney to Walter R. Varney; Ida M. Thompson to Ida M. Ellis; Ada Belle Chesley to Ada Belle Johnson; Myer Silverstein to Myer Silton; Fanny Silverstein to Fanny Silton; Maurice Z. Silverstein to Maurice Silton; Ronald Thompson Rogers to Ronald Thompson Scott; Ella Mildred Bronson to Ella Mildred Bergeron; William A. Davis to William A. Hayes; Arthur Mitchell Grondin to Ernest Mitchell Grondin; Libberatore Calvalcante Minichiello to Albert Mitchell; Simeon Max Krinsky to Simeon Kinsley

Belknap County - Marie Yvonne Jutras to Yvonne Eli (adpt.); Myrtle Bruneau to Myrtle Moore; Lora Alice LaClaire to Lora Alice Carr (adpt.); Laura Edith LaClaire to Laura Edith Carr (adpt.); Corinna C. Jones to Corinna C. Marston; Kenneth Winkley to Lewis Chesly Winkley;

[3/]   Chapter 281, 1929 N. H. Public Laws

1927-1929

Corinna C. Marston; Kenneth Winkley to Lewis Chesly Winkley; Kenneth Leroy Banfil to Kenneth Leroy Walker; Nettie B. Sanborn to Nettie Bickford; Myrtie E. Smith to Myrtie E. Kimball; Eleanor Jeanne McKean to Eleanor Jeanne Lane (adpt.); Norman Francis Bolduc to Norman Bolduc Simoneau (adpt.); Charlotte C. Elkins to Charlotte C. Guay; George H. Ericson to George E. Tenney; Rosamond F. Ashley to Nancy Althea Brown (adpt.); Florence M. Belisle to Florence M. Bellanger; Barbara Ellen Hicks to Barbara Ellen Harris (adpt.); Harold Lewis Pease to Harold Lewis Simpson (adpt.); Alice Martel Dumais to Alice Martel Gendron; Robert Dumais to Robert Gendron; Arnold Dumais to Arnold Gendron; Alma Dumais to Alma Gendron; Edgar Feather to Edgar Feather Lockwood; Isa B. Forbes to Isa B. Buswell; Helen Ivy LaMay to Mary Louise Ricker (adpt.); Robert Andrien Lacourse to Robert Andrien LeFrancois (adpt.)

Carroll County - Amy Plant [Van] Tassel to Amy Plant; William Van Tassel to William Plant; Margaret Plant Van Tassel to Margaret Plant; Pauline H. Lamontague to Pauline H. Robinson; Lenora Lamontague to Virginia Charlotte Haney; Charles Patch to Charles Parson Willey; Dorothy S. Rogers to Dorothy S. Roberts; Gwenedene May Moulton to Priscilla May Moulton; Harry Harlan Rhines to Harry Harlan Willey; Nathalie Eleanor Rousseau to Nathalie Eleanor Pendergast; Alma Jean Rousseau to Alma Jean Robertson; Lillian A. Peare to Lillian A. Wade; Merline Libby to Merlyne Louise Palmer; Paul Scott Emperor to Paul Scott Johnson; Edward Bruce Langley to John Glendon Clow; Virginia Claire McDowell to Virginia Claire Moore; Irene Marion Lamontague to Irene Marion Staples; Mary Elizabeth Severance to Mary Elizabeth Kennett; Virginia R. Abbott to Virginia Davis; Mary A. Moore Frost to Mary A. Moore

Merrimack County - Janie Rankin Rogers to Janie Rankin; William G. Hagar to William G. Happny; Laura Mary Mitchell to Laura Mary King; Annie Spencer Dunbar to Annie Spencer Wheeler; Arthur Edward Heath to Edward Arthur Heath; Irene I. Maki to Irene I. Olkkonan; Moses H. Kimball to Herbert M. Kimball; Paul Parker Metcalf to Paul Revere Metcalf; Maurice Tedovsky to Maurice Tedoff; Fannie M. Dickerson to Fannie M. Kilton; Jeannette Cofran to Jeannette P. Cofran; Ilona Evelyn Tucker to Ilona Evelyn Preston; Myla Stackpole to Myla Lola Mason; Elizabeth Nellie O'Connell to Elizabeth Cary

1927-1929

O'Connell; Mildred Neal Fitzsimmons to Mildred Neal Dunsford; Gustav Oberstebrink to Gustav Ober; Helen Healey to Mildred Irene MacLaughlin; Alfred Adelor Michaud to Maurice Alfred Garant; Edward Lynch to Edward McLaughlin; Elaine Frances Hopkins to Elaine Frances Bonnin; Lillian Elizabeth Lavoie to Lillian Elizabeth Campbell; Phillip Edmunds to Phillip Edmunds McIntosh; Almira Laporte to Madeline V. Cass; Cecile June Dennis to Cecile June Derby; Eleanor Jean Thorson to Eleanor Jean Graham; Richard Dennis Jenkins to Richard Dennis Stanley; Raymond Joseph Gordan to Raymond Joseph O'Brien; Iva Mae Sanderson to Iva Mae Johnson; Pearl Dennis Ray to David Porter; Russell Erwin to Donald Davis Chase; Earl Jay Bishop, Jr. to Earl Jay Griffin; Henry S. Keniston to Raymond Albert Brown; Francis Russell Bean, Jr. to Richard John Crane; Bernard Joseph Audette to Bernard Hill; Forrest Elmer Brown to Forrest Brown Barker; Grace Meader to Ruby Mabel Hill

Hillsborough County - Anastasia Koukos to Anastasia Fragoyanes; Thelma Boynton to Thelma Clemons; Eleanor Chasse to Eleanor Dionne; Frank Miner to Frank Miner Hayden; Marie Esther Sullivan to Marie Emilie Esther Poirier; Irving Geisler to Alan Davis Rogers; Doris T. Germain to Doris T. Paquette; Jeannette Fortier to Jeannette Lorraine Gosselin; Leendert Syx to Leendert Harry Rohner; Leo Steckute (also known as Leo Stickis) to Leo Kinduris; Phyllis McCarthy to Phyllis Peabody; Ronald Raymond to Ronald Forbes Gray; Alice Mae Laraba to Inez Mae Hanson; Evelyn Oakleaf to Evelyn Frances McDuffee; Frances E. Wilder to Frances Wilder Ryder; Charles William Hubel to Charles William Russell; Marilyn Gene McShane to Marilyn Jean Cox; Doris Ledoux to Simonne Guilmette; Mary Pearl Ida Ouellette to Mary Pearl Ida Corbin; Helen Davey to Shirley Frances Merrill; Madeline Clark to Mary Jane McCarthy; Dorothy Emond to Geraldine Dorothy Morin; John Wellington Drew, Jr. to John Drew Tjampiris; Beryl Jessie Hammond to Beryl Frances MacDuffie; Josephine Castagnini to Josephine Polidori; Mary Thomas to Mary Joron; Robert Thomas to Robert Joron; Leon G. Baril to Gerald Aubut; Charles Blanchette to Albert Levesque; Dorothy June Gobin to Dorothy June Hunter; Mary Marceline Audette to Mary Marceline Laurier; Carolus Coteneau to Carolus Laurier; Doris Estelle Staples to Barbara May Hewes; Mary Theresa Looney to Mary Looney Sullivan; Elizabeth McIntyre to Aimee Elizabeth Chartier; Beverley Ruth Fortier to Beverley

1927-1929

Marie Monette; Sylvia Fineblit to Sylvia Meltzer; Ralph Stewart Carleton to Ralph Stewart Boutwell; Eunice Bertha Briggs to Eunice Bertha Brown; Thomas P. Hennessey to Joseph V. Stribling; John O'Gara to John Wallace; Ernest J. Blodgett to Ernest J. Rioux; Theodore Matsis to Theodore P. Christou; Vasilios Matsis to Vasilios P. Christou; Albertine Rosamond Giroux to Alice Pepin; Mildred Norma Plante to Mildred Norma Merrill; Alice Mitchell to Alice Elizabeth Eastman; Frank Earl Chandler to Frank Earl Bamford; Mary S. Fitzpatrick to Mary Teresa Guay; June Ellen Lavigne to Mary Elizabeth Atwood; Marie Theresa Cecile Gosselin to Marie Theresa Cecile Simard; Marjorie E. Wheeler to Marjorie E. Graves; Marie Germaine Anna Lemire to Marie Germaine Anna Canning; Jeanette Isabelle Morin to Jeanette Marie Isabelle Valcourt; Eugene Sargent to Richard Eric Bergholtz; Mary Schellenger to Mary Catherine O'Neill; Eva Fortier to Doris Russell; Richard Buckley to John Richard Eivers; Deborah K. Love to Deborah K. Joslin; Holland B. Love to Holland B. Joslin; Esther Marcotte to Esther Gilman; John Franklyn Rezenders to Neil Edward Moriarty; Roland T. Fleming to Roland T. Lowell; Irene A. Carle to Irene A. Grant; Grace C. Millett to Grace A. Clark; Norma Kathleen Winkler to Norma Ernestine Winkler; Paulo Joanu Beltso to Peter John Belcher; Eva R. Robichaud to Eva R. Gaudette; Lloyd Lisherness to Lloyd L. Evans; Gretchen Campbell to Gretchen Ackerman Campbell; Erma Gladys Jeannotte to Erma Gladys Eaton; Ella Baum to Ella Wenzel; Arthur Edward Parkhurst to Arthur Spencer Parkhurst; Carl Francis to Carl Johnson; Florence Marjorie Kidder to Florence Marjorie Cross; Jean Baptiste Thiboutot to Valmar Thiboutot; Rose Herregodts to Rose Serues; Paul Papagianopoulos to James Cateras; Peter Papagianopoulos to George Cateras; Mary J. Remington to Mary J. Bartlett; Patricia Remington to Patricia Bartlett; Joseph Mederic Hermenigilde Desmarais to Ulric Joseph Desmarais; Gladys Myrtle McCarty to Gladys Peabody McCarty; Irma Anna Schneiderheinz to Irma Anna Neubert; Frederick Leblanc to Frederick White; Athanasios Tamposi to Nasi Nickolas Tamposi; Demetrios John Tegoutsios to Demetrios John Yiacas; Anthony Dubowsky to Anthony Dublow; Mary Dubowsky to Mary Dublow; Albina Dubowsky to Albina Dublow; Helen Dubowsky to Helen Dublow; Annie Dubowsky to Annie Dublow; Anthony Dubowsky, Jr. to Anthony Dublow, Jr.; George Lewis Adams to George Lewis Adamakos; Theodore Tenerowicz to Theodore Turner; Mary Tenerowicz to Mary Turner; Edward Tenerowicz to

1927-1929

Edward Turner; Stanley Tenerowicz to Stanley Turner; Philogene Breynaert to John P. Breynaert; Betsey L. Fowler to Betsey Lovejoy; Elizabeth Anna Duplessis to Elizabeth Bertha Anna Duplessis; Arthur Lyon Clement to Arthur Elmer Clement; Ernest Henry Daniels to Ernest Henry George; Alfred Sears to Alfred Gloddy; Dorothy Virginia Rogers to Dorothy Virginia Goodale; Alma M. Royal to Alma M. Johnson; Christos Kyriakakis to Chris Kyriax; Carl Werner Johansson to Carl Werner Johnson; Isabelle M. Houle to Isabelle M. Rood; Evelyn Mildred Smith to Evelyn Vaughan Smith

Cheshire County - Nellie Hooper to Nellie Hooper Shepard; Walter Francis Mason to Richard Charles Mason; Hazel Woodburn Morse White to Hazel Woodburn Morse; Clifton Averill Patnode to Clifton Averill Richards; Jeanette Mildred Derby to Jeanette Mildred Richards; Thelma Leonard to Thelma Mae Barrett; Norman Trudo to Milton Leroy Butler; Barbara Dorothea Boebel to Barbara Dorothea Dunham; Dorothy Althea Redstone to Dorothy Althea Randall; John Mientkievicz to John Dudzenski; Albert Henry Cunningham to Albert Henry DuVarney; Herbert Earl Thornig to Herbert Earl Day; Rosalie Marcia Lombard to Rosalie May Lombard; Francis Edward Burns to Richard Myron Rhoades; George Chakalos to Temolion Chakolos; Leon Noel Sharkey to Leon Noel Stearns; Doris Maher to Doris Curran; Dorothy Kenyon to Dorothy Kingsbury; Hattie Alice Hackett to Hattie Alice Stratton; Aileen Caroline O'Neil to Aileen Mary Foley; Daisy Healey to Daisy Joslyn; Ona George Ingalls to Ona George Brown; Lorenzo Alfred Michaud to Lorenzo A. Loring; Mary Litheland to Marion Fitzgerald; Lois Kay Piper to Nancy Nims Piper; Violet Appt to Violet Parker; Ralph Leonard Castor to Leonard Fred Castor; Minnie E. Todd to Minnie E. Crosby; Gladys May Whipple to Gladys May Toomey; Emma Belle Pasno to Emma Belle Brooks

Sullivan County - Robert L. Williams to Robert Charles Lockwood; Madeline Bliss to Madeline Brown; Mildred Madeline Osgood to Mildred Madeline White

Grafton County - George C. Akerman to George C. Akerman; Patricia Beaman to Patricia Caverhill; Marcelia L. Beede to Marcelia L. Beede; Ida May Boardman to Ida May Downer; Hannah Cayes to Hannah Pierce; Novella Cleveland to Novella Wender; Robert Earl Jaquith to

27

1927-1929

Maurice Calvin Estabrook; Mabel Lawrence to Mabel Clark; Blanche Lucia to Blanche Burnell; Myrtle Morse to Myrtle Morse; Walter Chester Munsey to Donald Calvin Jaquith; Flora S. Sawyer to Edna Myrtle Hanaford; Kathleen P. Sullivan to Kathleen P. Nutter; Nelson A. Thibodeau to Nelson A. Jaques; Dora M. Wright to Dora Melvina Elliott; Marland Russell Walker to Russell Clark Orton

Coos County - Theresa Conley to Theresa Aiellio; Everett W. Haney to Everett W. Simonds; Lorilda Desfosses to Lorilda Thibodeau; Phoebe Murray Tenney to Phoebe A. Murray; Fred Liebermann to Fred Loverin; Flora Liebermann to Flora Loverin; Mabel Liebermann to Mabel Loverin; Meyer Liebermann to Meyer Loverin; Etta Liebermann to Etta Loverin; Franklin J. Liebermann to Franklin J. Loverin; Milton Liebermann to Milton Loverin; Cecile R. Liebermann to Cecile R. Loverin; Dorothy Mae Tuttle to Dorothy Mae Smith; Joseph Amede Fournier to Amiede Peter Fournier; Arthur Delvern Marrs to Arthur Delvern Emerson; Pricilla E. Collins to Pricilla E. Pinette; Marie Amanda Blais to Florence Blais Clement; Ethel Harriet Read to Adeline Winona Johnson; Leonard Perry to Richard Perry Stevens; Tryphene Doherty to Tryphene Philips; Priscilla Pinette to Priscilla Washburn; Lina K. Maynard to Lina J. Kimball; Theresa Ross to Theresa McFarland; Marie Annette to Marie Annette Roy

Name changes made by the superior court in divorce proceedings:

Rockingham County - Anna R. Radford to Anna R. Matheson; Edna I. Paules to Edna I. Hill; Olive L. Trew to Olive L. Berry; D. Lucille Cloutier to Dorothy L. Rinalducci; Marion I. Charuk to Marion I. Coleman; Cora F. Platts to Cora F. Spaulding; Ellen Butler to Ellen Roberts; Mary E. Maloney to Mary E. Doucette; Lillie Bond to Lillie Currie; Catherine Ham to Catherine Case; Mildred Parent to Mildred J. Smith; Ida May Bond to Ida May Blaisdell; Mabel E. Thompson to Mabel E. Loukx; Mary Elizabeth Kingsbury to Mary Elizabeth Anderson; Gwendolyn Farmer Chilton to Gwendolyn Farmer; Mary A. Hanson to Mary A. Donaldson; Vivian J. Brown to Vivian J. Grover; Stella Perkins to Stella Gaidis; Alma W. Hersom to Alma W. Stevens; Monita Gray Lawton to Monita Gray

1927-1929

Strafford County - Louise G. Langmaid to Louise G. Dodge; Violet M. Rollins to Violet M. Scott; Marguerite E. Willand to Marguerite E. Phillips; Inez L. Pratt to Inez Lopez; Lily R. Sylvain to Lily R. Landry; Lillian M. Mithee to Lillian Maud Palmer; Nellie E. Fecteau to Nellie E. McCarron; Blanche M. Libby to Blanche L. Murray; Iva A. McCabe to Iva A. Downing; Ethel M. Carpenter to Ethel M. Remick; Bernice T. Gifford to Bernice Winkley Tasker; Rose E. Foss to Rose E. Herbert; Muriel Joyce Edgerly to Muriel Joyce Bannister; Ella Quimby to Ella Garland; Beatrice B. Young to Beatrice B. Maxfield; Marion Z. Cheney to Marion Z. Gerry; Lucille H. Rosenstiel to Lucille H. Downing; Mary S. Mann to Mary S. Weare; Clara A. LaBree to Clara A. Cooke; Elyse M. Osterman to Elyse M. Wallace

Belknap County - Emma Garneau to Emma Lovellee; Evelyn French to Evelyn Sartwell; Rosabel Blanche Graham to Rosabel Blanche Lamprey; Vivian C. Grieves to Vivian C. Andrews; Eva May Covey to Eva May Wentworth; Margaret Marchand to Margaret Borden; Bertha G. Constantine to Bertha G. Bacon

Carroll County - Junia I. Porter to Junia I. Irish; Tina Lucca to Tina Salvadori; Avis E. Peet to Avis E. Kennon

Merrimack County - Corrinne C. Connor to Corinne Carrier; Josephine Cable Kelley to Josephine C. Hamp; Ethel N. Colby to Ethel S. Newton; Lena W. Blaisdell to Lena L. Wyman; Luella Miller to Luella Hoit; Josephine H. Beaupre to Josephine H. Wells; Gertrude A. Gould to Gertrude J. Atkinson; Elinor Farwell to Elinor Nardini; Edna B. Simoneau to Edna B. Emerson; Mary Maria Randlett Davis to May Maria Randlett; Gladys R. Nichols to Gladys R. Welch; Clara E. Sammis to Clara E. Martin; Olive O. Nolan to Olive S. Ordeen; Cora A. Drew to Cora A. Baker; Louise E. Fitzgerald to Louise E. Veno

Hillsborough County - Marie Anne Therreault to Marie Anne Champoux; Viola B. Martin to Viola Edna Blair; Agnes Vezina to Agnes Kelly; Gertrude McConnell to Gertrude Mayou; Josepethine S. Smith to Josephine S. McNeil; Exima Alice Sinclair Boisvert to Alice Sinclair; Angelina A. Bilodeau to Angelina A. Lemay; Ruth Wilma Robertson to Ruth Wilma Grey; Julia Bouchard to Julia Desmarais; Bertha Pike to Bertha Frenier; Josephine Bangs to Josephine Huddleston; Paulette

29

1927-1929

Chailly Springer to Paulette Chailly; Nettie L. Lawrence to Nettie L. Griffin; Emma O. Eaton to Emma O. Larson; Corabelle Franklin to Corabelle Robbins; Daisy M. Day to Daisy M. Shaw; Maude B. Carter to Maude B. Elliott; Mary Vanderberghe to Mary Bolleyn; Hazel W. Gagne to Hazel W. Hitchcock; Amey E. Cote to Amey E. Bell; Winnie DeR. Morris to Winnie DeR. Pinkham; Julia Van Voast Burbridge to Julia Westerveldt Van Voast; Jennie Wiese McBride to Jennie Wiese; Marie Yvonne Sykes to Marie Yvonne Mathieu; Florence Agnes Kazlaris to Florence Agnes Gagnon; Alice Daoust to Alice Goudreau; Esther Bresnahan to Esther O'Brien; Mae Baum to Mae DeWaele; Ida E. Livingston to Ida E. Rollins; Agnes L. Gravel to Agnes L. Marson; Grace Kathan Thwing to Grace Kathan; Rose Labrecque to Rose Menard; Augusta V. Israel to Augusta V. Johnson; Myrtle Paquette to Phyllis O. Nichols; Cecile M. Hamel to Cecile M. Clement

Cheshire County - Susan M. Adams to Susan M. Murray; Marion V. Cobb to Marion G. Verrill; Elizabeth C. Collins to Elizabeth C. Bolt; Ruby E. Forbes to Ruby E. Deane; Mary Kansala to Mary S. Hryk; Lena M. Lancey to Lena M. Sharkey; Ida Spoon to Ida Gracie; Hazel M. Ward to Hazel M. McArthur; Cleora M. Ware to Cleora M. Leonard

Sullivan County - Pasqualena Maria Biagiotti to Pasqualena Maria Ciufo; Priscilla Margaret Stone to Priscilla M. Burrill; Bertha Florence (Ayer) Jerard to Bertha F. Ayer; Anne Abbie Crossett to Anne Abbie Newton

Grafton County - Laila B. Byron to Laila B. Albee; Madeline Hazel Russell to Madeline Hazel Harding; Pauline M. Jebb to Pauline M. Campbell; Doris E. Vetters to Doris E. Wilson; Clara C. Downing to Clara Adelaide Clemons; Eva M. Vigurs to Eva M. LaBrecque; Jennie Keith to Jennie Fisher; Mary M. Sousa to Mary M. Wheeler; Gwendolyn E. King to Gwendolyn E. Carbee; Florence E. Bowers to Florence E. Wilson; Adelie M. Boucher to Adelie M. Lacasse; Lottie M. Richardson to Lottie M. Kidder; Eva D. Nelson to Eva D. Kelley; Annie Kellam to Annie Reiter; Lulie M. Fenoff to Lulie M. Somers; Mildred Kelley Ball to Mildred Evelyn Kelley; Ruth Grant to Ruth Aldrich; Edna G. McLeod to Edna G. McIntyre; Anna F. Wright to Anna F. Champagne; Christie Mae Shepard to Christie Mae Lane

1927-1929

Coos County - Lesley Dorsey to Lesley King; Sarah A. Lynaugh to Sarah A. Wilson; Mary A. Dennis to Mary A. Blais; Helen McCarthy to Helen Keenan; Gertrude I. Withers to Gertrude I. Ingerson; Hazel Rowley to Hazel Ruby Chaffee; Evelyn Terrill to Evelyn Bushway; Mabel L. Joyce to Mabel L. Wedge; Hattie M. Sullivan to Hattie M. Currie

January 1929 to January 1931[4/]

Name changes made by the probate courts:

Rockingham County - Florence H. Leyden to Florence Boardman Hill; Frank Carroll to Frank Carroll Heselton; Carolyne Lois Trueman to Carolyne Lois Procter; Joyce Shockley Martin to Joyce Shockley Martin Peterson; Robert Ellsworth Lewis to Robert Ellsworth Bradley; Doris E. Gray to Doris E. Brown; Louise M. Churchill to Louise M. Task; Edna Mary Burke to Edna Mary Ames; Jean Warburton to Jean O'Brien; Alice Marie Taylor to Alice Marie Colliston; Annie M. Page to Anna M. Page; Esther Lillian Dockham to Esther Lillian Locke; Frederick Durand King to Charles Frederick Moberly Brine; Kissag Arslanian to George Ashland; Clara May Dockham to Jean Louise Hutchins; Mary Luetta Carlisle to Mary Luetta Nutting; Margaret Rand to Margaret Gatchell; Russell Walton to Russell Simpson; Mildred E. Letalien to Mildred E. Corson; Alexander Emerson to Emerson Alexander Gilmore; Helen Olive Meserve to Rita Theresa Tetreault; Rena May Lang to Rena Mae Bartlett; Barbara Lang to Barbara Lang Bartlett; Vivian Diener to Jeremy Howard; Bernard Ingraham to Bernard Edward Whidden; Elizabeth B. Clark to Elizabeth B. Webster; Stanley M. Dinkowski to Stanley M. Thompson; James W. Merchant to James Jacob Purington; Ruth Evelyn Allen to Ruth Evelyn Moore; Joseph Senneville to Wilfred John Brisebois; Ruth Messer Houle to Ruth Messer Ladd; Robert Foote to Edward Joseph Cleveland; Annette Ikan to Marilyn Annette Prolman; Barbara Alice Paulding to Barbara Alice Stevens; Francis Raleigh Grelish to Francis Raleigh Copeland; Anita Bassett to Anita Hurst; Pearl Evelyn Bassett to Pearl Evelyn Hurst

Strafford County - Arthur Michel Grondin to Ernest Michel Grondin; Simeon Max Krinsky to Simeon Kinsley; Libberatore Colnalcante to Albert Mitchell; Robert Hodgson to Robert Wendell Googins; Francis Woodrow Morrison to Charles Francis Morrison; Heinz Abraham to Heinz Brown; Leon Clifton Pike to Leon Clifton Howard; Agnes Christine Cilley to Agnes Christine Blaisdell; Ruth Lucinda Hodgdon to Ruth Lucinda Smiley

---

[4/] Chapter 250, 1931 N. H. Public Laws

1929-1931

Belknap County - Philip Thomas Beauchesne to Philip Thomas Huckins (adpt.); Faye Elaine Evirs to Faye Elaine Wakefield (adpt.); Ernest W. A. Wescott to Ernest Harry Young (adpt.); Marie Anna Parent to Marie Anna Morin (adpt.); Edith Helen Whalen to Edith Helen Tibbetts; Joseph John Hampel Whalen to Joseph John Hampel Tibbetts; Helen Maurine Winter to Helen Maurine Forbes; Herbert A. Fifield to Herbert A. Heath (adpt.); Etta Louise Wilkins to Etta Louise Ellis (adpt.); George Turcotte to George Piatkewicz (adpt.); John F. Garrigan to John F. Bennett (adpt.); Alan Beamish Taber to John Richard Tabor; Leonce A. Pilotte to Leonce Alphonse Paradis (adpt.); Miriam E. Maltais to Miriam Eugenie Tyler; Dorothy May to Dorothy May Young (adpt.); Donald Arthur Heath to Donald Arthur Heath (adpt.); Richard Baker to Richard Baker Downing; Kenneth Emerson to Lester Frank Potter (adpt.); Arnold E. Shirley to Arnold Shirley Goss (adpt.); Ellen F. Burroughs to Ellen F. Randell (adpt.)

Carroll County - Evelyn Glidden to Evelyn Huff; Frederick Crowell to Leon Rodman Warren; Florence Arlene Thurston to Florence Arlene Frost; Gene Louise Philbrick to Gene Louise Ward; Robert M. Meserve to Robert Littlefield Glidden; Gloria Constance McDonald to Gloria Constance Doyle; Cora E. Geary to Cora E. Avery

Merrimack County - Marion Grace Eaton to Grace Eulila Shaw; Donald Milton LaForge to Gerardo Donald Grimaldi; John Crawford Meagher to John Crawford Langlitz; ----- Plastridge to Mary Boyd Crockett; Jeannette May Anderson to Jeannette May Clarke; Robert Barnard to James Gordon Kittredge; Louie Joseph LaPointe to Louie Joseph Bonette; Alberta Guyett to Barbara Livingston Kittredge; Betty Sanborn to Janet Ruth Lorden; Walter Frederick Bailey to Graham Gordon; Marjorie Mae Burt to Marjorie Mae Cate; Barbara Gerald to Barbara May Ash; Dorothy Fernald to Dorothy Elaine Hall; Sylvia Alice Freeman to Cora Meredith Schoolcraft; Irving Stanley Marshall to Irving Stanley Cross; Eugene Everett Carroll to Leonard Alfred Stockwell; William King Carroll to William King Stockwell; John Gordon Chase to John Gordon; Francis Eugene Parshley to Francis Eugene Johnson; Barbara Anna Adams to Barbara Anna Field; Gordon Eugene Champion to Gordon Eugene Aiken; Edward Chase to Edward Wesley Heath; Edward Foisie to Edward Jones; Elva Noreen Smith to Joy Smith Harlow; Philip Allen Lowell to John Knowlton Beede; Florence

1929-1931

Dupuis to Margaret Louise King; Winnie Marguerite Whitcomb to Winnie Marguerite Whitcomb Emerson; Barbara MacNaught to Jane Porter; Ronald Noel Gelinas to Joseph Menard Roland Plante; Kenneth Wright to Harry Dayton Manning; Anna A. Wells to Anna A. Sargent; Richard Alfred Gould to Richard Alfred Heath; Beverly Van Neel to Janet McInnis; Willis Manley Peters to Willis Manley Spaulding; Roberta Goddard to Natalie Ann Clough; Geraldine Bean to Priscilla Jane Worthen; Kathleen R. Leemon to Kathleen R. Jordan; Richard Lincoln Burns to Richard Lee Metcalf; Bernice May Hall to Bernice May Roberts; Roderick Hughes to Roderick Hughes Bare; Eric Oberstebrink to Eric Ober; Emilie Oberstebrink to Emily Ober; Hildegarde Oberstebrink to Hilda Ober; Omega Frances Connor to Frances Belane Connor; Daniel George Hannington to Daniel Harrington; Carl D. Peverly to George D. Peverly; Aris Elizabeth Saltmarsh to Aris Elizabeth Davenport; Waldo A. Clement to Waldo A. Johnson; Celia B. Lemay to Celia B. Hayward; Arabelle M. Jewell to Arabelle M. Bailey; Christiana M. Shaw to Christiana M. Heartz; Royal A. McClary to Royal A. Ford; Charles W. Nelson, Jr. to Charles Brown Nelson; Ernest Elkins to Ernest Elkins Green; Leo J. Lambert to Noie Minnon

Hillsborough County - Susie Ellen Whitney to Susie Ellen Pelletier; John Rzeznikiewicz to John Ross; Philip Belavsky to Philip Belasco; Edna M. Burpee to Edna M. Basha; Blanche Eva Wilber to Betty Eva Wilber; Anna M. Gillan Bammann to Anna M. Gillan; Gordon Lee McLaughlin to Gordon Lee Conrey; Margaret Hope McLaughlin to Margaret Hope Conrey; Jessie S. Wentworth to Jessie S. Gilbert; Grosvenor Wendall Parker to Grosvenor Wendall Rice; Elise Ingalls (Gage) Norwood to Elise Ingalls Gage; Andrew John Wazniak to Andrew John Wayson; Irene A. (Pontbriand) O'Connell to Irene A. Pontbriand; Therese Cote to Therese Lamarche; Guy Charlie Demerse to Guy C. Miller; Holman Frank Blake, Jr. to John William Blake; Adam Valentine Ziemba to Joseph Valentine Adams; Mercedes Park to Mercedes McCormick Lacock; Lawrence Frederick Brown to Lawrence Frederick Reed; John Niziankowicz to John Janko; Elizabeth F. Rushton to Elizabeth Wagner; Beatrice Steuart to Beatrice Weightman; Theresa Francisca Prive to Frances Theresa Markey; Edward Joseph Kowalewski to Edward Joseph Richards; Cornelious Winter to John C. Reed; Janet Hodge to Janet Rae; Joseph Alfred Houle to Fred J. Hall; Sadie May Fisher to Sadie Reed; Maude Webster Adams to Maude

1929-1931

Beatrice Webster; Henri Noel Laganiere to Henry Paris; Stanley A. Borciak to Stanley A. Marshall; Alphonsine Dionne to Alphonsine Larochelle; Barbara Frances Flynn to Barbara Frances Calvert; William James Flynn to William James Calvert; *and the following through adoption*: Gloria Mitchell to Gloria Bellisle; Alice Bailey to Alice Triggs; Winslow Parker to Winslow Parker Triggs; Irene Guillot to Irene Marie Thibault; John Joseph McRell to Joseph Joseph (sic) Turcotte; Clarence McGinnis to Clarence Doherty; Romeo Jean Gagne to Robert Eugene Hitchcock; Iona Nereen Masters to Iona Nereen Warburton; Speridon Samalis to Speridon Docos; Evelyn Gelinas to Evelyn Olivette Theberge; Arthur Gerald Venne to Paul Joseph Bergeron; Edithe Mary Parker to Doris Mary Labarre; Alexandros Economides to Alexandros C. Papagianis; Rolland Gendron to Rolland Wilfred Benjamin; George Keith to George Philip Gosselin; Eva Louise Bishop to Eva Louise Currie; Nelly Emma Blood to Natalie Blood; Ernest Humphrey to Rogert R. Roy; Mary Bolleyn to Mary Van DeVelde; Marion Edna Beauvais to Marion Edna Heiden; Daniel Blanchette to James Daniel Patten; Mary Barbara Thibodeau to Rita Michaud; Earl K. Jackman to Edward Blanchard Batchelder; Andrew Lachance to Robert McCarthy; James Stovish to James Grealish; Geraldine Mary Devine to Geraldine Mary Jordan; Henry Lesniak to Hector Henry Prevost; Tanno E. Hill to Tanno E. Johnson; Alice Heselton to Alice Sullivan; Beatrice Lavoie to Beatrice Desclos; Gloria McNeil to Gloria Eklund; Richard Joseph Guillemette to Richard Leo Toussaint; ----- Anderson to John Bernard Whittemore; David Paul Lovett to David Paul Johnson; Jeanne d'Arc Raymond to Jeanne d'Arc Francoeur; Robert Sanford Knight to Robert Sanford Brown; Patricia Cass to Patricia White; Lois Taintor to Lois Ross; Catherine Louise Scott to Velma Catherine Newton; Richard Piper to Archie Donald Holloway; Phyllis Mary Cote to Rita Mary Michaud; Phyllis Miller to Phyllis Belle Carswell; Eileen Paquin to Mary Alberta Yvonne Savard; Howard McAlister to Howard Guy Watkins; Francis Albert Pelletier to Rosaire Beaulieu; Raymond Russell Unwin to Raymond Russell Blood; Mary Smith to Mary O'Hare; Alice Nadeau to Alice Fournier; Dora Foisie to Shirley Barbara Lawrence; Joseph Herbert Riley to Joseph Herbert Robinson; Paul Wayne Smith to Paul Wayne Keyser; Anthony Tomaselli to Melvin Robert Sibulkin; John Crawford to John Crawford Hayes; Mary Theresa Joan Anctil to Mary Theresa Joan Carriere;

1929-1931

James Frederick Towne to James Frederick Whitney; Harry H. Wheelock to Robert Albin Anderson

Cheshire County - Jeanette Mildred Richards to Jeanette Mildred Derby; Emilia Anttila to Dorothy Emilia Grube; Lilian Ruth Blair to Lilian Ruth Blair Sweeney; Barbara Jane (Davis?) to Barbara Jane Pike; Grace S. Beek to Grace S. Green; James Burnham McMaster to James Burnham Robbins; Marion Margaret Scott to Marion Margaret Mundell; Caroline Helen Hadley to Pauline Helen Hadley; Mildred A. Shea to Arlene Clarissa Greenwood; David Bernard Pitt to David Bernard O'Neil; Dorothy Mae McCann to Marion Mae Kinsman; Elizabeth Kenyon to Barbara Jean Raynes; Joseph Loiselle to Joseph Boulia; Wallace Fisher to Wallace F. Angier; Frances Ina Hill to Beverly Jane Luce; David Leighton Livingston to David Leighton Carpenter; Alice Swatzer to Roxana Louise Wyatt; Richard L. Connor to Donald Earl Wyman; Phyllis Arlene Brockway to Phyllis Arlene Duby; Lottie A. Lane to Charlotte A. Lane; Pearl Forcier to Theresa Pearl Pelletier; Mary Elizabeth Kiniry to Dorothy Ambler Welch; Joan Rosalie Adams to Joan Rosalie Stacy; Madge A. Hunt to Madge Alberta Hastings; William J. Bergeron to Gordon Floyd Walker; Eleanor Walker to Eleanor Ellinwood

Sullivan County - Betty M. Fogerty to Betty M. Young; Ruth Bruce to Ruth D. Delangis; Harry Bruce to Harry A. Delangis; Donald Bruce to Donald T. Delangis; Marion Lena Beckwith to Marion Beckwith Kibbie; Arnold Henry Beckwith to Arnold Beckwith Chapman; Alice Louise Tuttle to Marion Ruth Clark; Anna Theresa Kyne to Mary Theresa Richardson; Ernest Roland Downing to Ernest Roland Sturtevant; Donald Arthur Cross to Donald Arthur Scott; "Unknown Parentage" to June J. Economu; John Allen Rich to John Allen Walker; Richard Augustus Brown to Richard Collins Ruggles; Leona Annette Brown to Leona Annette Ruggles; Frank Wilbur Stevens to Marvin Burt Lindsay

Grafton County - Ralph Roy Avery to Ralph Roy Clifford; Dorothy Ella Buchanan to Dorothy Ella MacDonald; Louise M. Butler to Louise St. John Goodsell; Alfred E. Butler to Alfred Ira Goodsell; Arthur E. Butler to Charles Russell Goodsell; Elmer W. Butler to Elmer Butler Hassett; Marion M. Butler to Marion Butler Hassett; Susie Pearl Bugbee to Susie Pearl Tuxbury; Arlene Millicent Cowles to Arlene Millicent Cowles

1929-1931

Moody; Irene May Canfield to Irene May Austin; Alfred Napolin Collins to Alfred Martin Downing; Frederick Crocker to Frederick Eastman; Nelson Cota to Nelson Morrison; Hazel Crosby to Hazel Margaret Adams; Vernon Stackpole Davis to Vernon Davis Boyd; Dennis C. Fitzgerald to Dennis C. Shannon; Clara Holt to Clara Therese Goyette; Heber William Horam to Heber William Hull, 2nd; Lena O. Johnson to Lena O'Connor Johnson; Madison Karl Knighton to Madison Karl Boemig; Mayo Kenneth Laware to Oliver Charles Bean, Jr.; Laurence A. Laliberte to Laurence A. Myott, Jr.; Mary Slayton Nadeau to Mary Slayton; Shirley Fay Stevens to Shirley Stevens Estes; Wanita Francis Seeley to Wanita Francis Henderson; Joseph Harlin Tarbox to Harry Lewis Goodsell; Ruth Frances Whitney to Ruth Frances Montsie; Frederick Watson to Frederick Farrington; Doris Washburn to Doris Arlene Martin

Coos County - Eva M. Paquet to Eva M. Hicks; Gladys Blasland Rich to Gladys Blasland; Charlotte Virginia Notvig to Charlotte Virginia Johnson; Katherine Ann Larsen to Katherine Ann Johnson; Arthur G. Minah to Arthur G. Girard; Irene Chevrier to Irene Frechette; Joseph George Henry Arsenault to Joseph George Henry Morrisette; Simon Droskin to Simon Davis; Madeline Lacasse to Madeline Keroack; Dorothy Downs to Dorothy Hanson; Nicholas W. Corbett to Nicholas W. Brosius; Richard Raymond McGoff to Stephen Curtis Hook; Neil Lyman Perry to Lyman Perry Sweatt; Audrey Elizabeth Cole to Audrey Elizabeth Hilliard; Bernard Strout to Bernard Glenn Cole; Robert Ronald Beckwith to Robert Russell Garneau; Delvina E. Colby to Delvina E. Melbury; William George Chadburn to William George Laperle; Pearle Josephine Beauchemin to Pearl Joseph Benoit; Ethel Elizabeth Anderson to Ethel Elizabeth Hamilton; Walter Harris Oleson to Walter Harris Johnson

Name changes made by the superior court in divorce proceedings:

Rockingham County - Helen B. Pavey to Helen B. Conely; Elda E. Wallace to Elda E. Guyette; Ruth E. McNeely to Ruth E. MacKinley; Arlene Downing to Arlene Richardson Ricker; Bernice A. Gonin to Bernice A. Hamblett; Muriel S. Andress to Muriel Snyder; Beatrice M. Carnes to Beatrice M. Tewksbury; Anna H. Ryan to Anna Hollander;

1929-1931

Exilie Demers to Exilie Hamel; Bernice L. Morrill to Bernice L. Moore; Madeleine H. R. McLin to Madeleine H. R. Morgan; Bessie Donezan to Bessie Randall; Delia Chase to Delia Patmaude; Gertrude E. Robinson to Gertrude Elizabeth Ham; Pearl E. Pecunias to Pearl E. Wilcox; Isabella Craig to Isabella Fuller; Esther L. Jenkins to Esther L. Task; Nettie B. Jacobs to Nettie Beatrice Fletcher

Strafford County - Ida F. Kennedy to Ida F. Lough; Anna M. Boothby to Anna M. Beaudoin; Glenna A. Burleigh to Glenna A. Bryant; Gertrude E. Donovan to Gertrude Langmaid; Isabelle L. Stevens to Isabella Ricard; Martha E. Heckbert to Martha E. Fisher; Frances E. DeW. Sylvester to Frances E. DeWolfe; Ella E. Hester to Ella E. Brown; Irma Connell to Irma Grover; Althea Irene Connolly to Althea Irene Dame; Lucy Ann Kay to Lucy Ann O'Malley; Florence A. Boulanger to Florence A. Court; Elva P. Remick to Elva P. Holland

Belknap County - Mary E. Durgin to Mary E. Igel; Lada B. Menard to Lada Brown; Rintha M. Pettigrew to Rintha M. Bryant; Esther S. Wiswell to Esther Stickle

Carroll County - Leone E. Phinney to Leone Elfreda Thurston; Marie E. Smith to Marie Elizabeth Brantley

Merrimack County - Hazel B. Folsom to Hazel B. Cilley; Maud T. Bennett to Maud Towle; Irene Hayes Grant to Irene Wildred Hayes; Ella Heath Fagan to Ella Mavilla Heath; Beatrice Harriman Brown to Beatrice Mae Harriman; Lottie Pero to Lottie Cross; Gertrude E. Gilman to Gertrude Clark; Cora May Manning to Cora May Parshley; Elizabeth Morse Filspatore to Elizabeth Noble Morse; Lois J. Hamlin to Lois J. Keddie; Nanni J. Sullivan to Nanni J. Peterson; Gladys J. Haggerty to Gladys Moses; Elizabeth Hope Small to Elizabeth Hope Blood

Hillsborough County - Glenna Wares to Glenna Keirstead; Florette Delmore Class to Alice Florette Delorme; Mildred F. Cornell to Mildred F. Bent; Aimee Dora Dion to Aimee Dora Gagnon; Erma L. Greenwood to Erma L. Baker; Susie E. Knight to Susie Emma Annis; Corine Martin to Corine Cote; Doris Yeatter to Doris Tarr; Ruby I. Goodwin to Ruby I. Twiss; Blanche E. Piper to Blanche E. Thompson; Eva Katsalis to

1929-1931

Eva Boisvert; Lena Christidis also known as Helena Christidis to Lena Sturtevant; Lydia Soule to Lydia Buch; Florence Turrekens Terwoert to Florence Turrekens; Lily F. Tucker to Lily F. Stone; Laura E. Laschkowsky to Laura E. Nichols; Margaret Gallagher to Margaret E. Stickler; Irene K. Yates to Irene Foster; Rose Granz Schloth to Rose Granz; Anna I. Barry to Anna I. Dennis; Bernadette Katz to Bernadette Desbiens; Alma M. Meloon to Alma M. Rainville; Grace A. Massie to Grace A. Smith; Hazel W. Strong to Hazel B. Wilson; Eliza Franklyn Canning to Eliza Franklyn Tarrant; Mary Durkee to Mary Totten; Mary H. Hickman to Mary Elizabeth Harris; Helena K. Hickey to Helena Marguerite Kenney; Dorothy M. Cesarini to Dorothy M. Eaton; Jennie M. Somers to Jennie M. Docks; Alice Lawrence to Alice Lussier; Frances Slayback to Frances Thomas; Christina Athas to Christina Lafazanis; Julia A. George to Julia A. Tkacz; Ida D. Breault to Ida Paris; Jennie W. George to Jennie W. Beal; Gertrude Richmond to Gertrude Sibulkin; Valerie Moreau to Valerie Marcoux; Helen M. Durgin to Hellen Mollor; Myrtle B. Mayhew to Myrtle B. Nichols; Lena M. Hill to Lena M. Card; Mary Kenyon to Mary Fitzgerald; Grayce Brown Giles to Grayce Brown; Lena Gallagher to Lena Dolly Rainville; Cora A. Healey to Cora A. Corning; Ruth Fournier to Ruth Mason; Anna S. Lufkin to Anna S. Center; Bernice I. Chase to Bernice I. Williams; Ruth Allys Glines Bruce to Ruth Allys Glines; Arlene H. Bancroft to Arlene H. Proctor; Dorothy M. Robinson to Dorothy M. Desotell; Bernice F. Burton to Bernice F. Lintott; Tania Roberts to Tania Daniel; Eva Lillian Murray to Eva Lillian Cochran

Cheshire County - Edythe D. Brockway to Edythe D. Martin; Marion D. Wallace to Marion Stella Dickerman; Bessie Trask to Bessie Green; Lila M. Stone to Lila M. Brooks; Ella LaPointe to Ella Hatch; Elizabeth Isabelle to Elizabeth Beaudoin; Florence Edna Sullivan to Florence Edna Dewitt; Eleanor M. White to Eleanor Morris

Sullivan County - Luluma E. Lapoint to Luluma E. Cushmon; Myrtle Julia McCormick to Myrtie Julia LaFrance; Celia Anna Greenlaw to Celia Anna Johnson; Thelma E. Johnson to Thelma E. Negus; Mary E. Kebrich to Mary Evangeline Daigle; Dora S. Lesperance to Dora S. Brooks; Ethel M. Perkins to Ethel May Bean; Helen L. Townsend to Helen L. Jacobs; Emily C. Parker to Emily C. Collier; Vera Hastings to Vera Thomas; Nora M. McGrane to Nora Mary Chambers; Fanniebelle

1929-1931

Fowler to Fanniebelle Wilmarth; Jennie F. Atkins to Jennie F. Clarke; Irene S. Murray to Irene S. Simmons; Annie E. Hoyt to Annie E. Lees

Grafton County - Gladys V. Sanborn to Gladys V. Ingram; Mae L. Lester to May Lillian Lussier; Dora Caplan to Dora Rolstein; Dora Fecteau to Dora Lalonde; Betsey Burleigh Stevens to Betsey Burleigh; Mary Etta Phillips to Mary Etta Johnson; Lulie M. Fenoff to Lulie M. Somers; Mildred Kelley Ball to Mildred Evelyn Kelley; Ruth Grout to Ruth Aldrich; Edna G. McLeod to Edna G. McIntire; Anna F. Wright to Anna F. Champagne; Cristie Mae Shepard to Cristie Mae Lane; Anna M. Grenier to Anna M. Van Housen; Annabelle L. Goss to Annabelle L. Gardner; Eva D. Bishop to Eva D. Laramie; Nellie J. Stanley to Nellie J. Barnard; Elizabeth S. Burt to Elizabeth D. Spokesfield; Mary H. Van Curen to Mary Harriman Curtis; Flora B. Lanoix to Flora B. Berry; Ethelyn Millicent Bebler to Ethelyn Millicent Gilchrist; Carribel Lampro to Carribel Streeter

Coos County - Nellie F. Gilberson to Nellie Foster; Nellie Ward to Nellie Woodward; Seraphine G. Straw to Seraphine Gray; Mary A. Vallis to Mary Byrd; Esther Paradis to Esther Robertson

January 1931 to January 1933[5/]

Name changes made by the probate courts:

Rockingham County - Shirley Davis to Shirley Ruth Davis; Marion Little Batchelder to Marion Little Lane; George A. Atkinson to George Franklin Holmes; Marjorie Vesta Smith to Marjorie Vesta Grover; Carlyne Dawn Smith to Carlyne Dawn Grover; James McCullum to Jack Harold McLean; Camille Anne Houle to Camille Barbara Ladd; Linwood Herbert Howard to Linwood Greenwood Gage; Frank Zielinski to Frank Linscott; Victoria M. Zielinski to Victoria M. Linscott; John J. Zielinski to John J. Linscott; Joseph S. Zielinski to Joseph S. Linscott; Ann F. Zielinski to Ann F. Linscott; Jane Zielinski to Jane Linscott; Mary Zielinski to Mary Linscott; Merwin Woodburn to Merwin Thompson; Grace Henderson to Grace Morrissey; Roy Blake to Roy Blake Feinauer; Alfred Gilman Hemeon to Alfred Gilman Ripley; Maurice Kuchinsky to Maurice Kane; Ralph Buckman to Walter Olney McDuffee; Camille Leo Bergeron, Jr. to Leo Camille Byron; Iola DeCarlo to Iola Wason; William Swienton to Walter Albert Iwanicki; Chandler Power Skinner to John Clark Jacobs; Pearl M. Johnston to Pearl M. Levere; Bernice M. Johnston to Bernice M. Levere; Erma A. Johnston to Erma A. Levere; Galen B. Johnston to Galen B. Levere; Frances Hunton to Elizabeth Florence Harvey; Evelyn Alice Perkins to Evelyn Alice Kay; Richard Clayton Peckham to Richard Clayton Lynch; Erina Martinuk to Erina Martin; Ydonna Martinuk to Donna Martin; Olive Martinuk to Olive Martin; Michael Martinuk to Michael Martin; Peter Martinuk to Peter Martin; Samuel Martinuk to Samuel Martin; Sophie Martinuk to Sophie Martin; Alice L. Martinuk to Alice L. Martin; Robert W. Martinuk to Robert W. Martin; Victoria E. Zielinski to Victoria E. Linscott; John Weldon Chase to John Weldon Mettlach; Dorothy Elizabeth Oliver to Dorothy E. Greenman; Florence Ella McDonald to Florence Ella Walton; Robert W. Hurd and Robert Hurd Colburn; Charlotte L. Hurd to Charlotte Hurd Colburn; Annie Bell Davis to Pauline Sarah Gove; Florence V. Kunes to Shirley Mary Wheaton; Florence Rose LeClair to Florence Rose Mitchell; Mary Littlefield to Mary Philbrick; Jacqueline Wright to Beulah Mae Adams; Genevieve Margaret Uzarek to Genevieve Margaret Berry; Helen L. Tarlton to Helen L. Stanyan

---

5/ Chapter 282, 1933 N. H. Public Laws

1931-1933

Strafford County - Oliver R. Frye to Richard Thomas Holmes; Donald O. Day to Donald McCauley; Reed Casboris to Stanton D. Theodora; Bonnibel L. Wheeler to Bonnibel Elizabeth Orr; Margaret Gertrude Patch to Margaret Gertrude Roberts; Barbara Frances Murray to Barbara Ann Heath; John Marlin Buzzell to John Everett Joy; John Castricone to John Donald Couture; Margaret Wilkins to Margaret Sanborn; Gloria Louise Stackpole to Marilyn Claire Hurd; Bertha Hall to Bertha Call; Dora Josephine Parshley to Dora Josephine Perkins

Belknap County - Sarah V. Fugere to Sarah Vezina; Gloria Orlean Dantos to Gloria Mildred Vanderhoof (adpt.); Rose Anna Emiliana Guay Russillo to Evon Rosena Emiliana Guay Russillo; Lillian May Sampson to Lillian May Hodgdon (adpt.); Mary Elizabeth Bennett to Mary Elizabeth Maine (adpt.); Marie Elizabeth Abbott to Frieda Marie Elizabeth Abbott; Leslie A. Gould to Leslie Aaron Gould Gordon (adpt.); Alphonse Daoust to Henry Joseph Dauost; Virginia May Davis to Virginia May Shaw (adpt.); Chester Nordstrom to Edwin Michael Hodgson (adpt.); Marie Dodge to Marie Bliss Hodgson (adpt.); Caroline Faye Demeritt to Caroline Faye Demeritt (adpt.); Everett F. Ames to Kenneth Everett Chamberlain (adpt.); Edythe G. Chamberlin to Edythe G. Chamberlin (adpt.); Byron L. Tirrell to Byron L. Galloupe (adpt.); Priscilla J. Davis to Priscilla J. Sargent (adpt.); Helen E. Butterfield to Edith May Black (adpt.); Blanche L. Carisiti to Blanche Louise Cox; Evelyn May Carr to Joan Carr; Milton Arthur Wilson to Milton Arthur Wilson (adpt.); Dorothy Twombly to Dorothy Morin (adpt.); Miriam Kuronen to Marilyn Betty Parkey (adpt.); ----- Bishop to Elizabeth Esther Zanes (adpt.); Richard Jesse Robinson to Richard Jesse Canfield (adpt.); Lawrence Nickerson to Herbert Cecil Mudgett (adpt.); Roland Genest to Roland Genest Levasseur (adpt.); Rosamond Flack to Rosamond Florence Smith (adpt.); Albert Plaistard Blake to Albert Plaistard Blake (adpt.); Arthur Napoleon Boisvert to Arthur Napoleon Greenwood; Priscilla Shackleford to Priscilla Shackleford Cantin (adpt.); Ralph M. Shackleford to Ralph Shackleford Cantin (adpt.)

Carroll County - James Edward Kilgore to James Edward Army; Chester Cook to Chester George Stevens; Geneva Cook to Jane Colbath; Kenneth Knowles to Kenneth Garland; Una G. Thompson to Una G. Hutt; Arthur Johnson to George F. Ragna, Jr.; Louise M. Foster to Louise M. Hurd; Dorothy Emmons to Barbara Joyce Pike; Robert

1931-1933

Witham to David Earl Stillings; Shirley E. Coolidge to Shirley E. Larlee; Alice D. Merrow to Mrs. Frances Tuckerman

Merrimack County - Raymond H. Shaw to Raymond Herbert Manning; Anushaven George Sanders to Andrew George Sanders; Lucy Dustin to Lucille May Thompson; Catherine Quimby Taylor to Catherine Quimby Fredette; Kathryn Gross Kilburn to Kathryn A. Gross; Raymond S. Gillies to Raymond S. Pike; Forrest Evert Faris to Forrest Evert Boutelle; Florence Jean Pierce to Florence Jean Pierce Foster; Jean Lent to Jean Evelyn Nerden; Jane Virginia LaBombard to Jane Virginia Small; Louise Ann Roach to Betty Ann Roach; Jean Hazel Gordon to Frances Irene Adams; Roland Plastridge to Roland Barnard; Irene J. Olsen to Irene J. Young; Sylvester Wheeler to Sylvester Drew; Henry Joseph Morell to Henry Joseph Frederick DeLorme; Frederick J. Bowlan to Wallace Everton Brill; Harlan Straw to Harlan Floyd LaClair; David Arthur Smith to Thomas Boardman Sawyer; Doris May Garland to Doris May Johnson; June Violet Storrs to June Violet Storrs Wheeler; Robert Chapman to Robert Marshall Gulley; Dorothy C. Heath to Marjorie Louise Swetnam; Helen Agnes Ramsay to Helen Ramsay Lynch; Richard Bryant Ramsay to Richard Ramsay Lynch; Barbara Janice Wyman to Barbara Janice Wyman Girouard

Hillsborough County - Charles H. Towle to Charles H. Gallup; Marguerite Payeur to Marguerite Payeur Gagne; Donald Arthur Marston to Donald Arthur Nichols; Grace Margaret Sullivan to Grace Margaret Pritchard; Virginia Gertrude Twombly to Virginia May Peterson; Lillian Arlin Braga to Barbara Arline Latour; Harold Carl Hathaway to Carl Harold Pieritz; Mary Dorothy Bushman to Dorothy Silva; James Page to Clifford Wagne Johnson; Mary Fournier to Mary Jane Eivers; Aurele Beauregard to Aurele Catudal; Donald Eugene Ellis to Willard Laurence White; Robert Lacosse to Robert Lafreniere; Marie Edna Lacosse to Marie Eva Chouinard; Beverly Hathaway to Althea Kettelle; George Dana Lovejoy to George Dana Desroche; ----- Boyden to Theodore John Stone; Mary Agnes Barrett to Mary Loretta Ann Roy; Jack Marshall Jarest to Jack Marshall Gallagher; George Kenneth Hallett to George Kenneth Whiting; Mildred Laura Parsons to Mildred Laura Gutterson; Stanley Stewart Sturtevant to Stanley Sturtevant Grant; Marjorie P. Smith to Pauline Margaret Robert; Joseph Zemacoupis to Walter Prescott Bailey; Patricia O'Leary to

1931-1933

Doris Labarge; Joseph Emile Henry Pepin to Joseph Emile Henry Senneville; Henrietta Josephine Edmondson to Henrietta Josephine Page; Joseph Stribling to Joseph Steuerwald; Virginia Bessey to Margaret Swart; Marie Cecile Angers to Marie Cecile Dugre; ----- Allen to Lorraine Laporte; William Hawksworth to William R. Ford; Donald J. Lilly to Donald Lilly Clark; Floyd Elmer Carleton to Floyd Elmer Farnsworth; Norman Joseph Howland to Robert Leo Lowell; Marie Anne Gervais to Marie Anne Bienvenue; Hector Schellenger to Edouard Bonneville; Barbara P. Lathrop to Barbara P. Currier; Virginia A. Lathrop to Virginia A. Currier; Leonel Roy to Leonel Gagnon; Mary DeLourdes Joseph to Mary Eafrate; Philip Roy to William Marlowe; Francis William Conolly to Richard Glenn MacDonald; Priscilla Stetton to Lorraine Flanders; Frances Faye Crouse to Faye Etta Lange; Ernest Garceau to Ernest Garceau, Jr.; James Wallace Sawyer to James Timothy Spillane; Shirley Elizabeth Sturtevant to Elinor Grant; Marguerite Clair Maloney to Rita B. Nadeau; Patricia Ann Fortier to Patricia Ann Bricault; Mary Landers to Mary Hallisey; Edna Randlet to Edna Jacques; Carrie Dickinson to Carolyn Maud Streeter; Robert Parker to Robert Parker Nichols; John Frederick Keefe to John Frederick Fosher; Barbara Brown Day to Rose-marie Joan Sargent; Paul Brown Davis, Jr. to Paul Brown Watson; Patricia A. Fitzpatrick to Mary Flora Collier; Paul Gowing to Paul Henry Ouellette; Norman Russell McCutcheon to Norman Forbes Richards; Joseph Wilfrid Armand to Joseph Wilfrid Lafreniere; Mary Looney Sullivan to Mary Theresa Looney; Olive LaClair to Olive Gregg; Frederick Williams Bullen to Frederick Williams Potter; Harry Allen Prescott to John Allen Mack; Bernice Rockus to Marjory Jones; Abbie G. Cole to Abbie Clarica Gault; Nicholas J. Marcovicy to Nicholas J. Marks; Victoria Marcovicy to Victoria Marks; Emery Courtemanche to Emery Boyd; Francois Sebastien Isreal Bourgeois to Camille Sebastien Bourgeois, Jr.; Demetrios Pliakos to Demetrios Papamastasiou; Mrs. Adah L. Cote to Miss Adah L. Cote; Athanasios Pappachristos to Arthur Papachristos Mikolaj Hroniack to Mikolaj Bednarczyk; Marvin B. Belavsky to Marvin B. Bellows; Winslow Manchester Jackson to Winslow Manchester; Joseph Emanuel Lovci to Joseph Edward Lovesey; Joan Crawford Moir to Eleanor Mary Reilly; Mildred Reardon Gerow to Mildred Reardon; John Tubinis to John Dugan; Anthoula Moustakas to Anthoula Papademas; Servule Charrois, Jr. to Charlis S. Charois; Georgie H. Nealley to Georgie H. Merrill; Jacob Belavsky to Jacob

1931-1933

Bellows; Joseph Deskowicz to Joseph Landry; Paul Joseph St. Denis to Paul Joseph Fletcher; Sarah Morrill to Sarah Creeden; Grace Bennett Knowles to Grace R. Bennett; Eva Florence Richard to Eva Lillian Allard

Cheshire County - Pearl E. Brown to Pearl E. Thayer; Ellen L. Bowen to Ellen L. Moon; Russell M. Bowen to Russell W. Moon; Robert Billings Hubbard to Robert Penniman Hubbard; Charles Herbert Shedd to Charles Gale Shedd; Rose Mary Stackpole to Claire Agnes Stackpole; Lawrence Francis Brasier to Lawrence Francis Flynn; Robert Woods Huse, Jr. to Robert Woods Davis; Gertrude C. Sullivan to Gertrude C. Whitehead; Leslie Richard Jones to Stanley Alger Curtis; Wilmot Estes Mayhew to Burton Franklin Marshall; Henry Abraham Ojala to Henry Abraham Brooks; Charles Medvidofsky to Charles Medoff; Lona Grace Medvidofsky to Lona Grace Medoff; Frances Lathrop to Elizabeth Anne Hall; John Henry Toussaint to Paul Henry Toussaint; Alexander Brooks to Dale Ellis Wyatt; Lee Knowlton Robinson to Lee Knowlton Channell; G. Madeleine Beckham to G. Madeleine Quinn; Dalton Daniel Williams to Leason Daniel Dickinson; Dimitrios Germanos to James Jaffas

Sullivan County - Irma Rosenthal to Irma Zirdzin; Clarence Waldron to James Warren Hawley; Dorothy Mae Cunningham to Dorothy Mae Smith; William Childs to William Lussier, Jr.; Zebulun Henry O. G. Jordan to Henry Oliver Jordan; Isaac Budnitz to Isaac Budd; Raymond Thibodeau to Raymond Lee Vadney; John Patrick Bergland to John Patrick Hook; Marie Elizabeth Handly to Marie Elizabeth Reed; Charles Rodger to Charles Rodger Robertson; Irene Tarrien to Irene Virginia Clark

Grafton County - Alfred Bresette to Alfred Bresetts King; Lockwood Clyde Clifford to Lockwood Clyde Meyers; Peter Covell to Peter C. Cummings; Edwin Morse Coon to Edwin Morse Burton; Gwendolyn E. Dudley to Gwendolyn E. Emery; Hazel Pearl Dunlap to Hazel Pearl Powers; Robert Paul Eaton to Robert Paul Davison; Helen Fizette to Helen Post Fizette; Gladys Fizette to Gladys Fizette Lawrence; Arthur Ferrin to Peter Jackson Parkey, Jr.; Janice Mabel Fortier to Janice Mabel Brown; Edward Charles Gomez to Edward Charles Eastman; Paul Rockwell Holman, Jr. to Rockwell Holman; Stella Eleanor Lynch

1931-1933

to Dorothy Winona Frye; Gordon Richard Lindsay to Richard Dana Barton; Frank Evans Marden to Frank Evans Briggs; George Ernest Magny to George Ernest Manley; Audrey Keith Mackly to Roger Oscar Karpuk; Paul Bernard Mayette to Paul Kenson Mayette; Robert Presby to Robert Presby Cardinal; Edward B. Parker to Edward B. Tewksbury, Jr.; Elizabeth Rushton to Elizabeth Merchant; Geraldine Greta Roy to Geraldine Greta Kimball; Richard Randlett to Hector George Polson, Jr.; Alice Weeks Ross to Alice Weeks Abbott; Gustave Casper Shuck to Donald Frederick Seaman; Doris Marion Sanborn to Doris Marion Sanborn; Everett M. St. Lawrence to Everett M. Winslow; Edythe A. Varney to Edythe A. Dewing; Ruth Vien to Ruth Isabelle Lewis; Bernard M. Wilkie to Bernard Elmer Morse; Shirley Ann Wood to Shirley Ann Whitcher; Walter Earl Washburn to Walter Earl Lowell; Agnes Josephine Woodard to Agnes Josephine Dickinson; Marion Irene Young to Marion Irene Parker; Demetrios George Zertopoulis to James George Zertos

Coos County - Jeanne Elizabeth Melville to Jeanne Elizabeth Twitchell; Edward Thomas Pelletier to Raymond Dearborn; Lawrence Preston Hansen to Lawrence Preston Hansen Johnson; Bertha Beatrice Pelchat to Bertha Beatrice Vachon; Blanche Nugent to Virginia Kathleen Young; Phyllis Strong to Phyllis Ellen Rix; Theodore Ray Brown to Theodore Ray Wright; Gerald Leveillee to Leonce Bisson; Jacqueline Bessie Howland to Leona Bessie Forbush; Bethany Ann Hughes to Pierina Basile; Doris Thibodeau to Doris Lessard; Elizabeth Anne Morrissette to Elizabeth Anne Paquette; Shirley Ann Derosier to Shirley Ann Pace; Anita Louise Straw to Anita Louise Bryan; Stanley Dana Dodge to Stanley William McGee; Pauline LeBel to Pauline Goddard; Eleanor Christina Ferrari to Eleanor Christina Allard

Name changes made by the superior court in divorce proceedings:

Rockingham County - Cecelia S. Whitby to Cecelia S. Briggs; Elizabeth G. Davis to Elizabeth Greig; Grace A. Gilford to Grace A. Hill; Harriet E. Shirley to Harriet E. Pease; Dora A. Pinkham to Dora A. Graham; Selina Edith Thompson to Selina Edith Simpson; Florence Peckham Locke to Florence Peckham; Edith Grace McLean to Edith Grace Smith

1931-1933

Strafford County - Hattie E. Kenerson to Hattie E. Couture; Sibyl E. Bachelor to Sibyl E. Lord; Mabel E. Horne to Mabel E. Leavitt; Gertrude M. Otis to Gertrude M. Stone; Anna B. Foss to Anna B. Gray; Nellie Nadeau to Nellie McCarron; Mildred E. McAlister to Mildred E. Price; Anne S. Tuttle to Anne Sanborn; Mildred A. Burleigh to Mildred A. Tuttle; Alice F. Dodge to Alice F. Moore; Annette E. Howard to Annette E. Joy; Helena L. Lamontte to Helena L. Danahy; Edith M. Cole to Edith M. Haynes; Addie N. Garside to Addie N. McEwan; Cora M. Files to Cora M. Brunelle; Georgia A. Norwood to Georgia A. Morrill

Belknap County - Esther L. Corliss to Esther J. Lamphrey; Rose D. Chouinard to Rose D. Dufour

Carroll County - Gladys E. Cole to Gladys E. Kendrick

Merrimack County - Nanni J. Sullivan to Nanni J. Peterson; Gladys J. Haggerty to Gladys Moses; Elizabeth Hope Small to Elizabeth Hope Blood; Mabel W. Andrew to Mabel Wood; Ethel Blanchard to Ethel E. Lund; Thaylia Plummer Bullard to Thaylia Plummer; Nora Morgan Resse to Nora Morgan; Grace D. Rennie to Grace D. Owen; Caroline Goss Blandin to Caroline Goss McLouth; Susie M. Publicover to Susie M. Young; Mildred R. Hoadley to Mildred Savoy; Mildred N. Bourke to Mildred N. Dunsford; Bernice A. Pierce to Bernice Ashton; Mildred E. Blake to Mildred E. Burns; Doris B. Hall to Doris B. Tinkham; Bertha L. Corser to Bertha Lillian Gaskell; Corinne Wilma Blevens to Corinne Wilma Bouwman

Hillsborough County - Norma Elizabeth Corveau to Norma Elizabeth Michaud; Mary Hazel Elmes to Mary Hazel Bickford; Marie B. Danforth to Marie Battryn; Beatrice C. Larochelle to Beatrice Croteau; Mary M. Prescott Nason to Mary M. Prescott; Corinne Trepanier to Corinne Boisvert; Gertrude Wilson Valley to Gertrude O. Wilson; Violena Cutter to Violena Rancourt; Evelyn C. Paquette to Evelyn C. Raymond; Lena U. McAdoo to Lena U. Sargent; Dora J. Toumbas to Dora J. Dionne; Hattie Artimise Scribner to Hattie Arthemise Bergeron; Mary Grace George to Mary Grace Poole; Laura Fournier to Laura Fountain; Lois E. Currier to Lois E. Munson; Lena Duke to Lena Charpentier; Elizabeth R. Monast to Elizabeth R. Watkins; Beatrice Page to Beatrice Desrosiers; Marguerite H. Powers to Marguerite H. Wilkins; Estelle

1931-1933

Beadle to Estelle Cartlidge; Doris V. Reed to Doris V. Brown; Margaret D. LaBelle to Margaret C. Dinwoodie; Isabelle Buchanan to Isabelle Brien; Phaebe L. Dugas to Phaebe L. Boisseau; Evelyn Willey to Evelyn Bell; Louisa Agnes Gleason to Louisa Agnes Rollins; Evelyn M. Archibald to Evelyn M. Boardman; Doris M. Easter to Doris E. Mitchell; Madeline A. Borden to Madeline A. Douglass; Mildred Rooney to Mildred Pray; Margaret Wallace to Margaret Shea; Bernice L. Spaulding to Bernice L. Hanson; Delia Waldron to Delia Soucy; Phyllis Barker to Phyllis Wallace; Gretchen Seifert to Gretchen Koch; Eunice P. Miller to Eunice P. Hepill; Mildred E. Crockett to Mildred E. Burleigh; Ivie A. Trow to Ivie A. Rice

Cheshire County - Mary I. Baker to Mary I. Blodgett; Mabel Irene Claywood to Mabel Irene Kempton; Anne L. Croteau to Anne L. Beers; May Elmy Davidson to May Elmy Taylor; Ina O. Fitzgerald to Ina O. Valley; Marion E. Imm to Marion E. Brown; Sarah J. Swan to Sarah J. Nadeau

Sullivan County - Sarah Colcord to Sarah Ackroyd; Minna M. Walker to Minna Mary Boyce; Alice G. Moran to Alice Grace Walker; Mildred B. Marro to Mildred B. Colby; Ina I. Robbins to Anita I. Pushard; Cynthia J. Miles to Cynthia J. Cain; Helen B. Davis to Helen Beers; Jessie Oram Heath to Jessie Oram McKay

Grafton County - Mabelle Stone to Mabelle Downing; Myrtle E. Day to Myrtle Eva LaBombard; Katherine C. Plant to Katherine C. Weeks; Betsey Manchester to Betsey Johnson; Hazel G. Goodwin to Hazel G. Goodhue; Coletta Westling to Coletta Beston; Stella M. Bachand to Stella M. Barker; Bertha M. Jewell to Bertha M. Wetherbee; Marion A. Davis to Marion A. Sharon; Lucinda R. Bell to Lucinda R. Sutcliffe; Josie May Muchmore to Josie May French; Nellie L. Rancour to Nellie A. Leonard; Philona L. Keniston to Philona L. Downes; Mary B. McDuffey to Mary Florence Bates; Nina Vivian Talbert to Nina Vivian Farnham

Coos County - Evelyn Anctil to Evelyn Bushway; Ida Sidelinger to Ida Stewart; Madelene Parkhurst to Madelene Forbush; Edna Mae Fleming to Edna Mae Wilson; Harriet M. Rollins to Harriet M. Noyes; Doris M.

1931-1933

LaPlant to Doris M. Cook; Nettie Simpson to Nettie Shufelt; Olive J. Rich to Olive J. Nourse

January 1933 - January 1935[6/]

Name changes made by the probate courts:

Rockingham County - Bernard Vincent Jenkaites to Bernard Vincent Jennings; Elsie Beatrice Fudge to Mary Elizabeth Williams; Eileen Mary Casey to Eileen May Faucher; Pearl E. Trafton to Pearl E. Witham; John Donald Welch to John Donald Groetz; Florabel Evans to Florabel Gray; Walter Evans to Robert Gray; Marjory Evans to Marjory Gray; Dorothy L. Evans to Dorothy L. Gray; LeRoy Victor Hubley to Dona LeRoy Kimball; Hazel Jackson to Hazel Atkinson; Harold William Bjorklund to Harold William Burklund; Helen Frances Carroll to Helen Frances Adams; John Hildreth to John Robert Gilbert; Kathryn Kalinsky to Kathryn Kalens; Pauline Frances Kalinsky to Pauline Frances Kalens; Lulu C. Atherton to Hazel Atherton; Vesta E. Lenchte to Vesta E. Jewell; Alma Jean Robertson to Alma Jean Pendergast; Carol Ann Fraser to Carol Ann O'Hara; Geraldine Adams Loughlin to Gerald Adams Johnson; Frederick George Collum to Frederick George Kreuzer, Jr.; Ruth Leighton to Judith Wentworth; Swan Christian Hansen to Dwight Ferguson Crow; Frances Rita Bourinot to Rita May McCormick; Janet Dexter Barber to Janet Dexter Winchester; Beulah Alice Garside to Beulah Alice Kolvig; Donald Stephen Brooks to Donald Stephen Varnerin; Rodney H. Schakowski to Rodney H. Davis; Ada M. Schakowski to Ada M. Davis; Robert Francis Jarvis to Paul Chadbourne Jacobs; Stanislau Andrychowski to Andrew Jackson Stacy; Agnes Louise Andrychowski to Agnes Louise Stacy; Henry J. Conley to Ronald Paquette; Irene Constance Keene to Irene Constance Rand; Ernest Paul to Robert Charles Gillett; Anthony McClellan to Winston Grant Procter; Llewellyn Trevena to John Edward Reed; Frederick George Kreuzer, Jr. to Anton J. Johnson, Jr.

Strafford County - Anna Krinsky to Anna Kinsley; Thelma M. Wright to Thelma M. Hill; Robert Parshley to Norman Robert Boulet; Helen Frances Quint to Helen Frances Forbes; Abraham Eber Krinsky to Eber Kinsley; John Harold North to John Harold O'Neil; Barbara Lucille Chick to Barbara Lucille Rainaud; Jesse Robert Grant to Robert Grant Bickford; Robert Dupuis to Robert King; Barbara Louise Grass to Barbara Louise Roy; Jean B. Rainaud to Jean B. Kelly; Perley Albert

---

6/ Chapter 269, 1935 N. H. Public Laws

1933-1935

Barbara Louise Roy; Jean B. Rainaud to Jean B. Kelly; Perley Albert Clark to Perley Albert Clark Currier; Frances Roy to Frances Marie Grondin; Bertha I. Bean to Bertha I. Harris; Ronald Currier to Ronald Currier Lane; Louise Joyce Tuttle to Louise Joyce Marshall

Belknap County - Barrie Elaine Hanson to Barrie Elaine Martin; Mary F. Baker to Marie Flour DeLess LaHaise; Joseph Albert Boisvert to Audry Arthur Smith.

Changed by adoption: Priscilla Natalie Kimball to Phillis Natalie Stockwell; Dora Etta Bowden to Dora Etta Whitten; Delora Lacroix to Mary Delora Goyner; Robert Ervin Velmont to Robert Ervin Levoy; William Lacroix to Dolmar Elliott Whitten; Elizabeth M. MacDonald to Elizabeth May Rogers; Robert Earl Aldrich to Robert Earl Aldrich; Joan Beverly Dubois to Joan Beverly Bragg

Carroll County - Ethel R. Avedesian to Ethel Rollins Ballard; William J. Atwood to Angelo Cataldi; Richard Clayton Avedesian to Richard Clayton Ballard; Claude B. Dearborn to Clyde R. Dearborn, Jr.; Barbara Dunlap to Mildred Barbara Dearborn; John Louge Dow to John Dow Newton; Thomas Whitman Bartlett to Thomas Whitman Danforth; Roland G. Gray to Albert E. Haseltine; Clifton Leonard McCann to Billie Frederick Ritchie; Richard Allen Miller to Richard Allen Ridlon; Agnes Greta Orcutt to Agnes Greta Ritchie

Merrimack County - Clement Cyr to Paul Albert Richotte; Donald Charles Sanborn to Donald Charles Marston; Evelyn Rose Fleury to Evelyn Rose French; Gladys Coulson to Gladys Coulson Folsom; James Lockwood to James Harris; Kathleen Brown to Kathleen Ryan; Harland Cutler to Harland Cutler Tyrrel; Roland Ernest Hazelton to Roland Ernest Locke; Donald Nudd to Donald Hurd; Pauline Nudd to Pauline Hurd; Emily Louise Bethune to Emily Louise Sprague; Shirley Irlene Mason to Shirley Irlene Mack; Sarah G. Hodgman to Sarah C. Gillingham; Leon Joseph Serin to Leon Joseph Leclare; Ella Margaret Morrison to Ella Margaret Anderson; Beryle Center to Beryle McLaughlin; Marjorie Center to Marjorie McLaughlin; Grosvenor P. Hill to James Grosvenor Prentiss Hill; Elsie M. Lively to Elsie M. Severence; Marjorie Huston to Marjorie Holdsworth; Richard York to Allan McCrea Davis; Marie Agnes Bellerose to Marie Agnes McDonald;

1933-1935

Richard Frederick Curry to Richard Walter Smith; Ruth Louise Hicken to Ruth Louise Girdley; Virginia Mae Corbett to Virginia Mae Cruikshank; Carl Lawrence Plummer to Lester Tenison Gulley; Robert Allen to Robert Allen Chandler; Kenneth Nudd to Kenneth Hurd; Doris DeCota to Luanne Beverly Simpson; Josephine L. Alberty to Josephine L. King; Mona Gilman to Mona M. Thompson; Florence H. Hammond to Florence W. Harris; David Lee Attaya to David Lee Brown

<u>Hillsborough County</u> - Jean Lula to Jean Andrikowich; Honorious D. Classe to Norris D. Class; Yvonne Gonthier to Yvonne Lemay; Marie Anna Migneault to Blanche Marie Maranda; William P. Goodman, Jr. to William P. Goodman; Elias Papadoplos to Elias J. Papp; Hazel T. Guess to Hazel M. Towle; Rose Foster to Rosalind Foster; Edith Elizabeth Guilmette to Edith Elizabeth Broderick; Louise A. Ingelstrom to Louise A. Nickerson; John Edward Gurkowski to John Edward Gordon; Theodore A. Pappas to Theodore A. Christophil; Helen Zegarowska to Helen Kokoszka; Thelma Louise Provost to Thelma Louise Marshall; Vitul Belos to William Bellows; Stanley Belos to Stanley Bellows; Ernest Diemond to Arnold Diemond; Daniel Smith Marshall to Daniel Appleton Marshall; Richard Henry Vennott to Richard Henry Rogers; Helen Viola Drazkowska to Helen Viola Doyle; Robert Martineau to Robert Carignan; Clarence E. Goings to Robert Clarence Goings; Rodolphe J. Bernard to Peter J. Bernard; John Mason to John Melanson; Priscilla Ruth Bassett to Priscilla Ruth Parker; Ermanno Becchetti to Ermanno Cecchetti; Mae Louise McKenzie to Mae Louise Somerville; William J. Doschavich to William J. Dorson; Ellen E. Remick to Ellen E. Heath; Lillian M. Ennis to Lillian M. Leblanc; Ellen Leota Provost to Ellen Leota Marshall; Dorothy E. Garbarine to Dorothy Eastman; Irene A. Pappas to Irene A. Christophil; Aileen Mary Soraghan to Aileen Mary Hood; Chauncey Wallace Derbyshire to John Joseph Blakeley; Giovanni Piertrantoni to John Peter Anthony.

Changed by adoption: Consuelo Redden to Constance M. Sweeney; Theresa Mary Ledoux to Elaine A. Boilard; George Ernest Carpenter to George Richard Reney; a child given the name Mary Lorraine Josette Jeannotte; Catherine Dorothy to Catherine Dorothy Donovan; Bruce Darracott to Bruce Darracott Weston; a child given the name Russell Woollacott; Patricia Diane Denoit to Irene Lillian DuBois;

1933-1935

Edward G. Fischer to Thomas Edwards Cox; Ella Violet Hardy to Ella Violet Forbush; Baby Demers to Evangelos Panos Loukedes; Laurine Blanchette to Lorraine Pauline Blanchette; Richard Porter Doolittle to Wells Webster Whitney; James Hamilton Doolittle to Anthony Murdock Whitney; Marguerite Helen Vincent to Rita Agostini; George Lavallee to George Rheaume; Mona Annette Patten to Mona Annette Haywood; Clesson Marsh to Clesson Marsh Duke; Cleon Marsh to Cleon Marsh Duke; Mary Rose Richards to Marie Esther Lamb; Wallace George Gibson to Wallace McIntyre Walbridge; Lawrence Edward Muzzey to Lawrence Edward Stone; Helen Mary Boynton to Helen Mary Keddy; Philip Joseph Study to Philip Joseph Legendre; Arthur O'Neil to Arthur Donovan; Patricia DeGrandpre to Lea Vina Duval; Mary Galecki to Mary Kasper; Joseph Francis Houle to Leo Francis Couture; William Donald Sullivan to Donald Norman Larrivee; Leslie Eugene Boardman to Leslie Eugene Jones; Ronald Simoneau to Ronald Heywood Dubuc; Virginia Ann Smith to Virginia Ann Kilroy; Helen Jowders to Ileane Dorothy Hayes; Irene Denancourt to Helen C. Hebert; Josephine Regan to Judith Churchill; Judith Ann Healy to Elizabeth Jane Steuerwald; Richard Joseph Brochu to George Albert Chiasson; Joan May Schellenger to Joan May Grant; Richard Raby to Richard Arthur Holt; Angela O'Neill to Jane Martha Driscoll; Carolyn Irwin to Carolyn Louise O'Blenis; Raymond Gould to John Leonard Beeman; Teresa A. Carroll to Teresa A. Foley; Dickie Provencher to Donald Parker Dickinson; Stephen Meserve to Alfred R. Lavigne; Myrtle Lynch to Dorothy Myrtle Carlson; Mary Jane Riley to Mary Jane Merrill; Baby Reed to Carol Musk; William Smith to William Drolet; Rita Moran to Rita Moran O'Gara; Elizabeth Kudzma to Nancy Elizabeth Lee; Daniel LeClair to Joseph Edward Simoneau; Baby Locke to Myra Lois Folsom; Louis Huard to Frank Boyer, Jr.; a child given the name Barbara Ann French; Gloria Lavigne to Gloria Labore; Herbert Joseph Trumbull to John Dennis Hanchett; Franklin Moody Bushway to Arthur Eugene Hadley; Orville Fitts to Orville Richard Anttila; Arthur Joseph Lavoie to Arthur Joseph Provencher; Virginia Ann Kilroy to Virginia Ann Long; Joanne Wyatt to Joanne Aylsworth; Ruth T. Halley to Collette Nantel; Albert Vanasse to Albert Jacque LaBonte; Hester Mary Dupont to Hester Mary Landry; Rodney Robert Poisson to Richard R. Senecal; Rita Lorraine Gaudette to Rita Lorraine Collier; Ruby Lucille Chase to Ruby Lucille Bosley; Carol Barr to Carol Barr Hooper; Therese Lorraine Pinette to Therese Lorraine Ricard; Sophie Karkunis to Helen Peters;

1933-1935

Patricia Fitzpatrick to Frances T. Mailhot; Paulette Lamoreux to Anne Reney; Barbara White to Barbara Ann Walker; Lorraine Gertrude Grasset to Loretta A. Keenan; Maurice Dionne to Maurice Davis

<u>Cheshire County</u> - Dorothy Ellen Ewins to Dorothy Ellen Hastings; Thelma June Wisell to Thelma June Marsh; Charles W. Farrington to Charles W. Dean; Dustin Richards Hall to Hollis Richards Hall; Ruth Aravesta Hamilton to Ruth Aravesta Bunce Hamilton; Dorothy Harriet Freeman to Dorothy Harriet Garfield; Frederika Esther Marvin-Kauffmann to Frederika Maria Marvin; Joseph Babeu to Joseph Babbitt; Ellen Ruth Kauffmann to Ellen Ruth Marvin; Beryl Evelyn Grout to Beryl Evelyn Boynton; Kenneth H. Holbrook to Kenneth Randall Holbrook; Helen G. Pitt to Helen G. Roberts; Francis Ryan to Francis Willard Fosdick; Effie M. Ruffini to Effie May Mitchell; Mary Elizabeth Valenti to Mary Elizabeth Davis; Beverly Murray to Beverly Cahill; Bessie Cornelia Marvin-Kauffmann to Bessie Cornelia Marvin; Marion Brooks to Margaret Louise Davis; Margaret Hale Hamburger to Margery Hale Hamburger; Robert Francis Ruffini to Robert Francis Fairfield; David Ruffini to David Eugene Fairfield; Joseph Kercewich, Jr. to Joseph Kershaw; Helen M. Kercewich to Helen M. Kershaw; Edward W. Kercewich to Edward W. Kershaw; Ernest Haddad to Ernest Mossey; Emily J. Whitcomb to Emily J. Glendenning; Samuel Butterfield to Arthur Joseph Varville; Martha Jeanette Pair to Martha Virginia Moline; Charles Francis Baldwin to Charles Francis Brian Field; Raymond Joseph Vaillancourt to Raymond Joseph Wallace; Richard Gordon Bunce to Richard Bunce Hautenan; Viola Sivula to Viola Simpanen; Lawrence M. Guyette to Edwin Lawrence Marden; George Ellsworth McGrath to William Francis Majer; Irene E. Wilder to Carol Betsy Whitcomb

<u>Sullivan County</u> - George Dennis Kereazopoulous to George Dennis Kungulus; Fay Heath Falconer to Fay L. Heath; Richard Edward Myers to Donald Frenette; Leon Satinski to Leon Satin; Donald Kenyon to Ronald Stanley Dunbar; Gerald F. Godfrey to Gerald F. Bunker; Jean Marie DeGree to Jean Marie LaTour; Victor Albert Marcotte to Victor Willard McKenzie; Ronald Albert Marcotte to Ronald Willard McKenzie; Leroy George Parizo to Leroy George Pariseau; Ronald Ray Parizo to Ronald Ray Pariseau; Rose Mary Parizo to Rose Mary Pariseau; Harold Henry Parizo to Harold Henry Pariseau; Donald Frank Parizo to

1933-1935

Donald Frank Pariseau; Jacob Bayarsky to Jacob Bayer; Harry Bayarsky to Harry Bayer; Raymond E. Tobine to Raymond Eugene Lewis; Margaret Gohl Brown to Margaret Sheilman Gardner; Harriet Salinsky to Harriet Shulins; Selma Lindstrom to Selma Lind; Beverly Mae Martin to Beverly Mae Ordway; Ray Bergeron to Ray MacAdams; Floyd William Martin to Floyd William Ordway; Reta Jean Duguay to Joanne Jean Johnson; Angelo George Anastos to Anastasios George Anastos; Genieve M. Parizo to Genieve M. Pariseau; Edward W. Parizo to Edward W. Pariseau; Cleon E. Wright to Cleon E. Bartlett

Grafton County - Kenneth Russell Brisbois to Kenneth Russell Morse; Edith Derrington to Edith Herbert; Grace Elaine Dunlap to Maxine Kaye Lorden; Marion Louise Danforth to Marion Louise Downing; George James Moran to George James Downing; Joseph E. Therrien to John Rivers; Pauline May Baker to Pauline May Watson; William Edward Baker to William Edward Goss; Constance June Brusoe to Constance June Straw; Earl Howard Cook to Earl Cook Farnham; William S. Dunn, Jr. to William Shepard Lingley; Donald Robert Gingras to Elwin Donald Wilds; Stanley James Holt to Stanley Walter Peightell; April Waneita Hurley to April Waneita Bowlen; Harold Hay to Richard Harold Gazley; William Nickel to William Nichol; Bertha W. Oakes to Bertha M. Watson; Douglas Verril Sylvester to Douglas Alden Tabor; Thomas Charles Edgerley White to Tom Charles White

Coos County - Marie Therese Labbe to Marie Therese Drapeau; Marlene Freda Roberta Erickson to Marlene Frances Johnson; Peter Benedict Gaudet to Peter Benedict Whitcomb; Francis Clark Gaudet to Francis Clark Whitcomb; Jean Charlotte Gaudet to Jean Charlotte Whitcomb; Wilmer Rich Gaudet to Wilmer Rich Whitcomb; Christina May Burns to Christina May Monahan; Barbara Elizabeth Patch to Barbara Elizabeth Tully; Donald Mitchell DeRosia to Donald Mitchell Nocky; Francis Arthur Ernest Ricker to Francis R. Stevens; Isola Laperle to Isola Bergeron; Doris Couture to Doris Baker; Richard James King to Richard James Morin; Mabel May Kiser to Mabel May Oakes; Robert Sisco to Robert Henry Leach; Katherine A. Chase to Katherine A. Gainor; Sylvia Carroll to June Lillian Heath; Theodore Ray Wright to Theodore Ray Estes; Roderick R. Bisson to Roderick Boivin

1933-1935

Name changes made by the superior court in divorce proceedings:

Rockingham County - Ella Paterson to Ella Gertrude Emery; Zylphia Geneva Howard Seamans to Zylphia Geneva Howard; Arlene Blood to Arlene Walker; Jessie M. Ames to Jessie M. Rand; Anna C. Donovan to Anna C. Kennick; Jessie Mitchell Hatch to Jessie Morrison Mitchell; Lillian A. White to Lillian A. Howard; Leila G. Heckleton to Leila Gertrude James; Helen D. Palfrey to Helen M. Duncan; Mary E. Pike to Mary E. Hayes; Dorothy W. B. Batcheller to Dorothy W. B. Gardner; Marion Britt to Marion Lane; Anna M. Wilson to Anna Hansen; Lois K. Blizzard to Lois Killmer; Viney H. Clough to Viney H. Walton; Clara M. R. Morse to Clara Moody Ridgway; Marjorie B. Brown to Marhorie B. Cate; Margaret J. Harvey to Margaret J. James; Sylvia Peterson to Sylvia Parker McIntosh; Tillie M. Ohliger to Tillie M. Altvatter; Katherine F. McNabb to Katherine F. Currier; Lena Williams to Lena Kuchinsky

Strafford County - Marion F. Morrison to Marion F. Holmes; Beatrice C. Scanlan to Beatrice C. Perkins; Evelyn E. Cate to Evelyn E. Gardner; Marie Cleaves to Marie Tanner; Vera K. Varney to Vera K. Ketchen; Elena M. Rice to Eleanor Lillian Moore; Edna P. Glidden to Edna Pearl Tirrell; Mina F. Isaacson to Mina Mildred Forrest; Ethel F. Brown to Ethel F. Benner; Nellie May Gresty to Nellie May Taylor; Jennie M. Voinonatix to Jennie M. Wentworth; Lillian M. Burke to Lillian M. Dennett; Marcia M. Bell to Marcia Madeline Baxter; Marguerite E. Grant to Marguerite E. Phillips; Helen M. LaBrie to Helen M. Riley; Edith E. Kneiper to Edith Thompson; Esther Loring to Esther Smith; Bernice L. Garland to Bernice L. Glidden; Ernestine McKenney to Ernestine Sleeper; Jeanette Elizabeth Tonkin to Jeanette Elizabeth Saylor; Dorothy M. Demeritt to Dorothy M. Jackson; Eliza M. Cushing to Eliza M. Cook; Florence Baker to Florence Drew; Evelyn L. Judd to Evelyn L. Barton; Ella M. Tyler to Ella M. Brown

Belknap County - Helen P. McDougle to Helen S. Poole; Jennie Mae Murdock to Jennie Mae Cook; Mary J. Steele to Mary Jane Wilson; Agnes May Chase Shaw to Agnes May Chase; Mabel C. Plancon to Mabel Corbett; Caroline H. Glidden to Caroline H. Webster; Edna Smith Ball to Edna Smith; Alice Hoagland to Alice Rowell; Marion Frances Levoy to Marion Frances Sanders; Elizabeth Huff Jenkins to

1933-1935

Elizabeth M. Huff; Margaret C. Wilkins to Margaret C. Sawyer; Agnes L. Nadeau to Agnes L. Burnham

Carroll County - Olive E. Spooner to Olive E. Sinclair; Ruth J. Baker to Ruth Jenness; Lillian M. Bradley to Lillian M. West; Luella B. Perkins to Lulella B. McIntire; Lucy Helen Bolduc to Lucy Helen Currier; Dorothy E. Welch to Dorothy E. Moody; Harriet Fontana to Harriett Randall

Merrimack County - Una S. Morrison to Una S. Fuller; Eva Lapierre to Eva Belaire; Beatrice D. Grammont to Beatrice Diversi; Ann Sweeney Diversi to Ann Veronica Sweeney; Teresa D. Laird to Teresa Diversi; Margaret D. Durepo to Margaret Davis; Beatrice Wolfsohn to Beatrice Smith; Anna Belle Ellis to Anna Belle McGill; Jennie R. C. Thompson to Jennie R. Clark; Eunice M. Osgood to Eunice M. Ballard; Dorothy F. Olmstead to Dorothy F. Tippett; Esther Katherine Shultis to Esther Katherine Hartt; Gladys May Sargent Dearborn to Gladys May Sargent; Harriet Ferrin to Harriet Kennedy; Nina B. Corser to Nina Bean; Alma M. Emerson to Alma M. Berry; Anna Genevieve Millis Ash to Anna Genevieve Millis; Blanche A. Jacobs to Blanche DeForge; Clara G. Small to Clara Burns; Frances D. Brew to Frances D. Woodbury; Margaret Rose Huckins to Margaret Rose Venne; Mary A. Darrah to Mary A. Clark; Phyllis S. Savoy to Phyllis A. Stewart; Pauline Louise Stickles to Pauline Louise Davis

Hillsborough County - Carrie J. Clark to Carrie J. Shynott; Charlotte Mae Hawley to Charlotte Mae Barneetz; Leocadie Leblanc to Leocadie Moffette; Josephine Rose Prouty to Josephine Rose Buckminster; Corinne Laramy to Corinne Roy; Eleanor Cullinan to Eleanor George; Frieda M. Beadle to Frieda M. Dietlein; Grace Delores Coughlin to Grace Delores Bradshaw; Sarah J. Dow to Sarah J. Powers; Anna E. Lovering to Anna E. Eichorn; Blanche Sprague Heselton to Blanche Sprague; Mary Elizabeth Powers Smith to Mary Elizabeth Powers; Lylona D. Houle to Lylona D. Girard; Melverta F. Purington to Melverta F. Poore; Ethel E. Shoults to Ethel E. Rockwell; Bernice L. Crosby to Bernice L. Underhill; Thelma Palisoul to Thelma Cantrell; Edith Hannah Hutchinson to Edith Hannah Parkinson; Germaine Beaudoin to Germaine Clermont; Marcia Winefred Roll to Marcia W. Hill; Catherine I. Goodwin to Catherine I. Gross; Edith E. Chatel to Edith Eleanor

Nutbrown; Thelma Sturtevant to Thelma Tina Richards; Bessie R. White to Bessie R. Sario; Beatrice B. Messier to Beatrice B. Desclaux; Rebecca R. Lawrence to Rebecca Ruth Mushlin; Alice E. Brown to Alice E. French; Rowena W. Batchelder to Rowena A. White; Grace Doplace to Grace Blail Beaudet; Eloise Freeman to Eloise Marcus; Frances C. Byron to Frances A. Crowell; Marie Annette Hughes to Marie Annette Tasker; Edythe Early Lacy to Edythe Early Fournier; Demetra G. Brianas to Demetra A. Frangos; Nellie Hayford Smith to Nellie Hayford; Rose Bruno to Rose Pietrantoni; Eva May Gillette to Eva May Sweeney; Blanche E. Titus to Blanche Elizabeth Rogers; Amanda Vermette to Amanda Beaudoin; Daisy Lane to Daisy Campobasso; Ethel G. Hamilton to Ethel Gagnon; Grace H. Gill to Grace Florence Hadley

Cheshire County - Emma M. V. Bergeron to Emma Mary Venn; Theresa G. Chase to Theresa G. Crowley; Ruth Howard Currier to Ruth C. F. Howard; Elizabeth M. Doyle to Elizabeth Davis; Mary Hughes Geoghegan to Mary Hughes; Anna J. Graham to Anna J. Rudoff; Antonia A. Johnson to Antonia A. Jonaitis; Myrtle Annetta Lower to Myrtle Annetta Beal; Stella Stone Metivier to Stella Stone; Celia Parizo to Celia Melissa Nash; Gladys E. Smith to Gladys E. Peak; Myra E. Wilcox to Myra Evelyn Peel

Sullivan County - Ruby R. Belluscio to Ruby Raymond; Doris Elma Eastman to Doris Elma Blanchard; Reba M. Sposito to Reba Benson; Katherine D. Gregory to Katherine D. Magee; Jennie L. Davis to Jennie L. Call; Louise B. Moulton to Louise B. Greenwood; Mildred E. Luman to Mildred E. Trow; Claribel A. Cossett to Claribel Alford; Ruth (Briggs) Carroll to Ruth Briggs; Mary J. (Trow) Kendrick to Mary J. Trow; Emily Ruth Houde to Emily Ruth Stockwell; Clementine Boulerice to Clementine Dagenais

Grafton County - M. Alice Balben to M. Alice Waitt; Helen G. Gurney to Helen F. Gibbs; Thelma Howe to Thelma Sulloway; Delia Fox to Delia Goodwin; Martha Kelsea Chamberlin to Martha Louise Kelsea; Ruby K. Leach to Ruby K. Swinnerton; Rosa M. Rowe to Rosa M. Waterman; Dorothy Howard Carter to Dorothy Sybil Howard; Rebecca L. Richardson to Rebecca L. Williams; Esther Underwood to Esther Barr; Josephine H. Monica Welch to Josephine Helene Monica;

1933-1935

Kathleen S. Wells to Kathleen S. Mooney; Elsie M. Stewart to Elsie M. Pilotte; Blanche M. Bradley to Blanche M. Beattie; Doris L. Deroche to Doris L. Woolson; Ruth A. Thurlow to Ruth A. LaBombard; Edna Bailey Butterfield to Edna B. Bailey; Mildred V. Curran to Mildred V. Genna; Viola DeWitt to Viola Elizabeth Price; Gladys May Haywood to Gladys May Trumbull; Doris E. Salls to Doris E. Grace

Coos County - Sadie Leighton to Sadie Dowse; Evelyn Larkin to Evelyn Holmes; Lena May Pervere to Lena May Barber; Verna Rae Thomas to Verna Rae Newman; Miriam G. Foster to Miriam Gaynor; Selina M. Stone to Selina M. LaBonte; Georgia McPheters to Georgia Bell; Annie B. Dresser to Annie Cross; Marjorie Irene Bean to Marjorie Irene Gould; Anna Mae MacDonald to Anna Mae Leblanc; Florence S. McLaughlin to Florence Hazel Smith; Helen Eastman Lucchetti to Helen Lillian Eastman; Sally G. Holmes to Sally G. Hill; Ola M. Gallant to Ola M. Matthews

January 1935 - January 1937[7/]

Name changes made by the probate courts:

Rockingham County - Roger Ellis Whitney to Roger Ellis Preston; Robert Benson Kimball, Jr. to Benson Wheeler Brown; Marion S. Frost to Marion Louise Stevens; Lucy Catharine Stewart to Lucy Stewart Ross; Virginia O. Anderson to Virginia O. Nelson; Roger Douglas Clemons to Roger Edward O'Brien; Donald Boyd to Donald Eugene Boyd Austin; Frank William Loehn to Wallace August Loehn; Pauline Cora Florand to Pauline Cora Gosselin; Irene Rose Florand to Irene Rose Gosselin; Donald Warren to Donald Tatro; Eugene Raymond Tinker to John Edwin Neal; Dorothy Poland to Mary Theresa Lamoreux; Charles Lewis Smith to Floyd Palmer Smith; Jane Doe Stevenson to Mary Lou Grammont; Anna Mae Allen to Betsy Jane Marston; Kenneth Earl Morgan to Kenneth Earl Haley; Margaret Wenhold to Margaret Locke; Rhea Marie Dumais to Rhea Marie Lafrance; Harriet Tartalis to Sandra Dolores Parent; Evelyn Horne Collins to Evelyn Horne Brewster; Priscilla Faneras to Priscilla Powell; Pauline Faneras to Pauline Powell; Stanley S. Adamandares to Stanley S. Adams; Richard Gibbs Lapointe to Richard Gibbs Hammond; Todd Lee Wyman to Todd Lee Kyle; Philip N. Hutchings to Philip Arnold Broomfield; Peter Skopecki to Peter Kopecki; Nettie Skopecki to Nettie Kopecki; Joseph Skopecki to Joseph Kopecki; John Skopecki to John Kopecki; Teresa Brooks O'Leary to Teresa Brooks; Helen Heeney to Helen Hill; Everett Warren Johnson to Everett Warren Heath; Donald S. Anderson to Donald S. Thompson; Bessie Maude Hird to Betty Maude Hird; Doris Evelyn Shaw to Doris Evelyn Whitten; Harold Austin Trefethen to Harold Austin Kelleher; Chadbourne Wallace Quimby to Chadbourne Wallace Galt; Gail Quimby to Gail Kathryn Galt; Lillian E. Clark to Lillian E. Learnard; Barbara Virginia Cammett to Barbara Virginia Stamps; Eleuterio Iamele to Andrew Eleuterio Iamele; Mildred F. Proctor to Mildred F. Stevens; Wallace Crompton to Wallace Goldsmith Crompton; Myrtle E. Dennett Crompton to Blanche Myrtelle Crompton; Marlene Betty Adams to Alice Marilyn Furman

Strafford County - George Fisk to Charles Edward Weed; Clifford Alvra Butters to Clifford Alvra Young; Sally Anne Chimiklis to Yvette

---

7/ Chapter 256, 1937 N. H. Public Laws

1935-1937

McCann to Anita Evelyn Conners; Fannie Bailey Puffer to Frances Bailey Puffer; Jacqueline Ann Rodd to Jacqueline Ann Eldridge; Paul Shaw to Paul Shaw Herbert; Lois Stanton to Fredrika Hodgdon Kilburn; Sherman William Shirley to William Shirley Ballou; Charles Russell Turner to Charles Patnode Turner; Virginia Ruth Williams to Virginia Ruth Harris

Merrimack County - Stanley Arthur Fisher to Stanley Arthur Belanger; Margaret Mary Matte to Margaret Mary Ahern; Jacklyn Calleso to Jacklyn Chapman; Calvin Wesley Upton to Calvin Wesley Rollins; "Baby" Kirkpatrick to Janice Lucille Lewis; Richard LeBlanc to Richard John LeBlanc; Helen Prescott to Joyce Edith Howland; Maxwell Kerrick to Carroll Langdon Bristol, Jr.; Carol May McGrath to Nancy Deane Retter; Jeanne Ruth Gibbs to Jean Alicia Valliere; "Baby" Hill to Sidney Kynast Whiting; Robert O'Shaughnessy to Richard Coburn; Marian Louise Skinner to Marian Louise Cheney; "Baby" Giroux to Mary Joan Andrew; James Rodney Drake to Raymond Emerson; Viena Marie Halme to Viena Marie Halme Little; Jacqueline M. Smith to Jacqueline Mae Laramie; Jennie Florence Pettee to Jennie Florence Gray; Donald Herman Abbott to Donald Abbott Terrill; Robert Bruce Downing to Robert Bruce Ripley; David Marden to David Philip Marden; Isabelle Arville Bunce to Anne Miller Boutelle; Richard Francis French to Richard Francis Young; Norman Lapierre to Norman Lapierre Trottier; Beverly A. Maxson to Beverly Maxson Randall; Marilyn Ruth Heney to Marilyn Ruth Cressy; Mary Kathleen Heney to Mary Kathleen Cressy; Owen Elwyn White to Clarence Paul Stevens; Vera A. Blevens to Vera Dagmar Anderson; Vera A. Steele to Vera Althea Tuttle; Orvin Stanley Marsh to Vincent Stanley Marsh; Margaret Chandronait to Margaret Dubois; Carolyn Farnum to Carolyn Angie Farnum; Stephen White Gregory to Stephen White Winship; Joy Alice Smith to Joy Alice Clough; Alva Irving Leonard to Andrew Irving Anderson; Verne Roger Quinn to Verne Bernard Ingersoll; Frank Sherman Shepard to Robert Hersey Shepard; Marjorie McLaughlin to Marjorie Center; Louis Adelard LaMora to Louis Adelard Lamoureux

Hillsborough County - Frank Boyer, Jr. to Albert Louis Boyer; Helen Sedlewicz to Helen Sullivan; Hazel E. Murphy to Gloria Evangeline Nichols; Annie Sedlewicz to Annie Sullivan; Ruth M. Angus to Ruth M. Hall; Louis Raymond Beaupre to Louis Raymond Rioux; Charles

1935-1937

Cheney Schroeder to Charles Chute Cheney; Leda Gamache to Leda Dean; Joseph Henry Miller to Joseph Henry Miller Remillard; Fannie E. McGall to Fannie E. Robinson; Abraham Levine to John Lavigne; Phyllis Joan Rioux to Phyllis Joan Tobias; Ralph Irving Gaudreau to Irving Gaudreau Haselton; Louis Charles Andre Gaudreau to Louis Gaudreau Haselton; Joseph Paul Orlande Lemelin to Joseph Paul Orlande Anderson; Simos Vasilios Langas to Simos Vasilios Vasiliou; Avonia M. Rogers to Avonia M. Goethnee; Marie Albertine Brousso to Marie Albertine Bourcier; Euripede Hatzilelikas to Peter Hatzes; Dorothea Thompson Dubuc to Dorothea Thompson; Alta M. McClarty to Alta M. Foster; George F. Lavigne to George F. Reed; Beatrice Coburn to Beatrice Reed; Hendrick Kat to Hendrick Kate; Peter Slayton Straw to Ezekiel Albert Straw, Jr.; Isabella Marie Mayou to Isabella Marie Rood; Irene Theresa Sansouci to Irene Theresa Rau; Rose Helen Tremblay to Rose Helen Bergeron; Isabelle W. Winn to Isabelle W. Mahony; Burton Andrew Muzzey to Harland Andrew Muzzey; John C. Liliopoulos to John C. Lylis; Ernest J. Flannigan to Ernest J. Freeman; Ernest J. Flannigan, Jr. to Ernest J. Freeman, Jr.; Agnes G. Green to Diane Hunt; Madeline Lonergan to Madeline Hill; Joseph Archille LeClair to Joseph Archille LeClair de Francoeur; Delima Landry LeClair to Delima Landry LeClair de Francoeur; Leo Adelard LeClair to Leo Adelard LeClair de Francoeur; Rose Delima LeClair to Rose Delima LeClair de Francoeur; Florette Irene LeClair to Florette Irene LeClaire de Francoeur; Cecile LeClair to Cecile LeClair de Francoeur; Lois E. Mitten to Lois E. Watson.

Changed by adoption: Edward Read or Reed to Richard Boyer Anderson; Rose-marie Jean Sargent to Barbara Brown Day; William Kennedy to William Kennedy Foster; Doris Fuller to Doris Davis; Mary E. Roberge to Ann Filion; Reginald J. Therrien to Reginald P. Morin; Donald Allard to Edward J. Lehoullier; Flora May Graham to Flora May Smith; Marie Cecile Gertrude Thifault to Marie Cecile Gertrude Caron; Patricia Elaine Merrill to Margaret Gray Walbridge; Shirley Travis St. Denis to Shirley Travis Moller; Doris Frances Downey to Mary J. Easterberg; Donald Paul Oleson to Donald Earl Johnson; Mary E. Tondreau to Betty Ann English; Mary J. Beauregard to Patricia Ann Provencher; Theodore Doolittle to Theodore Joseph Degasis; William Burke to Robert Merrill Lagerquist; Phylis A. Deaette to Lorette Tanguay; Richard Labonte to Earl Edwin Mead; Roger A. Banden to

1935-1937

Roger S. Perreault; Leslie Garland Marston to Leslie Marston Kincaid; Roberta Baker to Lucille Claire Delude; Anne F. Brown to Jacqueline Maynard; Javern Manning to Alice Johnson Noyes; Joan Manning to Lucia Clapp Noyes; Rita Ann Robichaud to Rita Andrea Parent; John Elliot Innes to William MacDonald Battis; Baby Gould to Carrie Marie Lane; Laura Anne Cloutier to Patricia Laura Anne Cloutier; Ellen L. Downes to Ellen L. Fellows; Daniel Herbert Downes to Herbert D. Fellows; Gloria Marie Lucier to Gloria Marie Babel; Nureene Ouellette to Nureene Field; Pauline Rodier to Pauline Wilkaites; Reginald Storer to Reginald Storer White; Marie Therese Cecile Hamel to Marie Therese Cecile Gregoire; Armand Normand Bernard to Gaston Armand Bernard; Ronald G. Hutchinson to Ronald G. Fagnant; Betty Ryan alias Betty Ramsey to Elizabeth Ann Emerson; John Michael Morra to Frank Joseph Coco; Baby Regan to Jean Ann Buzzell; Delores Carol Ann Byrne to Dolores Carol Ann Wetherbee; Robert Fitzgerald to Robert James Roma; Patricia Laurent to Patricia Sanders; Baby Champagne to Peter Van Tetley; Lois Anne Ermalavich to Lois Anne Lalmond; Ruth Wilcox to Carol Stevens; Doris Ellen Lavigne to Doris Ellen Vaccarest; Marie Lucille Pauline Renaud to Marie Lucille Pauline Chaput; Valaria Menczywor to Valaria Puslecki; Mary J. Easterberg to Mary Joan St. Laurent; Donald McGuigan to James Donald Grenier; Theresa Elizabeth Powell to Theresa Elizabeth Cain; Phyllis Marie Davis to Phyllis Marie Powers; Pearl Marie Powell to Pearl Marie Cain; Gladys Beatrice Gamble to Gladys Beatrice Walker; Gladys Evelyn Davis to Joan Lucy Creel; Hazel Gertrude Davis to Hazel Esther Judkins; Gloria Faith Ashley to Muriel Gloria Tellier; Geneva Marie Holmes to Geneva Betty Reidy; Evelyn Reta Patten to Evelyn Reta Brown; Charlotte Mae Blood to Charlotte Mae Haight; Harriet Winona Gamble to Harriet Winona Manning; Albert Sansoucie to Albert Payant; John Robert Blakitis to Robert John Farland; Richard Carrigan to Richard Harold Bowden; Robert Carrigan to Robert Simonds Bowden; Ronald Osborne to Robert Louis Dube; Arthur R. Allaire to Joseph R. Minturn; Barbara Ann Burgess to Barbara Ann Boy; David Welch to Joseph R. Stuard; Robert Arthur Levesque to Robert Arthur Goulet; Mary E. Duquette to Shirley A. Truchon; Elizabeth Gladys Raymond to Elizabeth Gladys Brown; Dorothy Mae Jelley to Dorothy Mae Stewart; Baby Purdie to Harry Bradbury Musk; William Keefe to Robert Edward Goodfellow; Alfred J. Farland to Albert Joseph Sieradski; Joseph Albert Rouleau to Albert Henry Paquette, Jr.;

1935-1937

Lois Ann Beaubien to Lois Ann Moseley; Marion Christine Law to Patricia Ann Courtemanche; Marguerite A. Bowman to Mary Ann Bonin; Jacqueline Lorraine Rivard to Joan Dorothy Jorsan; Shirley Ann Barry to Shirley Ann Poehlman; Robert W. Doonar to Robert Donald Welch; Dolores Lorraine Hancock to Shirley Madeline Lones; Edward George Collette to Edward George Peterson; Arthur Roland Guimond to Arthur Roland Guerette

Cheshire County - Edgar Tieger to Edgar Teger; Mildred Pollard to Mildred Harriet Langdon; Lorraine Wilder to Lorraine Mae Benton; Chester Edward Chant to Chester Edward Venable; Anna May Miller to Anna May Stinson; Laura May Mundell to Laura Mae Whitman; Walter Baker to Walter John Croteau; Marilyn Ada Ayer to Marilyn Adah Ayer Beverly; Verna Mae Ayer to Verna Ayer Elwell; Constance Clark to Constance Nelson; Clayton Robert Gray or Clayton Robert Andrews to Roger Clayton Whipple; Audrey Mae French to Audrey Mae Dodge; Richard Elliot Shea to Morton Atwell Shea; Constance Maier to Constance Kostopoulos; Gladys C. Geiger to Gladys C. Egan; James Arthur Leslie to James Arthur Sibley; Kathleen Gloria Vargas to Kathleen Gloria Gooley; Viola Charlotte Vargas to Viola Charlotte Gooley; ----- Navish to Robert Earl Emery; Edward Allen Coombs to Edward Allen Symonds; Velda Joy Pickett to Velda Joy White; Joseph Arthur Doucette to Joseph Arthur Richard Doucette; ----- Sullivan to Richard Washburn Bates; Peter A. Kourevesis to Peter A. Karey; William Lessard to William Richard; Alfred Herbert Soderholm to Alfred Herbert Holmes; Bernice Baker Maxwell to Bernice Maxwell Graton; Robert Wilford Blain to Wilfrid Blain; ----- Sayers to Patricia Elizabeth Hoyt; Patricia Elizabeth Hoyt to Marilyn Elizabeth Hoyt; Norman Scott to Norman Georgina; Richard Scott to Richard Georgina; Beverly Rose Lurvey to Beverly Rose Willard; James Saunders to Charles Saunders; A. Lloyd Schurman to A. Lloyd Sherman; William Edward Howe to William Stowell Howe, Jr.; Gladys Raymond Piper to Ramona Gladys Gill; Daniel L. Louks to Daniel L. Glover; Evelyn Mary Warren to Evelyn Mary Freeman; Beverly Diantha Davis to Beverly Diantha Hale; Marion Alice Dean to Marion Alice Kenney; Jouerl Battashievch to Paul Bartashevich; Harry Portas to Roger Bartashevich; Lena Bartaskvic to Helen Bartashevich

1935-1937

Sullivan County - Ruth Johnson to Ruth Willis; Alice L. Louiselle to Alice L. Gillingham; Evelyn Vera Blaine to Evelyn Vera Leach; Ethel M. Atwood to Ethel M. Matthews; Bessie Mae Bunce to Bessie Mae Smith; Marjorie Melvina Barber to Marjorie Melvina Parizo; Rosamond Rollins to Louise Rollins; Prudence Evangeline Gardner to Prudence Evangeline Burke; Mary Chisholm to Mary Elizabeth Laber; Jane Elizabeth Walker to Jane Elizabeth Lacasse; Victor O. Parizo to Victor O. Pariseau; Fred G. Parizo to Fred G. Pariseau; Jennie S. LeGanger to Jennie S. Bryant; Fred Hoague to Fred Hoague Onley; Adam Jasiewicz to Adam Yasevitch; Gordon Thompson LeGanger to Gordon Thompson Bryant; Cora Natalie Damon to Cora Natalie Perkins; William Wade Damon to William Wade Perkins; Wilfrid Babeux to Wilford F. Babbitt; Francis Smith to Francis Mutney; Caroline E. Coutermarsh to May Elizabeth Woodward; Kenneth Lyford McCabe to Kenneth Robert Allen; Roi (Roy), Joseph Marie Leo to Leon Joseph Roy; Robert (Goodwin) Marsh to Robert Goodwin Pelletier; Patricia Arlene White to Patricia Arlene Lynch

Grafton County - Arlen Thornton Downing to Arlen Thornton Burke; Mildred Dodge to Mildred Byron; Edwin Austin Doremus to Edwin Doremus; Alvin Madison Emery to Alvin Madison Nichols; Richard W. Leo Grondin to Richard Willard Brunell; Kenneth Morrill Johnson to Kenneth Morrill Pelton; Ina Becker Lower to Ina Becker Allen; Maryellen Patricia Leonard to Maryellen Patricia Downes; Marjorie Augusta Tilton to Marjorie Augusta Gardiner; Clarence Louis White to Clarence Louis Strong; Gordon A. Besakiriski to Gordon Samuel Mascari; Beverly Ann Batchelder to Celia Ann Bassett; Jenness Stuart Bragg to Jenness Stuart Ware; Delcina W. Bennett to Delcina W. Page; Raymond Brooks to Marshall F. O'Connor; Leslie Harry Celey to Robert Eugene McKeen; Hubert Ferguson to Hubert Dryden Sycamore; Martha White Griffin to Martha White; Winifred Murphy to Constance Ann Hawes; E. Amedie Rouselle to Edward Arthur Boushey; Richard Sargent to Richard Richards

Coos County - Patricia Ann to Patricia Ann Bunnell; Mary Jane Lucchetti to Mary Jane Eastman; Norman Clark Stanley to Norman James Martin; Infant Morin to Omer Donald Leroux; Joseph Alexander to Joseph W. Barlow; Marie Clare Lucille to Marie Claire Lucille Collins; Mary Ellen Beady to Mary Ellen Williams; Frederick Parker Carpenter

1935-1937

to Parker Carpenter; Donald F. Walker to Donald F. Johnson; Eugenie Aurore Buber to Annie Jennie Buber; Patricia Ann Shea to Mary Francis Cecile Caron; Marie Anna to Anna Marie Dionne; Harriet Remick to Harriet Ross; Normand Roy to Rolland Bouchard; Rita Lois Parks to Rita Lois Monahan; Doris Morin to Doris O'Hearn; Alva Bell to Alva Gagnon; Doris Geraldine Roy to Doris Geraldine Morrissette; Dolores Mary Monahan to Dolores Mary Hammond

Name changes made by the superior court in divorce proceedings:

Rockingham County - Ruth D. Carkin to Ruth Dixon Philbrick; Harriet L. Connors to Harriet L. Drury; Ruth P. Rainey to Ruth P. Carlton; Pearl M. Scarponi to Pearl Mills; Lillian J. Aziz to Lillian J. Seavey; Cora Helen Davis to Cora Helen Meader; Esther Leah Task Elliot to Esther Leah Task; Hazel B. Martin to Hazel M. Butler; Doris J. Golter to Doris J. Moulton; Rose Katherine Jacques to Rose Katherine Marcuri; Winniefred H. Johnson to Winniefred H. Brewster; Norma Constance Tilton Houlihan to Norma Constance Tilton (Annulment decree); Idella A. Deal to Idella A. Gadis; Dorothy May Woodworth to Dorothy May Currier; Helen B. Palfrey to Helen B. Trueman; Calleope Pappas Condoninas to Calleope Pappas; Helen E. Hussey to Helen Batchelder; Hope Akerman Moran to Hope Akerman; Mary A. Muller to Mary A. Powers; Rosetta B. Vadeboncoeur to Rosetta B. Hoyt

Strafford County - Effie E. Dwire to Effie E. White; Julia M. Demeritt to Julia M. Trafton; Josephine B. Dearborn to Josephine B. Edgerly; Florence E. McSorley to Florence E. Martel; Helen R. Smith to Helen R. Johnson; Edna E. Streeter to Edna E. Bewley; Madeline E. Baker to Madeline Hudson; Evelyn E. Phillips to Evelyn E. Sevigny; Edith A. Blair to Edith A. Caverly; Geneva B. Corry to Geneva Bickford; Sadie A. Dodge to Sadie A. Dickinson; Ivadell M. Otis to Ivadell M. Nichols; Evelyn L. Holmes to Evelyn L. Walker; Mary O. Blair (otherwise known as Mary F. Plessas) to Mary O. Foss; Esther Randall to Esther Charles; Lois J. Shea to Lois J. Colby; Gertrude Pineo to Gertrude Clough; Evie Hussey to Evie B. Longley; Miriam P. Evans to Miriam Pascal; Pauline A. Jewett to Pauline Elizabeth Auger; Laura Keays to Laura Marcotte; Irene M. Smith to Irene M. Desautel

1935-1937

Belknap County - Marjorie A. Smith to Marjorie A. Oliver; Thelma L. Landry to Thelma Luella DeHart; Ethel Stoddard Bannon to Ethel Stoddard; Thalia L. Blackey to Thalia Louise Kimball; Annie Hughes Carroll to Annie Clara Hughes; Avis Cox Morrison to Avis M. Cox; Vera Campbell Dane to Vera Campbell; Pearl W. Provencal to Pearl W. Whiteman; Georgie M. Duquette to Georgie Margarete Farnham; Bernice P. Abbott to Bernice Robinson; Ivy M. Galloupe to Ivy M. Burleigh

Carroll County - Lena M. Drew to Lena M. Tappan; Ruth M. Bean to Ruth M. Potter; Vivian A. Prescott to Vivian A. Channell; Eleanor M. Woodmancy to Eleanor M. Thompson; Emma White to Emma Foster

Merrimack County - Nellie May Wheeler to Nellie May Allen; Clara L. Witham to Clara Lane; Margaret E. Martin to Margaret E. Cunningham; Elsie C. Angwin to Elsie Belle Colby; Gladys Cook Laird to Gladys Pauline Cook; Cathleen T. Rego to Kathleen T. Hayes; Mable Tebo to Mable F. Rogers; Victoria S. Wescom to Victoria S. Keniston; Edith G. Knox to Edith Nowell Grant; Stella Diversi Moore to Stella Diversi; Mary M. Reardon to Mary E. Mannion; Addie M. Lackey to Addie M. Edmunds; Stella F. Wheeler to Stella Philbrick Foster; Mabel Fern Klenke to Mabel Fern Colburn; Virginia Gray to Virginia Dolloff

Hillsborough County - Gara E. Wilson to Gara E. Brown; Lillian May Meader to Lillian May Hoague; Hazel E. Murphy to Hazel E. Nichols; Mary Staples Cote to Mary Staples; Amanda Blanchette to Florette A. Proulx; Alice D. Gormley to Alice D. Tirrell; Laura D. Carnes to Laura D. Carr; Beatrice Cora Shea to Beatrice Cora Roux; Minnie Denton Pazychuck to Minnie Denton; Harriet L. Bellofatto to Harriet L. Smith; Alice Y. Merrill to Alice Thelma Young; Gladys Stantial to Gladys Grenier; Clara Mae Cassidy to Clara Mae Tulin; Isabelle F. McLaughlin to Isabelle F. Miller; Ruth M. Chase to Ruth M. Smart; Mary Barrett Chilton to Mary Barrett; Laura A. Wheeler Dodge to Laura A. Wheeler; Josephine W. Schneiderheinze to Josephine Kendall Welch; Sophie Curtis to Sophie Daukas; Clara B. Ackermann to Clara B. Clough; Lucienne Durgan to Lucienne Corriveau; Joanna Gorczyca to Joanna Szemela; Linda Elizabeth Colburn to Linda Elizabeth Freeman; Bernice E. Atwood to Bernice E. Newcomb; Vera Smith Bennett to Vera Smith; Alice Mildred Sargent to Alice Mildred Chase; Luva Robinson to Luva

1935-1937

Blow; Maude Ann Roystan to Maude Ann Branch; Anna M. Dorval to Anna Marie Laventure; Dorothy Campbell Wilson to Dorothy Campbell; Aniela Flis to Aniela Janieszewska; Audrey Parker to Audrey Bishop; Evelyn May Jacques to Evelyn May Hall; Pearl M. Ziarko to Pearl M. Ingraham; Bernice Wheeler to Bernice Viola Stevens; Elizabeth Pearl Towne to Elizabeth Signor; Isabella Boisseau to Isabella Barrett; Jennie W. Clarke to Jennie Witham; Louise C. Farris to Louise C. Reynolds; Elizabeth W. Dee to Elizabeth Welch

Cheshire County - Marie I. LeClair to Marie Irma Hebert; Meredith L. Sanders to Meredith L. Stewart; Winifred F. Hudson to Winifred Frances Witham; Ruth Inez Seymour to Ruth Inez Whitcomb; Mildred M. Allen to Mildred E. Montgomery; June Bodwell to June Croft; Dorothy E. Miller to Dorothy E. Brooks; Pearl L. Lower to Pearl Lamber; Louise L. Hadley to Louise L. Perron; Geraldine T. Vaughan to Geraldine T. Lovering; Edda Renouf von der Marwitz to Edda V. Renouf; Blanche Lillian Winn to Blanche Lillian Plummer

Sullivan County - Rose H. McKenne to Rose H. Clark; Ethel Vine Chatsey to Ethel Vine Farnsworth; Edith M. Goodwin to Edith M. Ordway; Lillian D. Wallace to Lillian Dewey; Celia A. Kidder to Celia A. Johnson; Luella Mabel Wells Nolan to Luella Mabel Wells; Marion E. Corey to Marion E. Pitkin; Louise May Partlow to Louise May Gilson

Grafton County - Hazel N. Wilcox to Hazel N. Bliss; Grace R. Burnham to Grace Richardson; Ethel A. Norton to Ethel A. Lafoe; Esther Agnes Haggerty to Esther Agnes Riley; Laura C. Harrower to Laura M. Carter; Edith Knight to Edith Manchester; Odalite E. Johnson to Odalite E. Chesley; Lillian Mae Wheeler to Lillian Mae Rathburn; Ariel M. Smith to Ariel M. Marston; Florence M. Solberg to Florence Morin; Evelyn Estella Butman to Evelyn Estella Hayes; Sally LaBelle to Sally Louise Kendall; Mary F. Connery to Mary F. McLachlin; Zilpha A. Heinrich to Zilpha C. Avery; Gladys M. Barry to Gladys M. Fosie; Edith V. Aiken to Edith Violet Ruggles; Florence I. LaCourse to Florence I. Gault; Letha Elizabeth Conlin to Letha Elizabeth Nelson; Emma O. Blanchard to Emma O. Johnson; Josephine M. Phillips to Josephine Raymond; Estella H. Glover to Estella H. Greenhalgh; Florence Ellen Bressette to Florence Ellen Howland; Sarah A. Simonds to Sarah A. Dudley; Rena

1935-1937

Greenan Villeneuve to Rena Greenan; Ethel M. Tobin to Ethel M. Hopkins; Edna A. Ingalls to Edna A. Knights

Coos County - Veneda W. Parshley to Veneda Wheeler; Annie Mae Whitcomb to Annie Mae Bermis; Rita Sloane Ross to Rita Eleanor Sloane; Mary Taylor to Mary Anna Donnelly; Eliza Howe Tondreau to Eliza Anne Howe; Ruth B. Reed to Ruth B. Courser; Nathalie A. Dow to Nathalie Akers; Helen Willis to Helen Stahl; Verna G. Stevens to Verna G. Berry; Thelma Caird Witham to Thelma Caird; Clara C. Noyes to Clara E. Chamberlain; Hazel M. Reed to Hazel M. McClintock; Helen M. Donnelly to Helen M. Gould; Ruie R. Bunnell to Ruie R. Paige; Emma Louise Wells to Emma Louise Landry; Anne T. Predoehl to Anne Tankard

January 1937 - January 1939[8/]

Name changes made by the probate courts:

Rockingham County - Marion Amelia Allison to Marion Amelia Ewer; William Edward Allison to William Edward Ewer; Eva M. Hartford to Eva M. Thibeault; Baby Patterson to Nancy Neal; Jean Courser to Jean Courser Morrill; Jean Courser Morrill to Jean Ann Morrill; Maurice Kelley to Robert Franklin Kelley; Gertie ----- to Gertie Kuntz; Joseph Rocker, 3rd to Thomas Barr Rocker; Barbara J. Dockham to Margaret Rose Peterson; Richard S. Prescott to Wilfred Rowland Kimball; Shirley Adams Davis to Walter Adams Davis; William Richard Anthony to William Richard Dennison; Pluma Jane Boyd to Pluma Jane Fowler; Virginia Andrea Boyd to Virginia Andrea Fowler; Athanasios Aristides Marinopoulos to Arthur Marinos; Carrie W. Carlson to Carrie W. Raynes; Mary Ann Rogers to Elaine Frances Stevens; Veronica Nora O'Connor to Veronica Nora Critchley; Earl Jenvin Batchelder to Erle Nathaniel Priest; Phillip Burton Gough to Joseph Phillips Grave; Phillip Gerald Croft to Phillip Gerald Schubert; Riccardo Raffaele Papasotero to Ralph Rosa; Barbara M. Whiteaker to Barbara Mae Brown; Gloria Elaine Cookson to Nancy Rouner; George Oliver Cookson to Lucius Henry Chappell; David Mills Lawrence to Donald Guy Berry; Impi Jackson to Sally Ellen Scott; Edward Timothy Dwyer to Stephen Nathaniel Roberts; Anthony Andreus Coelho to Anthony Andrews; Elizabeth Andreus Coelho to Elizabeth Andrews; John Andrews Coelho to John Andrews; Walter Andrews Coelho to Walter Andrews; Mooney or Mendal Wexler to Murray Wexler; Lizzie Hill Downing Hartford to Elizabeth Hill Downing Hartford; Shirley Carol Dame to Shirley Carol Keller; William Litch Harrigan to William Litch Peek; Priscilla Locke to Priscilla Gorman; George Albert Locke to George Albert Gorman; Mrs. Ruth L. Fitts to Miss Ruth T. Lane; Reginald Jacques to Wallace Reginald Jacques; Baby Quigley to Joan Rosaline Berry; George Grace to Joseph Richard Grace; Dorothy Elinor Conrad to Dorothy Elinor Seavey

Strafford County - Sheldon Harold Halpert to Sheldon Harold Cook; John Herbert Moulton to John Herbert Carpenter; Nancy E. Pillsbury to Nancy E. Buswell; Samuel Ruggiero to Samuel Rogers; Leonel Wilfred

---

8/ Chapter 263, 1939 N. H. Public Laws

1937-1939

Deschants to Leonel Wilfred Fields; Marjorie L. Pickering to Marjorie L. Charrette; Lona Effie Burgess to Lona Effie McNeil; Richard Augustus McKay to Richard Augustus Donlon; Deborah May Morse to Deborah May Small; Everett Gordon Galloway to Everett John Galloway; Alberta May Nielsen to Yvonne May Aspinall; Mary Lora Estes to Mary Lora Dunlap; Grover Newbury to George Grover Newbury; Francis Joseph Crawford to Francis Joseph Carpenter; Joan Beverly Ostler to Joan Beverly Cassell; Roland Henry Drouin to Roland Henry Therrien; Jeannette Lefebvre to Jeannette Antoinette Brady; Mary-Rose Rachel Houle to Mary-Rose Rachel Vezeau; Janet Louise Mackey to Janet Louise Burleigh; Edvill B. Downing to Edvill B. Howland; Paul R. Geary to Paul R. Bowden; Barbara R. Geary to Barbara R. Bowden; Beverly E. Geary to Beverly E. Bowden; June Lorraine Huntsman to June Lorraine Deveau; Richard Gaffney to Richard Croft; Alice Irene Poisson to Alice Irene Fisher; Brenda O. Poisson to Brenda Ora Fisher; Ora M. Poisson to Ora Mary Fisher; Roland J. Poisson to Roland John Fisher; Robert Eugene Unglaub to Robert Eugene Dolph; Adolf Elias Unglaub to James Elias Dolph; Anna Katherine Unglaub to Anna Katherine Dolph; Jacqueline Joan Christie to Jacqueline Joan Christie Butterfield; Robert Morton Christie to Robert Morton Christie Butterfield; Shirley May Smart to Shirley May Peck; Ethel M. Bough to Ethel M. Whitehouse; Roberta Strafford Keller to Roberta Strafford Cassell; Helen Elizabeth Bough to Helen Elizabeth Caldwell; Marilyn Barbour to Geneva Marilyn Wentworth; Helen Louise Londo to Natalie Lorraine Jenness; Pauline Gagnon to Pauline Dubois; Roland Gagnon to Roland Dubois; June Gagnon to June Dubois; Aurel Gagnon to Aurel Dubois; Winifred Dorothy Tappan to Winifred Dorothy Knapp; Russell Edward Londo to Russell Edward Ellis; Bertha Hayes Atwood to Bertha Guernsey Hayes; George Paul Gray to William Edgar Gray, Jr.; Loretta Lorraine Trahan to Loretta Lorraine LaFrance

Belknap County - Glenna M. Estey to Glenna M. Buchanan; Lenona Elizabeth Huston to Leona Elizabeth Perry; Romeo DeBlois to Romeo Richard DeBlois; George F. Merrill to George Frederick Derby; Lorenzo A. Morin to Lorenzo Joseph Morin; Roselle M. Huntington to Roselle M. Torrey; Charles Henry Scott, Jr. to Charles Henry Morse.

Changed by adoption: Russell Emile Clairmont to Russell Emile Boissoneault; Gladys Perkins Bickford to Gladys Sargent Bickford;

1937-1939

Foster E. Varrell to Foster E. Varrell; George Walter Varrell to George Walter Varrell; Marjorie Woodward to Marjorie Woodward Ives; Priscilla Johnson to Priscilla Gurney; Germaine Prince to Germaine Prince; Napoleon Prince to Paul Prince; Anthony Joseph Bisson to Anthony Joseph Dupuis; Mary Jane Brosseau to Mary Jane Deslandes; Betty Caroline Fogg to Betty Caroline Cass; Barbara Louise Parsons to Barbara Louise Wheeler; Clifton William Reardon to Clifton William Fogg; Stuart D. Phillips to Stuart D. Phillips Stetson; Edmund F. MacQuarrie to Edmund Francis Fields; Robert James Breck to Charles O. Hopkins; Robert George Wallace to Robert George Casey; ----- Sampson to Cynthia Colby

Carroll County - Julia F. Davis to Julia F. Garland; Ellsworth Smith Ervine to Kenneth Grafton Evans; Earle Joseph Hilliard to John Leslie Taylor; Linnie Marie Mayott to Linnie Marie Thompson; John Frederick McLellan to John Frederick Starrett; Irving Howard Eaton to Richard Howard Charles; Leon E. Harriman to Ernest Carleton Bogle; Selma Fay Harriman to Fay Elizabeth Bogle; Earl Francis Chase to Earl Francis Hagar; Kirk P. Brewer to Kirk P. Read; Helen E. Floyd to Helen E. Herrick; Barbara M. Floyd to Barbara M. Herrick; Joseph Beauchemin to Arthur Joseph Bushman; Louise Beauchemin to Bertha Louise Bushman; Robert John Beauchemin to Robert John Bushman; Willis L. Lemorn to Willis Lemwood Nason; Levon Henry Takesian to Levone H. Takesian Fairbanks; Tobia Blake Brownrigg to Tobia Blake Brownrigg Goodson; Tuleta Tutt to Joan Zita Tutt

Merrimack County - Rosie M. Ireland to Rosie M. Jones; Ralph Withey to Harry Onley Lewis; Robert S. Borras to Robert L. Fickett; Everet Joseph Thayer to Everett Joseph Mozier, Jr.; E. Paul O'Connell to E. Paul Roberts; John William Zalanskas to John William Zorn; Paul Douglas deLahunta to Alexander deLahunta; Emily May Otto to Emily May Radcliffe Otto; Winifred Jewell to Winifred Bean; Bertie C. Tilton to Bert C. Tilton; Lois H. Holmes to Lois H. Heath; Kachadoor Kachadoorian to Benjamin Kane; Harry Lugsch to Harry Lugsch Wisner; Matthew F. Oliver to Matthew Frank Brown; Ibar Robert Derosier to Ibar Robert Lord; Woodrow John Derosier to Woodrow John Lord; Catherine J. Jenvey Lindsey to Catherine J. Jenvey; Dorothea Cecile Marie Chenette to Dorothy Cecilia Marie Chenette; Alpha Metivier to Alfred Metivier; Frederick L. Lancisi to Frederick L.

1937-1939

Lancey; Marion B. Lancisi to Marion B. Lancey; Nella D. Lancisi to Nella D. Lancey; Robert F. Lancisi to Robert F. Lancey; Dale Miner to Dale Miner Blandin; Mabel R. Dow to Mabel R. Scott; Arthur LaMora to Arthur Lamoureux; Louise C. Whipple to Louise C. Guptill.
Changed by adoption - Roger Chouinard to Roger Chouinard Leblanc; Harold Everett Thurber to Harold Everett Boulay; "Baby" Bergstrom to John Sanderson; Ronald Allen Barklay, Jr. to Ronald Allen Charles; Nancy Ann Files to Nancy Ann Files Gilson; Raymond Russell to Raymond Russell Marden; Charles P. Bessette to Charles Parker Corson; Jannette Nadeau to Jannette Couturier; William Marinelli to William LaClair; Lawrence Theodore Pero to Paul Arsenault; Barbara Elizabeth Adams to Barbara Elizabeth Reed; Shirley Belle Adams to Shirley Belle Reed; Virginia Belleveau to Clara Louise Boutelle; "Baby" Hill to Roger Lewis Whiting; Stuart Sanborn to Clarence Miles Boutelle; Priscilla Velma Brideau to Priscilla Velma Gosselin; Hilma May Jewett to Alice Ann Corbin; Paul Frederick Hoyt to Paul Frederick Clark; Janet Guertin to Beverly Janet Yeo; Katherine Odell Adkins to Katherine Odell Green; Marjorie Mae Murphy to Marjorie Mae Joyce; Elsie Margaret Bacon to Elsie Margaret Allen; "Baby" MacDonald to Richard Lawrence Sanderson; Dennis John Croft to Peter Blaisdell; Sylvia Pearl Fogg to Sylvia Pearl LaRochelle; Barbara Jeanne Hartman to Barbara Jean Comolli; Caroline Atta Smith to Patricia Ann Mundy; Roberta Goddard to Natalie Ann Clough; Donald Francis Savage to Donald Francis Savage Durost; Carl Edward Bent to Carl Edward Williams

Hillsborough County - Madeline Lonergan to Madeline Hill; Hector MacIsaac to Hector Homoleski; Eva Chatrai or Charter to Eveline Richer; Darrel Lamora to John Francis Lamora; Leopold Norton Booth to Lee Norton Booth; Joseph G. Biron to Joseph Larion; Lucien Raoul Beaulieu to Richard Lucien Beaulieu; George Albert Michaud to George Albert Graham; Diogenes Lioliopoulos to Daniel Lylis; Beatrice Ann Silva to Beatrice Ann Byam; Cecile B. Caron to Cecile Lorette Beaudet; Ernest William Charland to Ernest William Blake; Ida Lubin to Gussie Talent; Doris Glines Belmont to Doris Glines; Humphrey Edward DeSchuiteneer to Humphrey Edward Scannell; August DeSchuiteneer to August Scannell; August Edward DeSchuiteneer to Edward August Scannell; Julia Christina DeSchuiteneer to Julia Christina Scannell; Frank C. J. Dziadosz to Frank C. J. Jadosz; Charles Przybyla to Charles Prisby; Joseph H. Barbeau to Joseph

1937-1939

Bellefeuille; David Bernard Kaufman to David Kay; Peter H. Tsourides (Sourides) to Peter H. Landis; Stanley Kwiatek to Stanley K. Flower; Emerson Smith to Edward Emerson Smith; Joseph Pierre Menard to Joseph Pierre Maynard; William Henry Martin to William Henry Parker; Joseph Paul Emile DesGroseilliers to Paul Robinson DeGross; Alfred H. Raza to Alfred H. Ranger; Edward A. Raza to Edward A. Ranger; George A. Raza to George A. Ranger; Aime Raza to Aime Ranger; Doris C. Loughlin to Doris Charlotte McAuliffe; Roberta Gervais to Roberta Germas; Robert W. Perdue to Robert W. Hunter; Alfreda Joan Warcholik to Alfreda Joan Walker; Charles Karanikas to Charles Kearns; Alphonsine Goulet to Alphonsine Larochelle; Kimon Basil to Kimon Vasiliou; Theologia Lioliopoulos to Theo Lylis; Tanous Seibaha to Tanous Seibaha Saad; John Papalevizopoulos or Papalevizos to John A. Papp; Helen Papalevizou to Helen Papp; James Papalevizou to James Papp; George Papalevizou to George Papp; Catherine Papalevizou to Catherine Papp; Alexandra Papalevizou to Alexandra Papp; Joseph Alphonse Ferland to Alphonse Ferland Normand; Celina Caron to Celina Rock; Chow Shuck Yee to John S. Yee; Panagiotis Tempelis to Peter Spiretos; Efthemios A. Adamopoulos to Timothy Adams; Angelina Macri to Angeline Mary Costantino; Hermen Henrie L'Homme to John Joseph Manning; Neil Stanley Hodgdon to Donald Hodgdon Marshall; William Argeropoulos to Antonio Argeropoulos; Harold Malhoit to Wilfred Malhoit; Theodore Lioliopoulos to Theodore Lylis; Elsie A. Coldwell to Elsie C. Doyle; Wasyl Kott to Russell Kott; Thomas McGuigan to Thomas Guthrie; Mabel Zeisel to Mabel J. Frost; Robert Wallace to Robert Wallace Boyer; Paula Hidden to Paula A. Hiatt; Adolfena Smietana or Smietami to Ardele Krym; Felix Francis Smietana to Felix Francis Krym; John S. Caraphilakis to John S. Caraphil.

Changed by adoption - Richard Hayes Hickman to Richard Hayes Rogers; Marion S. Aldred to Marion S. Coons; J. Edward Aldred to J. Edward Coons; Marjorie W. Aldred to Marjorie W. Coons; Herbert A. Aldred to Herbert A. Coons; Bertha Alice Young to Alice May Tripp; Rita V. Simoneau to Marie Violette Rita Belanger; Norman Gabriel to Norman Gero; Richard Gabriel to Richard Gero; Paul Gabriel to Paul Gero; Charles J. Fournier to Robert Hadley Griffin; Alice Everhart to Florence Jane Lucas; Dorothy May Pepin to Dorothy May Blanch; David Keith Aldrich to Fred Lorraine Fottler; Robert Royal Brown to

1937-1939

Robert R. Flaherty; Florence Emma Gaudette to Florence Emma Francoeur; Donald Bruce Signor to Donald Bruce Steele; Joan Yvonne Brochu to Carola Joan Travini; Aldea Pearle Smith to Aldea Pearle White; Beatrice Ann Collins to June Elaine Brown; Adrian Glenwood Seavey to Adrian Glenwood Seger; Merritt F. Porter to Merritt Daniel Booth; Alice Bacon to Rosamond Woodruff; Robert Foster Walsh to Thomas Paul Bradford; Rene Andre Thibodeau to Rene Andre D'Amours; John J. Goonan, Jr. to John J. Dennis; Doris Klardie to Doris Hermsdorf; Georgette Cassista to Nancy Berube; Murielle Renaud to Pauline Lauretta Lavoie; Timothy John Chapman to Maurice William Godbout, Jr.; Josephine Mary Raymond to Kathleen Mary Mullen; Carol Mary Sanderson to Carol Mary Savoy; Baby Paquette to Maxine Ann Wainwright; Jane Davenport to Jane Taylor; Janet Marion Shaw to Janet Marion Rogers; Theresa Ann to Theresa Ann Lafontaine; Herbert Charles Blake to Herbert Charles Dallaire; Baby Lawson to John Lance Koenig; Ronald Baxter to Lewis Ronald Ashford; Robert Elude Castonguay to Robert Elude Cote; Joseph Alfred Gagnon to Joseph Alfred Gadbois; Stanley Lee Wilder to Robert Allen Vantine; Mary Margaret Brickley to Sonia Margaret Bernaiche; Robert Louis Sevigny to Robert Joseph Vachon; Huntley Joseph Tranfalia or Tranfaglan to Nikolaos Daskalopulos; Carol Tremblay to Marie Claire Rose Lemelin; William Lavallee to William Linehan; Baby Cloutier to Pauline Jeanne Duhamel; Faoth McIntosh to Faith Fox; June Wood to Helen Marguerite Copadis; Inez Fisk to Inez Webb; Douglas P. Scanlon to Donald Cote; Merilyn Huckins to Merilyn Ramsdell; Leonard George Doyle to Ronald Herbert Noyes; Doris Lillian Othot to Marie Leona Claflin; Barbara Jean Sheldon to Joan Barbara Rollins; Yvette Loiselle to Yvette L. Dufort; Robert Henry Latuch to Robert Henry Harwood; Davena Hartford to Sandra Eastman; Leo Raymond Tremblay to Rodney John Colasacco

Cheshire County - Preksfy Bartashievick to Wilfred Bartashevich; Isakka W. Bakka to Walter John Parker; Urho Isaac Maki to Earl Urho Mackey; Natalie Frances Greene to Natalie Frances Roberts; Alan Proctor Greene to Alan Proctor Roberts; Elsie G. Carter to Elsie G. Hornig; Walter Charles Corey to Walter Edson Clough; Marion Dorothy Gregory to Marion Dorothy Lafleur; Marion Shaw Manning to Marion Duffy Manning; Thomas Anthony Tartaglia to Thomas Anthony Tyler; Mary Heron to Shirley Ann Burgoyne; Baby boy Cyr to Robert Allen

1937-1939

Whitcomb; Marian E. Gates to Marian E. Lawrence; Joseph Alfred Guguy to Fred Alfred Duguay; Robert J. Drugg to Robert J. Qualters; Marie Libbarres to Helen Fotes Libbarres; Francis Metz to Francis Woodward; Bernice Viola Clough to Bernice Viola Woodward; Lucile W. Desgranges to Lucile Wilson Bedor; Richard Edmunds to Richard O. Stone; Grace Mae Stebbins to Shirley Grace Spencer; Louis Israel Medvidofsky to Louis I. Medoff; Rose G. Medvidofsky to Rose Gertrude Medoff; Maurice Medvidofsky to Maurice Medoff; Marshal Medvidofsky to Marshall Medoff; Alexander Robertson James to Alexander James; James Miles to James Hogan Beaulieu; Donald Koski to Donald James Allen; Reino John Hakala to Reino John Hackler; Shirley May Wood to Shirley May Ouelette; Lawrence Webster to George Lawrence Ryder; Francis Robert Stanley to Francis Robert Shulenbeger; Mary Ann Pelletier to Marianne Lorena Pelletier; Betty Lou Mantyla to Sally Jane Knight; Cynthia May Richardson to Yvonne Agnes Bushway; Rosie Kazanas to Jennie John Kazanas; Shirley Ann Rose to Carol Ann Rose; Viola Mae Heald to Viola Mae Vaughn; Dennis Page Fuller to James Lewis Crandall; Jacqualine Elizabeth Payne to Jacqualine Elizabeth Davis; August Honkamaki to August Maki; Evelyn Belle Bowhay to Evelyn Belle Foster; Elenor Frances Hewes to Eleanor Frances Campbell; Francis Morris Walker to John Thomas Moore, Jr.; ----- Wahlen to Wayne Weston Faery

<u>Sullivan County</u> - Madeline Madore to Madeleine Foisy; Harry John Pallas to Harry John Bowles; John Henry Spatz to John Henry Young; Harry W. Laprise to Harry W. Gross; Alexander Meczelski to Alexander Mitchell; Bertha Parizo to Bertha Pariseau; Thomas Francis to Thomas Francis St. Clair; Alice Gertrude Plummer to Alice Gertrude Chapman; Ada G. Coty to Ada G. Colby; Arthur J. Mayo to Untamo Penttila; Arvo Armas Peltonen to Arnold Armas Peltonen; Roy Bunker to Roy B. Parmelee; Margaret M. Malony to Margaret M. Croshere; Lee Robert Richardson to Ronald Edward Spooner; Conrad Higgins to Laurence R. Johnson; Oliver A. Lemere to Levi A. Lemere; Alik Koozanovich to Alexander Kowzan; Merritt Anderson Waterhouse to Merritt Tattrie; George John Kukolander to George John Starr; Marie Virginia Lawless to Louise Amanda Brunell; Angelina Jeanette Valenti to Angelina Jeanette Valenti; Catherine Constance Valenti to Catherine Constance Valenti; Milton William Ilhainen to Milton William Halainen; Kathleen Celarius to Kathleen Morgan

1937-1939

Grafton County - Raymond Allen Bissell to Raymond Allen Davio; Mathilde Brown to Mathilde Louise Skinner; Harold Bunce to James Wallace Lewis; Paul W. Carter, Jr. to Earl Sampson Howard; Edward Henry Conery to Wilfred Loren Smith; Leon Coty to Leon R. Saunders; Donald Courage to Donald Richard Noyes; Patricia Ann Doubleday to Patricia Ann Wolfsohn; Bertha Ellis to Viola Priscilla Gavel; Mildred Irene Gould to Mildred Irene Gould Foster; George Raymond Hobart to Elton William Wescott; Barbara Rae James to Barbara James Goss; Pauline McLellan to Pauline Angela Sweet; Edward Horace Pattee to Edward Standish Pattee; Hannah Mary Pennock to Billie Hannah Mary Pennock; Leslie Marston Reed to Leslie Reed Marston; Vernon Ned Trumbull to Vernon Ned Bergh; Priscilla Mae Wilkins to Carlene Priscilla Barton; Amelia Abdelnour to Amealia Samaha; Harleem Abdelnour to Harleem Samaha; Lora Abdelnour to Laura Samaha; Esther May Briggs to Esther Lucille Ray; Christina Carr to Christina Beth Jesseman; Beverley Ann Cady to Beth Ann Olsson; James Thurlow Colley to George Washington Ellis; Edris Davis Dzengelewski to Edris Davis Bowers; Stanley Edward Dzengelewski to Stanley Edward Bowers; Ughtree Newell Downing to Hugh Newell Downing; Marcia Edna Fuller to Marcia Edna Gay; Ralphie Jean Grenier to Robert Jean Allen; Robert Bruce Osmer to Robert Bruce Warcup; Murray Sargent, Jr. to Donald Ashworth Richardson; Evaline Lewis Samaha to Evelyn Samaha; Robert Prnce Schmohl to Robert Prince Houghton; Bertha May Schmohl to Bertha May Houghton; Charlotte Schmohl to Charlotte Houghton; Nancy Ann Stevenson to Nancy Lee Keniston; Margaret E. Whitman to Margaret E. Brown

Coos County - Junior Percival Johnson to Jon Percival Johnson; Everett E. Douse to Everett E. Palmer; Joseph Paul Hamel to Joseph Paul Bourassa; David G. Mattice to David G. Macloon; Edna L. Mattice to Edna L. Macloon; Sharon K. Mattice to Sharon K. Macloon; Francisco DiMaria to Frank DiMaria McGee; Clara Curtis to Claire Curtis; Lawrence A. Longstaff to Granville Aulis Longstaff; Marjorie Helen Queor to Patricia Alice Connolly; Gladys Eliza LaPlante to Gladys Elizabeth Hinman; Donald Edward LaMontagne to Donald Edward Arsenault

Name changes made by the superior court in divorce proceedings:

1937-1939

Rockingham County - Thelma F. Fontenot to Thelma F. Hersey; Alison I. Rowe to Alison Jean Ingalls; Helen Cooney Hallinan to Helen Cooney; Margaret Furman to Margaret Rocker; Mary F. Hamblett to Mary F. Blair; Sylvia Underhill Dollard to Sylvia Louise Underhill; Lillian Coburn Kieve to Lillian Coburn Emerson; Rosa D. Morse to Rosa D. Shoulders; Louise H. Niescier to Louise Frances Huntoon; Mary T. O'Leary to Mary T. Marshall; Dorothy V. Perfect to Dorothy V. Emery; Isabel (or Isabella) L. M. Rogers to Isabel (or Isabella) L. M. Kujeske; Marion D. Wetherell to Marion Dearborn Clark; Marguerite A. Witham to Marguerite A. Ball; Harriet H. Davis to Harriet H. Harrison; Norma Emma Coldwell Doherty to Norma Emma Coldwell; Irene M. Martel to Irene M. Sinclair; Laura J. Noel to Laura J. Gauthier; Beatrice Hartford Scarborough to Beatrice Hartford; Josephine Davison to Josephine Guiffrida; Beatrice Shaw Estes to Beatrice Shaw; Jennie B. Gordon to Jennie B. Hardy; Harriet B. Nicholson to Harriet L. Hodgdon; Marion D. Wetherell to Marion Dearborn Clock; Isabelle Beatrice Williams to Isabelle Beatrice Thompson; Alma Mary Pellegrino to Alam Mary Rainville; Harriett B. Cleeves to Harriett Prescott Bell; May Belle Triplett to May Belle Moody; Ethel P. Uhlig to Ethel Powers; Mertie Burrowes to Mertie Bunker Matthewes; Ida M. Dunton to Ida May Tivey

Strafford County - Jeannette G. Wilson to Jeannette G. Aiken; Isabelle Tracey Farley Schoonmaker to Isabelle Tracey Farley; Anne V. Folsom to Anne V. Jacobs; Yvonne M. Poulis to Yvonne M. Forgues; Alberta A. Roberts to Alberta A. Doyon; Evelyn M. Drouin to Evelyn Marie Daverio; Vivien M. Lagasse to Vivien M. Rothwell; Harriet E. Strachan to Harriet E. Hill; Doris A. Lieach to Doris A. Annis; Alexina Beaudoin to Alexina Plante; Ann L. Toomey to Ann L. Meader; Ruth A. Eastman to Ruth Atherton; Marjorie L. Cook to Marjorie L. Charette; Freda B. Martineau to Freda E. Burrows; Shirley Dickie to Shirley Pinkham; Clara May White to Clara May Kelley; Irma Rogers to Irma Grover; Emma M. Forbes to Emma M. Boulanger; Gladys Louise Tripp to Gladys Louise Mosely

Belknap County - Elizabeth Malouin to Elizabeth Wakefield; Gertrude Gagne Lapierre to Gertrude Nancy Gagne; Cecile West MacIntosh to Cecile Viola West; Elsie Staples to Elsie Roberge; Carrie Roy to Carrie Merrill; Dorothy Berry to Dorothy Belanger; Ruby B. Kimball to Ruby B. Keating; Emilienne L. Forrest to Emilienne L. Cormier; Mildred E.

1937-1939

Wasson Chaffin to Mildred E. Wasson; Beatrice K. Riley Sheldon to Beatrice K. Riley

Carroll County - Alice E. Cheney to Alice E. Philippe; Mary E. Cody to Mary Monahan; Irene A. Higgins to Irene Moriarty; Katherine F. Varney to Katherine F. Corson; Joanna M. Welch to Joanna M. Nickerson; Marilyn F. Brooks to Delmour E. Brooks

Merrimack County - Minerva C. Clark to Minerva C. Nickerson; Irene E. Tibbetts to Irene E. Oday; Irene M. Houle to Irene M. Martel; Lillian B. Andreevski to Lillian Broadhurst; Geraldine H. Stewart to Geraldine Hamilton; Nora Lundeen to Nora Mayhew; Priscilla Small to Priscilla Ruth Freitas; Irene C. Clough to Irene Bennett; Mona Caldwell to Mona Thompson; Gladys W. Burbank to Gladys May Wilson; Gertrude M. Hood to Gertrude M. Hodge; Blanche Gordon Fletcher to Blanche Gordon

Hillsborough County - M. Josephine Lavery to Mary Josephine Welch; Marie Louise Bisson to Marie Louise Belaire; Sylvia LaFountain Edison to Sylvia Ethel LaFountain; Emma Charait to Emma A. Wineberg; Florence E. Sibulkin to Florence Martin; Margaret Boivin to Margaret Zullo; Clara Martin Fitts to Clara Martin; Agnes G. Furman to Agnes G. Chauncey; Louise A. Barry to Louise A. Wamester; Alberta Rivard to Alberta Mitchell; Donna W. Colby to Donna A. Whittle; Jule Ivon to Jule Kelley; Valeda Burelle to Valeda Goodhue; Thelma King Jervah to Thelma King; Elsie Doyle to Elsie A. Coldwell; Jennie Giles to Jennie Kudolis; Emilienne Normand Mooney to Emelienne Normand; Delia Blaise to Delia Chartrand; Ethel Bourzikas to Ethel Sofatzis; Marguerite A. Locicero to Marguerite A. Wright; Anna H. McLaughlin to Anna E. Hubbard; Myra Smith Shirra to Myra Smith; Ruth C. Stanard to Ruth A. Christopher; Mary DeRome to Mary Garland; Bridget L. Allen to Bridget L. King; Mary E. Perry to Mary E. Emerson; Eva M. Meader to Eva M. Boisvert; Bessie Elizabeth Maynard Kapela to Bessie Elizabeth Maynard; Margaret J. Lamprinakas to Margaret J. Belrose; Mary A. McAllister to Mary A. McGuigan; Dorothy Elizabeth Cobb to Dorothy Elizabeth Kelley; Vera J. Deeg to Vera J. Robbins; Jeannette Bond to Jeannette St. Pierre; Grace Maud McQuillan to Grace Maud Bowler; Dorothy Josephine Colburn to Dorothy Josephine Fiske; Alice A. Delehanty to Alice A. Warren; Amy L. Benedick to Amy L. Tilton;

1937-1939

Blanche Rousseau to Blanche Bergeron; Harriet M. Friese to Harriet M. Barschdorf; Lida Kelley to Lida Dion; Rose Anna Valles to Rose Anna Desrochers; Amelia M. Guerriero to Amelia M. Bellefleur; Nellie Noel to Nellie Balukonis; Melverta Brooks to Melverta Poore; Rita Milliard to Rita Boldini; Beatrice L. Michaud to Beatrice L. Burelle; Marion M. Ford to Marion MacCann; Vera Owens Chesnulevich LeClair to Vera Owens Chesnulevich; Christine Denno to Christine Gianakos; Julia Korkovelos to Julia Gurska; Mildred Snarski to Mildred Adams; Elizabeth Gardner Freeman to Elizabeth Gardner Rodger; Esther H. Smith to Esther Hopkins; Alice K. Varnum to Alice Kuriger; Dorothy Emma Denison to Dorothy Emma Hoitt

Cheshire County - Pauline Laura Gordon to Pauline Laura Orkins; Edna Evelyn Ferguson to Edna Evelyn Bernier; Pauline B. Jarvis to Pauline I. Baker; Gladys E. Hayes to Gladys Evelyn Swain; Kathleen H. Duval to Kathleen H. Pollard; Beatrice Julia Cimone to Beatrice Julia LaPointe; Ellen LaDuca to Ellen Spydell; Josephine Carey Briggs to Josephine Carey; Florence Lee Barron Parsons to Florence Lee Barron; Evelyn L. Warner to Evelyn Lucille Lee; Bernice Eleanor Higgins to Bernice Eleanor Winn; Dorothy C. Stevens to Dorothy Lawler Cleghorn; Delia E. Killeen to Delia E. Webster; Mary M. Taylor to Mary Mlecezko; Florence Ophelia McGuigan to Florence Ophelia Bodware

Sullivan County - Marion O. Williams to Marion O. Smith (1936); Dorothy Anna Clement to Dorothy Anna Farnsworth; Ada B. Whittier to Ada B. York; Clare Florence D'Amante to Clare Florence Lower; Hazel E. Hill to Hazel E. Richardson; Lucie A. Wilson to Lucie A. Streeter; Josie M. Sheldon to Josie M. Schroeder; Christina A. Nagle to Christina A. Shea; Flossie L. Johnson to Flossie Ada LaBelle; Eva Baker Stebbins Whitney to Eva Baker Stebbins; Mary Anna Lepicier to Mary Anna Therriault; Grace E. Braley to Grace E. Bedell; Vina Guest to Vina E. Niles; Marcella Helen Martin to Marcella Helen Putnam; Katherine Smith Pfleiderer to Katherine Smith; Avis Cuthbert to Avis Reynolds; Hazel Bell Williams Morse to Hazel Bell Williams

Grafton County - Olive B. Straw to Olive B. Bush; Eva A. Dame to Eva A. Welcome; Alice Gray to Alice King; Goldie F. Sargent to Goldie F. Ford; Barbara L. Whipple to Barbara L. Bruce; L. Aileen Coghlan to L.

1937-1939

Aileen Kebrich; Bertha Hobbs LaMarre to Bertha Louise Hobbs; Myrtle H. Gardner to Myrtle Hodsdon; Alice D. Olsen to Alice D. Ladeau; Vera A. Stevens to Vera A. Straw; Althea Brown to Althea Gould; Nellie S. Pickering to Nellie Julia Sweet; Wilhelmine Haberer Girndt to Wilhelmine Haberer Hinnen; Lora E. Duplessis to Lora E. Goodrich; Beatrice Pollack to Beatrice Morrissette; Marguerite M. Barrett to Marguerite Maxine Bomhower; Flora Arline Renihan to Flora Arline Silsby

Coos County - Olive V. Temple to Olive V. Bennett; Vera E. Ball to Vera E. Lakin; Annie McGillivary Mason to Annie McGillivary; Alberta Gray Callan to Albert Gray; Clementine Evans to Clementine Asselin; Ruth Deal to Ruth Moss; Annie M. Arlinsky to Annie M. Rosi; Lillian A. Livingston to Lillian A. Bennett; Ruth Libby Barnard to Ruth Brenda Libby; Elsie R. Egan to Elsie R. Woodrow; Gertrude M. McGennis to Gertrude M. Willis; Serita Noyes Brinkman to Serita Noyes; Lillian Louks to Lillian Smith

January 1939 - January 1941[9/]

Name changes made by the probate courts:

Rockingham County - Joan Ann Walukinas to Joan Ann Gilkey; Mike Luchinsky alias Michael Lucinski to Michael Lewis; Beverly L. Lucinski to Beverly L. Lewis; Patricia Louise Chard to Patricia Ann Beers; Reginald Dunham to Reginald E. Kelley; Mary Elizabeth Wiggin to Dolly Austin Wiggin; Mertie E. Estabrook to Mertie Etta Whittier; Alfred Wightman to Alfred Wood Wightman; Harold G. Klauberg to Harold George Bowerfind; Roland Farrar to Roland Farrar O'Leary; Richard Farrar to Richard Farrar O'Leary; Robert Gardner Pender to Robert Gardner Vasselian; Wadislaw Biadacz to Charles Broderick; John A. Biadacz to John A. Broderick; Ella T. Biadacz to Ella T. Broderick; Marilyn K. Biadacz to Marilyn K. Broderick; Elaine M. Biadacz to Elaine M. Broderick; Josephine M. Biadacz to Josephine M. Broderick; John A. Biadacz, Jr. to John A. Broderick, Jr.; Margaret Stack to Margaret Haggerty; Wanda Kucharczyk to Wanda Baker; Muriel M. Norton to Muriel Gertrude Morton; Olive M. Christie to Olive M. Clark; Richard William Hallinan to Robert William Davenport; Patricia Ann Hallinan to Patricia Ann Davenport; William Edward Heffler to William Edward Powell; Katherine Louise Sprague to Barbara Grace Ingram; Warren James Ward to Warren James Perkins; Joseph T. Page to Leon T. Page; Carol Whitney to Carol Joyce Steady; James Henry Gaw to David James Fix; Mildred Marjorie Senter to Mildred Marjorie Hall; Dorothy M. Zoller to Dorothy M. Root; William Richard Zoller to William Richard Root; Peter Carrier to John G. Currier; Earle Grant Boutelle, Jr. to Grant Clarence Woodbury; Dorothy Faith Ann Johnson to Faith Ann Joslyn; Alfrieda Jeanette O'Brien to Alfrieda Jeanette Jarowsky; Dorothy Alice Labbe to Dorothy Alice Gilman; Nancy McLean to Nancy Fogg; Meyer Jacob Rosen to Milton Jack Rosen; William Samuel Heath to William Samuel Shepard; Josephine Freeman Tobyne to Josephine Freeman Tabor; Elizabeth Ann Gilman to Shirley Ann Preston; Robert Harold Marden to Robert Harold Byron; Beverly May Jameson to Beverly May Berry; Helen P. Larsen to Helen P. Shelton; Doris M. Larsen to Doris M. Shelton; Frances A. Larsen to Frances A. Shelton; Mary Elizabeth Diener to Mary Elizabeth Andrews; Theodore Bertram Diener to Theodore Bertram Andrews; Roberta G. L. Saffell

---

[9/]   Chapter 257, 1941 N. H. Public Laws

1939-1941

Bertram Diener to Theodore Bertram Andrews; Roberta G. L. Saffell to Roberta Louise O'Dare; Robert E. H. Saffell, Jr. to Robert Edward O'Dare; Everett B. Osgood to Charles Bailey Osgood; Preston Boyce Hawthorne to Preston Boyce Wares; Edith Frances Goulette to Edith Frances Keen; John Alexander Krukowski to John Alexander Cook; Richard Stanley Dorey to Richard Walker Corcoran; Ramona M. Williams to Ramona M. Pearson; Carol Ann Russell to Carol Ann Jackson; Laurel Elizabeth Webster to Laurel Elizabeth Knights; Hazel Madeline Corning to Hazel M. Sawyer; Fannie Belle Dearborn to Fannie Belle Johnston; Coy Sharleen Caswell to Coy Sharleen Hillyard; Janice Stevens to Janice Weston; Domenica Papasodero to Domenica Rosa; John Papasodero to John Rosa; William Papasodero to William Rosa; Ernest Papasodero to Ernest Rosa; Ernest George Carr to Ernest George Campbell

Strafford County - James Woodrow Prescott to James Woodrow Sewall; Willis M. Bartlett to Willie M. Tuttle; John Joseph Lever to John Joseph Rochon; Steven John Kruse to Steven John Merrill; Charles Issachar Ramsey to Charles Issachar Doeg; Jeannette Agnes Stewart Ramsey to Jeannette Agnes Stewart Doeg; Sandra Lee Nordine to Sandra Lee Morang; Donald Raymond Vachon to Edward Albert Richard; Olivette Frances Goodwin to Olivette Frances Murdock; Helynn Sandra Kopac to Helynn Sandra Cross; Armand Bernier to Armand Gilbert; Janice Leona Bean to Janice Leona Sanders; Threse C. St. Pierre to Threse C. Couture; Leon Samuel McCombe, Jr. to Jack Arthur Wallis; Morris Liptzer to Alfred Morris Lewis; Jeanette E. Liptzer to Jeanette E. Lewis; Bennett Leonard Liptzer to Bennett Leonard Lewis; Pearl Gloria Liptzer to Pearl Gloria Lewis; David Alonzo O'Conner to David Alonzo Smith; Edmund King to Edmund Douglas; James Arthur (Cole) Haskell to George Edgar Grondin; Maynard Joseph Vennard to Maynard Joseph Orr; Joan Elizabeth Woodman to Doris Elizabeth Preston; Joyce Vanessa Garland to Joyce Vanessa Haedt; Kysir Dowaliby to James Dowaliby; George Lefebvre to George Vincent; Marie Lefebvre to Marie Vincent; Arthur Lefebvre to Arthur Vincent; Walter J. Lougee to Jacob Walter Lougee; Walter W. Truman to Walter W. Fischer; Gerard E. Gagne, Jr. to John Paul Anthony Gagne; Albert Baxter to Leon Francis Davis; Willis A. Smith to Perley A. Smith; Constance Virginia Chard to Constance Virginia Nangle; Florence M. Cullen to Florence M. LeClair; Wilhelmine Rookey to

1939-1941

Wilhelmine Routhier; Joseph Louis Rookey, Jr. to Joseph Louis Routhier, Jr.; Rudolph Eugene Rookey to Rudolph Eugene Routhier; Marianne Rookey to Marianne Routhier; Marie Louise Rookey to Marie Louise Routhier; Leopold Nadeau to Leopold Lessard; Nicholas J. Micocci to Nicholas Joseph Caswell; Leon Ellis to Leon Hall; Roy Begley to Roy Whitlock Judd, Jr.; Jane Cancia Teaberg to Jane Cancia Willard; William Randall Ramsey III to William Lamar Hayes; Paul Secord to Robert Eugene Sanborn; Benjamin Kenney to Archie B. Canney; Arlene Osgood to Arlene Mildred Abbott; Gerald Miller to Gerald Ouelette; Ronald Francis Finnin to Ronald Francis Eastman; Barbara Rose Skillings to Barbara Rose Hurd; Jeannette Bertha Hebert to Jeannette Bertha Rouleau; Robert Augustine Lindsay to Arthur Robert DuBois; Joseph Leo Henry Peloquin to Leo Henry Cater; Rita May Dubois to Rita May Tibbetts; Walter Clyde Lea to W. Clyde Carden; Jacqueline Grace Evans to Jacqueline Grace Hamilton; Joseph Raymond Parent to Raymond Joseph Foss; Annie Gage Caldwell to Annie B. Gage; Gail Patricia Grant to Gail Penthia Wood; Senley Thomas Printy to John Senley Printy; Xavier Croteau to Joseph Hubert Leon Croteau; Minnie Etta Norris (McCrillis) to Minnie Etta Norris McCrillis

<u>Belknap County</u> - Florence E. Chamberlain to Florence Redman; Norma Lee Ratta to Norma Lee Rutta; Gladys E. Ratta to Gladys E. Rutta; Charles Hayford Stewart to Malcolm Alexander Rounds Stewart, Jr.; Frances Burke Goldstein to Frances Burke Gibson; Edward Goldstein to Edward Gibson; Nancy Ann Merrill to Nancy Ann Palm; Veronica D. Foley to Veronica D. Turley; Norman Edward Gonyer to Norman Edward Boucher; Rita L. Mack to Riva L. Mack; Jennie M. Moscardini to Jennie M. Cook; Edith S. Conley to Edith S. Johnson; Caroline Muriel Beckman to Muriel Caroline Beckman; William R. Smith to William Russell Downing; Lillian May Hodgson to Lillian May Smith; Marshall Locke to Marshall Ernest Locke; Philip Edward Tousignant to Philip Edward Dalton; John Paul Cranston to John Paul Bickford; Shoyloma Zulman Clevenson to Sam Solomon Clevenson; Edwin Michael Hodgson to Edwin Michael Darling; Wilfred Rouleau to Wilfred Plante.

Changed by adoption: Lionel Raymond Valliere to Lionel Raymond Valliere; George Theodore Valliere to George Theodore Valliere;

1939-1941

Richard Altomare to Kerrith Haddon King; Patricia Ann Avery to Patricia Ann Swain; Walter Everett Varney, Jr. to Walter Everett Varney Perkins; Mary Jane Seavey to Mary Jane Whitney; ----- Grimstone to Mary Ann Winkler; John Edmund Quinlan to John Edmund Hubbard; Ermus Fred Varney to Ermus Fred Ellis; Patricia A. Huckins to Sally Sue Sargent; Alfreda Alice Marden to Aldreda Alice Marden; Robert Lee Hobart to Robert Harry Avery; Mary Jane Rae to Mary Jane Haddock

Carroll County - Arthur Romeo Moore to Arthur Romeo Jette; Grafton Ralph Ward to Grafton Ralph Colbert; Bernard G. Tutt to Bernard Gunison Dudley Tutt; Helen Janet Steves to Sally Steves Davis; Addie B. Smith to Addie B. Hayes; Arthur J. Smith to Arthur J. Daurie; Roger Jackson to Roger Jackson Whittier; John Carpenter to John Gilman Carpenter; Rupert Clifford Hodgdon to Rupert Clifford Jones; Vernon Thomas Hodgdon to Vernon Thomas Jones; Mildred M. Drew to Madelyn Mildred Hoyt; Roland D. Emerson to Roland Dinsmore Dow; Georgette Hale to Georgette Percot; Henry J. Chandler, Jr. to Henry Archibald Meader; Leonard Ernest Demers to Leonard Ernest Charles; Kenneth Paige to Robert Kenneth Paige

Merrimack County - Walter Flanders Hunt to Francis Perley Hunt; Fred Arthur Paige to Fred Arthur Bailey; Hazel Billings Wheeler to Hazel Billings; Alice Bolkis to Alice Thompson; Beatrice Minnion to Beatrice Beaupre; Susan E. Huse to Elma S. Huse; Donald Day to Donald Riel; Nathan Edward Eastman to Nathan Currier Eastman; Kenneth Herman Juringius to Kenneth Herman Sheard; Rudolph Knoetzsch to Rudolph Knoetzsch Roody; Roger Pelletier to Roger Boudreau; Felicia Gertrude Knoetzsch to Felicia Gertrude Roody; Patricia Caroline Knoetzsch to Patricia Caroline Roody; Bertha L. Gaskell to Bertha G. Corser; George Calnan to George William Hall; Cora Alice Leo to Cora Alice Flynn; Aarne Jacob Wahamaki to Aarne Jacob Mackey; Doris P. Wahamaki to Doris Priscilla Mackey; Leonard J. Florence to Leonard J. Gray; Bernard Francis Sweeney, Jr. to Lance Douglas Sweeney; Basilios Tsekares to William Nichols Talmers; Ike Couffman to Isaac Kauffman; Harry B. Cohen to Hank B. Cains; Lewis M. Cohen to Lewis M. Cains; Rose L. Cohen to Rose L. Cains; Warren Harding Ginniss to Warren Harding Spofford; Carol Eugene Nudd to Carol Eugene Brown; Robert Louis Nudd to Robert L. Brown; Josiah Vose Fisher to Josiah Howe

1939-1941

Vose Fisher; Joan Alice Lamora to Joan Alice Woodbury; Fred Charette to Fred Carter; Arthur Forger to Arthur Leonard Newton; Lloyd Allison Wescom to Lloyd Allison Moulton; Martha L. Fretwell to Martha L. Morrill; Joseph Odilon Patoine to Joseph Odilon Desrosiers; Bessie E. Abruzzese to Bessie E. Simonella

Changed by adoption: Donald Alan Locke to Donald Alan Joy; Robert Bruce Hill to Robert Bruce Davis; Christine June Marcotte to Christine June Lewis; Pauline Patten to Pauline Dame; "Baby" Blackwell to Hugh Graham Cameron; David Roland Canfield to Stanley Philip Purtell; John Hart to John Joseph Bundy; Elizabeth Katherine Schriver to Elizabeth Katherine James; Tresa May Welch to Tresa May Foote; Robert William Welch to Robert William Foote; Elizabeth Rae Flint to Beverly Jane Howland; Robert Bruce McNally to Richard Paul Paveglio; Edmond J. Poire to Edmond J. Guay; Robert J. Poire to Robert J. Guay; Madeline May Laro to Madeline May Kelley; Sterling Victor Warren to Sterling Victor Blakeley; Mervin Dame Crommett to Mervin Dale Perkins; Constance Alger to Constance Alger Duclos; Ruth Miriam Olkonen to Ruth Miriam Paakkari; Jeffrey Pillsbury to Walter Robert Clark; Pamela Jean Scanlin to Margot Gibson Adams; "Baby" Potter to David Eugene Welch; Annabell E. Brideau to Annabell E. Demars; Barbara Florence Senise to Barbara Jean Moore; Patricia Duff to Patricia C. Partridge; Claire Lucille Fanny to Claire Lucille Labonte; Judith Merle McIntosh to Judith Merle Genest; Jean Demers (Fowler) to Jean Newell; Leon Norman Demers (Fowler) to David Parmenter Newell; Bruce Richard Doughty to David James Doughty; Judith Barbara to Judith Barbara San Antonio

Hillsborough County - Lawrence Verheyen to Andrew Lawrence Walsh; Annette Canane to Annette Rzeznikiewicz; Arnold Levine to Arnold Grevior; George Vlahopoulos to George Baroody; Ptefanos Vlahopoulos to John J. Baroody; Necolai Telicza to Joseph M. Tayloff; Malcolm Tibbetts to Joseph Malcolm Springfield; William Anderson Emmons to William Anderson Coleman; Roger Jackson Emmons to Roger Jackson Coleman; Victor Pappacostas to Victor P. Costa; Leo Francis Lariviere to Leo Francis Dubois; Alfred Gaudiase Leclair to Elzear Gaudiase Francoeur; Antonio Argeropoulos to William Hector Rouleau; Marguerite Prior to Marguerite Dunne; Ethel Frost Woods to Ethelyn Neal Frost; Mary Evelyn Dennis to Mary Evelyn Sullivan;

1939-1941

Andrew Muckuskie to Andrew McCuskey; Chester Muckuskie to Chester McKuskie; Wanda Muckuskie to Wanda McKuskie; Josephine Makowska to Josephine McKuskie; Adella Balzejewicz to Adella Sedlewicz; Lucille G. Owen to Lucille G. Lavigne; Waslow Walentukevicz to Walter Walent; Julius Kvaraceis to Julius Corosa; Joseph Aime Marcel Cormier to Ralph A. Cormier; Marguerite G. Murray to Marguerite G. LaBounty; Wasyl Szewczyszyn to Charles Szewczyk; Mildred Isabelle Van Duyne to Lynn Mildred Van Duyne; Edward Zbierski to Edward A. Comstock; Amber Chase Buholz to Amber Chase; Leo George Perras to Leo Arthur Perry; Joseph Eugene Maurice Gamelin to Joseph Eugene Maurice Lesieur; Agatha Miliauskas to Agnes Mills; Stedman Bradley Breed to Stedman Bradley Fottler; Charles Stanley Sakowich to Charles Stanley Stack; Siefar Bartosewie to Siefar Bortas; Stanislaw Kucharczyk to Stanley Ludwig Baker; Martha Emma White to Mattie E. Blood; Leo E. Bresse to Leonard E. Howard; Ronald Eugene Otis to Ronald Eugene Farland; Allen Wesley Sanders to Allan Griffith Saunders; George Perley Dow to Perley Doddridge Dow; Norma Nichols to Norma Willette; Elia Robinovitz to Elias Robbins; Helen Frances Blixt to Helen Frances Brown; Jane Daniels to Jane Doris Wheeler; Mary Limbourg to Mary Lynbourg; William Limbourg to William Lynbourg; Joseph Swiesz to Joseph Swiss; Anton Milasiewiez to Antanas Milas; Grace I. Bjurling to Grace I. Burling; Elmer Robert Bjurling to Elmer Robert Burling; Harriet E. Byam to Harriet Ellen Bryer; Elise Lehmann to Elise Lehmann Coppez; John Anthony Siedlewicz to John Anthony Sullivan; Everett Harrison Barnes to Alfred Dexter Barnes

Changed by adoption: Richard J. Flower to Richard J. Lamy; Thomas Psaltis to Thomas Lucas; Theoharis Psaltis to Harry Lucas; Margaret Mary McKenna to Janet Margaret Cloutier; Lorraine Cecile Desrosiers to Lorraine Patricia Lamothe; Baby Plowright to Nancy Porst Arthur; Rita Dorris to Helen Bachakouchos; Daniel Lee Patenaude to Daniel Lee Covill; Norrinne Teresa Sullivan to Norinne Teresa Crowley; Jean Murray to Mary Jeanne Ouelette; Judith Carrol Withstandley to Judith Carol Nahil; Baby Carpenter to Merton Don Fletcher; Carol Anne Boisvert to Carole Anne Tarullo; Arthur Sawyer to Paul Duffy; Baby Carpenter to Richard Allen Schneider; Joseph Albert Cloutier to Joseph Albert Zink; Frank Edward Boynton to Frank Eric Pfefferkorn; Carol Ann Bach to Marie Claire Elaine Caron; Philip Gagnon to Philip Joseph

1939-1941

Forrest; Joseph Plantier to Joseph Alphonse Levasseur; Edward Francis Bernard to Richard Evariste Pinard; Patricia Ann Duncan to Patricia Ann Desruisseau; Pauline Joan Leclair to Pauline Joan Lemay; Priscilla Ernestine Goodwin to Priscilla Ernestine Cheney; John Francis Hardy to John Francis Balban; Inis Margaret Hardy to Inis Margaret Balban; Baby Foster to Kathryn Ann Hastedt; Lucie R. Boulanger to Lucie R. Martin; Larry Grant Knapp to Larry Grant MacDougall; Baby McCarthy to Martha Weston Hammond; Margaret Doris Lavallee to Margaret Doris Rioux; Mary Edith Mabry to Mary Edith Sawyer; Marion Ella Hallstrom to Marion Ellen Rogler; Helen Maloney to Paula Jane Bozek; Marie Lillian Houston to Barbara Marie Hays; Baby Blidberg to Barrett Calvin Leete; Catherine Verge to Catherine Bellefeuille; Karlene Ann Woods to Constance Ann Bilodeau; Dorothy Jane Guilmette to Dorothy Jane Lawrence; Helen Joan Newcombe to Helen Joan Mizo; Robert L. Connelly to Millard Herbert Edwards; Suzanne Lucille Cutter to Barbara Richards; Mary Roberta Trudeau to Patricia Ann Gibbons; Carol Hickson Donelan to Carole Gertrude White; Albert William Briggs to Samuel Adrien Flanders; Paul Francis Beals to Paul Francis Freeman; Baby Kimball to Gregory Lawrence Cardinal; Baby McCarthy to Wanda Ann Boynton; Roland Joseph Poehlman to Roland Joseph Guillemette; Annie MacArthur, nee Baxter Archambeault to Annie MacArthur; Yvonne Rivard to Yvonne Loraine Beland; Sherman E. Starkweather to Richard Henry Cox; Emma Rose Belanger to Eva Ouellette; Pauline Proulx to Pauline Gage; Baby Norris to Robert Martin Wheeler; Jeanne D'Arc Proulx to Jeanne D'Arc Carrier; Geraldine Mary Jordan to Geraldine Mary McRae; Leslie Walker to Leslie Byron Nichols; Beryle Arlene Allen to Beryle Arlene Rowell; Robert Bernard Cormier to Robert Richard Ranalli; Margaret Mary Harte to Brenda Kelley; Norman Erene Paquette to Norman Erene Lefebvre; Robert Allen Sterner to Robert William LaPierre; Carol Anne Carrion to Vera Elizabeth Gove; Joseph Richard Roland Beliveau to Joseph Richard Roland Tremblay; Jean Phyllis Calhoune to Jean Phyllis Wagner; Isabelle Pailloucq to Isabel Robbins; Jean Pailloucq to Jean Robbins; Paul Ioshpa to Paul Robbins; Alfred Lemire to Alfred Albert Boulay; Steven Robert Abbott to Steven Robert Moody; Mary Lucy Alice Pickard to Mary Lucy Alice Bolduc; Marcelle Alice Robichaud to Marcelle Alice Letourneux; Stephen Loiselle to Stephen Connell; Helen Marguerite Andrews to Helen Marguerite Foskett; Donald Leazott to Donald Read; Arlene Frances Monaco to Arlene

1939-1941

Frances Smith; Natalie Francelia Winslow to Natalie Francelia Glines; Robert Veroneau to Gilbert Robert Boilard; Michael R. Guimont to Michael R. Binette; Jacqueline Ellen Decosse to Jacqueline Ellen Lovering; Shirley Morrison to Shirley Ann Gould; Barbara Louise Bartrum to Barbara Louise Tayloff; William John Novick to William John Jackson; Shirley Lagasse to Shirley Morisette; George Peterson to George Miller; Edith Smith to Oxley Doreen Elizabeth; Grace Bradis to Marlene Mullen

Cheshire County - Frances O. Flagg to Frances Odell Clark; Charles Babcock Caldwell to William Allen Caldwell; Harry Lewis Bedaw to Barry Lewis Bedaw; Leroy L. Parkhurst to Leroy L. White; Edward Miller Emmes to Edward Clifton Derby; Francis X. Curtin to Francis X. Watterson; Joyce Ann Richer to Joyce Ann Desrosiers; Mary Alice Willard to Mary Alice Bouvier; Irene Joan Roy to Irene Joan Dunn; Ralph Wallace Calkins to Ralph Wallace Britton; Frederick Palmer to Kenneth Clifford Foote; Evon Alice Berthiaume to Yvonne Alice Georgette Berthiaume; Patricia Johnson to Patricia Morley; Annie S. Mallila to Annie S. Lampinen; Barbara Louise Cyr to Barbara Louise Whitcomb; Edward Franklin Delory to Edward Franklin Cornwell; Bertha Delory to Bertha Cornwell; Edward Franklin Delory, Jr. to Edward Franklin Cornwell, Jr.; Paul Edwin Delory to Paul Edwin Cornwell; Mary Ellen Knapp Delory to Mary Ellen Cornwell; Baby Rosen to Carolyn W. Sleeper; Leland James Larrabee to Stanley Hiland Ring; Robert Charles Amsdam to Robert Charles Keddie; Merritt Giffin Dana to Marshall Merritt Dana; Olive H. Bryant to Olive A. Hunt; James L. Fay to Henry W. Fay; Paulina Anthanetta Holbrook to Paulina Anthanetta Lambert; Marilyn Ann Cutter to Marjorie Jane Scott; Walter Randall to Don Walter Randall; Baby Clark to Ward Fletcher Archer; Ronald Frank Cutter to Ronald Frank Reed; Elbra E. Fogg to Elbra E. Lamb; Marilyn Lois Simonds to Marilyn Lois Hudson; Mildred Smith to Judith Ann Mack; Arthur Philip Pelton to Arthur Philip Maki; Joseph Stanley McCormick to Joseph Stanley Christian; Edward Croteau to Edward Martin; Zoe Stamopoulas to Zoe Vrakatitsis; Dianne Fulton to Dianne Wilcox; Virginia Haigney to Merry Beth Russell; Sylvia Denise Kingsbury to Sylvia Denise Montgomery; Carol Dinane Record to Carolyn Dinane Carter; Ronald David Cole to Ronald David Toussaint; John Krystopowicz to John Kristof; Larry Edward Eastman to Larry Edward Anderson; Baby Merrifield to Sandra Gerda Johnson;

1939-1941

Etta L. Allen to Etta A. Lewis; Bernice Flora Pollard to Bernice Flora Tredo; Joseph Kubosky to Joseph Cook; Esther Kubosky to Esther L. Cook; Richard Kubosky to Richard Littlefield Cook; Murray John Patnode to Murray John Burt; Robert Deruisseau to Robert Joseph Collier; Allen to Dana Kinsman Foote; Theodore Frank Chabot to Theodore Frank Sheppard; Tony Salitski to Tony Seliskey; Helena Chensky to Helen Seliskey; John Saliskey to John Selisky

Changed by adoption: Margaret Ann Woods to Margaret Ann Woods; Edward Joseph Gilbert to Edward Joseph Gilbert

Sullivan County - Barbara Marie McGuire Fitts to Barbara Marie Fitts; Jennie M. Erskine to Jennie M. Dearborn; Patricia Faith Jennison to Patricia Faith Smith; Ellen Ann Jenkerson to Ellen Ann Streeter; Harry Lloyd Jenkerson to Harry Lloyd Streeter; Jeanne Ann Rollins to Jeanne Ann Nutting; Leo Serbian to Leo Dufferin; Barbara Anne Page to Barbara Anne Selmi; Normand C. Judd to Normand C. Brassaw; Ernest J. Babeux to Ernest J. Babbitt; Robert W. Barry to Robert Francis King; Fiorentino Marro to Rendy Michael Marro; Joseph Bordan Peterson to Joseph Bert Peterson; Dorothy D. Young to Dorothy D. Morse; Carole Ida Bythrow to Carole Ida Mardin; William Roach Wirta to William Roach; Shirley Learmouth to Shirley Lucile Caron; Howard Laurence Grenache to Howard Laurence Hutchinson; Edmond Lusier to Herman Lussier; Roberta May King to Roberta May Barker; Elias Ekman to George Eckerman; Julius Martin Stilson to Cecil Stilson; Konrad Anjou Kaukolander to Conrad Starr; Joseph Leo Dwire to Joseph Leo Merrill; Charles L. Lozo to Charles L. Mitchell; Hazel G. Lozo to Hazel G. Mitchell; Annie Mary Lozo to Annie Mary Mitchell; Martha Celina Lozo to Martha Celina Mitchell; Theresa Jane Lozo to Theresa Jane Mitchell; Joseph Omer Rousseau to Joseph Omer Brooks; Mary Alexandra Sakowich to Mary Alexander Rule; Julius Golofsky to Julius Gold; Charles A. Bouchard to Alfred A. Bouchard; Richard Owen Bythrow to Eugene Mark McGuire; Elfred Michael Fortune to Elfred Michael Otterson; Jairus Hammond Barnes to Jerome Clyde Barnes; Lawrence Barney to Lawrence Guy Dole; Gloria Jeanine Williams to Patricia Perry; George Arlinsky to George Arlin

1939-1941

<u>Grafton County</u> - Donna Mae Andreason to Norma Elizabeth Ward; Robert Abbott to Charles Richard Dixon; Sandra Beardsell to Carol Jane Funkhouser; Janice Elaine Bilodeau to Janice Elaine Harris; Marion Virginia Bromley to Marion Virginia Holinbrook; Edith Anne Chase to Ann Glazier; Frank Hazen Cook to Frank Hazen Paine; Donald Edward Cross to David Allen Roberts; Leslie Robert Devoe to Robert Lionel DesRoches; Barbara Louis Elliott to Joan Elaine Osgood; Janice May Flanders to Janice May Flanders; Stewart Frank to Richard Rainer; Evelyn Cerena Forbes to Judith Lynn Tyler; Mary Louise Goodwin to Mary Louise Goodwin; Dorothy Patricia Gillon to Dorothy Patricia Therrien; Hattie Irene Gilman to Harriett Irene Gilman; John Bruce Henault to John Parker Carr; James G. Haldane to James G. Stiles; Mary Elaine Harding to Mary Elaine Lee; Charles Lewis Joscelyn, Jr. to Gene Howard Chase; Francis Eugene Kimball to John Osgood Ellis; Arthur Bertrand Knight to Arthur Bertrand Knight, Jr.; Arthur Bertrand Knight, Jr. to Arthur Bertrand Knight, 2nd; Mary Jane LaPoint to Denise M. Longchamps; Richard Donald Mowers to Richard Donald Gallagher; Shirley Moulton to Shirley Hill; Alan Beverly Masslick to Alan Herbert; Donald McCabe to Donald Fillion; Fenton D. Moore to Fenton Hurley Bean; David John Napsey to David Clayton Flanders; Isabel Grace Newell to Ruth Ann Clark; Barbara Ann Powell to Barbara Ann Sycamore; Clarence F. Polaski to Nora Ivy Murphy; Ralph Ray Robins to Ralph Ray Streeter; Albert H. Rand to Robert Henry Rand; Charles Stevens to David Charles Capen; Laura Mae Stevens to Cynthia Anne Capen; Mary E. Stevens to Mary Elizabeth Jenkins; Harriet Elsie Burroughs Sherwood to Harriet Elsie Burroughs; Frederick Edward Schneider, Jr. to Frederick Edward Schneider, Jr.; Henry Stanley Stankiewicz to Henry Stanley Smith; James Stanton Walker to Richard Kimball Longchamps; Kathleen May Weller to Kathleen Mae Bronson; Charles Melvin Weed to Charles Melvin Weed Currier; Thedessa Olive Weed to Thedessa Olive Weed Currier; Lloyd R. White, Jr. to Lloyd R. Allen; Jay Field White to Jay Field Allen; Bertha J. Weller to Bertha J. Wiley; Margaret Audrey Whitcomb to Eleanor Arlenza Whitcomb; Marion Arleta Weller to Marion Arleta Fish

<u>Coos County</u> - Charlie Haisen to Jacob Charlie Jassop; Pauline LaBell to Pauline L. Keir; Mary Doris Guilmette to Mary Doris Waters; Leroy Llewellyn Mosher to Leroy Llewellyn Hatt; Marie Delia Dennis to Marie

1939-1941

Delia Sheehy; Albert Healy to Albert Healy Hickey; Helen Milbury Haley to Helen Milbury; Durward William Warren to Durward William Blair

Changed by adoption: Priscilla May Thompson to Priscilla May Gray; Elizabeth Ann Willson to Elizabeth Ann Prevost; George R. Smith, Jr. to George Smith Merrow; Eleanor Cora Glidden to Eleanor Cora Russell; Katherine Linnell to Katherine Dipucchio; Glenarron Delano to Glenarron Anderson; Robert King to Robert Bruce Parker; Patricia Ann Peterson to Patricia Ann Masters; William Dorr to Roy George Huntoon; Ernest Oscar to Ernest Oscar Dale; Richard Paul Gade to Richard Gade Williams; William Lester Booth to William Lester Terrill; Peter Parent to Guy Wayne Grady; Lucille Doris Merrill to Lucille Doris Filteau; Lillian Mary Napert to Lillian Mary Garon; Ronald D. LaClair to Clayton Ronald Larkin; Dorothea Gagnon to Dorothea Oleson; William Fred Lang to William Frederick Bowin

Name changes made by the superior court in divorce proceedings:

Rockingham County - Mildred W. Carano to Mildred Webber; Lucy Olive Michie to Lucy Olive Snyder; Alice M. Pratt to Alice M. Gove; Alice M. Rippy to Alice Hanson Markey; Annie T. Roche to Annie T. Fleming; Faoline H. Rylander to Faoline H. Colby; Ruby Marshall Langley to Ruby Marshall; Dorothy A. Merola to Dorothy A. Deroucher; Doris S. Moulton to Doris S. Spackman; Elinor S. Newhall to Elinor S. Piper; Dorothy Bonney Rowe to Dorothy Bonney; Dorothy Dunphy Vanden Molen to Dorothy Dunphy; Carrie Weatherly to Carrie E. Page; Hazel I. Manning to Hazel I. Patch; Martha Jennie Biester to Martha Jennie Whittemore; Ella Amelia Tucker to Ella Amelia Vondal; Hazel M. Buzzell to Hazel M. Butler; Abbie E. Dolton to Abbie E. Kosch; June S. Smith to June Standish Taylor; Elaine J. Gordon to Elaine J. Jordan; Marion F. Wetmore to Marion Flanders; Frances Langdon Bukata to Frances Langdon Henson; Esther Bessie Baker to Esther Bessie Fearer; Florence Hinckley Naylor to Florence Hinckley

Strafford County - Mabel Olko to Mabel Brown; Madeline G. Glass to Madeline G. Eastman; Martha David to Martha Costoras; Dorothy L. Webster to Dorothy L. Gilson; Gladys Grace Deal to Gladys Grace Edgerly; Catherine T. Croteau to Catherine T. Crennan; Arlene E.

1939-1941

Laverdiere to Arlene E. Knox; Jeannette I. MacDonald to Jeannette Irene Roberts; Beatrice V. Buzzell to Beatrice V. Woodman; Annie B. Kent to Annie B. Maloney; Adelaide C. Van Buskirk to Adelaide C. Janes; Enid H. Cook to Enid H. Hayes; Marion A. Mayott to Marion A. Wyatt; Helen B. Walsh to Helen B. Gagne; Frances L. Spiridondes to Frances L. Richardson; Marguerite Hildreth Hall to Marguerite M. Hildreth; Annie C. Brassaw to Annie C. Clement; Phyllis D. Braga to Phyllis E. Daggett; Roberta L. Mills to Robert L. Miles; Helen M. Hanson to Helen Marie Jeneau

Belknap County - Doris Geddis to Doris Dickson; Dora Mary Drouin to Dora Mary Tardiff; Margaret S. Hall to Margaret S. Taylor; Helen Beatrice Drury to Helen Beatrice Bousquette; Lilla G. Baker to Lilla B. Gould; Shirley M. Granger to Shirley M. Towle; Ludovica L. Schelin to Ludovica L. Williams; Esther K. Maynard to Esther Louise Kelley; Delsie K. Janssen to Delsie Knapp; Eleanor Jordan Crosby to Eleanor Mae Jordan; Lucille Cooney to Lucille C. Hamel

Carroll County - A. Gertrude Emerson to A. Gertrude Sturtevant; Mildred R. Libbey to Mildred Robinson

Merrimack County - Lillian B. Mattice to Lillian B. Browning; Bernice C. Filion to Bernice C. Brozeau; Freeda E. Reardon to Freeda E. Whiting; Irene M. Arthur to Irene M. Crowley; Lillian M. Archibald to Lillian Mae Kennedy; Dorothy O'Leary Duval to Dorothy J. O'Leary; Vivian R. Mercier to Vivian R. Vadney; Naomi B. Maltais to Naomi B. Wentworth; Mildred Breen to Mildred Chaput; Madeline L. Schott to Madeline Ellis; Elizabeth P. Bushey to Elizabeth Kimball Prescott; Ida Alice Beauley to Ida Alice Blodgett; Grace B. Decrow to Grace B. Smith; June O. Milligan to June Carol Orr; Lucy A. Buzzell to Lucy Airetta Cole; Thelma Leighton Schoch to Thelma Leighton; Olive N. Emerson to Olive Nettie Corey; Florence C. Young to Florence Dorothy Corriveau; Virginia M. Taylor to Virginia May Rines; Mildred E. Lindemulder to Mildred Denton; Bernice R. Daley to Bernice Ruth Young

Hillsborough County - Goldie Geraldine Wiggins to Goldie Geraldine Soper; Eleanor W. Harrington to Eleanor W. Welch; Mary V. Gaskin to Mary V. Conley; Barbara G. Adams to Barbara G. Davis; May Pearson Pierce to May Pearson; Violet Ledoux Hoyt to Violet Ledoux; Rose D.

1939-1941

Dodge to Rose Delia Bunton; Irene Peabody to Irene Lord; Frances Olive Howard to Francis Olive Mullikin; Thelma H. Teuber to Thelma Ham; Margaret Barrett Goudreau to Margaret Barrett; Ethel A. Duddy to Ethel A. Keefe; Theresa C. Carrick to Theresa Jozaitis; Elsie Keefe to Elsie Flanders; Pauline Lucille Fairfield to Pauline Lucille MacCormack; Estelle Durand to Estelle Rzeznikiewicz; Helga Warren to Helga Hutz Adams; Esther L. Bridgess to Esther L. Pitcher; Gertrude Marie Havey to Gertrude Marie Gauthier; Yvonne Hatch to Yvonne Lemay; Dorothy Gedenberg to Dorothy McKelvey; Marion M. Carrier to Marion Myrtle Cushing; Margaret F. Popple to Margaret B. Flagg; Rose Baron to Rose Chartier; Simone Olena to Simone Metropolis; Gene Nelson Atwood Cassidy to Gene Nelson Atwood; Ruth A. P. Kelley to Ruth A. P. Worthen; Lyn Allen to Lyn Brown; Ruth Hall Manolesco to Ruth Hall; Katherine M. Paquette to Katherine M. Healy; Jennie V. Jensen to Jennie Marie Valliere; Alice M. Spinks to Alice H. Murphy; Bernice Soter to Bernice Lucien; Irene Moore to Irene Camelbeek; Orma W. Fisher to Orma W. Wheaton; Lucille Billman to Lucille Dane; Elsie Hardman to Elsie Thompson; Caroline Sherburne to Caroline Mazur; Constance Fiske to Constance Smart; Vera E. Soucy to Vera E. George; Valida Girouard to Valida Bellefleur; Flora Mae Anctil to Flora Mae Belanger; Violet Larouche to Violet Anderson; Ruth Mason Kelley to Ruth Mason; Dorothy Evelyn Hunt Callahan to Dorothy Evelyn Hunt; Ella I. George to Ella I. Putnam; Doris Freelove Perdue to Doris Freelove Melcher; Beatrice O. Maybay to Beatrice Ora Denoncourt; Blanche A. Lajoie to Blanche A. Desjardins

Cheshire County - Nora Capen Wilson to Nora L. Capen; Eva Mary Lawrence to Eva Mary Desmarais; Elsie C. Wescome to Elsie Clara Lounder; Hazel M. Sprague Warn to Hazel M. Sprague; Mae D. Naromore to Mae D. Miner; Laura E. G. Lane to Laura E. Gauthier; Bertha Alice Conant to Bertha Alice Taylor; Mildred LaBombard Little to Mildred Marion LaBombard; Edith G. Champney to Edith G. Mathews; Mary Estey to Mary Eleanor Connor; Gladys May Baronoski to Gladys May Robb; Mary M. Underwood to Mary Marnell; Addie C. Wilbur to Addie H. Carter; Matilda A. Whitcomb to Matilda A. Hinds; Ruth P. Hoffman Rue to Ruth Phyllis Hoffman; Lois Lodelle Wojchick to Lois Lodelle Smart

1939-1941

Sullivan County - Nellie W. Burns to Nellie W. Hanley; Marion A. Pariseau to Marion A. Honny; Cora Lalibertee to Cora Roberts; Myrtle A. Chapman to Myrtle A. Yetman; Frances L. Dane to Frances L. Tulin; Ruby Kendall Hemphill to Ruby Kendall; Ruth E. Cassavaugh to Ruth E. Pettengill; Margaret V. Pariseau to Margaret V. MacIntyre; Hazel Lord Burns to Hazel Lord; Helene B. Light to Helene C. Baird; Celia B. Matson to Celia Bruce; Julie Eva Morse to Julie Eva Short; Virginia Ruuskanen to Virginia Taimi; Ada B. Maxfield to Ada B. Calkins

Grafton County - Eva Newell Schuck to Eva Newell; Eloise L. Delsanter to Eloise L. Marcus; Marguerite Sweet Wolfsohn to Marguerite Sweet; Madeline C. Boyd to Madeline C. McCue; Lila G. Neitz to Lila S. Goodwin; Alice Farr to Alice A. LaBombard; Marion Hoyt Mickelboro to Marion Hoyt; Mattie S. Cram to Mattie S. Dunham; Margot R. St. Lawrence to Margot Averill Robie; Jessie S. Woodman to Jessie N. Saulnier; June E. Brooker to June Esmar Stevens; Rita J. Dow to Rita Jane Somers; Evelyn D. Towne to Evelyn D. Grapes; Elizabeth B. Cutler to Elizabeth Kenny; Bertha L. Vaughn to Bertha L. Schrafft; Monica M. Valley to Monica M. Houghton; Margaret I. Lee to Margaret I. Moran; Lois G. Guernsey to Lois G. Gibbs; Doris D. Kebrich to Doris Doll; June P. York to June Pounder; Margaret E. Bowman to Margaret E. Cotnoir; June P. Enos to June P. Young

Coos County - Laura R. Hunter to Laura R. Hafford; Claire H. Balko to Claire H. LePage; Ethel Foster Hurd to Ethel Foster; Shirley R. Sawyer to Shirley R. Bryan; Geraldine G. Wiswell to Geraldine G. Belville; Agatha Robert to Agatha McKenna

Name changes made at the time of naturalization:

Strafford County - Joao Pereia to John Perry; Joseph Murray Ivanhoe Levesque to Maurice Ivanhoe Levesque; Hagop Garabed Banaian to Jacob Banaian; Cleopatra George Melonous to Clara George Melonous; Marie Leona Belonise Scrosati to Marie Leona Scrosati; Abdo Albert George to Albert George; Elias Shivel to Elias Khoury Hashem; Jan Piecuch to John Piecuch; Alexander Diamondis to Alexander Diamond; Kyreakos John Pastedenos to Charles John Pastene; Hattie Leona Gravel to Henrietta Leona Gravel; Francois

1939-1941

Elzear Pepin to Frank Elzear Pepin; Joseph Ovila Leon Alphonse Ferland to Leonard Joseph Ferland; Tom Joseph Abiseleah to Tom Joseph

January 1941 - January 1943[10/]

Name changes made by the probate courts:

Rockingham County - John Inman to Kenneth John Edward Cassell; Nona Marie Denyou to Nona Marie Healey; Philip William Denyou to Philip William Healey; Corienne Helen Peon to Corienne Helen Shea; Robert Chambers to Robert Philip Gratton; Joseph Jainkowsky to Joseph Jainkouwsky; Wayne Leonard Trider to Wayne Leonard Mitchell; Barbara A. Patch to Barbara A. Byrns; John Skibniowski also known as John Skibnoski to John Skibb; Maria Skibniowski also known as Maria Skiboski to Mary Skibb; Myron Mitchell Skibniowski also known as Myron Mitchell Skibnoski to Myron Mitchell Skibb; Estelle Irene Skibniowski also known as Stella Skibniowski to Estelle Irene Skibb; Genevieve Abbie Skibniowski to Genevieve Abbie Skibb; Mitchell Myron Skibniowski to Mitchell Myron Skibb; Ernest Chris Lenz to Clifford Ernest Bane; Warren Robert Dennis to Warren Robert Guptill; Elliot Akmakjian to Elliot Akmakjian Stevens; Mary Akmakjian to Mary Stevens; Elliot Dean Akmakjian to Elliot Dean Stevens; Audrey Joyce Akmakjian to Audrey Joyce Stevens; Teresa M. Sherman to Teresa Maria Rand Stevens; Celia L. Floody to Celia Carolina Lacross; William Frances Hawco to William Francis Hawko Dore; Anna Kucharczyk to Anna Baker; Stanislaw Stankiewicz to Stanley Stevens; Vicenta Stankiewicz to Virginia Stevens; Catherine Stankiewicz to Catherine Stevens; Mary Stankiewicz to Mary Stevens; John Joseph Stankiewicz to John Joseph Stevens; Emile Stankiewicz to Emile Stevens; Cynthia Aldrich to Cynthia Lee Mason; Lowell R. Atherton to Lowell R. Fox; Thomas Fuller to Clifford McCullough, Jr.; Wallerin Dummaskowski to Joseph W. Demasky; Robert Joseph Corcoran to Robert Charles Jeeves; Sandra Jean Merrill to Catherine Manley Farrington; Parmenas Nerbonne to Peter Nerbonne; Norma Louise Strout to Norma Louise Nudd; Donald Willard Underhill to Donald William Dollard; Benjamin Parker, Jr. to Benjamin Guiley; Donald K. Wheeler to Donald K. Roy; Elmer W. Collier to Donald Richard Collier; Mary Carroll Brown to Mary Carroll Leavitt; (Female Infant) Moody to Mary Susan Marston; Barbara Stevens to Barbara Stevens Fox; William James Penney to William James Crowley; Mary Margaret Chapman to Mary Margaret Zdeb; William E. Houston to William E.

10/ Chapter 243, 1943 N. H. Public Laws

1941-1943

Chapman to Mary Margaret Zdeb; William E. Houston to William E. Reagan; Diane Theresa Frandaca to Diane Theresa Bukata; William Allan Rogers to Walter Billie Stockman; Agere Albert Milette to Aga Bert Milette; Joseph Shilale to Joseph W. Wilbur; Roy Louis Taylor to Roy Louis Eldridge; Robert Arthur Hadley to Robert Arthur Balukas; Charles Sociates Tufts to Charles Socrates Arvenites; Albert Leo Dick to Charles Harry Ingram; David Nelson Myers, Jr. to David MacNabb Wells; Frances Louise Tucker to Frances Louise Morton; Louise D. Twombly to Louise D. Lahart; Gerald Craven to Gerald L. Hereux; Roger Haas to Roger Trafton; James E. Smith to James E. Davis; Daine Frances Blake to Nancy Walker; Marilyn Roberta Brigham to Bonalyn Carol Robinson; Mary Louise Madigan to Gail Elizabeth Harvey Cotter; Arthur Noto to Arthur Gobbi; Christopher James O'Leary to Chris O'Leary; Joseph Masialis to Joseph John Masellis; Richard LaMontagne to Richard Beaulieu; Elizabeth Ann Quinlan to Elizabeth Ann Dietrich; Barbara Ann Massa to Barbara Ann Mullins; Helen Wilson Frantz to Helen Ruth Wilson; Charles Henry Haley to George William Haley; Willis Leslie Worster to Raymond Peterson Ainsworth; Theodore H. Elms to Theodore Hanson Bradley; Vernard Albert Long to Vernard Albert Jenness Coleman; Robert Lee Vrettas to Robert Forest Garland; Marjorie Louise Bryant to Marjorie Louise Cummings; Aphrodite Legakes Deakoumakes to Aphrodite Deakoum; Evangelos Deakoumakes to Evangelos Deakoum; Henry J. Gotz to Henry J. Goss; Judith Ann Stafford to Judith Ann Dixon; Frances Rose Stafford to Frances Rose Dixon; Robert Edward Stafford to Robert Edward Dixon; Agnes Perry Moynihan to Agnes Perry; Verna Marie King to Verna Marie Middleton; Maryanna Michalska Krukowski to Maryanna Michalska Cook; Charles Frederick Mannell to Charles Fredrick Dunn; William Gerard Ward to Gerard William Jordan; Joan Seliga to Joan Smith; Walter A. Boulay to Joseph Walter Jameson; David Cohen to David Miller; Manuel Cohen to Manuel Miller; Helen Krukowski to Helen Cook; John Caswell to Chester M. Staples, Jr.; Nancy Ann Sawyer to Nancy Ann Kalens; Frank L. Smith to Frank L. Healey; Nancy Sherman to Louisa Goodwin Yeagle; Alfred Jackson Carden to Robert Andrew Batcheldor; Jane Vacilla Gaumond to Jane Vacilla Gouzoules; Barbara Ann Mahoney to Susan Louise Chase; Wladislaw Gzywacz to Walter Givetz; Assunta Szywacz to Susie Givetz; Dorothy Ernestine Hutchins to Dorothy Ernestine Graham; Junior Caswell Bartlett to James C. Bartlett; Earlan Atwood Barber to

1941-1943

Earlan Atwood Wetherbee; Rose G. LaPorte to Rose G. David; Marvin Arnold Carey to Marvin Arnold Dow; Leo E. LeBlanc to Leo E. White; Anna Barker to Anna Brooks Payn; Mary Jean Huntoon to Mary Jean Patch; Mary Constance Richards alias Mary Constance Nute to Mary Constance Hunt; Arlene Marie Fossett to Arlene Marie Chase; Charles Edwin Sargent to Charles Edwin Clow; James J. Cote to James Joseph Hill; Riley ----- to James William Riley; Mary Ann Sillery to Mary Ann Silveria; Martin J. Waleryszak to Martin J. Porter; Bertha E. Waleryszak to Bertha E. Porter; Martin J. Waleryszak, Jr. to Martin J. Porter, Jr.; Joann M. Waleryszak to Joann M. Porter; Donald J. Waleryszak to Donald J. Porter; John Burdg to Thomas Wilde; Henry Archers to Henry Klenke; Priscilla Booth to Priscilla Pennie Gingras; Norma Johnson to Norman Gingras; Richard Rand to Richard Rand Spinney; Harriet Jane Dolloff to June Harriet Nicholson; William Frederick Stickles to Frederick William Hatch; Charles Alexander Houle to Charles Alexander Wormwood; Hyman Albert Satowitz to Albert Hyman Sados; Malcolm H. Stewart to Robert H. Stewart; Khalil D. Barkha to Kalil D. Barka; David Delano Call to Eugene Francis Shapleigh; Eugene Francis Shapleigh to Robert Charles Call; Louis Arthur Schmalfuss to Charles Edward LeBlanc; Mary Linscott to Sharon Lee Reid; Norman Tracey White to John Tracey White; Roger Wells to Kenneth Robert McCollum; Slowinas ----- to Benjamin John Wallace; Beverly Bishop to Beverly M. Rosa; Jo Ann Bushy to Jo Ann Constance Bernard; Josephine Elizabeth Downing to Josephine Elizabeth French; Madelein A. Downing to Madelein Agnes French; Jerome Eugene Marshall to Jerome Eugene Lepore; Julius Lankoysky to Julius Lank; Leopoldo Giovanni Pieroni to Leo John Pieroni; Vincent Robert Kaczanowski to Vincent Robert Drake; Ralph Edward Shrague to Ernest Reginald Foote; John David Merrill to John David Marden; Betty Jane Queor to Betty Jane Hammond; Herman Albert Plouffe to Joseph Lawrence Pluff; Francis J. Hill to John F. Hill; De Witte Otho Hicksenhytzer to Robert Colvin Arnold; Charles Richard Estes to Charles Paul Elliott; Jane Elizabeth Courser to Jane Elizabeth Cash; William Lodge Courser to William Lodge Cash; Patricia Helen Kosky to Patricia Helen Johnson; Hormidas Cote to Middy Cote; Joseph Hector Pluff to Joseph Hector Plouffe; Casimir Nalewski to Harry Thomas Navelski; Louis Selime Langlois to Selime Louis Langlois; Ilene June Hersey to Ilene June Braum; Marie Clara Conlon to Pauline Clara Conlon; Kenneth Donald Mowatt to Kenneth Donald Langley;

1941-1943

Josephine Reitze Ratta to Geraldine Reitze Ratta; Vladislaus Szaine to Walter Shina; Wladyslawa Katazyna Shina to Ladia Catherine Shina; Arthur Leroy Hersey to Arthur Leroy Williams; Mary Louise Bailey to Mary Louise LeClair; Charles Frederick Bailey to Charles Frederick LeClair; William Anthony Bailey to William Anthony LeClair; Joseph E. Bergeron to Arthur Ernest Bergeron; William M. Emerson to William Emerson Roby; Catherine Mary Benedetto to Geraldine Mary Champagne; John J. Silva, Jr. to John J. Ridlon; Virginia M. Silva to Virginia M. Ridlon; Glen Colford Stewart to Glenn Colford Stewart; Grace Marie Beott to Teresa Gladys Doucette; Hervey Hebert to Hervey Abbott; Rose Ora Greenwood to Irene Rose Greenwood; Elsie Bertha Meehan to Elsie B. Weber

<u>Strafford County</u> - Richard Godfrey Cartee to Richard Godfrey Hough; Charles Michael Zervas to Charles Nichael Servas; Helen R. Zervas to Helen R. Servas; Eugene Zervas to Eugene Servas; Marie Zervas to Marie Servas; Janice Lillian Styles Fox to Janice Lillian Snipes; Margaret Elizabeth Shaw to Margaret Elizabeth Moore; Beatrice H. Bickford to Beatrice May Hartfiel; Denzil Ellsworth Senter to Denzil Fred Thayer; Norman Webster Senter to Norman Webster Thayer; Ralph Lewis Barnes to Ralph Lewis Conway; Larry Joy Mathews to Alston Laurel Wade; Beverly Mae Gage to Beverly Mae Black; Michael Peters to Michael Peters Hashem; Linda Taylor to Linda Ora Stevens; Lurana Audrey Wells to Lurana Audrey Mellott; Marlene Hamel (Towle) to Marlene Lebrecht; Kyreakos Pasthedenos to Charles Pastene; Clmina Virginia Pasthedenos to Clmina Pastene; Sevastula Pasthedenos to Elizabeth Ann Pastene; Theamandula Pasthedenos to Diane Katherine Pastene; John Pasthedenos to John Pastene; Charles Raymond Aller to Charles Raymond Hall; Usko Veli Zalo Oberg to Charles Frederick Oberg; Joseph Lilley to Joseph Bernard Young; Helen A. Hodgdon to Helen A. Barnes; Raymond Herbert Hamilton to Herbert Cope Skelly; Newell O. Frost to Norman Robert Bousquin; Mary Anne Shum to Mary Ann Nelson; Thelma Gardner to Mary Thelma Flynn; Fred J. Lessard to Alfred Joseph Lessard; Henry Chouinard to Richard Langdon Percy; Killil Abraham Shamoun to Charles Joseph Gabriel; Manfred Aryan James to Manfred Aryan Mathews; Joseph Mohammed to Joseph Ameen David; Sally Ann David to Donna Lee Mooreside; Robert Hall to Robert Varney; Mary Littlefield to Mary Beatrice Giberson; Althea Irene St. Jean to Althea

1941-1943

Irene Dame; Marie Claire Theresa Lagotte to Marie Claire Theresa Lagotte; Louis Aime Bourgeois to Louis Ameois Bushway; Habady Himeen Mohammed to Ablah David; Ameen Mohammed to Ameen David; Joseph David Wilfred Duquette to Louis Wilfred Duquette; Marie Lorraine Sylviane Hamel to Marie Lorraine Sylviane Ann Hamel; Carlisle Fred Seavey to Carlyle Fred Seavey; Jos Ovila Gregoire to Ovila Joseph Gregoire; Richard Peter DiNazzi to Richard Peter Duggan; Beatrice H. Eldridge to Beatrice H. Bradbury; Charles William Boeshaar to Charles William Bashaar; Gilbert Cooper to Gilbert Cooper Clough; Marie Theresa Florence Moison to Marie Theresa Florence Letarte; Mildred Belle Woodbury to Mildred Woodbury Hayes; Barbara Ann Spinney to Barbara Ann Sharrock; Mildred Garvin to Mildred Gauthier; William Lennon Vocha to William Lennon Boyd; Lena Madeline Baxter Robbins to Marcia Madeline Robbins; Victor Van Valley to Victor Van Johnson; Charles Nobert to Charles Henry Newbury; Louise Therese Nobert to Louise Therese Newbury; Leon Henry Nobert to Leon Henry Newbury; Sylvia Marcotte to Sylvia Beatrice Poliquin; Mary Laurea Pare to Mary Laurea Goulet; Nancy Elizabeth Goodwin to Nancy Elizabeth Horr; Kenneth Robert Owens to Kenneth Robert Owen; Pierre Labossiere to Walter Lawrence Gadoury; Nabucodor Nazire Marcotte to Albert Marcotte; Paul Willson to Paul Joy Willson; David Harley Willson to Charles Edward Willson; Spiriden ----- to Charles George Spiridondes; Allan Danforth Ruddy to Ronald Meserve; Paul Everett Wallingford to Paul Everett Downs; Arthur Ball to Arthur John Blanchet; Norma Jane Brock to Norma Jane Corbett; Almon F. Wing to Elmer Francis Thompson; Burton Louis Mahan to Burton Louis Lesperance; Francis Beals to Gardner Chamberlain; Allen Warren Nutt to John Dhu Allen; Franklin Owsley to James Wilfred Grigg; Roland Cullen to Roland Paul Cullen; Philip Beals to Phillip Jolly; Barbara Jean Kimball to Sally Ann Weathers; Napoleon M. Vachon, Jr. to Richard Mansur Rogers; Edward E. King to Edward E. Roy; Analda King to Analda Roy; Richard Keene to Richard Newton Bickford; Aida Elizabeth Butler to Patricia Elizabeth Butler; Mary Obeline Boucher to Emeline Boucher; Leo Joseph Lirette, known as Leo Joseph Marcotte to Leo Joseph Lirette; Jeanne C. Wentworth to Jeanne C. Hills; Joseph Henri Roy to Henry Francis King; Bernard Edson Cilley to Bernard Edson Chamberlain; Gordon Wayne Bruce to Gordon Wayne Geddis; Wallace Baxter to Wallace Woodbury Davis; Rudolph F. Minichiello to Rudolph Mitchell; Rita F. Minichiello to Rita Mitchell; Herve Lucien

1941-1943

Fredette to Herve Lucien Cole; Maheba Kalill Hughes to Josephine Mahanna Carlin Hughes; Haceboy Kalill Henson to Elizabeth Mahanna Carlin Henson

Belknap County - Dorothy Irene Cone to Dorothy Irene Williamson; Frederick Dwight Cone to Frederick Dwight Williamson; Joan Marsella Pray to Joan Marsella Cronin; Ella Louise Hopf to Ella Louise Lewis; Allan J. Lougee to Allan J. Westney; Richard William Patno to Richard William Poulin; Frances S. Osinski to Frances S. Davidson; Richard Putnam Lashua to Walter Richard Putman Lampman; Gordon Robert Metres to Robert Gordon Surpine; Robert Earl Perry to Robert Earl Poire; Gertrude Mary Perry to Gertrude May Poire; Marguerite Marilyn Mozroll to Marguerite Marilyn Niles; Stephen Sztucinski to Stephen Stephens; Weston Lorenzo Wiggins to Robert Lorenzo Wiggins; Wesley Josiah Wiggins to Richard Josiah Wiggins; Elaine Sztucinski to Elaine Stephens; Katherine Sztucinski to Katherine Stephens; Harold Bordo Mitchell to Harold Bordo Lampman; Helmer Joseph Corriveau to Edmund Joseph Corriveau; Gaston Paul Jodoin to Gaston Paul Jodoin; William Earl Scheuerfeld to William Earl Holmes; Jeanne Claire Shackelford to Jeanne Claire Pooler; Eslie Leonard Smith to Leonard Eslie Smith; Marie Jeanne Richard Laroche to Marie Jean Richard Stone; Philias Henry Laroche to Philip Henry Stone; Biruta Alexandria Prokop to Biruta Helen Prakapas; Euripides Hatzekelekas to Peter Hatzes; Carl Frederick Peterson to Carl Frederick Wright; Ross Milan Smith to Thomas Milan Smith; Robert Eugene Morin to Eugene Joseph Morin; Male Peck to Wallace Wrisley; Jacob Lawrence Lewis to Jay Lawrence Lewis; Pantale Contos to Lee Karatsanos; Harry A. Morse to Harry Alver Morse; Jos. Aimee Theberge to Aime Armand Theberge; Earl Looman Tuffts to Earl Luman Chamberlain; Josephat Dulac to Richard Joseph Dulac; Philip Ray Maban to Philip Ray Davis; Jonathan Edgar Page to Edward Joseph Page; Ludwig Heimis to Louis Alfred Heinis; Louise Trojano to Mary Louise Trojano; Edward Warren to William Warren; Joseph Meachem to Joseph Treaushure Mitchell; Marion Contos to Marion Karatsanos; Joseph Freddy Laroche to Alfred Simpson LaRoche; Ivers Pearl Haskell to George Ivand Haskell; ----- Campbell to Archie Lenwood Campbell; William Rudolph Farra to Rudolph Farra Wilson; Katherine Helen Contos to Katherine Helen Karatsanos; Joseph Jean Guy Parent to Joseph Jean Guy Cantin; Franz Milton Paine to Frank Milton Paine;

1941-1943

Clyde Lemoine Baker to Lloyd Lemoine Baker; Martin Feuerstein to Martin Feuerstein; Raoul Jean Thomas Xavier Morin to Ralph John Morin; Mary Evelyn Lasheway to Mary Evelyn Peavey

Changed by adoption: Joan Marie LaCross to Joan Marie Weir; unnamed to Janet Colby; ----- Beaudoin to Peter Barrett Sargent; Clyde Martin Lacroix to Frank Richard Smith; Daron Rae Willoughby to Susan Pauline Mooney; Jeanne Louise Annair to Jeanne Louise Segole; Lois Alberta Annair to Lois Alberta Segole; Warren Chester Buchanen to Warren Paul Cutting; David Albert Taylor to David Albert Plant; Iola Belle Lacroix to Iola Belle Smith; Rena May Heath to Rena May Heath; Carl Thompson to Carl Hamilton; Harvey James Rollins to Harvey James Forsyth; John Arthur Pearl to John Arthur Bragg; Francis Leighton Vittum to John Conrad Haven; Joan Burdick to Joan Clough; Lewis Warren Tassinari to Lewis Warren Mayo; Jennie Marie Wallace to Jennie Marie Blackey; Constance Mary Dion to Constance Mary Dion; Pauline Dorothy Moulton to Pauline Dorothy Robinson; Robert E. Foster to Robert Earl Emerson; Shari Lynn Connors to Shari Lynn Gray; ----- Novia to Leo A. Barton, Jr.; Robert A. Runnells to Robert A. Runnells; Joseph Rudzinski to Joseph Roubo; Roger Albert Eryou to Roger Albert Dow; Howard J. Buttman to Howard J. Lank

<u>Carroll County</u> - Otto Grant Kramer to Robert Grant Kramer; Pauline F. Brackett to Pauline Frances McCrillis; Felix Joseph Loville to Felix Joseph Lavely; Severino Fernandez to Severino Jean Fernandez; Mildred F. Towle to Mildred F. Johnson; Florence B. White to Florence Ella Beede; Carlotta D. Bragg to Carlotta Direne Ames; Clarence Wilbur Drew to Clarence Wilbur Davis; Francis Ford Manley to William Ford Manley; Lester E. Thompson to Lester Eldridge; Lila Goldie Ward to Fay Lane Ward; Alberta Mae Potter to Alberta Mae Bean; Vernon Eugene Bickford to Vernon Eugene Pecunies

Changed by adoption: Ernest Richard Gagne to Ernest Gagne Moore; Margaret Anne Clough to Margaret Anne McBride; Cherolyn Ann Ward to Cherolyn Ann Vittum; Barbara Louise Murray to Barbara Louise Knox; Harry Harlan Willey to Harry Harlan Rines; Frank Fox to Frank Fox Chambers; "Baby" Meldrum to Norman Whittier Turner, Jr.; Sandra P. Seeley to Sandra P. Massey; Wendell E. Smith to Wendell Everett Dodge; Bertha Anne Taylor to Bertha Anne Brown

1941-1943

Merrimack County - Thena E. Peterson to Thena Loveland Eaton; Edna MacEachran to Edna Myrick; Arthur Brown to Arthur Leach; Frank George Daniels to Lester George Daniels, Jr.; Janet Stoneham to Janet Jackson; Donald W. Odell to Donald W. Flanders; Stella Mary Gielarowski to Stella Mary Giles; Samuel Adler to Sidney Adler; Beatrice P. Hueftline to Beatrice P. Heflin; Martin H. Hueftline to Martin H. Heflin; Elizabeth E. King to Elizabeth King Remington; Clifford Allen Downs to Clifford Allen Rogers; Lewis John Peters to Wesley John Howard; Henry C. Pichette to Harry C. Pichette; Richard Herbert Savage to Charles Herbert Deane French; Ena Davis Hillsgrove to Ena Davis; Joseph Harry Ouimet to Harry Joseph Wilmot; George Arnold Halcombe to George Arnold Osgood; Alice McNally Haggerty to Alyce McNally Haggert; Lloyd Robert Haggerty to Lloyd Robert Haggert; Annie Pinker to Annie Rousseau; Merle Irving Eastman to Merle Montana Eastman; Jeannette T. Noury to Jeannette T. LeBlanc; Frederick G. Reagan to Harry Frederick Reagan; William H. Plummer to Henry William Saltmarsh; Roger Cone to Roger Fred Durgin; John Craig to John Dalziell Craig; George Henri Roy to George Henry King; David Oscar Clemons to David Oscar Clemons Higgins; Clayton Adams to Clayton Arnold Frenette; Victoria Jenness to Victoria Ann Moody; Joseph Victor Bouffard to Joseph Wade; Gwen E. Hibbert to Gwen Ella Hayes; Robert William Hunt to Robert William Barrett; Alvin Francis Angwin to Alvin Francis Johnson; Octave J. L. Lauzier to Leo Colle; Eunice M. Sanborn to Eunice M. Leavitt; Harold Jerome Alley Street, Jr. to Harold Stowell; Joan Barbara Howe to Joanne Barbara Howe; David Porter to Ervin David Porter; George Rochou to Joseph William Finan; Beverly May Baker to Beverly Mae Merrill; Walter Daniel Scribner to Walter Daniel Bailey; Efthemios Nicholas Tseckares to Frederick Nichols Talmers; Joseph Raymond Hamby to Joseph Raymond Chandler; Joseph Charles Caughey, Jr. to William James Dawson; Sherman Ellsworth Campbell to Sherman Ellsworth Campbell Linen; Francis P. Hunt to Walter Flanders Hunt; Felix Albert Purull to Felix Albert Purrell; Gerald Ray Wilkinson to Gerald Ray Gilmore; Russell W. Cox to Russell W. Quimby; Charles J. Tousner to Charles J. Tousignant; Robert Vincent Benton to Robert Vincent Gilpatrick; Bartley Harold Desmond to Joseph H. Elliott; Ayling John Chilton to Herbert J. Adams

1941-1943

Changed by adoption: Barbara D. Cook to Barbara Delia Sullivan; Rebecca Ann Goodfellow to Cynthia Stewart Lyford; Bruce Earl Jellerson to James Earl Foote; Curtis Maynard to Laurence Worthen Rowe; Gertrude Paul to Gertrude Mims; Fairfax Hatch to David Wilson Rowe; Frederick Maurice Wood to Frederick Norman LaBrie; John Chester Stewart to John Chester Baker; Albert Theodore Renee to Albert Theodore Audet; Robert James Fraser to Robert James Andrews; Marcel J. Shulman to Marcel J. Tyrrel; Victoria Mae Brockman to Victoria Ann Decato; Marion Ruth Hewey to Marion Ruth Roy; Nancy Jean Lucia to Nancy Jean Davison; Carol Ann Peppler to Sandra Dean; David Barry to David Anson Boyce; Roger Clarence Brissette to Roger Clarence Gregoire; Paula Earleen Mayhew to Paula Earleen Corliss; Paul Clayton Weatherbee to Clayton Paul Mitchell; Cecil Dean to Cecil Dean Currier; Warren Harding Ginniss to Warren Harding Spofford; Clifford Frick to Clifford Lefebvre; Norman J. Soucy to Norman J. Geary; Richard E. Brown to Richard E. Rhodes; Virginia Rose Longley to Virginia Rose Severance; Neal Ellis Morrison to Neil Ellis Coulson; Sandra Lee Bassett to Sandra Lee Garland; Katherine Tucker to Katherine Belle Fortune; Thelma Fay Weatherbee to Faye Ann Bonette; Ronald W. Hurd to Kenneth Stevens Haskell; Constance Theresa Couturier to Constance Theresa Coleman; Richard Arnold Discoe to Richard Arnold Davison; Theresa Gloria Gilbert to Teresa Gloria Smith; Robert Francis Nye to James Robert Anderson; Robert Gilbert to Robert Dragon; Rose Marie Ring to Patricia Ann Perry; Tammy Ann LaDuke to Janice Elaine Gile; "Baby" Giles to Chester Thompson Brown; Charles Albert Georgina to Charles Albert Connor; James Edward Page to James Edward Magoon; Carol Beatrice Perron to Carol Beatrice Downing; Sandra Jean Perron to Sandra Jean Downing; Robert Lewis Brown to Robert Lewis Dukette; William Jenovese to Donald William Terrell; Raymond Mayo to Raymond Collerette; David H. Demeritt to David H. Waldo; Marion Elsie Rollins to Marion Elsie Waldo; Patricia Ann Rollins to Patricia Ann Waldo; Beverly Ann Sargent to Beverly Ann Simonds; Glenn Orson Dockey to Glenn Orson Hornberger; Mary Josephine Ellis to Sandra Jean Sabin; Jan Sanborn to Jane Ellen Proud; Judson Ward Colby to Judson Ward Crawford; Edwin Prantilla to Edwin Walden; Eino Prantilla to Eino Walden; Freddy Sawyer, alias Freddy Soucy to William Dominique Levesque; Leo Soucy, alias Leo Souci to Leon Levesque; Thomas Varney to Thomas Rush

1941-1943

<u>Hillsborough County</u> - Earle Livingstone to Earle Sheldon; Robert Charles Heselton to Robert Charles Clark; Agnes Mary McCarthy Warcholik to Agnes Mary McCarthy; Aurelia West to Aurelia Fitzpatrick; Ursula May Eaton to Ursula May Lavigne; Leo St. Onge to Leo Roy; Susan Juliette Johnson to Susan Juliette Gagnon; Joseph Louis St. John to Joseph Louis Gagnon; Walter Frederick Johnson to Walter Frederick Gagnon; Elizabeth Brown to Elizabeth Gagnon; Ellen Maki to Ellen Marie Myllymaki; Isabella Louise Goonan to Isabelle Louise Jensen; Lillian Sawyer to Lillian Levesque; Rosario Louis Sawyer alias Soucy to Rosario Louis Levesque; Hanna Johnson to Hannah Ekdahl; Robert V. Clancy to Robert W. Cuddihee; Aime Levi to Amos Drouse; Anthony J. Siedlewicz to Anthony J. Sullivan; Alvina Baum Hecker to Rena Baum Hecker; Mary Andruchuck to Mary Andrews; Elizabeth E. Patterson to Elizabeth E. Sterling; Stanwood Patterson to Stanwood Sterling; Theodore Warcholik to Theodore Walker; Iwan Luczkewicz to John Luckers; Gosta Sven Siguard Evert Romberg to Gosta Evert Romberg; Russell Champagne to Russell Henry Gadbois; James William Dimmick to James William Darrah; Mordkho or Mordcha or Mortachai Jankelewitz Robinowitz to Morton J. Robbins; William Zwezila to William Zeeler; Stanley J. Zwezila to Stanley J. Zeeler; Harriet Maria Osmer to Anna Maria Osmer; Eva A. Brooks to Eva A. Hollins; Florence Mary Roberge to Mary Florence Marden; Victor Warcholik to Victor Walker; Mathew Milewski to Michael Mills; Urshula Milewski to Urshula Mills; Eloza Wolcowski to Alonzo Wolkowski; Josef Sanger to Joseph Jacob Sanger; Elmer Newman Austin to Newman Elmer Austin; John Ivarnoff to John V. Ivanow; Malvina Levesque or Leveck to Malvina Levesque; Raymond Gamache to Raymond Trimble; Joseph Yvan Lester Ryan to Joseph Ivan Lester Demers; Anne Marie Osmer to Anne Marie Morse; Theos Pierpoint Alsop to Thomas Pierpoint Alsop; Mildred Gerew to Mildred Reardon; Robert J. Chretien to Robert J. Caron; Henry A. Bazylewicz to Henry A. Basil; Sebastien Bourgeois to Camille Sebastien Bourgeois; Joseph Whitney to Edward Furman; Leo Cayer to Leo Blanchette; Fortula Stavrou to Judy Stavrou; ----- Peecha to Robert John Mahoney; Archie Carl Lord to William Alfred Lord; Xenephon Prutsalis to Andrew Prutsalis; James Thomas Johnson to James Thomas Patton; Edna Mumford to Edna Tirrell; Joseph Roland McNicol to Joseph Roland McNichols; Janvier Rousseau to Gustave Rousseau; Linwood Allen Morrison to Roy Elmer Hall; Reymert Ragnvald Madsen or Matsen to Ray Madison; Arthur J.

1941-1943

Chabot to Robert Walsh; Barbara Drozdoff to Barbara Anne Hunting; Kastantos Stanskouskis to Constantine Steger; John Staszkawskits to John Steger; Stanislaus Stanskoukis to Steven Jeremiah Steger; Andrew Malik to Stanley Malik; William Robert Alexander to Robert Alexander Emerson; Achiel Beeckman or Achille Beeckman to Charles Achiel Beeckman; Stanislaw Betlej to Stanley J. Betley; Chresoula Anagnostou to Chresoula Anastas Anthony; Helen Anagnostou to Helen Anastas Anthony; George Anagnostou to George Anastas Anthony; Adolphe Guay to Adolphe Lafond; Joseph Alphonse Michaud to William Alphonse Michaud; Athanasios Nicholas Pistolas to Arthur Pistolas; Hans Popp to Henry George Johansen; William Walentutuawicius to William Walent; Sophie Walentutuawicius to Sophie Walent; Philorum Clarence Dubois to Clarence P. Woods; Joseph J. Sisko to Joseph William Sheska; Evelus Vasyabedient to Evelyn Varger; Nicolaos G. Hondrogiannis to Nicholas J. Hondrogen; Wilho Eineri Beders to William Einar Bedders; Solomon Greenblatt, Jr. to Solomon Taube; Celina Marie L'Italien to Celina Marie Maynard; George Kostas to George Hajicostas; Boleslaw Robert Smietana to Robert Michael Krym; Elaine Arlene Delisle to Elaine Arlene Reardon; Alfred Liberty to Alfred Joseph Laliberte; Dimitrios Pleatsekas to James Pleatsikas; Haralambos Theodoropoulos to Arthur George Theros; David Sklarsk to David Sklar; Lucien Boudreault to Lucien Boudreault Pinet; Steven Z. Metrakas to Steven Metrakes Lester; Henry Clayton Stone to Henry Barclay Stone; Aleph Urville Yergeau to Paul Aleph Yergeau; Edward Noyes to Edward Francis Tierney; Wilfred Vernon Noyes to Wilfred Vernon Tierney; Mildred Noyes to Mildred Tierney; Apostolos Kokulis to Paul Kokulis; Muriel C. Noyes to Muriel C. Tierney; George Wilfred Lexner to Wilford MacKenzie Martin; Cournelious Winters to John Reed; William Deeb to William Debb Nicholas; John Degasis to Bolic Alexander Degasis; Vytautas Boleslovas Aukstulevicius to Vit Thomas Akstull; Leo Gilbert Lajoie to Gilbert Leo Dumas; Joseph John Ferrera to Joseph John Gilinsky; Shirley June Ferrera to Shirley June Gilinsky; Elefthareos John Folis to Tully John Folis; Demetrios Gregoriou Karamitopoulos to James Georeg Carros; Eftstatios Hrisantheas alias Chrisantheas to Strates Christy; Michael Paskiwicz to Michael Paskevich; Harold Jackson French to Harold Jackson Fowle; Edmund Jozaitis to Edmund Jositis; Leo Edward Jozaitis to Leo Jositas; Koula Vassil Pachajakis to Kay Vassil; Madeline Pachajakis to Madeline Vassil; Doris Zeeler to Doris

1941-1943

Marguerite Labounty; Ronald Sylvio Chommard to Ronald Slattery; Louis Kalmonowith to Louis Harold Camann; Sefania Raczki to Christine Raczski; Delzina Cordelia Soucy to Joyce Marie Soucy; Helen B. Lamontagne to Elaine B. Lamontagne; Lillian DerHovhanesian to Lillian Injian Derr; Avedis H. DerHovhanesian to Avedis H. Derr; Joseph Achile Gourd to Joseph Archile Gould; Lucia B. Gourd to Lucia B. Gould; Leonora Goulson to Leonora Cousins; Lois Jacqueline Roux to Lois Jacqueline Heselton; Judith Sandra Roux to Judith Sandra Heselton; Morris Feuerstein to Morris Firestone; Anthony J. A. Wolkowski to Anthony J. A. Wolkow; Demetrios Papanastasiou to James Pappas; David Solomon Casbe to David Solomon David; William McCarthy to William Francis Parker; Frank Lavigne to Frank Kruczek; Pearl J. Luczkewsycz to Pearl J. Luckury; Mary A. C. Laflamme to Mary A. C. Fahey; Helen Goonan to Helen Connor; Joseph Elzear Dube to Leo Paul Dube; Willie Saxton to William Louis Saxton; Peter Spiretos to Peter Debelis; Leo Joseph Dufour to Leo Joseph Linehan; Adelard Guichard to Adelard Dichard; Henry Raymond Walker to Henry Raymond Jordan; Robert Hanson to Robert Hanson Moffitt; George Edward Popp to George Edward Johansen; Henry Mills to Henry Smith; Joseph Wilfrid LaMarche to Alfred Joseph LaMarche; Leon Gibson Roberts to Leon Gibson Phinney; Thomas Alphee Dufour to Thomas Francis Linehan; Joseph Edward Oliver to Joseph Edward Morin; Ovide Petit to Ovide Petit Mitchell; Paraska Luczkiewicz to Pearl J. Luckury

Changed by adoption: Norah Jean Cutts to Jean Nora Stimson; Frances Agnes Bailey to Donna Mae Kirsch; Esther Marie Charpentier to Constance Maria Colasacco; Baby Knowles to Stephen Franklin Flanders; Mary Louise Travers to Judith Alice Willard; Paul Ernest Marquis to Ernest Joseph Barbeau; Richard Joseph Michaud to Wilfred Paul Lachance; Baby Ronan to Kathleen Estelle Young; Rita Jutras to Rita Gelinas; Claire Jutras to Claire Gelinas; Madeleine Roberge to Madeline Theresa Bouchard; Mary Jane Hilson to Mary Jane Sastous; Baby Mickielevich to Jay Kendall Nichols; Ruth Athelia Wilson to Ruth Athelia Towle; Edna J. S. Dana to Edna J. Riddel; Louis J. Smith to Louis J. Marshall; Robert Joseph Richard to Robert Joseph St. Cyr; Baby Dion to Berthel Frederick Johnson, Jr.; Dorothy Mary Joyal to Nancy Ann Gatto; Marie Houle to Marie Marceau; Bernard Richard Watkins to Normand Paul Gosseline; Pauline Atkins to Pauline Mae

1941-1943

Foster; Jeannette Naomi Carter to Jeannette Naomi LeClaire; Edwin Clayton Partridge to Jon Edwin Nichols; Margaret Elizabeth Foster to Margaret Elizabeth Knowles; Arthur Richard O'Hare to Arthur Richard Stockley; George Henry Clermont to George Henry Bourque; David Osmer to James David Wheeler; Richard Earl LaBranche to George Richard Earl Dubois; Female Infant to Beverly Ann Grigas; Paul Quinn to Paul Reilly; Marie Jeannette Fortin to Marie Jeannette Lamontagne; Pauline Alice Fortin to Pauline Alice Lamontagne; Alfred Kenneth Scofield to Alfred Kenneth Barbour; Russell L. Lilly to Russell L. Sylvester; Edward Ronaldo Thayer to David Allan Bruce; Charles William Savage also known as Charles William Murphy to Charles William Margaritis; Robert Lionel Blanchette to Ronald Lionel Rivard; Russell Keefe to Russell Lucier; Rita Clouette Beaudette to Rota Regina Roux; Georges Robert Desrosiers to Georges Robert LaFleur; Jean Rose Marchetti to Jean Rose Krzyzanowski; Arthur Armand Cardin to Arthur Durling Corliss; Robert Drolet also known as Robert Tardiff and Robert Robidas to Robert Tardiff; Margaret Elizabeth Johnson to Margaret Elizabeth Chipman; Nancy Theresa Marchion to Jacqueline Obin; James Stewart Murphy to Donald Stuart Arthur LaTourette; Robert Eugene Taboske to Robert Eugene Taboske Fallgren; Thomas Wayne Worthley to Wayne Thomas Ring; Baby Bellinger to Diane Elizabeth Steady; James H. Demanche also known as James H. Grover to James Lizotte; Henry Lachance to Henry Bilodeau; Barbara June Kelley to Barbara June Morse; Robert Andrew Lariviere to Robert Andrew Lupien; Joseph Nalette to John Joseph Mayhew; Baby Puras to Sheila Jane Brown; Robert Francis Schmidtchen to Robert Francis Rogier; Lionel Routhier to Lionel Simard; Everett Campbell to David Francis Totte; Arthur Joseph Russell to Arthur Joseph Russell Boisseau; Gail Frances Cochran to Elizabeth Cochran Knudsen; Pierrette Jacqueline Gingras to Pierrette Jacqueline St. Pierre; Baby Bocon to Joan Marcelia Tracy; William Pickett to William Briand; Norman Joseph Morrissette to Norman Joseph Curran; Cleo Alberta Raza to Cleo Alberta Davis; Irene Delsie Raza to Irene Delsie Davis; Eveline May Nelson to Evelyn May Davis; Robert Valley to Robert Fisher; Ernest Hubert Brodeur to Ernest Hubert Chaput; Marie Claire Brodeur to Marie Claire Soucy; Elaine Rose Normandeau to Elaine Rose Paradis; Louise Mae Allen to Louise Mae Claveau; Marie Alice Lorraine Janice McDonald to Marie Lorraine Janice Page; Dolores Agnes Lavallee to Dolores Agnes Roy; Roland

1941-1943

Henri Soucy to Roland Henri Pelletier; Freda Nason to Freda Claveau; Francis Edgar LePage to Francis Edgar Small; Baby Hurd to Richard Terry Swenson; David O'Brien to David J. Fox; Robert Aurelian Grenier to Robert Aurelian Beaudin; Barbara Ann Dyer to Barbara Ann Fowle; Rocky Edward Thompson to Robert Bruce McClarty; Doris Levesque to Doris Pelletier; Lucille Laliberte to Lucille LaJoie; Roger Laliberte to Roger LaJoie; Walter Dyrkacz, Jr. to Walter Zinis; Carol Ann McDonald to Carol Anne Fitzpatrick; Baby Goss to Edmund Irving Elgart; Raymond Edward Lawrence to Raymond Edward Kecy; Baby Croteau to Florence June LeMay; Lucie Courteau to Louise Rheault; Barbara Ann Grew to Barbara Ann Connor; Baby Leclerc to Raymond Edward Penn, Jr.; Mary Theresa Sievers to Mary Theresa Denoncour; Catherine May Benson to Frances Catherine Hayden; Robert Francis St. Hilaire to Robert Francis Schambier; Emile L. Corriveau to Emile L. Arguin; Yolande Carmene Corriveau to Yolande Carmine Arguin; Gerald Arthur Corriveau to Gerald Arthur Arguin; Wesley James Cote to Wesley James Greeley; Elizabeth Ann Signor to Elizabeth Ann Moses; Mildred Gardner to Ruth Hildred Martin; Ronald Elliott to Ronald Elliott Bellemare; Baby Bernard to Patricia Alice Thompson; Shirley Ann Stevens to Marjorie Ann Thurlow; Esther Arlene Delisle to Esther Beatrice Luce; Joyce Eleanor Miller to Joyce Eleanor Bailey; Baby Otis to Tanya Lyn Spiracos; David Verne Rich to David Verne Letendre; Mariette Paris to Mariette Dignard; Mary Rita Gill to Rita Goudreau; Claudia Ann Piotrowski to Judith Catherine Smas; Phyllis Donahue to Phyllis Brown; Robert Duane Harrell to Robert Duane Buchanan; Harold Paine to Clayton Milton Hall; Joyce Ellen Grant to Marjorie Ann Kay; Starr Joan Ann Salter to Evelyn Rosamond Webb; Clifford Arthur Gates to Henry Arthur Osborne; John Manoleros to John Wardner; Ronald Leo Levesque Renaud to Ronald Leo Roy; Mary Claire Simoneau to Mary Claire Ring; Henry Desilets to Henri Charles Gagne; Robert Charles Ziemba to Robert Charles Schlottmann; Betty Lou Beaudoin to Therese Yvonne Beaudoin; Raymond Joseph Pepin to Raymond Joseph Cote; Richard Ellmore Warren to Richard Taylor Murphy; Rita Marguerite Smith to Rita Marguerite Levesque; Robert Cadieux to Robert Ronald Bernard; Richard Lloyd Durant to Richard Lloyd Coady; Charles Bradley Stearns to John Perley McGrath; Robert Wayne Breton to Robert Wayne Grant; Robert Wilfred Vanasse to Robert Wilfred Martineau; Carol Ann Gilbert to Carol Ann Nerbonne; Lois Clorine Stevens to Lois Clorine Nelson; Gene Wheeler to Richard

1941-1943

Redmon Russell; Nicholas Coronis to Nicholas Edward Warring; Homer Theodore Worcester to Homer Theodore Ford; June Elaine Worcester to June Elaine Ford; Paul Carey to Stephen Blaisdell Norwood; Andre Duplessis to Kenneth Arnold Boone; Renie Rochfort to Raymond St. Jean; Beverly Waillancourt to Nancy Plante; Frank Thomas Moody also known as Thomas Rosewell Moody to Frank Thomas Wells; Sylvia Belle Clifford to Sylvia Belle Blaisdell

<u>Cheshire County</u> - Cynthia Townsend to Patricia Mae Gauthier; Audrey Helen Caron to Audrey Helen Oksanen; Francis C. Wilder to Frank C. Parker; Hendra Prita Hendrickson to Helen Prita Holt; Patricia Ann Wilber to Patricia Ann Bloom; Gordon A. Courure to Gordon Albert Neaves; Bonar L. Erickson to Bonar Lee Koski; Verna M. Knox to Gertrude Louise Knox; Lawrence LaWayne Wilder to Lawrence LeWayne Pratt; Beverly J. Hubbard to Sandra Jane Hubbard; Arthur Cyr to Barry Gorges Pearson; John Dana Redington to John Skinner Redington; John E. Tillman to John E. Pratt; Donna Marie Patenaude to Donna Marie Lindsay; Guerino Didomenico to William Dedo; Alfred Edmund Scott to Alfred Edmund Dingman; Bradley C. LaValley to Bradley Chester Pratt; Gordon F. Lapierre to Gordon Francis Spinelli; Ruth Anna Lapierre to Ruth Anna Spinelli; Joan Shover to Mary Elizabeth Bushway; George Michael Tellia to George Michael Tellier; Donald V. Record to Donald Record Inglis; William Francis Dupree to William Francis Dupree; Sterling R. Valley to Gary Robert Green; Constantine Zahos to Charles E. Zahos; James H. Pelkey to James H. Graves; Alfred Papineau to Alfred John Harper; John R. Joudrey to John Robert Oman; Elaine Wood to Elaine Winn; Leda Bergeron Ladam to Leda C. Bergeron; Walter C. Abrahamson to Walter C. Hanson; George E. Williams to George E. Nason; Lee B. Dow to Leigh Burton Dow; Louis Laware to Louis Whitcomb; Raymond N. Huse to Raymond Neal Wheeler; Damon W. Stevens to Damon W. Stendor; Bette A. Barrett to Betta A. Crouse; Elizabeth A. Perrault to Elizabeth Ann Handy; Everett H. Littlefield to Everett Henry Chaplin; Guy Dunn to Charles Ernest McCray; Joan Ann Lecuyer to Joan Ann Stone; Charles Arthur Nicolas to John Arthur Nicholas; Loretta I. Blanchard to Loretta I. McRae; Marjorie Nelson Thompson to Marjorie Ann Nelson; Romeo Frederick King to Robert Frederick Clay; Cecil Winfred Barrett to Cecil Winfred Wilson; Michael Person to Michael Johnson; Beatrice Ann Patenaude to Beatrice Ann Lepitre; Ronald Girard Betz to Ronald

1941-1943

Girard Doyle; Carol Betz to Carol Doyle; Daniel E. Betz to Daniel E. Doyle; Eleanor V. Betz to Eleanor V. Doyle; William H. Betz to William H. Doyle; Mary B. Merry to Ruth Boyea Merry; Chester Keniskman to Chester F. Kingsman; Eleanor Gertrude Moynahan to Eleanor Gertrude Joyce; Norris E. J. Moynahan to Norris E. J. Joyce; Durward Lawre to Durward Charles Whitcomb; Richard M. Letourneau to Richard Oliver Duval; Baby Boy Andrews to Donald Merle Prevost; Kenneth P. Desrochers, adopted, no change; Geraldine Ruth Parks to Patricia Margaret Calef; Ruth K. Babkirk to Ruth K. Babcock; William W. Babcock to James William Babcock; Harold Francis Martin to Harold Francis Henchey; Cynthia Jane Turner to Cynthia Jane Kathan; Carl V. Belluscio to John Carl Belluscio; Josef Krystopowicz to Joseph Kristof; Anne Krystopowicz to Anne Kristof; Francis Krystopowicz to Francis Kristof; Harold J. Lang to Jeffrey Russell Cleary; Gerald A. Nallett to Gerald Alfred Bussiere; Eleanor Taylor to Eleanor Taylor Mason; Carl Hanson to Carl Robert Fairbanks; Sergius Polewik to Frank Kay; Alfred L. Castor to Alfred L. Castaw; June Beverly Stone to June Beverly Brown; John J. Matthews to John Roger Matthews; Reginald A. Davis to Reginald Arthur Karr; Shirley M. Davis to Shirley May Karr; Lawrence R. Pinney to Lawrence Ray Burnham; Thomas J. Bergeron to Gerard Joseph Arseneault; Richard A. Clarke to Richard A. Crossman; Claire Mary LaCoille to Elaine Mary LaCoille; Albert Frank Thayer to Albert Frank Bailey; Pauline L. Corey to Pauline Louise Caron; William J. Minor to William Joseph Ford; Donald W. Chase to Donald William Ball; Melvin S. Bushia to Melvin S. Bushey; James A. Griswold to James Albert Ingalls; Albert Tolman to Odella Tolman; Mike William Zmaskie to Michael William Zeminsky; Melvina Pellerin to Eleanor Lavina Pellerin; Francis Driscoll to Francis DeMars; Josephine Katherine Black to Josephine Katherine Bogumiloff; Harold V. Lambert to Verne Harold Lambert; Marie M. King to Margaret Evelyn King; Leslie L. Robbins, Jr. to Leslie Robert Robertson; Norman R. LeBracque to Norman R. Weeks

<u>Sullivan County</u> - Kathleen Holbritter to Joan Gladys Spooner; John Richard Ihalainen to John Richard Hallin; Sandra Jean Howard to Sandra Jean Posey; Wesley Gardner Brailey to Charles Gilbert Brailey; Leslie Gilbert Odell to Leslie Gilbert Lewis; Dana Guy Boisoneau to Dana Guy Herbert; Ephraim Russell to Jack Harding; Austin Robert Carr to Austin Robert Waters; Doris Louise Archambault to Doris

1941-1943

Louise Lepicier; Charles W. LaPierre to Fred Davis Barnes; Sylvia May Carley to Sylvia May Hatch; Theodore E. Vickarey to Theodore E. Smith; Abe Bennes Hirsch to Benjamin Abe Hirsch; Shirley Evelyn Green to Shirley Evelyn Noakes; Oscar Arthur LaPlante to Harry Oscar LaPlante; Joanne Carole Williams to Joanne Carole Page; Joy Ann Ducharme to Joy Ann Jenkins; Marjorie Marie York to Marjorie Marie Stevens; Elsie May Thurber to Elsie May Barton; Arthur J. Parizo to Arthur J. Pariseau; John Kazanowich to John Kowzan; Clarence O. LeBlanc to Clarence LeBlanc Paulette; Ernest A. LeBlanc to Ernest LeBlanc Paulette; Harlan Ernest Ryan to John Henry Lunderville; Robert Cote to Robert Lane; Glenn Foster Grimes to Glenn Foster Niles; Matti Kankolander to Matti Starr; Pauline Pearl Duguie to Pauline Pearl Abare; Archie Richard Whittemore to Archie Richard Cox; Onni Ernest Pesola to Ernest Onni Pesola; Daniel Courtamarthe or Daniel Courtemanche to Daniel Philippe Palmer; Gladys Ruth Moran to Ruth Merle Edminster; Kenneth Fontaine Goodrow to Kenneth Joseph Fontaine; George Davidson to George Raymond LaTulippe; Joseph Armand Boisvert to Joseph Armand Greenwood; Rolland F. Burch to Roland F. Pratt; Helen Estella Oikari to Helen Estella Hendrickson; Amos E. Provencal to Amos E. Russell; Omer M. Provencal to Omer M. Russell; Oney Z. Provencal to Oney Z. Russell; Reita D. Provencal to reita D. Russell; Roberta L. Provencal to Roberta L. Russell; Lucille Josephine Welch to Lucille Mary Normandin; Marie Virginia (Hebert) Hansen to Ada Virginia Hansen

<u>Grafton County</u> - John Henry Abbott to Howard Davis Bennett, Jr.; Leon Ammel to Leon Laware; Meredith Una Avery to Meredith Mary Elaine Demers; David Applebaum to David Appleton; Margaret Boss to Margaret Holinbrook; Alan Frederick Brooks to Alan Frederick Elwood; Lynne Alfreda Belleau to Linda Spafford; Helmut Hans Bielschowsky to John Hans Biel; Daniel A. Carlin to Daniel Andrew Stevens; Arthur Sherman Chase to Arthur Sherman Muchmore; Ethel E. Dow to Ethel E. Downing; Beverly Ann Eastman to Beverly Ann Lanning; Richard Oliver Elliott to Richard Oliver Prescott; John Galloway to Lawrence John Gazley; James Henry Godin to Richard James Fields; Ruth Marion Gravett to Ruth Marion Wright; James Francis Guay to Stephen Josselyn Young; Ralph Johnston Gordon to Ralph Johnston Beaman; Arthur Harlow to Kenneth Hugh Sensinig; Mary Ellen Hoyt to Frances Ellen Cobb; Albert Helm to Albert Helm

1941-1943

Meyers; Theodore F. P. Mooney to Theodore F. P. Mooney; Joseph Raymond Ordway to Raymond J. Kelly; Irving Leo Plant to Leo Ernest LeClerc; Christie E. Parker to Christine E. Parker; Teresa Emily Revoir to Teresa Emily Glode; Bruce Robert Sanborn to Robert Bruce Folsom; Gabrielle Silverman to Michelle Silverman; Clifton Whitney to Clifton Barden; Boyd Kenneth Conery to Boyd Elmer Leavitt; Alma Bertha Conery to Marian Smith Robbins; Dudley E. Corey to Dudley E. Russ; Evelyn A. Corey to Evelyn A. Russ; Marilyn Phyllis Corey to Marilyn Phyllis Russ; Brenda Louise Dicey to Ruth Marie Sharp; Donald Bruce Doyle to Donald Bruce Blake; Marion Norma Flagg to Marion Norma Clark; Roy Hutchins to Roy Nelson Andrews; John Joseph Hill to Warren Ivings Garland; Frederick David Haughn to Dale Frederick Keniston; Richard Ward King to Donald Ward King; Foster Lowell to Foster George Cook; Leonard Lemay to Leonard Prech; Richard Talbot Lariviere to Richard Charles Bisson; Patricia M. LaVoice to Patricia M. Young; Arthur Andrew Macropal to Andrew Arthur Bullard; Edna Jean Newell to Edna Jean Berry; Jean Nelson to Martha Gale Chamberlin; Wanda Isabelle Peckham to Alice Lorraine Merchant; Donald L. Patenaude to Robert Leo Patenaude; Roland Ralph Romprey to Roland Ralph McNeil; Ross E. Sylce to Ross Earl Seace; Pauline Mae Shields to Pauline Mae Boisvert; Nancy Rae Sleeper to Nancy Rae Woodward; James Earl Santy to James Earl Kinne; Wanda Lee Schofield to Wanda Lee Sanborn; Ratha Roy Tobine, Jr. to Alfred Pillsbury; Robert Saville Varney to Robert Jackson Varney; George D. Wood to Donald Hazen Woodward; Elizabeth H. White to Elizabeth Jane Healy; Baby Willson to John Neale Richardson

<u>Coos County</u> - Alfred N. Rainville to George A. Rainville; Donald Murry Sandelin to Donald Murry Jordan; James B. Pearlstein to James Clark Burrill; Marion Peterson Monahan to Marion Peterson; Robert Stiles to Robert Baird; David Lionel St. Georges Montambeault to Lionel David Tardiff; Alice Hissen to Alice Jassop; Nazreea Hassan to Isadora Jassop; Theresa Haisen to Theresa Jassop; Donald Leslie Hawes to Donald Leslie Fogg; Norma E. French to Norma E. Barnes; Joseph Octave Anthanase Cloutier to Arthur Joseph Couture; Jeanette Mary Long to Jeanette Mary Nadeau

Changed by adoption: Lillian Mary Napert to Lillian Mary Garon; Norman Majorique Doyon to Norman Majorique Baker; Priscilla Azila

1941-1943

Doyon to Priscilla A. Baker; Betsy Ann York to Betsy Ann Steinbruch; George T. Lindgren to Alan Leason Martin; Edith Margaret Timmony to Margaret T. McLaughlin; Edward Littlehale to Willard Elwood Cameron; James Littlehale to James Howard Cameron; Ronald David Thurlow to Ronald David Buckley; Edwin Lee McKeage to Edwin George Hapgood; Richard Brian Jodrie to Arthur Irving Webber, Jr.; Gracia Bedard to Gracia Lemieux; Stephen Eugene Rowell to Stephen Eugene Hickey; "Infant" Dresser to Judy May Burbank; Valerie Annette Ridgewell to Valerie Annette Leighton; Sandra Fay Johnson to Sandra Fay Keating; Stanley Chapley to Stanley Pettingill; Pauline Hazel Chapley to Pauline Hazel Pettingill; Philip Arthur Morse to Donald Silas Miner; Marie Ann Baron to Mary Ann Veilleux; Paul Vincent Alphonse Breton to Paul Vincent Alphonse McCready; Minnie Helen Hart to Minnie Helen Martel; Henry George Leighton Couturier to Henry George Daniels; Roy Spreadbury to Guy Maure; Linda Gail Hicks to Linda Gail Nourse; Mary Elizabeth Shores to Mary Belle Knapp; Roberta Bennett to Sandra Jean Burgoyne; Leonard Lincoln Desilets to Leonard Lincoln Lowe; Beverly Fern Wheeler to Beverly Fern Young; Edward Pearl Wheeler to Edward Pearl Young; Sandra Rae Blodgett to Sandra Rae Dumas; Francis R. Stevens to Francis Ricker; Ernestine Wheeler to Ernestine Jessie Clogston

Name changes made by the superior court in divorce proceedings:

Rockingham County - Anne E. Hamilton to Anne Elizabeth Skelly; Dorothy S. Heger to Dorothy M. Shaw; Julia S. Lynch to Julia S. Danley; Phyllis Mabel Meloon to Phyllis Mabel Trefethen; Edith M. Mosher to Edith M. Rowe; Antoinette A. Stevens to Antoinette Gendron; Mary A. Trafton to Mary A. Fudge; Nellie B. Bower to Nellie B. Purdy; Vivien G. Broes to Vivian G. Howard; Margaret J. Craft to Margaret Johnson; Emily Florence Dambrino to Emily Florence Wilson; Maude D. Fogg to Maude D. Moulton; Caroline G. Fowler to Caroline E. Gynan; Concetta Marie Guarino to Concetta Marie Rando; Gertrude C. Knowles to Gertrude C. Eaton; Evelyn Pennewaert to Evelyn Johnson; Jennie C. Scamporino to Jennie Colombo; Christine Soteros Syrios to Christine Soteros; Ethel M. White to Ethel M. Burley; Elisabeth Verna Williamson to Elisabeth Verna Tierny; Christine P. Nelson to Christine Harriet Phelps; Virginia C. Sebastian Long to Virginia C. Sebastian (Annulment); Beulah Moore to Beulah Marsh;

1941-1943

Phyllis Madeline Marks to Phyllis Madeline Webb; Ella T. Loughlin to Ella T. McKinnon; Marjorie Leah Popoff to Marjorie Leah Brayton; Dorothy C. Hall to Dorothy Catherine Ballou; Pauline Hearrin to Pauline Paul; Mae J. Shapleigh to Mae J. Armstrong; Thelma F. Jackson to Thelma B. Florence; Shirley C. Churchill to Shirley C. Blake; Harriet R. Phillips to Harriet R. Littlefield; Dorothy Grace Ogden to Dorothy Grace Holt; Julia E. St. John to Julia E. Moody; Mary Ethel Sullos to Mary Ethel Merrill; Jane Bukata Dixon to Jane Bukata; Barbara Frances Fickett to Barbara Frances Stubbs; Pauline T. Gilchrest to Pauline Thelma Graham; Ruth Olive Jestings to Ruth Olive Stacey; Gertrude Lee Montanye to Gertrude Lee Belmont; Beatrice H. Scarborough to Beatrice Elizabeth Hartford; Edith C. Stevens to Edith Cummings Mellen

Strafford County - Alice E. Johnson to Alice E. Staples; June M. Merrill to June M. Nichols; Lucy Marie McElroy to Lucy Marie Bureau; Madelene A. Woods to Madelene A. Copp; Doris MJ Tebbetts to Doris MJ Lacasse; Jean Beaudette to Jean Nevers; Helen Susan Tinker to Helen Susan Caswell; Olive Ruth Lenfest to Olive Ruth Porter; Alberta G. Hinson to Alberta G. Labbe; Minnie A. Currier to Minnie A. Hamel; Lena F. Moreau to Lena F. Ellis; Annie Mae Gibbs Chasse to Annie Mae Gibbs; Ruth E. Lewis Bowman to Ruth E. Lewis; Effie E. Dwire to Effie E. White; Barbara E. Wiggin to Barbara E. James; Elmina Pastene to Elmina Begin; Muriel L. Munsey to Muriel L. Turner; Aimee H. Knight to Aimee H. Robertson; Marjorie Lucille Grenier to Marjorie Lucille Burrows; Evelyn B. McKenna to Evelyn Bourdage; Frieda Iona Demers to Frieda Iona Dwyer; Mary Pauline Draper to Mary Pauline Stevens; Eleanor F. Sylvester to Evelyn F. Masury; Lillian A. Trott to Lillian A. Norton; Lorraine A. Bridges to Lorraine A. Casey

Belknap County - Alice Mae Prince to Alice Mae Peabody; Cora J. Higgins to Cora J. Bracy; Dorothy Mae Norton to Dorothy Mae Ainsworth; Velma M. Audet to Velma M. Teft; Jessie Frances Ness to Jessie Frances Burley; Ida Bernice Stone to Ida Bernice Rollins; Mabel C. O'Shea to Mabel C. Wilkins; Elizabeth Malouin to Elizabeth Wakefield; Vernila Louise DeMar to Vernila Louise Merchant; Elizabeth E. Daigneau to Elizabeth E. Greene; Marion P. Baker to Marion Phelps; Valena Nadeau to Valena Babineau; Marie M. Trudeau to Mary M. Lapitre; Charlotte Adelaide Jefferson to Charlotte Adelaide Whittpenn;

1941-1943

Clara Bunnell Howser to Clara Bunnell Gulley; Oreille E. Marston to Oreille E. McWilliams

Carroll County - Margaret Blackwood to Margaret Curtin; Bessie H. Herbert to Bessie H. Kimball; Grace H. Conliff to Grace H. Floyd; Eva D. Demeritt to Eva Ethel Emerson; Helen M. Brown to Helen M. Runnels; Bernice Mills Nickerson to Bernice Mills

Merrimack County - Mildred V. Rogers to Mildred V. Haney; Clara Lucier to Clara Wing; Ora Temple to Ora Langevin; Ruby L. Colburn to Ruby L. Virgin; Lucy T. Boulay to Lucy Ann Tsaridis; Myrtol M. Trainor to Myrtol M. Chapman; Esther Aurora Colby to Esther Aurora Paveglio; Marie Thompson Stimmell to Marie G. Thompson; Pauline M. Hoit to Pauline M. Swain; Pauline P. Roberts to Pauline P. Leavitt; Geneva F. Lodge to Geneva Grace Fisher; Helen H. Kropp to Helen H. Goldman; Laura Gaynor to Laura Presby; Evelyn L. Anstett to Evelyn L. Cross; Harriett A. Sanders to Harriett Isabella Albee; Erdine M. Blais to Erdine Marguerite Kimball; Olga C. Rines to Olga C. Quintiliani; Florence L. Tucker to Florence L. Gerald; Louise L. Weatherbee to Louise E. Leonard; Evelyn A. Cilley to Evelyn A. McGown; Dorothy P. Hassett to Dorothy Jardine Perkins; Hazel Evonne SanSouci to Hazel Provencher; Mae Mansfield Noyes to Mae Louise Mansfield; Helen M. Morris to Helen Mary Johnson

Hillsborough County - Elizabeth V. Wilson to Elizabeth V. McHugh; Jeanette E. Aman to Jeanette E. Reimer; Orpha Gregoire to Orpha Beland; Philomene Daneault to Philomene Racourt; Eva W. Holmes to Eva W. Bemis; June Irene Greeley to June Irene Rich; Barbara Anne Connors to Barbara Anne Dane; Violete R. Watkins to Violete Renaud; Doris Clark to Doris Anderson; Thelma G. Frear to Thelma C. Goodwin; Sylvia Arline York to Sylvia Arline Heino; Doris M. Ciechon to Doris Morrell; Ollie LeRoy Young to Ollie LeRoy Camp; Frances K. Berry to Frances Gile Kilton; Phyllis L. Philbrook to Phyllis L. Slate; Marjorie D. Ziarko to Marjorie D. Glover; Mary E. Sullivan to Mary E. Reilly; Ruth T. Angus to Ruth T. Estes; Cynthia E. Clifford to Cynthia Erskine; Mildred Ferguson to Mildred Felch; Natalie Donahue to Natalie Williams; Bertha H. Shedd to Bertha Mae Hilchey; Mildred Bonney to Mildred A. Walker; Thelma LeBlanc to Thelma Gertrude Dickie; Anna Stanczak to Anna Palenska; Fannie Hilton to Fannie Mason; Emilienne

1941-1943

Carrier to Emilienne Rouleau; Mary Louise Paquette to Mary Louise Houle; Mikalina B. McCarthy to Mikalina Balkus; Helena A. Riel to Helena Alice Parkhurst; Lucille Tassinari to Lucille Beland; Corine M. Savageau to Corine M. Stuart; Hermina Dostie to Hermina Beaulac; Stella D. Guzman to Stella Delia Royer; Violet Blakeley to Violet Cousins; Elsie Sharby to Elsie Yeaton; Gladys S. Cushman to Gladys Stiles; Ollie Nowakowski to Ollie Wix; Edith B. DesRochers to Edith B. Bellefleur; Alice LaFrance Woods to Alice LaFrance; Charlotte Avery to Charlotte Lavigne; Viola B. Dugas to Viola B. Davis; Cecile Fortier to Cecile Demeule; Stella P. Tucker to Stella Polar; May Fober to May DeWaele; Rose Tambakiss to Rose Bienvenue; Verretta Ouellette to Verretta Austin; Laurette Carelli to Laurette LeComte; Roberta Ceil to Roberta Morrill; Margaret E. Eastman to Margaret Emerson; Nathalia Turcotte to Nathalia Gagnon; Yvonne Carette to Yvonne Letourneau; Sabra Ellen Murray to Sabra Ellen Weatherbee; Fannie K. Baraby to Fannie K. Axton; Mary Blekitis to Mary Mozitis; Edith J. Abbott to Edith J. Hanley; Addie D. Kimball to Addie M. Dalton

<u>Cheshire County</u> - Doris Forsyth to Doris Luce; Josephine Couillard to Josephine Stevens; Sarah Callahan to Sarah Northrup; Catherine Eleanor Cheney to Catherine Eleanor Fowler; Mary Rose Carey to Mary Rose Pollard; Nellie Gertrude Hale to Nellie Gertrude Sawtell; Mildred R. Crossman to Mildred Rose Curtis; Eulela Chesley Wallace Longever to Eulela Chesley Wallace; Evelyn Mary LaPlante King to Evelyn Mary LaPlante; Ida E. Barrett to Ida Augusta Edwards; Jessie C. Wilson to Jessie C. Schlichting; Thelma V. Bucheri to Thelma V. Leonard; Hope Armitage Williams to Hope Armitage; Mary M. Giguere to Mary Martina Weeks; Elsie Buckley to Elsie Rich Morris; Mildred MacCollom Allison to Mildred MacCollom Felix; Gladys A. Thompson to Gladys A. Denico; Mary Rita Blair to Mary Rita Doyle; Doris B. Gale to Doris M. Brazer; June W. Asbury to June A. Wetherbee; Rachel Victoria Vanni to Rachel Victoria Abare; Marion Loumina MacDonald to Marion Loumina Paradise; Vera Proctor Whitman to Vera Mae Proctor; Millicent A. Prevost to Millicent Alma Crossman; Virginia R. Parsons to Virginia Irene Richardson; Leona P. H. Davis to Leona P. Hastings

<u>Sullivan County</u> - Frances Dudley Taylor to Frances Dudley; Donna W. Bean to Donna W. Small; Mabel I. Case to Mabel I. Simpson; Avis L.

1941-1943

Winter to Avis L. Brown; Ruby O. Rowell to Ruby O. Wilson; Martha I. Charles to Martha I. Clark; Elizabeth Plunkett to Elizabeth Jacobson; Elizabeth T. Chase to Elizabeth Thelma Martel; Eda W. Williams to Eda W. Lindquist

Grafton County - Marion B. Bump to Marion B. Moulton; Ruth Elizabeth Pappas to Ruth Elizabeth Griggs; Elizabeth G. Wright to Elizabeth G. George; Kaye Fales to Katherine Fifield; Violet E. Nelson to Violet E. Spence; Nina C. Coulter to Nine C. Fellows; Marion L. Paquette to Marion L. Blodgett; Geanoula Mary Tkagut to Geanoula Mary Lougis

Coos County - Louise Knox to Louise Gale; Annette Couture DeChamplain to Annette Couture; Marion Pickford to Marion Ann Howland; Gertrude Pillsbury Dorr to Gertrude Clark Pillsbury; Winifred Temple Bouchard to Winifred Virginia Temple; Rita Pearl Nault to Rita Pearl Lacroix; Anastasia Radsky to Anastasia Sulloway; Leona Pearl Guilmette to Leona Pearl Pelchat; Mabel Buoniconti to Mabel Blake; Auralie B. Lefebvre to Auralie Beatrice Glines; Elsie Diane Nevins Colman to Elsie Diane Nevins; Vivian R. Swift to Vivian Rosalie Bacon

January 1943 - January 1945[11/]

Name changes made by the probate courts:

Rockingham County - Marjorie Frances Brown to Marjorie Frances Tuttle; Margaret Laura Dexter to Margaret Laura Waning; Baby Field to Jonathan Adams Aldrich; Antonina Drobisewskia to Jane Elizabeth Drobisewski; Peter Bosiniss to Peter Henry Bosen; John B. Simes alias John B. Quirk to John B. Simes; Florence Ellen Meatty to Florence Ellen Mullikin; Charlotte Priscilla Charuk to Charlotte Priscilla Coleman; Kenneth A. Hooper to Kenneth A. Carter; Paul Robert Bascom to Robert Webb; Mary E. Kingsley to Mary E. Wilbur; Archie B. Carson to Archie B. Corson; Josephine M. Carson to Josephine Martha Corson; Harold W. Carson to Harold Wesley Corson; Irene G. Carson to Irene Gertrude Corson; Alexandria Sophia Chloros to Alexandria Sophia Beleski; William Lester Courage to Lester William Courage; Harold L. Max to Harold L. Mosney; Mary Edith Pike to Doris Elizabeth Pike; Justus Lang to Julius Lang; Emma Christina Lang to Christine Emma Lang; Donald Raymond Waleryszak to Donald Raymond Bruce; Herbert Franklin Joslyn to Herbert Franklin Harrington; Ella Dorothy Joslyn to Dorothy Ella Harrington; Herman F. Joslyn to Herman Forrest Harrington; Ella Martha Simpson to Martha Ray Simpson; Francis Zielinski to Francis Robert Linscott; Clyde C. Rich, Jr. to Clyde R. Seavey; Rose Turcotte Demers to Rose M. Turcotte; Donald Allen Chance to Donald Allen Rea; David Eugene Graeher to Phillip Nicholas Barrett; Nancy Ann Morin to Patricia Ann Comeau; Harlene Harriet Caswell to Harlene Harriet Szabo; Richard Daniel Woodbury to Richard Daniel Wells; Ruth R. Turner to Ruth R. Robinson; George Albert Locke to George Albert Gorman; Priscilla Margaret Locke to Priscilla Margaret Gorman; Elizabeth Mae Gleason to Elizabeth Mae Nudd; Ervin Eidler to Robert Samuel Eidlow; George Wells to George Dupuis; Joseph Telesphore Moreau to Peter Joseph Moreau; Roland Stevens to Roland Bowden; Albert P. West to Albert Philbrick; Seley Crosbie to William Seley Crosbie; Robert Allan Gordon to Robert Gordon Phinney; Robert Libby to Robert Libby Chadbourne; Walter Lewis Pelletier to Walter Lewis Dorman, Junior; Arthur Pluff to Arthur Albert Plouffe; Katherine Ruth Packard to Katherine Ruth Eaton; Paulette Ann Hart to Paulette Esther Thyng; Harry Gould Costello to Harry Gould Rogers;

11/ Chapter 241, 1945 N. H. Public Laws

1943-1945

Paulette Esther Thyng; Harry Gould Costello to Harry Gould Rogers; Helen Beatrice Shaner to Helen Beatrice Smith; Luigi Bizzoachi to Louis Raymond Bizzoachi; Alton Buttner Nickerson to Alton Nickerson Beals; Albert Raymond Fluck to Albert F. Raymond; Margaret Reina Richard Fluck to Margaret Richard Raymond; Anita Bolduc Levesque to Anita Emelie Bolduc; Mary Karipi to Annette Millicent Karippey; Joseph Krystoic to Joseph Benjamin Christy; Ruth K. Alessi to Ruth Virginia Kanada; Sophoclis Hapchis to Sophoclis Hapsis; Barbara Rowena Ressler to Barbara Rowena Smith; Robert John Bennett to Robert John Martel; Dorothy Morin to Dorothy Anderson; Eugene Anthony Wilcox to Vaughan Michael Yeagle; Jacqueline Ann Cook to Jacqueline Ann Price; Jane Louise Burns to Jane Louise Reynolds; David Alden Ligthbody to David Alden Knowles; Joan Elizabeth Lightbody to Joan Elizabeth Knowles; Jean Catherine Lightbody to Jean Catherine Knowles; Donna Bernadette Pollard to Bernadette Charlotte Wilson; Alice Ingham Whiting to Alice Ingham Hunter; Lillian Emma Bates to Lillian Emma Knights; Virginia Caswell Dow to Virginia May Caswell; Louise Silvia to Patricia Ellen McCarthy; Joyce Virginia Weldon to Joyce Virginia Dunlap; Reginald Fulton Weldon, Jr. to Reginald Fulton Dunlap; George Gerald Davis to George Gerald Ross; Gilbert H. Bennett to Gilbert H. Veilleux; Fred Alvin Johnson to Fred Arthur Sheaff; David Francis Bogan to George L. Marshall, Jr.; Andrew Stancisko to Andrew Stancisco; Baby Kahill to Wilfred Maurice Peloquin; Paula Jean Leger to Paula Jean Brisson; Jacqueline Alice Clapp to Jacqueline Alice Abbott; Joanne Hutchins to Joanne Troutman; Kenneth Newbury to Kenneth Troutman; James J. Figerle, Jr. to James J. Perkins; Joseph Cadotte to Joseph H. Caswell; Kerwin David Olden to Homer Henry Davison; Robert James Belmonte to Robert James Lannon; George Litchfield Kenney to George Whitfield Kenney; Francis Michael Oltman to Frank Forbes; Baby Lenneville to George Dewey McCain, Jr.; Baby Archambault to Betsey Ann Squire; Patricia Gail Hawkins to Patricia Louise Witham; Philip Stanislaw Bourk to Philip Stanley Bourque; Abraham Fox to Earle Fox; Baby LaCoss to Sharyn Kay Couch; Betty Jeanne Gowan to Betty Jeanne Grant; Aurise Alberta Laramie to Aurise Alberta Hersom; Vivian Madelyn Shaner to Vivian Madelyn Smith; Patricia Ann Mixer to Patricia Marion Gratton; Richard Don Gurganus to Richard Don Levis; Robert Earl Stevens to Robert Earl Irvine; Linda Elaine England to Linda Elaine Smith; Joseph Albert O'Brien, Jr. to Joseph Albert Whities; Paul Davis to Paul Erwin

1943-1945

Noyes; James W. Knight to James Winthrop Hale; William F. Knight to William Francis Hale; Cecil Padgett Hodson to C. Padgett Hodson; Jean Montville to Jean Philbrick; David Keith Read to David Keith Mandigo; Cynthia Diann Hill to Cynthia Helen Bibbey; Lawrence Frank Brown to Lawrence Frank Hayes; Brenda Mae Gorton to Brenda Mae Martell; Joyce Peterson to Joyce Beverly Cooper; Dorothy Linda Perry to Dorothy Linda Franz; Lawrence Sidney Cohen to Lawrence Sidney Coleman; Joyce L. Sweeney to Joyce L. Clark; Thomas Russell Cook to Thomas Wesley Lyle; Sandra Drayton to Sandra Johnstone Cerutti; Lilly May Gill to Rosalie Eldredge; Carl Edward Morin to William Edward Malloy; Nancy Jean Warner to Nancy Jean Jenne; Annabelle Gertrude Hedgepeth to Annabelle Gertrude Witham; William Clifford Baptist to William Clifford Nau; Rodney Eugene Gannett to Rodney Eugene Hooper; Karen Claire Kimball to Karen Claire Quimby; Madeline Figerle to Madeline Perkins; Robert Paul Herbert to Robert P. Cammett; William Francis Beaumont to William Francis Wyman; Roberta Ann Craigie to Marion Reid Gilchrist; Howard George Kimerling to Howard George Malloy; Richard Frederick Waas to Richard Frederick Keezer; Robert Lee Rollins to Robert Lee Florence; Baby girl Hamilton to Constance Rae Howell; Dorothy V. Chaisson to Dorothy V. Dixon; Kathryn Beebe Birtwell to Kathryn Beebe; Richard Joseph Barry to Richard Joseph Laughton (Granted May 12, 1942)

<u>Strafford County</u> - June Ann Hayes to June Ann Nickerson; Zoe Evelyn Papageorge to Zoe Evelyn Constantopoulos; Hannah Moran to Joanna Elizabeth Moran; Alice Frances Chase to Frances Chase Hurd; Edgar Willis Laughton to Edgar Laughton Smith; Alexina Flora Rousseau Noel to Clara Rousseau Noel; Robert Lewis Gray to Robert Lewis Bridges; Mary Leduc to Mary Duke; William Leduc to William Duke; Marie Leocadie Ouellet to Leona Leocadie Ouellette; Constance Bisson to Constance Maurice; Joseph Leodar Normand to Leo Joseph Normand; John Francis Beamish to John Francis Beamis; Joseph Octave Cote to Joseph Richard Cote; Napoleon Vachon to Paul Rogers; Gustave Adolphe Nasman to Gustave Adolphe Nesman; Joseph Gilbert to Herman Emile Pouloit; Kleopatra Daeris to Claire C. Daeris; Billie Jackson to James Graham Kittridge; Mavis Blanche Hodgdon to Mavis Blanche Young; Patracia Ann Hatch to Patricia Ann Ross; Marylin Edith Brown to Marilyn Edith Cann; Joseph Louis Alfred St. Lawrence to Alfred Joseph St. Laurent; Alice Mansour Hashem to

1943-1945

Alice Mansour; Josephine Mansour Hashem to Josephine Mansour; Sarkis Mansour Hashem to Sarkis Mansour; Alcide Etienne Mansour Hashem to Alcide Etienne Mansour; Henry Richard Leonard to Henry Richard Perkins; Erileen Gertrude Pickering to Erileen Gertrude Goodwin; Ruth Eleanor Beaudoin to Ruth Eleanor McDaniel; Virginia Lillie Degrace to June Helen Ferrigan; Joseph Cook to Joseph Cook Currier; Trudy Goldbaum to Trudy Gould; Peter Adamopoulos to Peter Adams; Mary Labrecque Carkins to Marie Rose Carkins; Jean Joseph Chasse to John Paul Chasse; Donat Grondin to Albert Donat Grondin; Allie C. Conner to Winfred Leslie Bunker; Bernard J. McGee to Bernard Joseph Ferrigan; Robert Douglass, Jr. to Ronald Walter Jaffarian; Helen M. Ellison to Helen M. Ainsworth; Theodore Russell Therrien to Russell Theodore Therrien; Emma Mary Smith to Irene Mary Smith; James Gordon Cameron to Harold Evan Mitchell; Norman Desilets to Norman Richard McKone; Norma Rose Wallingford to Norma Rose Burroughs; Michael Robert Lewis to David Dennis Demers; Chellis Carroll McAllister to Chellis Carroll Weeks; Electa Louise Twombly to Electa Louise Shattuck; Mary Anna Laguerex Bernier to Mary Anna Lagueux Bernier; Annabelle Sandra Arnold to Annabelle Sandra Martineau; Francis J. Smith to Albert Hall Mercier; James Woodrow Sewall to Samuel Harry Sewall; Lumina Proulx Gouin to Minnie Gouin; Wesley George Columb to Wesley George Harris; Leslie Roy Columb to Leslie Roy Harris; Mary Ellen Couturier to Mary Ellen Taylor; Alfred Leo Couturier to Alfred Leo Taylor; Joseph Marcotte to Joseph Jestude; John Marcotte to John Jestude; Louis Paul Deschenes to Paul Louis Deschenes; Charles William Piercy to Charles William Clement; Joan Agatha Wolski to Joan Agatha Atwood; Patricia Lee Boucher to Patricia Lee Hobbs; Dona Clark to Dona Byerly; Betty Ann Maxfield to Betty Ann Treahey; John Frederick Kneeland to Frederick Mullen Steadman; Gary Robert Hall to Gary Robert Button; Katherine Marie Elizabeth Hamel to Katherine Marie Elizabeth Mondoux; Graziella Bergeron to Donalda Grazielle Bergeron; Kenneth Stokes to Kenneth Stokes Arnold; Glenn Raymond Hughes to Carl Lee Whitehouse; Archille Oditton Italion to Archille Arthur de l'Etoile; Marie Alice Moore to Alice Mary Moore; Joseph Albertus Leblond to George Albert Leblond; Malcolm Bruce Strauss to George Malcolm Wood; Frank Joseph Couillard to Joseph Manuel Couillard; David Court to David Foster Bennett; Pauline Joyce Wilkinson to Pauline Joyce Sanborn; Harriett May York to Patricia Ann Worden; Dolores June

1943-1945

Corson to Jacqueline Ann Mailot; Mildred L. York to Mildred L. Hawkins; Fred Willard Corson to Fred Willard Mailhot; Molly Rosemond Leighton to Maureen Rosemond Leighton; George Francis McEnnis to Robert Samuel Bernier; Donna Marie Parent to Jean Ann Adams; Raymond Whittaker to Raymond Bragdon; Loretta Mary Hughes to Loretta Mary Taylor; Kenneth Howard Paige to Kenneth Howard Nichols; Gale Van Wart White to Martha Jane Kelsey; Caroline Faith Brunkard to Myrla Joy Mitchell; Ernest E. Humphreys to Ernest E. Sheltry; Dolores Joy Fitzherbert to Dolores Joy Colbroth; Omer George Anthony Mailhot to John Mason Worley; Gladys Ella York to Gladys Ella Kelley

Belknap County - Frantz Milton Paine to Frank Milton Paine; Clyde Lemoyne Baker to Lloyd Lemoyne Baker; Martin Feurstein to Martin Feuerstein; Raoul Jean Thomas Xavier Morin to Ralph John Morin; Mary Evelyn Lasheway to Mary Evelyn Peavey; Eunice Zilla Shurbert to Eunice Lilla Blanchard; Richard Szalajeski to Richard Stanley Szalajeski; Charles Collins Clifford to Clifford Collins Clifford; Muriel Fern Thompson to Muriel Fern Moody; Ellen Morin to Helen Mary Morin; Pauline Louise Gagnon, alias Benoit to Pauline Louise Gagnon; Jean Edwina Gagne to Jean Edwina Wing; Ralph Lovely to Frederick Ralph Paquin; Frances W. Farra to Frances W. Wilson; Alvin Morse to Irving Gardner Morse; Leola Mae Floros to Leona Mae Floros; Helen K. Lugliani to Helen K. Bronson; Peter Joseph Grabowski to Peter Joseph Graham; Phillip Gignac Couture to Philip Gignac Couture; Blanche May Ringer to Marie Blanche Ringer; Albert George Orens to Albert George Joseph LaPierre; Floyd Harold Paradee to Clyde Harold Claflin; Leonard Alvis Martinetz to Leonard Richard Kean; Rena Agnes Lang to Rena Ada Pickering; Joseph Patrick Allen to Joseph Patrick Francis Allen; Virginia Durgin to Virginia Holden; Joseph E. Z. Johndeo to Joseph E. Dumas; Madelene Shirley Dufield to Madelene Shirley Riley; Vivian Rita Guyer Goyette to Vivian Rita Guyer Cyr; Stanley Richard Willmott to Stanley Richard Griffin; Ernest Ulysse Jacques to Joseph Ernest Jacques; Armand Alphonse Morin to Armand Joseph Morin; Richard Morin to Richard Joseph Morin; Isabelle S. Jones to Isabelle S. Blake; Carl Ange to Carl Angers

Changed by Adoption - Joseph Rudyinski to Joseph Roubo; Roger Albert Eryou to Roger Albert Dow; Howard J. Buttman to Howard J.

1943-1945

Lank; Louise Ida Lyman to Louise Ida Littlefield; Marcia Evelyn Kitchen to Marcia Evelyn Hamel; Donald Williams to Donald William Clouthier; Arnold Bolduc to Arnold Bolduc; Gail Lynn Chadwick to Gail Lynn Scarboro; Jeralyn Jane Middaugh to Jeralyn Jane Cornish; Raymond Husband, Jr. to Raymond Bagley; Gary Daniel Moses to Gary Daniel Brown; Glenn Irving Moses to Glenn Irving Brown; Robert John Storrs to Robert John Lamere; Carol Ann Walker to Carol Ann Walker; Donald Leon Willett to Donald Leon James

Carroll County - Ann L. Mathers to Ann Clara Titus; Mary V. Lewis to Mary V. Gibson; George Arthur Lewis to George Arthur Gibson; David C. Lewis to David C. Gibson; Donald P. Lewis to Donald P. Gibson; Clarence Wesley McClellan to Charles Stuart McLellan; Marilyn Ann Baker to Marilyn Ann Nason; Edward Bruce Brown to Edward Bruce Nason; Ronald Wayne Brown to Ronald Wayne Nason; Robert Francis Brown to Robert Francis Nason; Roberta Frances Brown to Roberta Frances Nason; Lionel Giles to Lyle Giles; Tonita Ethel Lougee to Tonita Ethel Buchanan; Lloyd Sprague Hammond to Lloyd Francis Stevens; Romona Jean Lewis to Romona Jeanne Bunker; Frances H. Marsh to Frances H. Kennett; Norma Klug to Norma French; Babara Jean Klug to Babara Jean French; George Ernest Klug to George Ernest French; Helen Klug to Helen French; Lawrence Arnold Clough to Lawrence Arnold Newhall; Raymond Bishop to Raymond B. Brown

Changed by Adoption - Blanchard child of Wolfeboro, N.H., to Linda Joyce Davis; Winn child of Boston, Massachusetts to James Oliver Bovaird; Irene Lucille Beal to Irene Lucille Pippin; Priscilla Maude McGraw to Priscilla Maude Washburn; Edward Fratus to Kenneth M. Fox; Rita Ann Howard to Rita Ann Hutchins; Mary Louise Hodsdon to Mary Louise Gorman

Merrimack County - Franciszek Piwonski to Frank Piwonski; Allister Hirtle to Sterling Allister Hirtle; Teresa Gloria Smith to Teresa Ann Smith; Bertram Schubert to Basil Bernd; Raffael Schubert to Siegfried M. Bernd; Marie Alice Elizabeth Jennings to Elizabeth Ellen Jennings; Robert S. Ellis to Robert S. Fanny; Elsie C. Koopman to Elsie Colby; Caro Lucia Allen to Caro Lucia Arsenault; Reino Jarvi to Ervin Reino Nelson; Isabelle C. Phillips to Isabelle Claire Babb; Charles Royce Ackley to Charles Royce Harvey; Raleigh M. Nudd to Raleigh M.

1943-1945

Brown; Stanislava Mary Giles to Stella Mary Giles; Irma Jean Ash to Irma Jean Rell; Maynard Wayne Brackett to Wayne Brackett Nicoll; Harry B. Lafferty to Harry Ernest Sharkey; Robert Forbes French to Robert Forbes Copp; Maryanne Stanley to Marianne Stanley; Hazel Adelaide Fellows Tucker to Hazel Maude Fellows Tucker; Alfred Edward Holden to Alfred Edward Halden; Joseph F. Davian to Joseph F. King; Patricia Ann McGuigan to Patricia Ann Walerstein; Alan Michael Abramowitz to Alan Michael Abrams; Beatrice E. Abramowitz to Beatrice E. Abrams; Jack Abramowitz to Jack Abrams; Foster Rand to Richard Leon Rand; Joseph Wilfrid Couturier to Alfred Joseph Taylor; Gerald A. Cannon to Gerald A. Little; Elinor G. Chagnon (Shonyo) to Elinor G. DeAngelis; Judith Anne Payne to Judith Anne Rand; Cora M. Roby to Cora M. Osgood; Marian Ruth Sanderson to Marian Ruth Townsend; William John Caveney, Jr. to William John Beaupre; Richard Harold to Richard Harold Dustin; Pauline Greene to Pauline Scarponi; Stephany Kartaczewicz to Stephany Victoria Kart; Gertrude E. Annis to Elizabeth G. Davis; Mary E. Warren to Mary Ellen Rogers; Robert Dudley Paul to Robert Dudley Bell; Arthur Richard Boyd to Arthur Richard Abbott; David Mansfield Boyd to David Mansfield Abbott; Arlen Carl Bujnievicz to Arlen Carl Benning; Audrey Jane Bujnievicz to Audrey Jane Benning; Lorraine M. Bujnievicz to Lorraine M. Benning; Paul Edward Gates to Paul Edward Himes; Maxine Barbara Kenniston to Maxine Barbara McLeod; Duane A. Wormbrand to Duane A. Windemiller; William Francis Vondell to William Francis Strobridge; Nathaniel Mortimer Mahoney to Nathaniel John Mahoney; Carol Hunt Matson to Carol Matson; Henry Frederick Robert to Henry Frederic Gignac

Changed by Adoption - Irene McGaffigan to Irene McGaffigan Drew; Charles Edwin Wentworth to Paul Conrad Gustafson; William Henry Eaton to William Henry Farmer; Margaret Elizabeth Fielding to Hope Chisholm; Lester Robert Leavitt to Lester Robert Page; Patricia A. Heath to Patricia A. Rounds; Helena Richard Foster to Helena Richard Holbrook; Joan Nancy Townsend to Joan Nancy Holbrook; John Harvey to Robert Carr Stimson; Gilbert Graeme Holt to Gilbert Welch; Patricia Mary Ann Overs to Blair Bamford; Katherine Proctor to Sally Elizabeth Roberts; Oral Codere to Oral Diane Bourbeau; Patricia Ann Lees to Patricia Ann Bureau; Eugene Allard to Eugene Laramie; Robert Francis Cliche to Robert Francis Drouin; Joanne A. Buzzell to Joanne

1943-1945

A. Culberson; Francis Clifton Charnock to Francis Clifton Cass; Rose Marie ----- to Rose Marie Adams; John Ernest Elliott to John Ernest Hemeon; Elaine Pappanickola to Elaine Walter; Jacqueline Mae Louthan to Jacqueline Mae Brown; Andrew Stewart to James Gordon Silver; Judith Arlene Beebe to Judith Arlene Storrs; Dorothy May Fitts to Dorothy May Nutter; Priscilla Elsie Neary to Priscilla Elsie Wood; Richard Allen Goss to Richard Allen Bishopric; "Infant" Roy to Albert Andre Boulay; Jacqueline Ann Dickey to Jacqueline Ann Lesmerises; Leroy Hillman Pratz to John Stanley McGilvray; "Baby" Robinson to Vincenzo Paul DePalma; Patricia Ann Cushman to Janet Parker; Christie Ann Gage to Christie Ann Beane; Judith Carol Hayes to Judith Elliott Morse; Agnes M. Knight to Agnes May Tripp; George P. Knight to George Page Tripp; Loretta Marie Nelson to Diana Elizabeth Lewis; Dorothea Mae Cole to Dorothea Mae Baker; David Healey to David Frank Brown; Margaret Jean York to Amy Welcome Blaisdell; Nancy Grover to Nancy Louise Jaastad; Warren J. Hall to Warren Hall Barker; Earl M. McKean to Earl M. Spooner; Theresa Brown to Theresa Liberty

<u>Hillsborough County</u> - Henri Courtemanche to Henry Albert Courtemanche; Genevieve Glancy O'Grady to Genevieve Glancy; Peter Banaskevich, Jr. to Peter Banis; Doris Banaskevich to Doris Banis; Emma D. Wallace to Emma D. Nichols; Normand Ernest Rivard to Normand Ernest Ouellette; Helen J. Papadoplos to Helen J. Papp; Paul B. Holland to Paul B. Young; Adam J. Krsytopowicz to Adam J. Kristoff; Robert William Jarvis to Robert William Basoukas; Albert Feurstein to Albert Firestone; Constantinas Mirmingis to Charles Mirmingis; Oscar Joseph Perras to Oscar Joseph Bilodeau; Mary Sedlewich to Mary Katherine Sullivan; Merton Douglass to Merton George Briggs; Elaine Emma Theriault to Elaine Emma Richard; Amelia M. Snow to Amelia M. Rioux; Charles Morris Feurstein to Charles Morris Firestone; Paul Abraham Feurstein to Paul Abraham Firestone; Tadeus Irmalowicz to Frank Yarmalovich; Domithilda Stepanionis to Dorothy Patricia Stepanon; Constantine Pappas to Charles Arthur Pappas; Donald Powers Hughes to Donald John Ladd; Joanne Hughes to Joanne Ellen Ladd; Ramard Chester Baldwin to Raymond Clinton Baldwin; Edward Farmer to Edward Francis Miller; Agnes Ploch to Agnes Gackowski; Adam Ploch or Plocharcyk to Adam Gackowski; Fernand Beaudoin to Richard Fernand Beaudoin; Marguerite Elizabeth Marston to Marguerite Elizabeth Walker; Frank

1943-1945

Y. Tong to Frank Tong Joyce; Israel H. Feuerstein to Harold Israel Firestone; Nile Clyde James to Nile Clyde Miller; Marcella Simpson Charois to Bernadette Ernestine Charois; Wladsylaw Syrek to Edward Joseph Syrek; Peter John LaMotte to Peter John Lamothe; Louis Barowski to Edward Barowski; Rachel Rota Raby to Rochelle Rita Raby; Gertrude K. Haas to Thirzo K. Haas; Gertrude A. Chouinard to Gertrude A. Clark; Marie Jeanne Rose Godin to Jeanne Rose Pelletier; Francena May Dandley to Francena Grace Dandley; Marietta Priscilla Lizotte to Priscilla Valliere; Edmund T. Potvin to Edmund Thomas Parson; William Whittet to William Whittet Turnbull; Dorothy Eva Whittet to Dorothy Eva Turnbull; Eva Georgianna Boulanger to Loraine Marie Boulanger; Emile Paul Dionne to Emile Paul Dion; J. Dolard Robert L'Heureux to Robert Dolor L'Heureux; Francois A. Menard to Archibald F. Maynard; Peter William Sadauskas to Peter William Sudosky; Catherine Luckwryz to Catherine Luckury; Richard John Kaline to John Papagien; Demetrious Anagnostopoulos to James Anagnost; Joseph J. Betlej to Joseph J. Betley; Marcelle Lamy Audet to Marcelle Lamy; Arthur Frederic Horne to Frederick Arthur Horne; Leo Bertrand Romeo DesRochers to Rome Leo DesRochers; Katherine Harrises to Katherine Harris; Marie B. L. Lucier now Sullivan to Isabel L. Sullivan; Malteades Harrises to Melty John Harris; Marion Ray O'Brien to Marion Rae McCann; Peter Chlorianopoulos to Peter Chloros; Maria Calamargetou to Mary Margetou; Theodore Calamargetou to Thomas Theodore Margetou; Evangelina Calamargetou to Evengeline Margetou; Berontia Ustin to Bertha Lapin; Venetia Calamargetou to Venetia Margetou; Lionel George Beaulieu to Leo George Beaulieu; Serasine LePage to Alice LePage; Robert Roger Lambert to Roger Lambert; Ralph B. Austin to Ralph B. Worcester; Ralf Hakansson to Ralph Ernest Larkinson; Jeremiah Louise Gingras to George H. Gingras; Louise Sarpi to Louise Lavoie; Louise Stulginskas to Louise Stulgis; Bronislaw Stulginskas to Bruno Stulgis; Anita Stulginskas to Anita Stulgis; Janice Eleanor Egan to Shirley Anne Egan; Dorothy Ada Bosse to Dorothy Ada O'Brien; Robert Aldo Morenghi to Robert Aldo Moreno; Joseph Henry Bean to Joseph Henry Lefebvre; Joanne Ruth Bennett to Joanne Ruth Vigue; Evangeline Jane Kosowicz to Wanda Jane Kane; Joseph Elphie Ouellette to Elmo Alphe Ouellette; Elizabeth C. Beattie to Elizabeth C. Jackson; Joseph Louis Gerard Donald Tellier to Donald Joseph Louis Gerard Tellier; Yvette Lemay to Yvette Gonthier; Yvonne Lemay to

1943-1945

Yvonne Gonthier; Marion Tatro to Marjorie Marshall; Joseph Elias Maurice Ronaldo Lemelin to Maurice Elias Lemelin; Stanislaus Joseph Morton to Stanley Joseph Morton; Constantinos Plechekos to Constantine Charles Pleatsikas; Antonios Mesaelis to Anthony Macenas; Joseph Henry Cazzot to Joseph Henry Caza; John Warren Gonsalves to John Palreiro; Honora Maria Sullivan to Maria Josephine Sullivan; Carl Henry Innie to Kenneth Bradley Innie; Wilfrid Adrien Caron to Wilfrid Adrien Rodier; Henry Zajaczkowski to Henry Zankowski; Antoinette Mary Theriault to Antoinette Mary Provencher; Toivo Matthias Kankaanpaa to Tovio Matti Kangas; Marie Delima Victoria Gagnon by marriage Pelletier to Rose Delima Pelletier; Lucille Merrill to Lucile Merrill; Regina Perras to Regina Krajewski; Louis Peter Stiko to Louis Peters; Anna Royer Banks to Anne Royer Banks; Marie Bura to Marie Russell; Saul Zozofsky to Saul Stone; Rose Cereier to Rose Cerier; Joseph Philippe Adelard Lanoie to Joseph Philip Adelard Lanoie; Roman Chester Staniszewski to Roman Chester Stanley; Robert Odilon Rouleau to Robert Odilon Ouellette; Joseph Hermenegil Boudreau also known as Hermenegil Boudreau to Joseph Herman Boudreau; Alice Antoinette Cannon to Alice Antoinette McCabe; Annie Maria Sullivan to Anna Marie Sullivan; Warren David Sandwell to Warren David Bodge; George Peter Poulas to Peter T. Koufopoulas; Gregoire Girard to Joseph Girard; Sofia Petriw to Zonia Petriw; Zella F. Spiracos to Zella E. Franklin; Shirley Alice Eileen McInnis to Shirley Alis Arline MacInnis; Tanya Lyn Spircos to Tanya Lyn Franklin; Stanley John Czarnosz to Stanley John Carson; Agnes Lillian Ingeborg Frans to Agnes Lillian Ingeborg Johnson; Bertha Zazofsky to Bertha Stone; Grace Margaret Gaura to Grace Margaret Cote; Joseph Alfred Irving Pelletier to Irving Fred Pelletier; Joseph Albert Adrien Ricard to Andrew Joseph Ricard; Bolaslov Bogdan to Benjamin Walker Bogdan; Nancy N. Sutherland to Nancy N. Hurlburt; Stanley P. Poplawski to Stanley P. Laski; Christina Margaret Schricker to Christina Margaret Klardie; Evanthia Marines to Evanthia Makarias; Spiridoola Lappas to Dora Berry; Theodore George Asteriou to Theodore George Astaire; James Gorham Polk to James Gorham Aston; Edna Jane Lakr to Edna Jane Dolzko; Bennie Owsiuk to Benny Olsen; Marie Rose Paquette to Rose Marie Allaire; Andrew Zarmarkupos to Andrew Watson; John Kurylak to John Kurylock; John J. Macuilevicious to John J. May; Soterios G. Plentzas to Joseph Plentzas; Lefterois Flioras to Ted Floras; John Miloszek or Milosl to John Mills; Ronald Edward Chagnon

1943-1945

to Ronald Edward Martin; Gordon Keith Chagnon to Gordon Keith Martin; Thornburn W. Warde to Thorburn W. Hills; LaBaeles W. Warde to LaBaeles W. Hills; Ordre T. Warde to Ordre T. Hills; Joseph Frederick Baril to Frederick Joseph Berry; Helen Nellie Butler to Helen Nellie Murphy; Hay Kuhn Wong to Hay Kuhn Lee; Helen Rzeznikiewicz to Helen R. Herbut; Robert W. Boulanger to Robert W. Lee; Charlotte Nellie Masztal to Charlotte Nellie Gervaise; Ladislaw Guerski to Walter Gurska; Victoria Anne Krystapowicz to Victoria Anne Kristoff; Fannie Barbara Wheeler to Joann Barbara Wheeler; Sherry Baird to Daniel Manning Hazard; Beverly Ann Grzymski to Beverly Ann Noel; Agnes D. Gackowski to Agnes Paris; Walter Aksztulewicz to Walter Akstull; George Leo Feurstein to George Leo Firestone; Hanna Johnson to Hannah Ekdahl; Albert Romani to John Henry Romani; Armand S. Couturier to Arnold Sylvio Taylor; Marguerite Couturier to Marguerite Taylor; John Valopulus previously petitioned as Ptefanos Vlahopoulos to John J. Baroody; Irving George Barnard to Irving Morrill Barnard; Bibian Cote Piper to Bibian Cote; Stanley Malinowski alias Millinuski - Malinoski - Malinowsky or Mallinosk to Stanley Uzdavinis; Antonina Malinowski alias Millinuski - Malinoski - Malinowsky or Mallinowski to Antonia Uzdavinis; John Malinowski alias Millinuski - Malinoski - Malinowsky or Mallinowski to John Uzdavinis; Rita Malinowski alias Millinuski - Malinoski - Malinowsky or Mallinowski to Rita Uzdavinis; Joanne Lou Zazofsky to Joanne Lou Stone; Frances Gale Zazofsky to Frances Gale Stone; Janet Fay Zazofsky to Janet Fay Stone

Changed by Adoption - Sylvia Belle Clifford to Sylvia Belle Blaisdell; Frederick C. Butler to Frederick Butler Elliott; Harold Edward Moore to Harold Edward Jones; Mona Mae Campas to Mona Mae Poirier; Peter George Campas to Peter George Poirier; Betty Jane Grant to Betty Jane McAfee; Marcel Paul Roland to Marcel Paul Roland Janelle; Rita Richard to Rita Richard Hewitt; Gerard Mercier to Gerard Rheaume; Joseph Robert Beckford to Joseph Robert Lavarnway; Carl Henry Stewart to Carl Henry Innie; Rita Lorraine Michel to Jeannine Phylis Bruneau; Mary Ruth Nettie Noels baptized as Irene Fleurette Vaillancourt to Irene Fleurette Froton; William Joseph Heron to William Joseph Rogers; Clarence George Gobin to Clarence George Rodier; Lorraine Harrison to Lorraine Philbert; Michael Hall to Robert Joseph Jenkins; Brenda Jane Buffelli to Brenda Jane Taylor; Mary E. White to Mary Elizabeth Gardner; Rita Rose Hood to Rita Rose Cyr; Helenmary

1943-1945

Boire to Helenmary Mack; Joan Ella Nickerson to Joan Ella Brooks; John William Smith to Joseph Harrison Kennard; Mary LeBorgne to Dorothy Marie Roux; Baby Chappell to Robert William Tate; Baby Hamilton to James R. Lavigne; Eva Wilkinson also known as Eva Belair to Eva Belair; David James Parlon to Donal Brenden Tobin; Baby Heath to William Oliver Mason, Jr.; Daniel Robert Dufour to Daniel Robert Flynn; Harold Edward Moore to Harold Edward Jones; Ernest Demers to Roger Ernest Plourde; Peggy Ann Bush to Peggy Ann Hall; Roy Walter Harriman to Roy Walter Hall; Margaret Janet MacDonald to Janet Margaret MacDonald; Dolores Niziankowicz to Dolores Sophia Timbas; Daniel Theodore Pappas to Daniel Theodore Roberge; Albert Leon Dube to Albert Leon Larochelle; Francis Sanders to Francis Sanders George; Agnes Caverly to Agnes Kennedy; Russell E. Dunn, Jr. to Russell E. Caron; Beatrice Vadeboncoeur to Beatrice Chase; John Ford to Richard Willwerth Gillespie; Joseph Insogna to Thomas Ignatius Kiley; Alfred Allen to Alfred Bosse; Robert Roger St. Pierre to Robert Roger Wajda; Robert Guptill to Robert Horatio Ball; Catherine Mary O'Leary to Patricia Margaret Flynn; Barbara Nicholi Champoux to Maureen Lois Gibbons; Yvette Jean Pitcher to Shirley Jean Pethick; Marie Irene Germaine Savageau to Marie Irene Germaine St. Jean; Paul Joseph Grogan to Robert Starita; Richard Raymond Genest to Richard Raymond Letendre; Shirley Ann Carley to Shirley Ann Salvail; John Kiritsis to John Francis Lakeman; Baby Poole to Mary Alice Reagan; Thomas William Kelly to Thomas William Levesque; Raymond Roger Gamache to Raymond Roger Francoeur; Gianakis Marvrellis to John Hartofelis; Michael James St. Cyr to Ernest Anthony Trahan; Mark Paul St. Cyr to Edward Joseph Trahan; Fotini Mavrellis to Fotini Hartofelis; Beverly Jewell Bucy to Beverly Bucy Parks; Deanne Teresa LaFontaine to Deanne Teresa Webster; Mary Ardelia Starumpski to Mary Ardelia Baio; Peter Christopher Holland to Peter Christopher Cordatos; William Arthur Thomas to William Arthur Saxon; Donald Sinkervitch to Donald Zibolis; Dorothy Ellen Bellefeuille to Dorothy Ellen Burnham; Baby Buchanan to Martha Anne Wood; William Angelo Marino, Jr. to James Howard Smith; Alfred Allard Clough, Jr. to Norman Alfred Field; Grace Frances Lepetre to Grace Frances Henderson; John Carter to David Collin Ainsworth; Ronald Underwood, Jr. to Ralph Andrew Ashton; Cynthia Lee Otis to Elaine Christine Schubert; Carl Harold Packer to Carl Harold Bienvenue; Richard Allen Packer to Richard Allen Bienvenue; Thomas Bernard

1943-1945

Stokel to Anthony Thomas Zdon; Robert Francis Robbins to Robert Francis Burden; Gerald Haley to Gerald Francis Shea; Maurice Richard Roberts to Janes Dana Clark; Anne-Marie Elizabeth Rush to Anne-Marie Elizabeth Tucker; Robert McLaughlin to Grover Robert Bohan; Norman David LaPlante to Norman David Sanborn; Robert Daniel Marion to Donald Purlee Greenough; Maureen Olive to Maureen French; Irene Marie Tremblay to Irene Marie Legendre; Janice Diane Croteau to Janice Diane Collette; Alfred Ernest Caldwell to Alfred Ernest Lemire; Sandra Louise Merchant to Sandra Louise Blackey; Robert Chase Hunt to Robert Chase Collins; Beverly June Hunt to Beverly June Collins; John Francis Hunt to John Francis Collins; Betty Jean Kirk Green to Betty Jean Walsh; Charles Joseph Caron to Charles Joseph Michie; Wayne Allan Connor to Wayne Allan Eaton; Mary Ellen Davis to Mary Ellen Hampton; Dorothy E. Robbins to Dorothy E. Gray; Louis Girard Zoes to Louise Girard Field; Roger George Zoes to Roger Girard Field; George Dennis Zoes to George Dennis Field; George Minasian to George Mougamian; Howard Irving Wirtanen to Howard Irving Beaubien; Therese Deschamps to Therese Roy; John Kirk to Edward Ralph Martin; Sandra R. Berube to Sandra R. Gagnon; Robert W. McGettigan to Robert W. Duda; Virginia Oikelmus to Virginia Aho; Dorothy Louise Pitcher to Dorothy Louise Pethick; Theresa Ann Lafontaine to Theresa Ann Tansey; Therese Madeleine Bourque to Therese Madeleine Cote; Baby Laro to Margaret Regina Warren; John Robert Bourque to John Robert Patch; Mary Elizabeth Lawrence to Mary Elizabeth Coons; Grover Clifford Battye to Grover Clifford Morrill; Gail Elizabeth Adams to Gail Susan Desrosiers; Pauline Rita Anderson to Pauline Rita Bouchea; Charlotte Theresa Maloney to Charlotte Theresa Crisp; Joseph Roland William Guertin to Joseph Roland William Young; Robert Arthur Guynn to Robert Arthur Stewart; Donald James Miles to Donald Miles Clough; Janet Ann Belair to Janet Ann McQuade; William Henry Andrews to Carl Bullard; Donald J. Francis, Jr. to Donald J. Cross; Robert Theodore Glannon to Robert Theodore Flodin; Henry Charles Ricard to Henry Charles Heath; Phyllis Gray to Mary Jane Dunbar; Irene Elizabeth Chase to Irene Elizabeth Fellows; Lilja Raakel Kuusisto to Lilja Raakel Raitanen; Kathryn Presby to Colleen Theresa Kendrigan; Sandra Lee Burpee to Diane Claire Grigas; Clarence Leo Ricard to Clarence Theodore Jameson, Jr.; Paula Arline Case to Paula Arline Mudge; Mary Ann Tagalakis to Mary Ann Connor; Baby Judkins to Lauralee Willard; Christine May Fulton

1943-1945

to Christine May Ryan; Sidney Rosen to Sidney Diamond; Robert Burns, Jr. to Robert Dennis Bergeron; Marie Frances Griffin to Marie Frances McNeil; Infant Roy to Sylvia Marie Eva Couture; Thomas Clark to Richard Henry Baribeau; Patricia Ann Sheridan to Patricia Ann Tellier

Cheshire County - Susie M. Bates to Maud Eva Bates; Myrtle E. Matson to Myrtle E. Hammond; Gerald M. Jones to William Lyle Cummings Jones; Richard W. Rice to Richard Warren Denico; Allan Roy Chambers to Alan Roy Chambers; Jean P. Lonie to Jean Pearson Tolman; James Miles to James H. Beaulieu; Stephen P. Heil to Bernard James Heil; Jacob Hakola to Jacob Hackler; William M. Hakola to William M. Hackler; Demetrius C. Stamos to James Charles Stamos; Phyllis K. Thayer to Phyllis Ruth Doran; Robert D. Brock (Murdock) to Robert Domenico Contri; Ida Pauline Sherry to Dolly Beverly Stalbird; Newell J. Pair to Newell J. Paire; Male Wirein to Walter Harold Dodge; Baby Bergstrom to Lee Richard Hazeltine; Laura M. Doody to Dorothy May Doody; Earl W. Pregent to Donald William Pregent; Dorothy Kostopoulos to Dorothy Kostas; Irene Kostopoulos to Irene Kostas; George Kostopoulos to George Kostas; Pauline Kostopoulos to Pauline Kostas; Mary Elizabeth Walker Hobson to Ruth Walker Hobson; Agnes Krystofowiecz to Agnes Kristof; Warren A. Willard to Warren A. Robinson; Joseph A. Berthiaume to Joseph A. Barcomb; Peter Doyle to Elliott Case Beveridge; Lucy S. Parry to Lucy Shaw Mitchell; Donald C. Sharkey to Donald C. Stearns; Bette Ann Crouse to Bette Ann Class; Harlan E. Crouse to Harlan Eugene Class; Stuart Lane Butler to Stuart Lane Currier; Roselyn F. Petitt to Roselyn F. Carpenter; Robert W. Knowles to Robert W. Pickering; Carolyn M. Warner to Carolyn M. Page; Marjorie M. Nelson to Marjorie M. Brown; William David Edward Sherrad to Wm. David Edward Thompson; Maurice Simkovetz to Maurice Quint; John Murray to John Murphy; Caroline Ann Murray to Caroline Ann Murphy; Richard B. Fullam to Richard Thomas Beauregard; Richard Thomas Beauregard to Thomas Bradley Beauregard; Janice A. Woodward to Janice Arlene St. Germain; William G. D. Prairio to William Joseph Prairio; Isabelle A. Doyle to Isabelle Ann Royce; Philip M. Doyle to Philip Melvin Royce; Charles H. Tuomi to Charles Henry Tielinen; Walter E. Ellis to Walter Edwin Mackey; June Dubal to June Diana Simonds; Otto Johnson to Arvo Matti Johnson; Freddie Maki to Fred Matthew Mackey; William P.

1943-1945

Croteau to William Paul Springer; Lawrence ----- to Lawrence John Enright; Ernest W. Preston to Ernest William Rhoades; Charles J. Gobeil to Charles John Taylor; Ivan L. Foley to William Foley Coughlin; Charlotte R. Stone to Charlotte Ruth Cox; Francis F. Derosier, Jr. to Francis William Davis; Norman Bruce Derosier to Norman Bruce Davis; Frank E. Grostein to Frank Elmer Parkhurst; Lorriane E. Gauthier to Lorraine E. Gauthier; Richard Louis Eno to Richard John Eno; Raymond E. ladd (not changed); Mary P. Woods to Mary Elaine Payeski; Barbara J. Cook to Barbara Jean Brayman; Shirley Anne Cook to Shirley Anne Brayman; Arthur J. Roy to Leonard Onesime Roy; Ronald D. Boyle to Donald Donovan Higgins; David N. Cullinane to David Niles Garland; Ellen C. Atkins to Helen Christo Atkins; Julian Hurd Ellis to Earle Julian Ellis; Arthur Alfred Muhlenbein to Arthur Alfred Deters; Jeanne Barbara Vaillant to Jeanne Barbara Richter; Goldie MacPregent Amlaw to Lillian Mary Pregent Amlaw; Ronald Paul Fish to Ronald Paul Fish; Richard Allen Primeau to Bruce Lee Guillow; Bradford Allan Howard to Bradford Allan Hulslander; Alvin Gene Garfield to Alvin Gene Watson; James Stacey Robertson to James Gordon Yendell; Mary Ann Robertson to Mary Ann Yendell; Cedemis Duvall to Sidney Duval; Emedio Joseph Dedomenico to Meo Joseph Dedo; Peter Bassett to Kenneth Wayne Marshall; Loretter Felix Howard to Loretter Feliz Whiting; James Francis Delisle to Francis James Delisle; Deborah Dean to Deborah Dean Bartlett; Angelino DiBernardo to Angelo David DiBernardo; Howard W. Sears to Howard William Hubbard; Kristoq Miti to Kriste Dimitri; Faith Agnes Lescord to Faith Agnes Ball; Alan P. Keough to Patrick Alan Shulenberger; Catherine Ann Kiniry to Catherine Ann Spinelli

<u>Sullivan County</u> - Ronald Francis Jordan to Ronald Francis Palmer; Reva Avis Godfrey to Reva Avis Beland; Jessie E. Hall to Jerrie Elenore Hall; Joan L. Gray to Joan L. Cabral; Elizabeth Monahan to Elizabeth Rebecca Glynn; Donna Marie Baxter to Joanna Marie Brown; Robert Joseph Maloney to Robert J. LeClair; Alice Allene Black to Ileene Alice Black; Clinton Irving Guy Johnson to Irwin Clinton Philbrook; Doris A. Johnson to Doris A. Philbrook; Gary James Johnson to Gary James Philbrook; Eugene Neil Frazee to Eugene Neil Gagnon; Sylvia Mae Knight to Sylvia Mae Karins; Shirley Marie Knight to Shirley Marie Karins; Reynold Salmela to Reynold Salmela Styles; ----- Serviss to Virginia Josselyn Young; Edward Nelson Blanchard to

1943-1945

Edward Nelson Clow; Uno Jalmar or Elmer Mackey to David Elmer Mackey; Walter M. Avery to Cleveland Farewell; Beverly Ann Bellinger to Beverly Ann LaRouche; Helen Edith Clough to Thursa Mae Clough; Robert Ashton Price to Robert Joseph Desfosses; Erwin L. Nerenberg to Erwin L. Lane; Arlene Margaret Merton to Arlene Margaret Connolly; John Stephen Hilty to John Stephen Dustin; Sharone Lee Niles to Sharone Lee Rhoades; Branislawa Adamowitz to Felicia Evelyn Adams; Anna M. T. Lauste to Miriam Anne T. Laustee; Carolyn Marie Koivisto to Carolyn Marie Murgatroy; Patricia Mae Doucette to Patricia Mae Blaine; Frederick Ernest Hewey to Frederick Ernest Blaine; David Albert Brown to David Albert Blaine; Shirley Anne Cleveland to Shirley Ann Swan; Duane George Baraw to Duane George Latvala; Robert Lee Slattery to Thomas Robert Brown, Jr.; Clayton George Paris to Clayton George Roy; Robert William Small to Robert William Keneson; Mary Leonora Bergeron to Rita Leonora Bergeron; Ida Hannah Shulins to Ann Ida Hannah Shulins; Ellen Mary Breed to Mary Ellen Breed; Richard Henry Peacor to Richard Henry Howard; Helen Winifred Joy to Helen Winifred Hawkins; Elizabeth Ann Sanborn to Elizabeth Ann Austin; Verna Mae Demars to Verna Mae Roy; Paul L. Hutchins to Perl Llewellyn Hutchins

<u>Grafton County</u> - Helen Mary Austin to Charlotte Susan Parker; Kenneth Edward Allard to Kenneth Edward LaMott; Clifford Arland Bruce to Clifford Albert Smith; Donald Alan Burlock to Brian Charles Smith; Ronald Bruce Burlock to Bruce Everett Smith; David Allen Bresnahan to Terrence Neil St. Germain; Shaben Louis Corey to Paul Louis Corey; Linda M. Corey to Linda May Ingalls; Flora Isabel Ford Clevenson to Rebekah Florah Ford Clevenson; Barbara Jean Crowley to Barbara Jean Wallace; Diane Lea Ducharme to Marcia Mary Somes; Marion B. Hall to Marion Lucille Blodgett; Wendell John Holt to Robert Wendell Holt Hadley; Marion Lepa to Frank Lepa; Thomas F. McMahon to Thomas Francis Belisle; Clifford Moulton to Clifford Roger Champney; James Edward Michaud to James E. Harnish, Jr.; Martha C. Merrick to Martha C. Paselt; Richard Wayne Provencher to Richard Wayne Day; Christine Raczka to Elizabeth Mary Blais; Carole Leona Savage to Carole Leona Fournier; James Dominous Sheridan to Thomas Erwin Ball; Doris Marie Stebbins to Doris Marie Ball; Paul Reaves Stanford to Paul St. Francis, Jr.; Barbara Eileen Thurston to Barbara Eileen Macy; Robert Evan Wright alias Robert Tortorelli to

1943-1945

Peter West Cooney; Dennis LeRoy Willey to Willard Howard Beckley; Cimone Mina White to Lillian Marion White; Baby Brown to John Harrison Hall, Jr.; Beverly Ann Boynton to Beverly Ann Gilpatric; Curtis Carson to Curtis Carson Rock; Irwin George Conery to George Douglas Taylor; Marilyn Norma Conery to Marilyn Taylor; Arthur Conner to Arthur Ranald Bailey; Sara Esther Conner to Sara Esther Bailey; Sandra Jane Conner to Sandra Jane Bailey; Baby Carey to Peter Edwards Carr; Althea M. Cheney to Althea E. Moulton; Calvin Lee Colburn to Calvin Lee Raymond; Judith Lee Finan to Judy Hughes; Janice Mae Goodwin to Janice Mae Cass; Robert Frank Harrison to Robert Frank Revoir; Ruth M. Harrison to Ruth M. Revoir; Patricia Ireleen Hartwell to Patricia Eileen Bedell; Mary Rose Jette to Mary Rose Swain; Paul Joseph to Russell Joseph Gwynn; Clifford Junior Martyn to Clifford Harry Martyn; Sheila Lee Madore to Sheila Lee Fields; Marvel Katherine Palmer to Marvel Katherine Guyer; Marjorie Janet Parent to Marjorie Janet Aldrich; David A. Palmer to David A. Mallard; Mary Phyllis White to Mary Phyllis Goodwin; Carol Ann Weeks to Carol Ann Pierson

<u>Coos County</u> - Alice Ledger Theriault to Alice May Ledger; Normand Caron to Normand Nadeau; Francis Murphy to Francis James Brill; Neil Edberg to Neil Boucher; Margaret Mary Ryan to Margaret Mary Sheridan; Pasquale V. Ferrari to Edward Victorio Ferrari; Richard Leonard Sargent to Richard Leonard Merrick; Lorette Adrienne Dumais Audet to Lorette Adrienne Dumais; Linda Ann Blake to Linda Ann Savage; David Wolfgang Bernheimer to David Wolfgang Bernay; Priscilla Beatrice Elvira Spencer to Priscilla Beatrice Whittum; Alice Young LaDuke to Alice Young; Richard Arnold Flower to Richard Arnold Streeter; Charles Antony Malasky to Charles Antony Malas; Hilda Simonds Hayes Malasky to Hilda Simonds Hayes Malas; Marian Clarkson Weinberg to Marion Lamere Clarkson; Joseph Bouchard to Ned Pelletier; Ruby M. Samson to Luba M. Samson; Earl John Shaw to John Earl Shaw

Changed by Adoption - Wallace Daniel Reed to Wallace Daniel Maker; Barry McKee to Barry McKee Stauffer; Lois Annette Wormell to Lois Annette Johnson; Judith Day to Marie Joan Suzanne Martel; Wallace E. Nicholson to Harold Chester Bowker; Nancy Lou Long to Nancy Lou Cole; Natalie Iris Drown to Natalie Iris Harriman; Rosalie Marie Drown

1943-1945

to Rosalie Marie Harriman; David Arnols Covio to David Arnold Vallee; Alice Arlene Robinson to Beverly Mildred Boudle; Arlene Stanford (known as Beatrice Caroline Blodgett) to Arlene Nadeau; Robert Sproul to Marshall Alvern Thurlow; Emile Ernest Morel to Emile Ernest Pelchat; Lucienne Germaine Morel to Susan Germaine Poisson; Maureen Jennie White to Maureen White Kier; Leonard Landon Blake to Lenord Erwin Egan; Nancy Elizabeth Boutin to Nancy Elizabeth Daley; Phillip Aaron Swift to Philip Aaron Young; Rita Doris Francoeur to Rita Doris Watson; Theresa Thomas LeBrun to Theresa Dubeau Lebrun; Mary Lee Richards to Mary Lee Nichols; Wilfred Roger Joseph Veilleux to Wilfred Roger Joseph Couture; Robert Wilson Shute to Robert Wilson Dow; Albert Langlois to Colindale Peter Brigham

Name changes made by the superior court in divorce proceedings:

Rockingham County - Irene O. Galinsky to Irene Oden; Verna May Webster to Verna May Packard; Alice Sabins to Alice Staples; Kathryn Howard Fairchild to Kathryn Elizabeth Howard; Dora Alberta Shapleigh to Dora Alberta Graham; Dorothea Mae Bilbao to Dorothea Mae Johnson; Virginia M. White to Virginia M. Turney; Becca Halprin to Becca Miller; Elinor B. Moulton to Elinor Clarissa Bachelder; Geraldine R. Ratta to Geraldine Elizabeth Reitze Heywood; Florence B. Callahan to Florence E. Bennett; Sophie Antonelos to Sophie Pappas; Louise Entwistle to Louise Etheridge; Madeline E. Gordon to Madeline Edith Smith; Dorothy T. Hall to Dorothy Belle Todd; Jessie S. Hemm to Jessie Stacy; Ruth Atwell Hodgdon to Ruth Atwell Goodell; Doris Keen to Doris Philbrick; Sadie L. King to Sadie L. Pickering; Barbara E. Pierce to Barbara E. Trefethen; Janet E. Plante to Janet E. Tatham; June Beals to Edith June Odiorne; Eileen May Garant Perron to Eileen May Garant; Clara E. Pollard to Clara E. Mee; Cora Mary Rosa to Cora Mary Rainville; Helen R. Rinalducci to Helen Raedell Hankins; Ellen Barati to Ellen Trzinska; Beulah A. Gilbert to Beulah Rumrill; Frances Cox Grover to Frances Cox; Rita M. Hamm to Rita Margarita Moreau; Ruth deR. Moulton to Ruth E. deRochemont; Ann Doreen Pennewaert to Ann Doreen Francis; Clarabelle E. Reschke to Clarabelle E. Wooldridge; Cecil Moeckel to Cecil Dussault; Laura M. Patterson to Laura Mardorcheo; Mary Elizabeth Batchelder to Mary Elizabeth Hutchings; Elizabeth D. Bushey to Elizabeth Thompson; Marjorie V.

1943-1945

Flynn to Marjorie V. Grover; Louise J. Harnowski to Louise Josephine Hurley; La Vena Mae Mathews to La Vena Mae Mock; Mavis R. Miller to Mavis R. Williamson; Madelyn E. Paige to Madelyn E. Knowles; Constance Pappalardo to Constance Zangari; Marjorie H. Ross to Marjorie H. Clark; Lorenda M. Small to Lorenda Mae Dow

Strafford County - Marie Anna Poulin to Marie Anna Roy; Marie C. R. Boulanger to Cora Roy; Corine M. Joyal to Corinne Marie O'Donnell; Elizabeth F. Garland to Elizabeth Francena Caverly; Edith Marion Ashland to Marion Edith Trainor; Alice J. Alford to Alice Varney Jones; Margaret L. Flint to Margaret L. Bell; Helen Pray Dunlap to Helen Pray; Georgia E. Agnew to Georgia Ellen Dame; Bessie Louise LaFleur to Bessie Louise Smith; Emma Irene Thompson to Emma Irene Gray; Lucy A. Bureau Vachon to Lucy A. Bureau; Katherine E. Krisiak to Katherine E. Coyne; Evelyn H. Labonte to Evelyn H. Corliss; Marie Blanche Ida Mitchell to Marie Blanche Ida Routhier; Elizabeth A. Peavey to Elizabeth Spear Aldrich

Belknap County - Vernila Louise DeMar to Vernila Louise Merchant; Elizabeth E. Daigneau to Elizabeth E. Greene; Marion P. Baker to Marion Phelps; Valena Nadeau to Valena Babineau; Marie M. Trudeau to Marie Martha Lepitre; Charlotte Adelaide Jefferson to Charlotte Adelaide Wittpenn; Clara B. Howser to Clara Bunnell Gulley; Orellie E. Marston to Orellie E. McWilliams; Claire G. McClary to Claire Gallagher; Lillian Edith Lessard to Lillian Edith Hebert; June I. Moran to June I. Merrill; Philomene B. Burres to Philomene B. Wilson; Doris J. Phillips to Doris J. Cate; Evelyn B. Fortier to Evelyn B. Harvey

Carroll County - Ruth Bickford Londa to Ruth Bickford; Barbara L. Flanders to Barbara Louise Goodrich; Violet G. Irish to Violet Esther Graham; Geraldine P. Nickerson to Gladys Geraldine Pascoe

Merrimack County - Glendel N. Thurston to Glendel Carole Nichols; Georgia A. Naughton to Georgia Allen; Eunice M. McKenzie to Eunice M. Ballard; Carol B. Patch to Carol B. Smith; Rose M. Pearl to Rose Place; Mary E. Ellis to Mary E. Bartlett; Sylvia I. Boomhower to Sylvia I. Russell; Virginia St. Armand to Virginia R. Merchant; Naomi B. Hermanson to Naomi B. Wentworth; Rose Anna Senneville to Rose Anna Plante; Ruth Martin Cherry to Ruth Fairbanks Martin; Harriett

1943-1945

Louise Sutton to Harriet Louise Clark; Jeanette T. LeBlanc Morgan to Jeannette T. LeBlanc; Arlene M. Shattuck to Arlene M. Webber; Esther Simpson to Esther S. Carter; Susan B. Bartlett to Susan Victoria Colby; Audrey Taylor Hill to Audrey Taylor

Hillsborough County - Emilienne A. Bailey to Emilienne Alice Normand; Veronica Smith to Veronica Mathews; Mildred Welch to Mildred Upham; Mary Eickman to Mary Smith; Helen D. Mailhot to Helen Duncan; Leah V. Basham to Leah V. Davis; Katina Douklia Pialtos to Katina Douklia; Fernande V. Johnson to Fernande Gertrude Veilleux; Katherine E. O'Reilly to Katherine E. Cox; Thelma Golfinos to Thelma Zerbinos; Margaret E. Heron to Margaret E. Celen; Salome Vieira to Salome DeFreitas; Anna Crosby otherwise known as Anna Olson to Anna Rajotte; Evelyn Regan to Evelyn Babcock; Helen Gorey to Helen Putnam; Caroline J. Stoklosa to Caroline J. McGuire; Edith Strandberg to Edith Hale; Gladys F. Fagnant to Gladys Rose; Phyllis Shirley to Phyllis Elaine Whidden; Lorraine Pelissier to Lorraine Corinne Laplante; Eva Pelletier to Eva Blais; Marie A. Demers to Marie A. Glaude; Gertrude M. Freeman to Gertrude M. Sullivan; Phyllis R. Lowell to Phyllis R. Rabadeau; Marie Alma Senechal Moreau to Marie Alma Senechal; Olive Cassarino to Olive Irene Banks; Virginia K. Mallek to Virginia Krupa; Helena A. Whitney to Helena Alice Parkhurst; Peggy Harisiadaes to Peggy Vallas; Mary Phyllis Rahmanop to Mary Phyllis Brown; Yvonne Neudeck Gelb to Yvonne Neudeck; Phyllis M. Pollock to Phyllis M. Steere; Leona White to Leona Segal; Helen L. LaPointe to Helen L. Hirschman; Sylvia Charron to Sylvia Cohen; Anna M. Spence to Anna M. Tamulonis; Barbara M. Beattie to Barbara M. Werden; Juliette Boivin to Juliette Provost; Yvonne Poehlman to Yvonne Patnaude; Marion Haase to Marion Harrison; Gladys May White to Gladys May Whitney; Ruth D. Lapierre to Ruth Genevieva Dionne; Mary Laure St. Pierre to Mary Laure Despres; Helen A. Titus to Helen A. Walsh; Patricia Collette to Patricia Young; Emma LaPlante to Emma Prassler; Irene E. Turner to Irene E. Paradis; Matilda Pearle Tumblin to Matilda Pearle Selig; Alice Filteau to Alice Deslaurier; Rose Barlow to Rose Duquette; Jennie W. Wyman to Jennie W. Witham; Grete P. Johnson to Grete P. Hansen

Cheshire County - Helen M. Ingalls to Helen Marguerite Bartlett; Louise C. Jarvis to Louise C. Rudolf; Palma Lecuyer to Palma Pellerin;

1943-1945

Florence E. Butterfield to Florence E. Tedford; Toini Irene Taylor to Toini Irene Jurva; Lillian E. Girouard to Lillian Everline Campbell; Miina Raatikainen to Miina Oja; Alta M. Forcier to Alta Muriel Beaudoin; Erma D. Dixon to Erma Mae Durant; Myrtle H. Toomey to Myrtle J. Hazleton; Laura E. Cardinal to Laura Emma Fortier; Rosanna D. Boyea to Rosanna Dinagan; Jennie Wilhelmina Steman to Jennie Wilhelmina Heinonen; Linda Ryan to Linda Ascani

Sullivan County - Esther H. Coots to Esther Haswell; Mary Wuorela (also known as Mary Kanerva) to Mary Kanerva; Ruth E. Hastings to Ruth E. Niles; Margarette E. White to Margarette E. Parker; Hazel M. Dubreuil to Hazel M. Taylor; Dorothy M. Jondro to Dorothy M. Wilkins; Lois M. Foisy to Lois M. Tashro; Eunice M. Clements to Eunice M. Cairns; Katherine M. Carey to Katherine M. Burbee

Grafton County - Grace P. C. Stetson to Grace Greenia; Virginia Enid Murphy to Virginia Enid Conrad; Natalie Inez Bonfilio to Natalie Inez Howard; Delma Evelyn Jordon to Delma Evelyn Dunkerton; Stella J. Thompson to Stella M. Jackson; Rosamond Elizabeth Brown to Rosamond Elizabeth Hazeltine; Martha Adams LeVoy to Martha Adams; Bessie A. Thornton to Bessie A. Eastman; Thelma H. Williamson to Thelma H. Fisher; Rena G. Cilley to Rena G. Goodell; Marjorie Daniels Place to Marjorie Daniels; Edith Sippell McFarland to Edith Sippell; Louise A. Bacon to Louise Anna Butman; Shirley Horrocks to Shirley Ayer Pearson; Velma A. Hill to Velma A. Corey; Hazel Adams Matevier to Hazel Emma Adams; Mabel M. Elmora to Mabel M. Hathorne; Eleanor R. Simpson to Eleanor Roelse; Virginia E. Beamis to Virginia E. Hartwell; Alta C. Bardill to Alta Croft Perry; Claire D. Silverstein to Claire Dunleavy; Dorothy M. Gray to Dorothy May Jordan

Coos County - Beatrice J. Thibodeau to Beatrice Therrien; Jeannette Lawrence Myers to Jeannette Lawrence; Lucille May Merritt to Lucille May Thibeault; Elizabeth T. Crawford to Elizabeth Caroline Tilton; Veneda Wheeler Buzzell to Veneda Eunice Wheeler; Eunice C. Taylor to Eunice Chappell; Katie B. Hersom to Katie B. Ball; Ellen Mildred Hopps to Ellen Mildred Portigue

January 1945 - January 1947[12/]

Name changes made by the probate courts:

Rockingham County - Louisa Burgess to Barbara Louise Burgess; Sarah June Heath to Sarah June Willey; Loren Austin Fernald to Loren Austin Tuttle; C. Padgett Hodson to Carey Padgett Hodson; Virginia Lowell Molte to Virginia Green Lowell; Isadore Stein to George Isadore Stein; Marshall Goodwin Pecker to Charles Goodwin Parker; Philip August Schmuck to Philip August Phillips; Laura Aldea Schmuck to Laura Aldea Phillips; Florido Richard Katsanos to Floros Nicholar Katsanos; Anastasios Marinopoulus to Anast Marinos; Stanley Kliewinski to Stanley Lewis; Catherine Etta Kliewinski to Catherine Etta Lewis; Robert Kliewinski to Robert Lewis; Mary Ann Kliewinski to Mary Ann Lewis; John Henry Paules to Phyllis Mae Gammon; Dorothy L. Sargent to Dorothy Brewster; Minnie M. Kuntz to M. Denne Kuntz; Francesca Randall Dobson to Francesca Randall Mitchell; George May Watts to Georgia May Watts; Stanislaus Pis to Stanley Pizz; Genevieve Berry Malone to Genevieve Berry; Margaret L. Stevens to Margaret L. Barton; Marguerite E. Thomas to Marguerite Elizabeth Wendell; Jesse William Carter to William Jesse Carter; Steven Robert Gento, Jr. to Steven Robert Blinn; Marie O'Brien to Marie Roy; Andrew Joseph Ganitos to Andrew Joseph Pelletier; Mary Elizabeth J. Davenport to Betty Jean Davenport; C. Kenneth Mandigo to C. Kenneth Mann; Vivian Y. Mandigo to Vivian Y. Mann; David Keith Mandigo to David Keith Mann; Hubert Joseph Vallier to Hubert Joseph Downing; George W. Fowler to Daniel W. Fowler; Marjorie Ann Call to Marjorie Ann Westgate; Lena Belmonte to Lena Lannon; Wtadjitaf Maskwa to Arthur Joseph Maskwa; Robert E. Weber to Robert E. Webber; Ruth B. Farcas to Ruth Bernice Cummings; Joan E. Strandell to Joan E. Howard; Joseph Hector Plouffe to Hector Joseph Plouffe; Isabella Kujeska to Isabella Rohr; Marian P. Williams to Marian Mort Palmer; Eva E. Mason to Eva E. Kennett; Lizzie May Fowler to Elizabeth May Fowler; Lorraine M. Felch to Lorraine M. Knowles; Nicholas Karamaplas to Nicholas Kay; Grace Elizabeth Karampalas to Grace Elizabeth Kay; Sandra Lee Karampalas to Sandra Lee Kay; Ernest C. Angelos to Ernest C. Owen; Rose Mitchell Carr to Rose Mitchell; Chester W. Dowe to Chester W. Dow; Norma Jean Gillespie to

---

[12/] Chapter 330, 1947 N. H. Public Laws

1945-1947

Chester W. Dowe to Chester W. Dow; Norma Jean Gillespie to Normagene Gillespie; Laurance Alan Morgan, Jr. to Christopher Alan Morgan; Boleslaw Pahutsky to William Joseph Trosky; Hyman Fisher to Herbert Hyman Fisher

<u>Strafford County</u> - Anne Shirley Susmann to Anne Victoria Sussmann; Richard Paul Lambert to Joseph Leo Lavigne; Margaret Loretta McSorley to Margaret Loretta Gailey; Albert E. Maynard to Albert Edward Barcomb; Linda Lee Osborn to Linda Lee Baxter; Eva Emma Cushing to Eva Emma Lindbom; Frederick William Trongeau to Frederick William Goodwin; Arlene Lorraine Kirouac to Arlene Lorraine Dobbins; John Regis Cote to Robert James McKenney; Roland James Morse to Roland James Baxter; Baby Lamontagne to Ronald Almon Snell; William Thomas Smith to James Frederick Meader; David Allen Hebert to David Allen Gagne; Diane Carol Marshall to Diane Marshall Davenport; Leo Joseph Desjardins to Roy Leo Gardner; Marie Cecile Godin to Judith Kate Weathers; Jacqueline Marie Guy to Jacqueline Marie Foster; Martha Susan Asadoorian to Miriam Brooks; Marie J. LaFay to Marie J. Valley; Linda Lee Grotty to Linda Lee Ochs; Richard Poisson to Richard Hussey; Dorothy Priscilla Buker to Dorothy Priscilla Lapete; Norma Louise McNeil to Norma Louise Paul; Patricia Ann Cormier to Priscilla Rachel Landry; Marie Auron (Lambert) Babin to Palma Ora (Lambert) Babin; Ronald Devoid to Ronald W. Nichols; Donald Devoid to Donald A. Nichols; June Page to June P. Nichols; Paul Woodbury Wheeler to Paul Woodbury Knight; Robert Carlton Collins to Robert Carlton Berry; Dianne Alice Guptill to Dianne Alice Randall; David Butler to Peter Donald Weathers; June P. Nichols to June Louise Nichols; William R. Ellis to William R. Mountford; William White to William Mailhiot; William Francis Mullins to William Francis Morrison; Robert Elmer Walbridge to Robert Elmer Marble; Germaine Stella Carignan to Germaine Stella Glassburn; Mary Jeanne Desgroseilliers to Patricia Ann Hughes; Thelma Louise Collins to Thelma Louise Verville; John Joseph Szabo to John Joseph King; Louise May Chesley to Lois May Chesley; Joseph Basil Roux to Joseph Wheeler; Pauline Chesley to Pauline Ida Chesley; Brian Richard Robinson to Brian Richard Voge; Elizabeth Ann Hebert to Elizabeth Ann Gagne; Albin Joseph Kozminski to Albin Joseph Kozminski Malin; Marcia Louise Kozminski to Marcia Louise Malin; Edward John Paul Gulubicky to Edward John Paul Grieg; Vera Pauline

1945-1947

Fannie to Carol Florence Nutbrown; Jerry Willie Locke to Jerry Willie Brown; Kenneth LeRoy Howland to Kenneth LeRoy Nisonger; David Raymond Howland to David Bliss Nisonger; Grace May Allard Blaylock to Grace Helen Blaylock; Dolores Marian Lacasse to Dolores Marian Tebbetts; Donna Marie Locke to Donna Marie Rodney; Stig Henry Wilhelm Andreason to Stephen William Andreason; Eleanor M. Hopps to Eleanor M. Horr; Theodore Papadopoulos to Theodore Pappas; Baby Anderson to David Earl Paisley; Lillian M. Smith to Katherine Elaine Donahue; Richard Ryan to Richard Andree Thivierge; Olga Munson Ladin to Olga Munson Lacy; Maxwell H. Ladin to Maxwell H. Lacy; Jeanne Elizabeth Fusco to Jeanne Elizabeth Timmons; Beverly Adele Fusco to Beverly Adele Timmons; Albert Guy Fusco to Albert Guy Timmons; J. Alfred R. Couture to Richard Alfred Couture; Florence Anita Graves to Florence Anita Barcomb; Jane Rose Doucette to Jane Rose Hayes; Peter Jason Lover to Peter Jason Fernald; Joyce May Patterson to Joyce May Gray; Joseph Henry Brown to Warren Howard Perry, Jr.; June Ann Kelley to June Ann Brazis; Carol Anne Young to Carol Ann Marcoux; Jan Cheryl Cullinan to Jan Cheryl Adams; Shirley Ann Hughes to Ency Ellen McCormack; William Frederick Gray to William Frederick Connor; Mary Lois Demers to Mary Lois Grondin; Carol Marie Pichette to Carol Marie Harris; Wayne Chesley Grenier to Wayne Chesley Keays; Patricia Marie Burleigh to Patricia Marie Howard; Margaret Ellen Marquis to Margaret Ellen Pearson; Shirley Louise Hall to Virginia Louise Hall; Richard Hugh Kidder to Richard Hugh Caverly; Edward Norris Kidder to Edward Norris Caverly; Gloria Jean Haycock to Gloria Jean Nichols; Blandine Rose George to Pauline Rose George; Suzanne Gosselin to Barbara Jean Gagne; Donna Louise Glidden to Donna Louise Tarmey; Raymond Francis Williams to Raymond Francis Jussila; Joseph Martin Curran to Martin Joseph Curran; Carole Anne Cummiskey to Carole Anne Bradfield; Prudence Lee DuBois to Bonnie Ellen Mills; Thomas Arthur Stacy to Thomas Arthur Gray

<u>Belknap County</u> - Soterios Palathiotis to Samuel Pallas; Joseph Norman Breton Manning to Norman Joseph Breton; Bella Turlis to Bella Tatakes; Eileen Germain Tong to Eileen Germaine Tong Joyce; Joseph Patrick Altomare to Joseph Patrick Altomare Joyce; John DeMatha Altomare to John DeMatha Altomare Joyce; Victor Emanuel Tong to Victor Emanuel Tong Joyce; Rita Emily Tong to Rita Emily

1945-1947

Tong Joyce; Francis Tong to Francis Tong Joyce; Edward Orville Skinner to Edward Joseph Skinner; Marie Rita Laramie to Marie Bertha Laramie; Barbara May Maxwell to Barbara May Gray; Joseph Wilfred Turcotte to Wilbrod Joseph Turcotte; Donald Arthur Riel to Arthur Donald Riel; Andrew Johnson to Andrew Dolphus Johnson; Arthur Harry Johnson to Arthur Carlton Johnson; Florence Emerson Drew to Florence Emerson Rich; Lucian Gay to Lucien Maurice Guay; George Roland Cardinal to Roland George Cardinal; Joseph Francis Pilote to Frank Pelotte; Robert S. MacDonald to Robert S. Bastraw; Joseph Renault Garneau to Ronald Joseph Garneau; Virginia Maureen Sanders to Virginia Maureen Andrews; Bernice Prudence Elliott to Jerre Elliott; Rose Dora Croteau to Pauline Mary Croteau; Harold Lester Bruce to Harold Lester Brazeau; Kyle Sorrell to Frederick Kyle Sorrell; Elinor Seeley to Eleanor Louise Seeley; ----- Perry to Lorraine Jeanne Poire; Laonia Vallia to Lionel E. Valliere; Daniel G. Watson to Daniel Webster Watson; Esther C. Drury to Esther V. Nixon; Arthur Samson to Armand Paul Samson; Jessie Elizabeth Worcester Jones to Elizabeth Worcester; Mildred L. Murray to Mildred L. Whittey

Changed by Adoption - Raymond Walter Davis to David Merlin Robinson; Pamela Jane Brackett to Jane Clark Riel; David Edgar Isrealian to David Edgar Piper; Beverly Richardson (alias Brooks) to Loris Mae Stone; Theresa M. Morin to Theresa M. Dunn; Virginia Estelle Hanson to Virginia Estelle Holmes; Norman Lewis Wescott to Norman Lewis Jones; Edward George Beattie to Edward George Greemore; Robert Lee Avery to Robert Lee Smith; Richard Raymond Craig to Richard Charles Robinson; Melvin John Knowlton to Ronald Alex Young; Roland G. Ellis to Roland Cleveland Dow; Foster Eddy Varrell to Foster Eddy Varrell; Frank Ernest Eldridge Fowler to Frank Ernest Eldridge; Harold Paul Enwright to Harold Paul Keniston; ----- Hersey to Barbara Pence Mooney; Marie Bliss Hodgson to Marie Bliss Darling; Raymond R. Heath to Raymond R. Fowler; Robert C. Heath to Robert C. Fowler; John Sullivan to John Harold Jones; Richard George Page to Richard George Page; Evelyn Gladys Michaud to Evelyn Gladys Fisher; Bill Sylvester Bascom to Bill Sylvester Waldo, Jr.; Raymond Clinton Johnson to Raymond Clinton Thurston; Edward C. Lecour to Edward Paul Dupuis; Ernest Robert Morrison to Edward Robert Morrison; Joseph Sikorsky to Joseph A. Rowell; Mary Jean Harvey to Karenann Elizabeth Carr; Joanne Learned to Joanne Bean;

1945-1947

Dorothy Beede to Dorothy B. Ellis; Frederick L. Varney to Frederick Varney Moulton; Rose Louise Blackey to Rose Louise Fugere; Henry Julian Fournier to Henry Julian Lemieux

Carroll County - Merle Eugene Smith to Merle Eugene Severy; Jessie A. Ambrose to Pansie A. Ambrose; Otis Conrad Ross to Conrad Ross McCormick; Dorothy Dawn Robinson to Betty Jean Robinson; Barbara Nelson to Barbara Bowles; James Lawrence Pratt to James Lawrence Plummer; Frank Harrison Pratt to Frank Harrison Plummer; Reginald Edward Clancy to Reginald Edward Williams; William Martin to William M. Ainsworth, Jr.; Neal Malcom Rogers to Neal Malcom Hansen; Eric Daniel Hughes to Eric Daniel Corrow; Andrew Lucien Elliott to Richard James Cotton; James Robert Perry to James Rand Edgerly; John David Perry to John Worthy Edgerly

Merrimack County - Harold N. Carey to Harold Arthur Falmer; Charles J. Kolioburdas to Charles James Thomas; James Thomas Kolioburdas to James Thomas; Marion Ruth Kolioburdas tp Marion Ruth Thomas; Ruth Emma Kolioburdas to Ruth Emma Thomas; Irene M. Winslow to Irene M. Perreault; Irene Lorraine Marie Bertrand to Marie Irene Lorraine Stokes; Hazel Mae Barbrick to Hazel Mae Honey; Norman Arthur Letendre to Norman Arthur Pelletier; Howard Russell Beane to Russell Howard Beane; Donaldine Achia Bayley to Nancy Mildred Lees; Alice G. Bushway to Alice Donna Guimond; Anne Carol McDonald to Anne Carol San Soussi; Lombard deGuern Nyman to Lombard deGuern Rice; Holman Witson to Nazzer Aleem; Ernest Earl Bartley to Ernest Earl Plourde; Joseph Edward Nardini to Frank Joseph Nardini; Mildred B. Kenney to Mildred B. Hawthorne; Ellice F. Fannie to Ellice F. Andrews; Evelyn Gertrude Gile to Evelyn G. Dalton; Ethel M. Dunbar Lunt to Ethel M. Dunbar; Nancy Mahomet to Nancy Estelle Mahmot; Joan Louise Bishop to Joanne Louise Bishop; Myrna Selina Howe to Myrna Starratt Howe; Frank J. Karwocki to Frank J. Sullivan; Alice M. Mitchell to Alice Mary Gignac; Thelma Lynn Hitchcock to Madoline Lynn Hitchcock; Andrew J. Karwocki to Andrew J. Sullivan; Carrie E. Ames to Carrie E. Bacon; Frank Gustav Seligson to Frank Gustav Seldon; Elizabeth Juliane Auguste Seligson to Elizabeth Juliane Auguste Seldon; George Herman Lorenz Seligson to George Lawrence Seldon; Walter Flanders Hunt to Francis Perley Hunt; Ethel Manning Walters to Ethel Manning; Dorothy M. Osborne to Dorothy Mary Ford;

1945-1947

Bertha May Park Lamson to Bertha May Park; Reginald Crosby to Reginald Lee Pierce; Dorris Crosby Boyce to Dorris Templeton Boyce; Dorothy Kay Frost to Dorothy Kay Dyment; Angele Lawrencia Toussaint to Angele Lawrencia Rondeau; Marilyn E. Jones to Marilyn Elizabeth Abbott; Mamie Gordon Matott to Mamie G. Gordon; Fernande Douphinett to Fernande Margaret Roy; Margaret S. Boyle to Margaret S. Frost; Lois H. Gantz to Lois Leslie Hammond

Changed by Adoption - "Baby" Gagnon to Robert Roch Ouellette; Angelina Edith Ciarla to Rosemary Ann Coderre; Raymond Arthur Roy to John Ronald Tasker; Robert Williams to Robert Calvin Linscott; Robert Bixby to Robert Bixby Liberty; "Baby" Housman to Robert Rush; Martin Arthur Thornton to Martin Arthur Bowden; John Bragg to Rexford Booth Sherman; Edward H. Marshall, Jr. to Edward H. Marshall; Jean Olive Gould to Jean Olive Berry; Joanna Marie Pieroni to Joanna Marie Masson; "Baby" Lougee to Sonia L. Sydeman; Beverly Mae Grimes to Beverly Mae Ulman; Joseph Paul Marchand to Joseph Paul Gagnon; Beverly Ann Smith to Beverly Ann Taylor; Robert Coburn Fratus to Robert Arthur Coburn; John Cotton to John Robert Fridell; Kent Holmes to Jeffrey Charles Proctor; Barbara Ann Jervah to Lynn Bamford; Carol Ann King to Carol Ann Robinson; Elizabeth Ann Moody to Patricia Elaine Young; John Elliott Plaisted to Charles Eaton Haynes; Richard Douglas Collins to Richard Douglas Denis; Alton David Mooney to Alton David Emery; Francis Clyde Mooney to Francis Clyde Emery; Gail Elizabeth Littlefield to Dorothy Anne Giles; Douglas E. Bickford to Douglas E. Fields; "Baby" Kendall to Jane Alma Stewart; Sharon Lee Smith to Sharon Lee Munsey; "Baby" Cusson to Helene Ann Fortin; Phyllis Jane Elliott to Tashia Edith Elliott; Harriet Kilkis to Harriet Mae Dillon; William Kilkis to William Arthur Dillon, Jr.; Doris Loraine Muzzey to Doris Loraine Carter; "Baby" Thompson to Gerard Roy Boulay; Donna Lorraine Merrill to Donna Lorraine Yeaton; Adele Hasler to Mary Jean Chamberlin; Hope Latham to Hope Latham Holt; Yvonne Therese Lemay to Kris Tina McLaughlin; Ernest Blackman to Levi Ernest Nichols; Rebecca Ann Ciarla to Rebecca Ann Hall; Karen Cecelia Hall to Karen Cecelia Beard; Stanley Burton Hoyt to Stanley Burton Kenney; Myrna Huntington to Carolyn Colby; Robert Allen Lemay to Robert Allen Breslin; "Baby" Wiersma to Barbara Ann Chase; "Baby" Crawford to Bruce Robert Crawford; Teresa Sleeper to Betty Ainsley Griggs; Eldon Roger LaDuke to Eldon Roger Duclos; Robert

1945-1947

Howard Jondreau to Robert Charles Sabin; Emile Arthur Belanger to Raymond Arthur Bradley; Mary Jeannien Francis Gendron to Mary Jeannien Francis Morin; Sharon Lee Armstrong to Sharon Lee Kane; Nellie Gertrude Demers to Nellie Gertrude Meeker; Wayne Douglas Price to Wayne Douglas Gilbert; Jacqueline Morin to Jacqueline McCormick; Paul Morin to Paul McCormick; Dorothy Ann Vanasse to Dorothy Ann Dostie; Diana Cancia Vanasse to Diana Cancia Dostie; Molly Alice Devoid to Molly Alice Zagamy; Robert Alan Ash to Robert Alan Lockwood; Wanita Mae Tanner to Wanita Mae Smith; Joyce Ann Tanner to Joyce Ann Smith

Hillsborough County - George Leo Feurstein to George Leo Firestone; Robert Arnold Saidel to Robert Marcus Saidel; Shirley E. Harding to Shirley Evelyn Sanderson; Wong Suey Hee also known as James Wong to Wong Suey Hee; Joseph Anthony Piaseczny to Joseph John Piaseczny; Albert Homer Gordon to Albert Homer Foster; Robert W. Lee to Robert W. Boulanger; Joseph Stanley Batura to Joseph Stanley Gawel; Stella Babalas to Stella Ballas; Pauline deNault Dondale Elliott to Paule Dondale Elliott; Joseph Henri Albert Ledoux to Henry Albert Ledoux; Mame Tempeli to Mamie DeBelis; Evangeline James Pitarys to Evangeline James; Bronca Yarmotowich to Bronca Yermal; Enoch Richard Nessen to Richard Enoch Nessen; Catherine N. Ouellette to Catherine N. Staite; Julius Cherkas or Czerkis to Julian Charkis; Anthony Daukas to Paul Toli Daukas; Nellie Walenkrikenic also known as Nellie Valentukievicz to Nellie Walent; Joan Beattie to Joan Carpenter Jackson; Julia Bucloveci to Julia Buslovich; Juwel A. A. von Schmiterlow to Jewell Ann Monroe; Lillian Florence Lavoy now Lones to Ruth Eileen (Lavoie) Lones; Pearl Ida Pethick to Pearl Ida Corbin; Grace Maud Piwowarczyk to Grace Maud Bowler; Henry Charles Ryll to Charles Henry Ryll; Odia Lessard St. Francois to Claudia Lessard St. Francois; Kastonta Swaracki to Kastanta Dvareckas; Raymond G. St. Laurent to Raymond G. Maher; Koula Mavrougeorge to Betty George; Zelma Dorothy Snowman to Sallie Knowlton; Lucille Bennett to Lucille Binette; Alexandra Huntington to Sandra Alexandra Huntington; Joseph Morissette to Dorilla Morissette; Marie Lorraine Lucille Hipsher to Lorraine Lucille Godbout; Edmond Armand Roland Lemery also known as Edmond N. Lemery to Armand Edward Edmond Lemery; Philip Edward Poisson to Edward N. P. Fisher; Evangeline Shea to Lillian Evangeline Shea; Adeline Skwarzynski to Adella

1945-1947

Skwara; Mary Alice Theresa Freese to Theresa Mary Freese; Helen Anna Chiuszcz to Helen Anna Chrusz; Carl Casper Cohen to Carl Casper Conrad; Helen Selma Maki to Helen Selma Manninen; Mary June Palnaire to Frances Louise Palriero; Knapp L. Vallas to Larry Knapp Vallas; Robert Paine to Robert Stuart Marsh; Elsie Ann Dery to Elizabeth Ann Dery; Martha Petryczkowycz to Martha Petry; John Petryczkowycz to John Petry; Wasyl Petryczkowycz to Wasyl Petry; Gordon Petryczkowycz to Gordon Petry; Mary Petryczkowycz to Mary Petry; Paul Allen Zeeler to Paul Allen Gallup; Marie Estelle Vivian Lally to Vivian Lally; Irma Louise Todt to Erma Louise Todt; Ellen Naomi Greene to Ellen Naomi Sherwin; Helyn A. Sedlewich to Helyn A. Sullivasn; Ferdinand Frank Kisiolek to Ferdinand Frank Tomashevski; Joseph Walter Rotkiewicz to Joseph Walter Rock; Joseph Pinet to Joseph Pinet Merton; Virginia F. Prichard to Virginia Frank; Alice L. Weinstein to Alice L. Winston; Kenneth Michael Weinstein to Kenneth Michael Winston; Madeline Karen Weinstein to Madeline Karen Winston; Manuel Weinstein to Manny Winston; Fannie Steckewicz to Frances Stitzgerald; Vasilios Apostopoulos to William Apostolos; Margaret McCrink to Margaret Wentworth; Joseph Romeo Lemelin to Romeo Alfred Lemelin; Nadia Buxton to Nadia Dalpra; Milda Jean Leavitt to Jean Forrest Leavitt; Phillip Anthony Saj to Phillip Anthony Sage; Mary Ann Saj to Mary Ann Sage; Alexander Joseph Saj to Alexander Joseph Sage; Leona Vivian Alter to Naomi Leona Vivian Alter; Martha Stanley Saj to Martha Stanley Sage; Emile Leo LaBonte to Emile Leo Lavallee; Katie A. Ryan to Hilda Grace Ryan; Vesalis P. Tsitsos to William P. Tsitsos; Raymond J. Zajaczkowski to Raymond J. Zankowski; Thrassivolos C. Louis Lioliopoulos to Louis C. Lylis; Stergios Apostologoulos to Stephen Apostolos; Pauline Matsopoulos to Pauline Matsis; Barney B. Labunsky to Barney B. Laben; Mary Stepanionis to Mary Anne Stepanon; Edward Stepanionis to Edward Joseph Stepanon; Helen Steponovitch Davis to Helen Stepanon Davis; Mathew John Matsopoulos to Mathew John Matsis; Benny Joseph Krystopowicz to Benny Joseph Kristoff; Wallenty Krzewski to Walter Walent Krewski; Arthur John Matsopoulos to Arthur John Matsis; John Matsopoulos to John Matsis; Frank J. Urgelevicz to Bruce Brenner; Peter Naczas to Peter Natches; Evangelos N. Anagnostopoulos to Van Anagnost; Richard James Daniels to James Robert Rock; Marie Ida Buchesne Brown to Anita Buchesne Brown; Gordon Lee Conrey to Gordon Lee McLaughlin; Fred Hilton Colby to Fred H. Colby Walker;

1945-1947

Francis Michael Dimick to Francis Michael Darrah; Genevieve Mariana Szostakiewicz to Genevieve Mariana Kenick; Teofil John Szostakiewicz to Theodore John Kenick; Mecislaw J. or Mieczyslaw Polchlopek to Matt J. Polk; Barbara M. Tuttle to Barbara M. Frye; Samuel Tabachnick to Samuel Taylor; Nancy Morse Mansfield to Nancy Stewart Morse; Raymond Clarence Gauthier to Raymond Ernest Gauthier; Florence Eva Sumner to Florence Eva Gage; Alphe Paul Emile Melancon to Paul Emile Melancon; Doris Duperron to Doris Bisson; Edward Joseph Gilman to Edward Joseph Guilmain; Arthur German Henderson to Arthur Robert Henderson; Niki Tsourides to Victoria Tsourides; Frances Januzewski to Frances Jackson; Wilfred Roland Raymond to Wilfred Raymond Berube; Lylona Dorothy Whalen to Lylona Dorothy Girard; Constantinos Sakellariou to Charles John Sakellarides; George Wong to Wong Teung Gwong; Thelma E. Green to Thelma E. Crockett; Roselda Claire Berle to Roselda Claire Gebo; Theodora Davis to Theodora Zissis; Sterge A. Papacostas to Sterge A. Costa; Leo Normand Gagnon to Norman Leon Kierstead; William Petryczkowicz or Petrykoz to William Ryan; Lillian Caroline Labombarde to Lillian Caroline Rapsis; Margaret Swart to Margaret Beasom Swart; Marjorie Johnson Dube to Marjorie Johnson; Constance Prudden to Constance Thurber Prudden; Deonizy Krzewski to Daniel Krewski; Bronica Rucz to Bernice Ruez; Wasyl Zylak to Russell Zela; Mikolaj Zyla to Nickey Zela; Saul Gorenstein to Saul Gordon; Peter Zyla to Peter Zela; Alfred Joseph Cossette to Alfred Joseph Biron; Romuald Joseph Champagne to Romeo Joseph Champagne; Leo E. Nusenoff to Leo E. Nason; Rose Marie Peters to Mary Jane Osborne; Doris E. Carter to Doris E. Sanborn; Americo des Santos to Americo Santos; Walter Charles Saj to Walter Charles Sage; Esther Boulanger to Esther Stone; Lillian Mabel Balcom to Lillian Mabel Boynton; Sheila Marlene Pockell to Sheila Bonnie Pockell; John A. Maksymiec to John Adolph Marker; Victoria Xenetimenus Devolites to Victoria Xenas Devolites; Annette Laurie Albrewczenski to Annette Laurie Albren; Fay Collier Nadeau to Fay Laura Collier; Michael Richard Shomsky to Michael Richard Stevens; Ludwik Albrewczenski to Louis F. Albren; Joseph Armand Robert to Armand Joseph Robert; Joseph Alfred Maurice Dupre to Ernest Arthur Lamontagne; Harilaos Demos to Harry Demos; Eleanor Lorraine Stefonowicz to Eleanor Lorraine Stefen; James Gilbert Stefonowicz to James Gilbert Stefen; LeRoy Len Stefonowicz to LeRoy Len Stefen; John G. Bouboulica to

1945-1947

John G. Bolos; Demetrios J. Boubouikas to James Bolos; Robert Lee Kreps to Robert Lee Holden; Zenny Owsink to Zenny Olsen; Panos Stamelos to Peter Stamelos; Wanda Jane Kane to Wanda Jane Kosowicz; Costas Dempelis to Charles Dembelis; Aaron Sumner Marcus to Alan Sterling Marcus; Chan Shui Tong to Charlie Toy Kem; Mary Rose Auger Goulet to Louise Marie Rose Auger Goulet; Kenneth Neal Bishop to Kenneth Neal Pigeon; Jeanette Helen Leary to Jane Helen Leary; Lydia Pilkowicz to Lydia Pokultinis; Laurentia Anastasatos to Laura Anaston; Madeline Carol Doherty to Madeline Carol Dexter; Bruce Davis to James Bruce Davis; Annette Laurie Albrenczenski to Annette Laurie Albren; Ina Hamblin Bureau to Ina Augusta Hamblin; Marjorie L. Doody to Marjorie L. Lambert; Cynthia Claire Bronwen Chappell to Bronwen Claire Chappell; Lucille I. Kusiak to Lucille I. Jauron; Margaret S. Cushing to Margaret S. McCormack; Euridiki P. Karahalios to Everedeke Caris; Fred Kajzy to Fred Keyza; Lucille V. Roberts to Lucille Vincent; Michael Petryczkowycz to Michael Ryan; Yanina Owsink to Anita Olsen; William Edmond L'Homme to William Edmond Manning; Bibian Cote Piper to Bibian Cote; Robert Joseph Butler to Robert Joseph Johnson; Doris Shaw Walters to Doris Shaw; Maurice Martin to Maurice Grugnale

Changed by Adoption - Mary Zienisz to Mary Cormier; Francis Roland Boily to Francis Roland Desmesmeules; Baby Rayno to James William Hall; Shirley Chase to Karen Anne Miles; Brenda Brown to Brenda Ruth Gossler; Terrance Dawson to Terrance Joseph Perrino; James Thomas Layfield to James Thomas Lessard; Mary Fitzgerald to Mary Linda Lee Menter; Alan David Amey to Robert Lewis Clark; Eugene Donald Samson to Eugene Donald Garand; Normand Charles Samson to Norman Charles Garand; Theresa Ouellette to Theresa Hackett; Nancy May Burnham to Nancy May Chandler; Betty Lou Rouleau to Denise Marie Grondin; Elaine Jacqueline Marquis to Elaine Jacqueline Theriault; Edward Simpson to Edward Allard; Baby Bell to Gary Michael Hook; Reginald Billy to David Peter Ouellet; Donald Stanley Koehler to Donald Stanley Sanborn; Lucille Rita Koehler to Lucille Rita Sanborn; Joseph Leonelle Rudolph Huot to Rudolph Lionel Allaire; Joseph Pollock to David James Hosking; Brian Harvey to Brian Paige Bush; Mildred Jean Dansevich to Theresa May Roulx; Eleanor Pearl Leavitt to Eleanor Pearl Cushing; Arthur Paris to Francis Joseph Arthur Prevost; Fernand Jules Paris to Fernand Jules Prevost; Marlene Mae

1945-1947

Kingsbury to Shirley Louise French; Natalie Jean Blumberg to Linda Dwinell; Ronald Dudley to Richard Clarke; Joseph Patrick O'Rourke to Joseph Patrick Wagner; Richard Faro also known as Bergeron to Richard Leo Pratte; Baby Aiken to Cecily Esther Fowler; Rodney J. Pennington to Rodney Pennington Swanson; Pauline Elaine Tack to Pauline Elaine Proulx; Edward A. Whittemore to Edward A. Donnelly; Baby Raymond to Karen Phyllis Howland; Baby Gustitus to Jeannette Lucille Gatto; James Joseph LaBranche to Norman Edward Lampron; Baby Tirrell to James Franklin Barnard; Thomas Hembly Buchan Sydserff to Thomas Corrigan; Alan Francis LeRoux also known as Moffett to Alan Francis Kesterson; Howard Wendell Brown to Howard Wendell Grant; Donald E. Jones to Donald E. Berry; Maurice Suprise, Jr. also known as Pelletier to Maurice Gendron; Mary Ann Gallagher to Mary Ann Calderwood; Juliette Dube to Juliette Blais; Loraine Dube to Loraine Blais; Pauline Dube to Pauline Blais; George Markarian to George Emmons; Garald Lee Abel to Gerald Lee Germain; James Thrasher to Robert James Houle; David Malcolm Carter to David Malcolm Carter Naismith; Barton Warren Hedrick to Barton Warren Chabot; Marie Valcourt to Marie June Knight; James Robet Caron to Rodney Clarence Stone; Judith Elaine Brown to Constance Patricia Breton; Baby Robertson to Nancy Jane Warren; Alfred LeRoy Raymond to Alfred LeRoy Whitney; Charles Raymond Duerbitz also known as Falin to Charles Raymond Shannon; Patricia Anne Fulton to Patricia Anne Case; Shirley Ann Dufresne to Shirley Ann Greenlaw; Donna June Gelardi to Donna Re Starita; Frances Jones to Susan Jo Letzkus; Ann Huddleston to Ann Sheldon Fisher; Jane Owens McClure to Jane Austin Doty; Terry Veane McKee to Terry Veane Signor; Karol Tine Yianahopolas to Robert George Carignan; James Edward Sornberger to James Edward Doyle, Jr.; Pamela Joyce Goodall to Pamela Joyce DeLorme; Alice Porter to Ellen Alice Donnelly; Jeanot Konigs to Jeanno Cholette; Leon Albert Dionne to Leon Albert Prince; Philip LaPointe to Philip Savageau; Alice Mary Grimard to Alice Mary Dextras; Jo Anne Rowman to Jo Anne Battistelli; James Robert Trottier to Donald Paul Dubois; Cynthia Lee Hutson to Cynthia Lee Dugas; Marie Ellen Jenks to Marie Ellen Farrington; James Edward Clark to James Edward Schuessler; Robert David Briand to Robert David Webster; Paul Hamson to Kenneth Brigham George; Dolores Theresa O'Sullivan to Nancy Przybyla; Alice McGovern to Betty Ellen Greenwood; Wayne Burton Gorman to Wayne Burton Hartwell; Earl

1945-1947

Kenneth Rivers to Earl Kenneth Anderson; Nellie Butler to Nellie Murphy; Raymond Emery Marcoux to Caliph Girard; Erma B. Claxton to Erma Bernadine Townsend; Patricia Ann Ireland to Patricia Ann Manning; Baby Cummings to Ronald Taylor Rogers; Richard Henry Connor to Richard Henry Parmenter; Marie Ann Ruest to Marie Anna Anderson; Walter Edmund Maple to Walter Edmund Castro; Sandra Carol Ditmore to Sandra Carol Voth; Sean David Foley to Richard Paul Allaire; Francis Fecteau to Francis Parent; Phillip Roland Gray to Phillip Roland Stickney; Ronald Lawrence Gray to Ronald Lawrence Stickney; Frank L. Hartshorn, Jr. to Roger Lee Lagasse; Linda Lee Patkus to Tamisan June Little; Richard Clinton Mousseau to Richard Clinton Leonard; Shirley Ann Joy to Shirley Ann Lazotte; Marilyn Kay Kenyon Kovach to Marilyn Kay Auger Kovach; May Enid Marcotte to May Enid Coffin; Marion Stella Dickerman to Margaret Kennard; Charles Francis McGowan to Raymond Robert Marquis; Norma Lee Bolduc to Norma Lee Sosnowski; Baby Sadowski to Walter J. Harrington, 2d; Baby Neilsen to Peter John Heikkila; Thomas J. Kenyon, Jr. to Thomas J. Auger; Eva Rose Shirley Paul to Shirley Eva Rose Dyer; Richard Gene Daigle to Richard Arthur Lessard; Anthony Robert Marcotte to Anthony Robert Spinelli; Alfred William Paul, Jr. to Alfred William Dyer; Garry Schellenger to Gary Cote; Anne Elizabeth Harris to Anne Elizabeth Harris Bishop; Carol Esta Wilkinson to Carol Esta Collins; Baby Westerhoff to Robert Edward Reagan; Phyllis Morrissette to Phyllis Duguay; Andrea Lee Vaillancourt to Andrea Lee Hautsch; Joseph Oliver Maurice Daigle to Maurice Joseph Janelle; Doris Marie Duval to Marie Doris Beverly Menard; Joanena Mae Bugbee to Joanena Mae Salvas; Judith M. Karstok to Judith M. Parzych; Patricia Ann Reed to Patricia Ann Faulkingham; Thomas Lashua to Lawrence Harold Knudsen; Baby Laroche to Barbara Aline Scholth; Thomas Manley Sharpe, 3rd to Thomas Manley Peck; Linda Ann Rodonis to Linda Ann Flanders; Irene Pauline Gagnon to Irene Pauline Plaurd; Bruce Errol Hart to Paul Scott Pendleton; Baby Mack to Jo Leslie Bechard; Virginia Louise Salo to Janice Vianne LaPierre; Merline Jessie Cody to Merline Jessie Dyer; Marie Joan Gelinas to Marie Joan Hurd; Theresa Doris Beaulac to Doris Theresa Janelle; Louise Rachel Forcier to Louise Rachel Robbins; Jeannette Boulay to Jeannette Malenfant; Anne Mae Albert to Anne Mae Fournier; Doris Lussier to Nancy Ann Winter; Joan Rita Bourque to Beverly Rita Burns; Yvette Cecile Bolduc to Yvette

1945-1947

Cecile Gregoire; Marie-Jeanne Carmen Laverdiere to Carmen Laverdiere

Cheshire County - Philip Patterson to Harry J. Patterson; Mary Hyla Waite to Hyla Marie Waite; Raymond Ernest Wilson to Raymond Everett Wilson; Donna Lee Wadsworth to Donna Lee Wadsworth; Barbara Christine Smith to Barbara Christine Miles (Flagg); Mary Castaw to Lucinda Mary Castaw (Bouffard); Elena Micaroni to Elena M. Colantonio; Alice Bartoscheyce to Tatiana Alice Bartaschevich; Verner Nelson Edoff, Jr. to Nelson Verner Edoff; Rudolph Nelson Buffum to Rudolph Nelson Flanders; Philip Austin Hubbard to John Austin Hubbard; Vargey L. Dombrowski to Roger Stanley Dubriskie; Robert James Stoodley to Robert James Croteau; Francis Clifford Burrell to Francis Clifford Paquette; Maude Twitchell to Olive Maude Twitchell; Louise Ann Kennedy to Louise Ann Porter; Catherine Emily Soucise to Catherine Viola Soucise; Paul Kenneth Freeman to Paul Kenneth Daniels; James R. Lavigne to James Roland Holt; Mitchell Robert Bradbury to Robert Mitchell Bradbury; Frank Exavier Wilcox to Frank Exavier Turcotte; Cyrille Alphonse Wilcox to Cyrille Alphonse Turcotte; Henry George Wilcox to Henry George Turcotte; Charles Wescott Giles to Hollis Whitcomb Abbott; Robert Francis Farinoli to Robert Francis Shepard; Lawrence Herbert Bisonette to Lawrence Herbert Karson; Henrietta Lindquist Bissonette to Edith Henrietta Karson; Lawrence Eno Bissonette to Lawrence Eno Karson; Carol Betsey Whitcomb (maiden name) to Irene Elizabeth Wilder (maiden name) (Towsley); Charles Walter Howland to Donald Charles Kellom; Grace Evelyn Whitcomb to Grace Evelyn Kelley; Virginia Alice Bitters to Virginia Alice Luce; William Ancil Dorais to William Ancil Dailey; Anthony John Tasoulas to Christo John Tasoulas; Sara Franklin Ripley to Sally Franklin Ripley; Alfred Joseph Minkiewicz to Alfred Joseph Kelley; Marilyn Louise Babineau to Marilyn Louise Britton; Phyllis Jeanne Watson to Phyllis Efland Watson; Beverly Ann Poisson to Beverly Ann King; Sandra Ann Hall to Sandra Ann Davis; Patricia Louise Beam to Patricia Louise Bissell; Amedeo Sabatini, Jr. to David Boynton Staples; Barbara M. Hall to Barbara M. Sargent; Beverly Lorraine Richards to Beverly Lorraine Lessard; Philip Joseph Crecco to Philip Joseph Collins; Nastsia Julia Olinsky to Judith Olinsky; William J. Bedaw, Jr. to William J. Bedard; Parayula K. Kontinos to Eugenia K.

1945-1947

Kontinos; Marfoula Zahos to Morfia Georgia Zahos; Richard Harold Worcester to Richard Harold Whittemore; Antonia Laura Knapp to Antonia Barbara Knapp; Frank B. Mills to Avanda Elmer Meader

Changed by Adoption - Edward Thomas Case to David Stephen Calef; George Edward Robbins to George Edward Wilson; Paul Henry Barard to Henry Paul Desrosiers; Joyce Ruby Fennessy to Joyce R. Bingham; Doris Irene Mattson to Doris Irene Tielinen; William Foley to William Foley Coughlin; Sherry Lynn Horton to Sherry Lynn Carey; Thomas Woodward to Leonard Bursey Fuller; Douglas Lee MacKenzie to Douglas Lee Good; Oscar J. Thayer, Jr. to James Joseph Audet; Gardner Guillow Smith to Gardner Guillow Wyman; Jane McHardy Bland to Jane McHardy Leverich; Richard H. Columb to Richard Horace Wilder; Beverly Jean Dicey to Beverly Jean Reason; George Arthur Cole to George Arthur Hall; Richard Norman to John Leroy Blood; Laura Patricia Thayer to Laura Patricia Doran; Barbara Newell to Barbara Keenan; Arnold John Pelletier to James Arthur Beauregard; Anita Agnes Dutton to Anita Agnes Donnelly; Vichi Marie LaFarr to Mildred Marie Marcott; Joel Alan Braverman to Joel Alan Brault; Larry Wayne Bissell to Edward Meehan Elliott; Bonnie Lee McCollester to Bonnie Lee Abare; Joyce Elaine Weeks to Joyce Elizabeth Knapp; Arthur M. Economu to Arthur M. Dunlap; Robert G. Economu to Robert G. Dunlap; Gail Ann Patnode to Gail Ann Boudrieau; Jean Christina Hovaness to Jean Christina Brandt-Erichsen; Warren Frederick Chamberlin to Warren Frederick Pierson; Robert Allen Salatas to Robert John Tedford; Donna Jean Forsyth to Donna Jean Carey; William Chris Jean to Nicola Tachi Tjimaki; Richard Parks to Richard Charles Skiffington; Jane Doe to Nancy Virginia Holt; Richard Edwin Duval to Richard Edwin Pickford; Judith Ann Morse to Lee Plaisted Hanna

<u>Sullivan County</u> - Richard Allen Howe to David John Nutting; Roger Mack to Roger Mack Nichols; Richard Reid to Kern Warren Rhoades; Katherine Suko to Katherine Mantia; Josie Kawzowicz to Josephine Ann Kawzowicz; Tamara Carylin Hodder to Carylin Sturgis; William Webster Vandergrift to Billey B. Van, Jr.; Blanche Theresa Mignault to Theresa Melcher; Marie Violet Mignault to Violet Melcher; Cleomenis Anastasios Fragopulos to Cleo Anastasios Franklin; Georgia Vina

1945-1947

Fragopulos to Vina Racheotes Franklin; Elaine Cleo Fragopulos to Elaine Cleo Franklin; Peter Ernest Fragopulos to Peter Ernest Franklin; Doris Elizabeth Merton to Doris Elizabeth Connolley; Larry M. Petrin to Larry Maurice Trepanier; Charlotte Marie Desiderio to Charlotte Marie Thibodeau; Mary Pikielnez to Mary Soja Johnson; Robert Maurice Rideout to Robert Maurice Caron; Virginia E. Smith to Virginia E. Brown; Mary William Milios to Mary William Miller; Stanley William Milios to Stanley William Miller; Alexander William Milios to Alexander William Miller; Theophile Niebrzydoski to Teofil Nebrydoski; Jadwiga Niebrzydoski to Jadwiga Nebrydoski; Joanne Niebrzydoski to Joanne Nebrydoski; Donald Dubrieul G. to Donald G. White; Francis Desmond to Frank E. Desmond; Rose Marie Clow to Rose Marie Eastman; Sandra Bond to Sandra Silver; Joan P. Belair to Joan P. Small; Robert Earl Freeman to Robert Earl Freeland; Tarmo Tapio Taimi to Thomas Tapio Taimi; Sandra Jane Howser to Nancy Ruth Ainsworth; Paul N. Murphy to Paul N. Goyette; Chloe A. Murphy to Chloe A. Goyette; Carol Ann Maskell to Shirley Louise Benner; Evelyn Lorraine Kennison to Evelyn Lorraine Dahms; Paul Francis Richards to Paul Francis Hart; Helen Elizabeth Baker to Betty Ann Gorman; Gary Victor Gagner to Gary Victor Small; Frederick G. Gunn to Frederick M. Gunn; Joy Ann Clarke to Joy Ann Kinney; Jerry Wayne Smith to Jerry Wayne Huston; Rocco John Avery to Rocco John Tetreault; Francis Alfred Avery to Francis Alfred Couture; Anthony Albert Avery to Anthony Albert Sanford; Donald I. Sanborn to Donald I. Manning; Lawrence Gonsalves to Lawrence Converse; Donald Paul Bond to Donald Paul Pederson; George Everett Colby to George Everett Blue; Florence Lillian Foote Howard to Lillian Florence LaRue Howard; Helen E. Koivista to Irene Helen Koivisto; Lee June Pride to Lee June Moore; Guy Arthur Page to Robert Arthur Page; Francis Alexander King to Francis Alexander Taggart; Lee Andrew Christensen to Lee Andrew Carroll; Lee Andrew Carroll to Lee Francis Carroll; Michael Gary Bowker to Michael Gary Walker; Stephen Gerard Champagne to Andre Descoteau; Cecil Dan Nutting to Cecil Dan Currier; Patricia O'Connor to Patricia Pelton; Robert Carlyle Nichols to Robert Carlyle LaClair; Valma Loring Nottage to Valma Ray; Kenneth John Margeson to Marc Albert DeRobertis; Francis S. Brownell to Francis S. Collins; Carol Ann Coyer to Carol Ann Gendron; Helen Fisette Bellinger to Helen Kinney Bellinger; Joseph Philip Fisette to Robin Joseph Philip Kinney; Janet Lee Hamel to Janet Lee Thalasinos; Ann Ida Hannah Shulins to Anne Meredith Shulins;

1945-1947

Donna Elizabeth Sheehan to Donna Elizabeth Boemig; Clair Rosemary Coles to Claire Rosemary Pomeroy; Neal Oakes Fairbanks to Neal Oakes Rice; Hugh Knight, Jr. to Hugh Barker; Judith Ann Tallman to Jane Louise Dustin; Velma M. Bean to Velma M. Lafountaine; Sadie M. Wilson to Sadie M. Fedelski; Myrtle E. Fountain to Myrtle Edith Ogden; Anna H. O'Rourke to Anna H. Erickson; Gladys Young to Gladys Stockholm; Emily Van Dusen to Emily Szalucka; Gertrude A. McPhee to Gertrude A. Hentschel; Alice F. Tenney to Alice F. Mason; Jeannette E. Kimball to Jeannette E. Dunn; Betty Kebalka to Elizabeth Rollins; Gertrude A. Moylan to Gertrude L. Ahern; Eleanor Y. Chapman to Eleanor M. Young; Bessie Hyman Ratner to Bessie Hyman; Beverly Elizabeth Lewis to Beverly Elizabeth Dewey; Georgeana R. Spoone to Georgeana R. Powell

<u>Grafton County</u> - Romolus Amorosino to John Amorosino; Malcolm Vance Armstrong to Malcolm Armstrong Lackey; Marilyn A. Bennett to Marilyn A. Batchelder; Harold William Baldwin to Harold William Sanders; Rutherford Philip Bagley to Philip Rutherford Bagley; Gordon Joseph Baillie to Gordon Joseph Stuart; Beverly Florence Bedard to Beverly Florence Thibodeau; Burl Louis Bedard to Burl Louis Thibodeau; David Edward Bedard to David Edward Thibodeau; Archie Raimond Bowles to Raimond Bowles; Hugo Lapquist Cox to Jon Eldon Cox; Robert Curtis Clark to Robert Curtis Lower; Arthur J. Cranshaw to Arthur James Cranshaw Borry; Alice Helen Douglass to Janet Caro St. Lawrence; Merton Elwin Dunham to Merton Elwin Lovely; Ronald Fields to Ronald Converse; Baby Gile to Russell Dow Rankin; Roland J. Gamache to Roland J. Gault; Francis William Geeb to Charles William Tarr; Baby Humphrey to David Anthony Picozzi; Jane Haskell to Jane Gibson; William Lee Hart to Howard Hollis Whitcomb; Sandra Mae Hall to Sandra Mae Seamans; William Haskins to William George Wayne Peabody; Gilbert Warfield Haley to Max Gilbert Haley; Richard Jackson to Wendell Lear Woodward; Melinda Ann Jordan to Linda Louise Hill; Henry Thurston Johnson to Richard Ashley Maynard; Catherine Ann Kolinsky to Catherin Ann Belanger; Gene Arthur Langmaid to Gene Arthur French; Mona Ann Leach to Paula Grace Leavitt; Dianna Theresa LaFlamme to Norma Jean Clough; Baby Ludgate to John Robert Bailey; Beverly Joan Leonard to Beverly Joan White; Daniel Carlisle LaBonte to Karl Edwin Kelly; Marilyn Morris to

1945-1947

Esmeralda Wendy Triller; Sharlene Jean Merrill to Sharlene Olney Young; Linda Anne Marrone to Linda Anne French; Dorothy Fay McCollum to Dorothy Fay Downer; Mildred L. McCollum to Mildred Louise Downer; Bertha Geneva Mulherin to Brenda Mulherin; Barbara Muir McAuliffe to Barbara Virginia Muir; William Carrol Martinez to Richard Earl Gray; Mary Ann Marcotte to Mary Lydia Hill; Baby Boy Olsen to David Andrew Brown; Jacqueline Pratt to Jacqueline Ellis; Reginald Bruce Page to Bruce Reginald Miller; Marie Sonja Pare to Janet Lee Bisson; Patricia Ann Putnam to Kay Cooney; Gordon Earl Roberts to Gordon Earl Hannett; Katharyn Evelyn Saari to Catherine Melissa Brown; Richard Lewis Semons to Richard Lewis Barnes; Cecile May Stevens to Cecile May Landry; Richard Wayne Smith to Richard Arthur Fletcher; Henry Roger Smith to Michael Elgin Andross; Winona Mae Spaulding to Winona Mae Paro; Lorraine Jean Splude to Lorraine Jean Haynes; Jeanne Marion Smith to Jeanne DeWoody Gile; Luther Lyall Williamson to Frederick Luther Williamson; Douglas Willard to Mary Wesley Triller; Edwin Webb to Charles Franklin Carle; Allen L. Weeks to Allan Davis Emerton; Janice Elaine Weeks to Janice Elaine Emerton; Bertha Mae Wiggin to Bertha Mae Martin

Coos County - Grace M. Hurlbert to Grace M. Keach; Lillian M. Provencher to Lillian Tremaine; Gladys M. Rice to Gladys Mae Gove; Florence Beverly Griffeth to Florence Beverly Hartford; Mary E. Lewis to Mary Maloney; Doris C. Nolet to Doris C. Levesque; Laura B. Rosenberg to Laura B. Hunter; Berta H. Brigham to Berta Hope Kingston; Elizabeth L. Mahan to Olive Marie Larrivee; Roland Houle to Roland Theriault; Doris Eva Aube to Doris Eva Aubey; Angie Bernadine Martin to Bernadine Martin; Natalie Twitchell to Natalie McRae; Raymond Johnson to Raymond Nichols; Paul Jean Jalbert to Paul Leon Gilbert; Annie Nora Lebnon to Nora Labnon; Faheem Lebnon to Norman Michael Labnon; Barbara Corey to Barbara Labnon; Elias M. L. Corey to Louis Michael Labnon; Monassa Lebnon Corey to Morris Michael Labnon; Elizabeth Labnon to Alice Labnon; Michael Lebnon Cory to Michael Labnon; Anna Means Lepage to Anna Blanche Means; Marjorie Florence Holman to Marjorie Florence Betz; Roland Donald Rowell to Roland Donald Young; David Wolfgang Bernay to David Wolfgang Bernheimer; Laura Dauphinais to Laura Dauphney; Clifford Walter Dauphinais to Clifford Walter Dauphney; Robert Thomas

1945-1947

Lonsdale to Robert Thomas McGee; Lebnon Michael Corey to Anthony T. Labnon; Tonia Lebnon Corey to Daniel Anthony Labnon; Martin Niemi to Martin Temple; Joseph Armand Philemon Couture to Joseph Armand Philemon Rousseau; Roy E. Bishop to Roy E. Merrow; Maria Elvira DiProspero to Marie Elvira Frechette; Ronald Leslie Jalbert to Ronald Leslie Gilbert

Changed by Adoption - Donald Edward Welch to Donald Edward Flynn; "Infant" Murphy to Charles Joseph Dickey; Catherine Janice Fuller to Catherine Janice Connary; Priscilla Ann Fisk to Priscilla Ann Parker; "Infant" Smith to Bonnie Dae Spencer; David Arthur Vincent to David Arthur Giroux; Rose Irene Pelchat to Rose Irene Leclerc; Leonard Ronald Leach to Ronald Joseph Dandeneau; Diane Mary Page to Mary Gertrude Yvonne Caron; Priscilla Fern Willey to Susan Althea Erickson; Leonard Ronald Joseph Nolet to Roland Joseph Routhier; Allen Barbin to Richard Robert Patrick; Rita Rose Marie Landry to Rita Rose Marie Suffill; "Annette" ----- to Annette Napert; Stephen Hapgood Mills to Stephen Hapgood Shoff; Rita Rose Marie Remillard to Rita Rose Marie Nadeau; "Patricia Ann" ------ to Mary Ann Massey; "Baby" Gagne to Judith Elaine Groves; Dorothy Jean Murphy to Francis Ann Lajoie; Richard James Cozzi to Richard James Dionne; Joseph Floribert Auger to Richard Joseph DeBlois; "Baby" Coe to James Eric Brown; Nancy Anne Bickford to Nancy Anne Mortenson; Alice Mary Frabee to Alice Mary Cote; Agnes Ann Frabee to Agnes Anne Cote; George Robert Houley to Robert Gerald Michaud; "Baby" Hayes to David Pickering Morse; Patrick O'Neil to Patrick O'Neil Connelly; Diane Childs to Marianne Keir; "Infant" McGinnis to Leonard Lawrence Morel

Name changes made by the superior court in divorce proceedings:

Rockingham County - Virginia A. Berlin to Virginia A. Stevens; Vivian H. Frink to Vivian G. Howard; Dorothy J. Petro to Dorothy J. Winn; Edythe M. Tessicini to Edythe L. Holt; Helen B. Cox to Helen B. Heskett; Elizabeth Liberty to Elizabeth Baker; Beatrice L. Sturtevant to Beatrice L. Brown; Frances P. Alain to Frances P. Emery; Velma E. O. Arsenault to Velma E. O. Senter; Esther M. Bangs to Esther M. Davis; Frances A. Barry to Frances A. Dion; Emma E. Buckley to Emma E.

1945-1947

MacLean; Rose V. Hubbard to Rose V. Barthelemy; Mildred Raitt Parker to Mildred C. Raitt; Helen M. Gammon to Helen M. Cotnoir; Phyllis I. Gately to Phyllis I. Ashford; Phoebe H. Gray to Phoebe H. McLane; Olive Horton to Olive O'Leary; Ninetta Kozlowski to Ninetta Luce; Mary F. Brite to Mary F. Smith; Adeline Evelyn DiAngelis to Adeline Evelyn Novelle; Geneva B. Downing to Geneva Bartlett; Valentine M. Erickson to Valentine J. Marcuri; Alice L. Heger Felch to Alice L. Heger; Christine M. Lasher to Christine M. Heacock; Martha Josephine Parks to Martha Josephine Rice; June Semple to June Bond; Mary L. Spinelli to Mary Louise Trefethen; Virginia Constance Zahn to Virginia Constance Stafford; Shirlie A. Lydon to Shirlie A. Arnold; Evelyn A. McQuarrie to Evelyn A. Ross; Josephine J. Novak to Josephine Jewell; Geraldine Frances Wagner to Geraldine Frances Trafton; Charlotte J. Cole to Charlotte Jeanette Wendell; Rita Edwards to Rita Federick; Florence M. Keough to Florence M. Gray; Beatrice I. Blais Cole to Beatrice I. Bliss; Elizabeth M. King to Elizabeth M. Harvey; Margaret Allen to Margaret Kelley; Ethel Mae Charious to Ethel Mae Jones; Victoria Ginalski to Victoria Tomaszewska; Nancy G. Goodwin to Nancy G. Hoyt; Thelma P. Groder to Thelma P. Ingalls; Frances Marjorie Huseby to Frances Marjorie Trefethen; Norma F. Lenane to Norma L. Frost; Barbara Virginia Noble to Barbara Virginia Harvey; Hazel M. Shina to Hazel M. Nichols; Barbara H. Willette to Barbara Helen Paul; Emma J. Eriksson to Emma J. Nelson; Shirlie E. Perkins to Shirlie E. Rowe; Adrienne Delphine Watts to Adrienne Delphine Rioux; Shirley Ellen Welch to Shirley Ellen Webber

Strafford County - Pearl G. McDonough to Pearl G. Lewis; Mary P. C. Proulx to Mary Pauline Clairmont; Irene P. Gagne to Irene P. Nault; Priscilla R. Labonte to Priscilla R. Maine; Georgia Zorbas to Georgia George; Violet G. Allison to Violet Eastman; Joyce E. Putt to Joyce Elizabeth Brown; Marilyn M. Robbins to Marilyn M. Clark; Cecile Carignan Johnstone to Cecile Carignan; Florence M. Seneca to Florence M. Jimerson; Rose D. Habel to Rose Delima Hebert; Mattie M. Speco to Mattie M. Riley; Mildred Esther Watts to Mildred Esther Hyllman; Barbara E. Quimby to Barbara E. Bennett; Lillian M. Wakefield to Lillian M. Chapman; Freda B. Jackson to Freda E. Burrows; Germaine G. Holland to Germaine G. Goupil; Lois A. Wallingford to Lois Appleton; Gabrielle M. Smith to Gabrielle M. Elliott; Winifred B. Lincoln to Winifred Elois Bowley; Marjorie L. MacKenzie to

1945-1947

Marjorie Louise Charette; Marion H. Potts to Marion Hall; Barbara M. Pickup to Barbara H. Masury; Thelma F. Haywood to Thelma Fay Thompson; Eunice Thayer Young to Eunice E. Thayer; Chrysanthe Athans to Chrysanthe Constantopoulos; Theresa M. Champagne to Theresa M. McCabe; Lillian A. Girard to Lillion A. Norton; Ellen Harmon Michaud to Ellen Harmon; Joan W. Kelly to Joan W. Carry; Lena R. Forcier to Lena R. Routhier; Ruth R. Smith to Ruth R. Shaw; Myrtie L. Watson to Myrtie L. Gould; Anna A. Otis to Anna A. Hutchins

Belknap County - Alberta T. Bush to Alberta T. Kellock; Mildred Julia Clark to Mildred Julia Hamel; Laurette Messier Cotton to Laurette Messier; Fitzpatrick Dufour to Patrick Dufour; Leona M. Gagnon to Leona M. Rollins; Geraldine M. Gleason to Geraldine M. Peary; Catherine H. Israelian to Catherine H. Matthews; Rena C. Marcouex to Rena C. Laplante; Cora E. Provencal to Cora E. Towns; Yvonne Savage to Eva Savage; Loretta M. Smith to Loretta M. Drowns; Phyllis Marion Smith to Phyllis Marion Crockett; Thurley A. Spooner to Thurley A. Trumbull; Rita Bernadette Dion to Rita Bernadette Fortin; Pearl E. Reed to Pearl E. Flanders; Caroline Greenwood Johnson to Caroline Charlotte Greenwood; Roxanna H. Lancaster to Roxanna Harmon; Nellie C. Royal to Nellie C. Bryant; Elizabeth Rausch Merrill to Elizabeth Rausch; Mabel C. Scarborough to Mabel C. Potter; Doraine E. Dodge to Doraine E. Batchelder

Carroll County - Beatrice M. Stillings to Beatrice M. Sleeper; Mae S. Capri to Mae E. Stanley; Ona I. Knight to Ona J. Bond; Isabel R. Vaughn to Isabel Rector; Ruth E. Welch to Ruth E. Pearson

Merrimack County - Alberta E. VanDenburgh to Alberta Eleanor Sims; Gladys T. Sanborn to Gladys Collins Towle; Irene F. Breckney to Irene F. Fleury; Mary B. Badger to Mary E. Besse; Miriam S. Nelson to Miriam Alma Stover; Barbara M. Kimball to Barbara May Crawford; Mildred F. Mussey to Mildred F. Tucker; Alice J. Meeks to Alice J. Cass; Marion G. Banks to Ruth Marion Prowse; Jennie F. Johnson to Lennie F. Burdick; Dorothy Louise Nunes to Dorothy Louise Wing; Victoria L. French to Victoria L. Reid; Annie L. Campbell to Annie L. Stewart; Helen Cheney Miller to Helen Cheney; Agnes D. MacCowan to Agnes D. Farnum; Dorothy L. Andberg to Dorothy L. Rogers; Ida Ruth Bonner to Ida Ruth Brent; Dora F. LaFerte to Dora F. McGarey;

1945-1947

Isabelle Gaillardetz to Isabelle Albert; Bertha W. Sprague to Bertha Margaret Williams; Eva Annette Wing to Eva Annette Oakes; Gene Grow Dykeman to Gene Patrick Grow; Nellie Anderson to Nellie Wescott

Hillsborough County - Cynthia Clifford to Cynthia Erskine; Mae Dorney Westerdahl to Mae Dorney; Mary L. Stevens to Mary Lyon; Lucille Douville to Lucille Lessard; Marie A. Turcotte Isabelle to Marie A. Turcotte; Nellie W. Lyons to Nellie W. Hanley; Marion R. Stark to Marion R. Talbot; Lauretta Duclos to Lauretta Frenette; Alice M. Grant to Alice M. Paul; Blanche Katulak to Blanche Kozacki; Janet Szemela to Janet Gilbert; Helen Firestone Parker to Helen Firestone; Laurence Y. Blake to Laurence Y. Lamothe; Emily Stantial to Emily Battersby; Mary Ann MacDonald to Mary Ann Buxton; Jeanne P. Pouliot to Jeanne P. Boisvert; Marie A. Somers to Marie A. Chouinard; Marion H. Sargent to Marion Edna Hersey; Virginia Dolores Ann Piecuch to Virginia Dolores Ann Morey; Marie L. Fleury to Marie L. O'Brien; Elizabeth R. Tanczos to Elizabeth R. Watkins; Evangeline Moulton to Evangeline Hines; Myrtle Lee Puckett to Myrtle Lee Barnes; Ellen French Odekirk to Ellen French; Phyllis Von Iderstine to Phyllis Tuttle; Mada Pritchard to Mada Harriman; Leovina Alice Cullinan to Leovina Alice Worth; Lois Drabinski to Lois Allen; Florence Pierce to Florence Deroche; Ethel A. Brown to Ethel Anna Keefe; Dorothy Mae Kennedy to Dorothy Mae Wilson; Regina L. Guichard to Regina L. Dichard; Margaret E. Carder to Margaret E. Young; Blanche Irene Daneault to Blanche Irene Granz; Frances J. Garabedian to Frances G. Johnson; Lillian E. Clark to Lillian E. Putnam; Dorila U. Fraser to Dorila Ursula Wilson; Alyce Moore to Alyce Williams; Germaine A. Vachon to Germaine A. Theriault; Celeste Fyffe to Celeste Melin; Ethel P. Boucher to Ethel P. Wordios; Edna V. Trudeau to Edna V. Stone; Barbara R. Simons to Barbara R. Seymour; Ethel S. Nicholson to Ethel M. Sprague; Claire L. Roy to Claire L. Lambert; Adella Zautra to Adella H. Jazel; Ella Huskie Legault to Ella Huskie; Dorothy M. Dorsett to Dorothy M. Ralph; Lillian P. Walsh to Lillian P. Mayou; Helen E. Cutting to Helen E. Morrell; Beverly Pelletier to Beverly Clark; Ursula M. Bagley to Ursula M. Couture; Marian Burke to Marian Shaw; Anita Elise Mitchell to Anita Elise Levesque; Theresa Dempsey to Theresa Lucier; Alberta M. Jacob to Alberta May Burbank; Irene Niquette to Irene Biron; Eva Ouellette to Eva Levesque; Marion E. Clark to Marion E. Coney;

1945-1947

Helen Rogers to Helen Sullivan; Florence B. Minott to Florence B. Horton; Helen Mary Kofer to Helen Mary Bruno; Margaret B. Marquis to Margaret B. Jacobson; Dorothy Bergeron to Dorothy Hartshorn; Charlotte Ames Gallo to Charlotte Ames; Arlene P. Harriman to Arlene P. Pierce; Yvette Francoeur to Yvette Ricard; Irelean English to Irelean Moulton; Daisy F. Matthews to Daisy F. Burpee; Charlotte B. Brazelton to Charlotte Bargiel; Doris M. Toscano to Doris M. O'Brien; Betsey S. MacDonald to Betsey Adams Schadt; Marion Grace Gauthier to Marion Grace Dunican; Antoinette Prince to Antoinette Ermalovich; Rita Naro to Rita Savoie; Beatrice R. Rahmanop to Beatrice R. Allen; Ruth E. Brown to Ruth E. Felch; Juliette Lloyd to Juliette Gagne; Emilienne O. Gabirel to Emelienne O. Lajoie; Muriel Bertha Grauer to Muriel Bertha Gouin; Dorothy Rudisill to Dorothy Murphy; Genevieve E. Cherry to Genevieve E. Waters; Alexina M. Peppin to Alexina Marie Lussier; Jeanne C. Dufour to Jeanne C. Theriault; Lena Marie Gallagher to Lena Marie Rainville; Mae Hayes to Mae DeWaele

Cheshire County - Doris Lambert Phillips to Doris Lambert Wyman; Bernice Elnora Lavigne to Bernice Elnora Holt; Catherine Amelia Hemeon to Catherine Amelia Champney; Beverly Maranda Warriner to Beverly Maranda Phelps; Theresa Shirley Lampman to Theresa Shirley Ward; Avis L. Simons to Avis Leona LaBelle; Phyllis M. Tyo to Phyllis Marie Kent; Virginia A. Read to Virginia Alice Goodrum; Ida Berman to Ida Tenofsky; Betty Miller Canavan to Betty Miller; Hulda M. Norton to Hulda May Morrill; Margaret E. Howard to Margaret Elizabeth Russell; Jeanette P. Navish to Jeannette Louise Parizo; Ethel I. Sizemore to Ethel I. Cutter; Bertha D. Heil to Bertha Dostilio; Irene M. Deyo to Irene Marie Lamoreux; Amy Demerse Burns to Amy Dodge Demerse; Gloria L. Goodell to Gloria Mae Lane; June P. King to June P. Howland; Eleanor M. MacDonald to Eleanor M. Vigneault; Lila E. Fuller to Lila E. Wilder; Dorothy W. Calkins to Dorothy W. Marchand; Mildred T. Barron to Mildred T. Solomon; Lena Shine to Lena Sharkey; Elizabeth Jean Fair to Elizabeth Jean Briggs; Anna S. Conway to Anna Sanstock

[Sullivan County - not reported]

Grafton County - Vivian B. Shortt to Vivian L. Brown; Isabelle H. Perron to Isabelle Hutchinson; Eleanor Worthley Dickinson to Eleanor

1945-1947

Worthley; Charlotte M. Howard to Charlotte Adele Marchetti; Ruth Ann St. Pierre to Ruth Ann Dow; Ida Sargent to Ida Davis; Mary A. Davio to Mary A. Hansen; Esther Louise Lynde to Esther Louise Taylor; Helen R. Mason to Helen R. Soper; Anita M. DeMosh to Anita M. Blake; Anna H. Cleveland to Anna Louise Harriman; Pauline E. Roy Barbin to Pauline E. Roy; Marion Louise MacKenzie to Marion Louise Logan; Allene C. Phelps to Allene C. Brown; Robby N. Franklin to Robby Naomi Williamson; Marion L. Lucas to Marion L. Laythe; Marjorie D. Moses to Marjorie Dyke; Edwina Elizabeth Sippell Rowland to Edwina Elizabeth Sippell; Helen P. Adams to Helen Pinard; Alice Fuller to Alice Allen; Bernadette Sullivan to Bernadette Harvey; Henrietta R. Plummer to Henrietta Evelyn Rainey; E. Pearle Lebeaux to E. Pearl Dexter; Eleanor Swett Kramer to Eleanor Jane Swett; Barbara C. Higgins to Barbara C. Burnham; Inez E. Bellerose to Inez E. Kenney; Marie E. Allen to Marie E. Woods; Mary B. Ziter to Mary A. Brouillett; Evelyn H. Harris to Evelyn Hammond; Harriett R. Baker to Harriet R. Munroe; Martha Keniston Thompson to Martha Keniston; Isabel E. Acorn to Isabel Evans; Winona B. Eastman to Winona Walker; Cora W. McCarthy to Cora Belle Whitehouse

[Coos County - not reported]

INDEX

The following index of surnames makes reference to the sections in which those names appear. The number at the beginning is the first year of the relevant section. For example, 43-R-d, refers to the lists for 1943-1945. The capitalized letter or letters is the county in which the event occurred. These are as follows:

- B - Belknap
- Ca - Carroll
- Ch - Cheshire
- Co - Coos
- G - Grafton
- H - Hillsborough
- M - Merrimack
- R - Rockingham
- St - Strafford
- Su - Sullivan

The final letter makes reference to whether the name change was made by the Probate Court, "p", or by the Superior Court in conjunction with a divorced proceeding, "d". In addition, one year's listing includes name changes made during or after the naturalization process, with an "n".

One important caveat is that the same surnames often appear more than once in a given section, particularly in the probates. Often entire families would have their names altered. Further, these names may not be listed consecutively, so the entire section should be reviewed.

Abare - 41-Ch-d, 41-Su-p, 45-Ch-p
Abbott - 23-R-p, 25-G-p, 27-Ca-p, 31-B-p, 31-G-p, 35-B-d, 35-M-p, 39-G-p, 39-St-p, 39-H-p, 41-R-p, 41-G-p, 41-H-d, 43-M-p, 43-R-p, 45-M-p, 45-Ch-p
Abdelnour - 37-G-p
Abel - 45-H-p
Abiseleah - 39-St-n
Abraham - 23-St-d, 29-St-p
Abrahamson - 41-Ch-p
Abramowitz - 43-M-p
Abrams - 43-M-p
Abruzzese - 39-M-p
Ackermann - 35-H-d
Ackley - 43-M-p
Ackroyd - 31-Su-d
Acorn - 45-G-d
Adamakos - 27-H-p
Adamandares - 35-R-p
Adamopoulos - 25-St-p, 25-H-p, 37-H-p, 43-St-p
Adamowitz - 43-Su-p
Adams - 23-R-p, 27-H-p, 27-Ch-d, 29-Ch-p, 29-G-p, 29-H-p, 29-M-p, 31-R-p, 31-M-p, 33-R-p, 35-R-p, 37-M-p, 37-H-p, 37-H-d, 39-H-d, 41-M-p, 43-M-p, 43-St-p, 43-H-p, 43-Su-p, 43-G-d, 45-St-p, 45-G-d
Adkins - 37-M-p
Adler - 41-M-p
Aggelon - 41-St-n
Agnew - 43-St-d
Agostini - 33-H-p
Ahern - 35-M-p, 45-Su-p
Aho - 43-H-p

Aiello - 27-Co-p
Aiken - 29-M-p, 35-G-d, 37-St-d, 45-H-p
Ainsworth - 41-R-p, 41-B-d, 43-St-p, 43-H-p, 45-Ca-p, 45-Su-p
Akerman - 27-G-p, 35-R-d
Akers - 35-Co-d
Akmakjian - 41-R-p
Akstulewiz - 25-H-p
Akstull - 25-H-p, 41-H-p, 43-H-p
Aksztulewicz - 43-H-p
Alain - 45-R-d
Albee - 27-G-d, 41-M-d
Albert - 27-R-p, 45-H-p, 45-M-d
Alberty - 33-M-p
Albren - 45-H-p
Albrenczenski - 45-H-p
Albrewczenski - 45-H-p
Alden - 23-Co-p
Aldred - 37-H-p
Aldrich - 27-G-d, 29-G-d, 33-B-p, 37-H-p, 41-R-p, 43-R-p, 43-G-p, 43-St-d
Aldridge - 25-H-p
Aldworth - 25-Su-p
Aleem - 45-M-p
Alessi - 43-R-p
Alexander - 35-Co-p, 41-H-p
Alford - 33-Su-d, 43-St-d
Alger - 39-M-p
Allaire - 35-H-p, 43-H-p, 45-H-p
Allard - 31-Co-p, 31-H-p, 35-H-p, 43-M-p, 43-G-p, 45-H-p
Allen - 23-St-d, 23-H-p, 25-G-d, 25-St-d, 25-M-d, 25-Su-d, 27-R-p, 29-R-p

Allen - 31-H-p, 33-M-p, 35-B-p, 35-R-p, 35-G-p, 35-Su-p, 35-M-d, 35-Ch-d, 37-G-p, 37-Ch-p, 37-M-p, 37-H-d, 39-Ch-p, 39-H-p, 39-Ch-p, 39-G-p, 39-H-d, 41-St-p, 41-H-p, 43-H-p, 43-M-p, 43-B-p, 43-M-d, 45-H-d, 45-G-d, 45-R-d
Aller - 41-St-p
Allison - 37-R-p, 41-Ch-d, 45-St-d
Alsop - 41-H-p
Alter - 45-H-p
Altomare - 39-B-p, 45-B-p
Altvatter - 33-R-d
Aman - 41-H-d
Amazeen - 25-B-d
Ambadges - 35-St-p
Ambrose - 45-Ca-p
Ames - 25-H-p, 25-Ca-d, 29-R-p, 31-B-p, 33-R-d, 41-Ca-p, 45-M-p, 45-H-d
Amey - 45-H-p
Amlaw - 43-Ch-p
Ammel - 41-G-p
Amorosino - 45-G-p
Amsdam - 39-Ch-p
Anagnost - 43-H-p, 45-H-p
Anagnostopoulos - 43-H-p, 45-H-p
Anagnostou - 41-H-p
Anastas - 25-M-p
Anastasatos - 45-H-p
Anaston - 45-H-p
Anastos - 33-Su-p
Anctil - 29-H-p, 31-Co-d, 39-H-d
Andberg - 45-M-d

Anderson - 23-H-p, 23-Ch-p, 27-R-d, 29-H-p, 29-Co-p, 29-M-p, 33-M-p, 35-R-p, 35-M-p, 35-H-p, 39-Ch-p, 39-Co-p, 39-H-d, 41-M-p, 41-H-d, 43-H-p, 43-R-p, 45-H-p, 45-St-p, 45-M-d
Andreanopoulos - 25-St-p
Andreason - 39-G-p, 45-St-p
Andreevski - 37-M-d
Andress - 29-R-d
Andrew - 31-M-d, 35-M-p
Andrews - 27-B-d, 35-Ch-p, 37-R-p, 39-H-p, 39-R-p, 41-M-p, 41-Ch-p, 41-H-p, 41-G-p, 43-H-p, 45-M-p, 45-B-p
Andrikowich - 33-H-p
Andross - 45-G-p
Andruchuck - 41-H-p
Andrychowski - 33-R-p
Ange - 43-B-p
Angelos - 41-St-n, 45-R-p
Angers - 31-H-p, 43-B-p
Angier - 29-Ch-p
Angus - 35-H-p, 41-H-d
Angwin - 35-M-d, 41-M-p
Ann - 35-Co-p
Anna - 35-Co-p
Annair - 41-B-p
Annette - 27-Co-p
Annis - 23-Co-p, 25-R-d, 29-H-d, 37-St-d, 43-M-p
Anstett - 41-M-d
Anthony - 33-H-p, 37-R-p, 41-H-p
Anton - 23-R-d
Antonelos - 43-R-d
Antonia - 25-Co-p
Anttila - 29-Ch-p, 33-H-p

Apostolgoulos - 45-H-p
Apostolos - 45-H-p
Apostopoulos - 45-H-p
Applebaum - 41-G-p
Appleton - 41-G-p, 45-St-d
Appt - 27-Ch-p
Aptt - 23-Ch-d
Arbour - 23-M-d
Archambault - 41-Su-p, 43-R-p
Archambeault - 39-H-p
Archer - 39-Ch-p
Archers - 41-R-p
Archibald - 31-H-d, 39-M-d
Argeropoulos - 37-H-p, 39-H-p
Arguin - 41-H-p
Arlin - 39-Su-p
Arlinsky - 37-Co-d, 39-Su-p
Armand - 31-H-p
Armitage - 41-Ch-d
Armond - 25-H-p
Armstrong - 23-Ch-p, 41-R-d, 45-M-p, 45-G-p
Army - 31-Ca-p
Arnold - 41-R-p, 43-St-p, 45-R-d
Arps - 27-R-p
Arsenault - 29-Co-p, 37-Co-p, 37-M-p, 43-M-p, 45-R-d
Arseneault - 41-Ch-p
Arslanian - 29-R-p
Arthur - 25-H-p, 39-H-p, 39-M-d
Arvenites - 41-R-p
Aryell - 23-H-p
Asadoorian - 45-St-p
Asbury - 41-Ch-d
Ascani - 43-Ch-d
Ash - 25-B-p, 29-M-p, 33-M-d, 43-M-p, 45-M-p

Ashcroft - 23-Ch-d
Ashford - 25-G-p, 37-H-p, 45-R-d
Ashland - 29-R-p, 43-St-d
Ashley - 27-B-p, 35-H-p
Ashton - 31-M-d, 43-H-p
Aspinall - 37-St-p
Asselin - 37-Co-d
Astaire - 43-H-p
Asteriou - 43-H-p
Aston - 23-B-p, 43-H-p
Athanasiou - 41-St-n
Athans - 45-St-d
Athas - 29-H-d
Atheron - 33-R-p
Atherton - 25-H-p, 37-St-d, 41-R-p
Atkins - 29-Su-d, 41-H-p, 43-Ch-p
Atkinson - 25-H-p, 27-M-d, 31-R-p, 33-R-p
Attaya - 33-M-p
Atwood - 27-H-p, 33-Ca-p, 35-Su-p, 35-H-d, 37-St-p, 39-H-d, 43-St-p
Aube - 45-Co-p
Aubey - 45-Co-p
Aubut - 27-H-p
Audet - 41-M-p, 41-B-d, 43-H-p, 43-Co-p, 45-Ch-p
Audette - 27-H-p, 27-M-p
Auger - 35-St-d, 45-H-p, 45-Co-p
Aukstulevicius - 41-H-p
Austin - 23-Ch-p, 29-G-p, 35-R-p, 41-H-p, 41-H-d, 43-H-p, 43-G-p, 43-Su-p
Avedisian - 33-Ca-p
Avery - 23-G-p, 25-Ca-p, 25-H-p, 29-Ca-p, 29-G-p, 35-G-d, 39-B-p, 41-G-p,

Avery - 41-H-d, 43-Su-p, 45-B-p, 45-Su-p
Axton - 41-H-d
Ayer - 23-H-d, 27-Su-d, 35-Ch-p
Ayers - 23-G-d
Aylsworth - 33-H-p
Aziz - 35-R-d

Babalas - 45-H-p
Babb - 23-St-d, 43-M-p
Babbitt - 25-St-d, 33-Ch-p, 35-Su-p, 39-Su-p
Babcock - 41-Ch-p, 43-H-d
Babel - 35-H-p
Babeu - 33-Ch-p
Babeux - 35-Su-p, 39-Su-p
Babin - 45-St-p
Babineau - 41-B-d, 43-B-d, 45-Ch-p
Babkirk - 41-Ch-p
Bach - 39-H-p
Bachakouchos - 39-H-p
Bachand - 31-G-d
Bachelder - 43-R-d
Bachelor - 31-St-d
Bacon - 25-B-d, 27-B-d, 37-H-p, 37-M-p, 41-Co-d, 43-G-d, 45-M-p
Badger - 23-H-p, 45-M-d
Bagley - 43-B-p, 45-H-d, 45-G-p
Bailey - 23-H-d; 23-R-p; 25-B-p, 29-M-p, 29-H-p, 31-H-p, 33-G-d, 39-M-p, 41-Ch-p, 41-R-p, 41-H-p, 41-M-p, 43-G-p, 43-H-d, 45-G-p
Baillie - 25-M-p, 45-G-p
Baine - 23-R-p
Baio - 43-H-p

Baird - 39-Su-d, 41-Co-p, 43-H-p
Bakaian - 23-H-p
Baker - 23-Ch-p; 25-H-p, 25-H-d, 27-M-d, 29-B-p, 29-H-d, 31-Ch-d, 33-G-p, 33-B-p, 33-Co-p, 33-St-d, 33-Ca-d, 35-St-p, 35-H-p, 35-Ch-p, 35-St-d, 37-Ch-d, 39-H-p, 39-R-p, 39-R-d, 39-B-d, 41-R-p, 41-Co-p, 41-B-p, 41-M-p, 41-B-d, 43-M-p, 43-B-p, 43-Ca-p, 43-B-d, 45-Su-p, 45-G-d, 45-R-d
Bakka - 37-Ch-p
Balban - 39-H-p
Balben - 33-G-d
Balch - 23-B-p
Balcom - 45-H-p
Baldwin - 33-Ch-p, 43-H-p, 45-G-p
Balko - 39-Co-d
Balkus - 41-H-d
Ball - 25-Co-d, 27-G-d, 29-G-d, 33-B-d, 37-R-d, 37-Co-d, 41-Ch-p, 41-St-p, 43-Ch-p, 43-H-p, 43-G-p, 43-Co-d
Ballard - 33-Ca-p, 33-M-d, 43-M-d
Ballas - 45-H-p
Ballou - 35-Ca-p, 41-R-d
Balukas - 41-R-p
Balukonis - 37-H-d
Bamford - 27-H-p, 43-M-p, 45-M-p
Bammann - 29-H-p
Banaian - 39-St-n
Banaskevich - 43-H-p
Bancroft - 29-H-d

Banden - 35-H-p
Bane - 41-R-p
Banfil - 27-B-p
Banfill - 25-G-p
Bangs - 27-H-d, 45-R-d
Banis - 43-H-p
Banks - 43-H-p, 43-H-d, 45-M-d
Bannister - 27-St-d
Bannon - 35-B-d
Baptist - 43-R-p
Baraby - 41-H-d
Barard - 45-Ch-p
Baras - 23-St-p
Baratelli - 25-M-p
Barati - 43-R-d
Baraw - 43-Su-p
Barbarossa - 25-Ch-p
Barbeau - 37-H-p, 41-H-p
Barber -33-R-p, 33-Co-d, 35-Su-p, 41-R-p
Barbin - 45-Co-p, 45-G-d
Barbour - 25-Co-p, 37-St-p, 41-H-p
Barbrick - 45-M-p
Barclay - 23-R-d
Barcomb - 43-Ch-p, 45-St-p
Barden - 41-G-p
Bardill - 43-G-d
Bare - 25-M-p, 29-M-p
Bargiel - 45-H-d
Baribeau - 43-H-p
Baril - 27-H-p, 43-H-p
Barka - 41-R-p
Barker - 23-H-d, 23-G-d, 25-Ch-p, 27-M-p, 31-H-d, 31-G-d, 39-Su-p, 41-R-p, 43-M-p, 45-Su-p
Barkha - 41-R-p
Barklay - 37-M-p
Barlow - 43-H-d

Barlow - 35-Co-p
Barnard - 29-M-p, 29-G-d, 31-M-p, 37-Co-d, 43-H-p, 45-H-p
Barneetz - 33-H-d
Barnes - 39-Su-p, 39-H-p, 41-St-p, 41-Su-p, 41-Co-p, 45-G-p, 45-H-d
Barney - 39-Su-p
Barnhart - 23-G-d
Baron - 39-H-d, 41-Co-p
Baronoski - 39-Ch-d
Baroody - 39-H-p, 43-H-p
Barowski - 43-H-p
Barr - 33-H-p, 33-G-d
Barrett - 23-H-d, 27-Ch-p, 31-H-p, 35-H-d, 37-G-d, 39-H-d, 41-Ch-p, 41-M-p, 41-Ch-d, 43-R-p
Barron - 37-Ch-d, 45-Ch-d
Barrows - 23-Su-p
Barry - 29-H-d, 35-H-p, 35-G-d, 37-H-d, 39-Su-p, 41-M-p, 43-R-p, 45-R-d
Barschdorf - 37-H-d
Bartaschevich - 45-Ch-p
Bartashevich - 35-Ch-p, 37-Ch-p
Bartashievick - 37-Ch-p
Bartaskvic - 35-Ch-p
Barthelemy - 45-R-d
Bartlett - 23-B-d; 25-R-p, 27-H-p, 29-R-p, 33-Ca-p, 33-Su-p, 39-St-p, 41-R-p, 43-Ch-p, 43-M-d, 43-Ch-d, 45-R-d
Bartley - 45-M-p
Barton - 27-R-p, 31-G-p, 33-St-d, 37-G-p, 41-Su-p, 41-B-p, 45-R-p
Bartoscheyce - 45-Ch-p

Bartosewie - 39-H-p
Bartrum - 39-H-p
Bascom - 43-R-p, 45-B-p
Basha - 29-H-p
Bashaar - 41-St-p
Basham - 43-H-d
Basil - 37-H-p, 41-H-p
Basile - 31-Co-p
Basoukas - 43-H-p
Bassett - 25-St-p, 29-R-p, 33-H-p, 35-G-p, 41-M-p, 43-Ch-p, 45-B-p
Batchelder - 23-G-d, 25-Ch-p, 25-B-p, 29-H-p, 31-R-p, 33-H-d, 35-G-p, 35-R-d, 37-R-p, 43-R-d, 45-G-p, 45-B-d
Batcheldor - 41-R-p
Batcheller - 33-R-d
Bates - 31-G-d, 35-Ch-p, 43-Ch-p, 43-R-p
Batholomee - 35-B-p
Battashievch - 35-Ch-p
Battersby - 45-H-d
Battis - 35-H-p
Battistelli - 45-H-p
Battryn - 31-H-d
Battye - 43-H-p
Batura - 45-H-p
Baum - 27-H-p, 27-H-d
Baxter - 25-B-p, 33-St-d, 37-H-p, 39-St-p, 41-St-p, 43-Su-p, 45-St-p
Bayarsky - 33-Su-p
Bayer - 33-Su-p
Bayley - 45-M-p
Bazylewicz - 41-H-p
Beadle - 31-H-d, 33-H-d
Beady - 35-Co-p
Beal - 25-B-p, 29-H-d, 33-Ch-d

Beals - 39-H-p, 41-St-p, 43-R-p, 43-R-d
Beam - 45-Ch-p
Beaman - 27-G-p, 41-G-p
Beamis - 43-St-p, 43-G-d
Beamish - 43-St-p
Bean - 23-H-p, 23-Ch-d, 27-M-p, 29-M-p, 29-G-p, 29-Su-d, 33-St-p, 33-M-d, 33-Co-d, 35-Ca-d, 37-M-p, 39-St-p, 39-G-p, 41-Ca-p, 41-Su-d, 43-H-p, 45-B-p, 45-Su-p
Beane - 43-M-p, 45-M-p
Beard - 23-H-p, 45-M-p
Beardsell - 39-G-p
Beattie - 33-G-d, 43-H-p, 43-H-d, 45-H-p, 45-B-p
Beaubien - 35-H-p, 43-H-p
Beauchemin - 29-Co-p, 37-Ca-p
Beauchesne - 29-B-p
Beaudet - 23-H-p; 25-R-p, 33-H-d, 37-H-p
Beaudette - 41-H-p, 41-St-d
Beaudin - 41-H-p
Beaudoin - 23-H-p, 29-St-d, 29-Ch-d, 33-H-d, 37-St-d, 41-B-p, 41-H-p, 43-H-p, 43-St-p, 43-Ch-d
Beaulac - 41-H-d, 45-H-p
Beauley - 39-M-d
Beaulieu - 29-H-p, 37-H-p, 37-Ch-p, 41-R-p, 43-H-p, 43-Ch-p
Beaumont - 43-R-p
Beaupre - 27-M-d, 35-H-p, 39-M-p, 43-M-p
Beauregard - 25-H-d, 31-H-p, 35-H-p, 43-Ch-p, 45-Ch-p

Beauvais - 29-H-p
Bebler - 29-G-d
Becchetti - 33-H-p
Bechard - 45-H-p
Beckford - 43-H-p
Beckham - 31-Ch-p
Beckley - 43-G-p
Beckman - 39-B-p
Beckwith - 29-Co-p, 29-Su-p
Bedard - 41-Co-p, 45-Ch-p, 45-G-p
Bedaw - 39-Ch-p, 45-Ch-p
Bedders - 41-H-p
Bedell - 23-M-p, 37-Su-d, 43-G-p
Beders - 41-H-p
Bednarczyk - 31-H-p
Bednard - 23-G-d
Bednarz - 23-H-p
Bedor - 37-Ch-p
Beebe - 43-R-p, 43-M-p
Beeckman - 41-H-p
Beede - 27-G-p, 29-M-p, 41-Ca-p, 45-B-p
Beek - 29-Ch-p
Beeman - 33-H-p
Beers - 31-Ch-d, 31-Su-d, 39-R-p
Begin - 41-St-d
Begley - 39-St-p
Belair - 43-H-p, 45-Su-p
Belaire - 33-M-d, 37-H-d, 39-H-p
Beland - 41-H-d, 43-Su-p
Belanger - 25-R-p, 25-Co-d, 35-M-p, 37-H-p, 37-B-d, 39-H-p, 39-H-d, 45-M-p, 45-G-p
Belasco - 29-H-p
Belavsky - 31-H-p
Belcher - 23-R-p, 27-H-p

Beleski - 43-R-p
Belford - 25-G-p
Belisle - 25-H-p, 27-B-p, 43-G-p
Beliveau - 39-H-p
Bell - 27-H-d, 31-H-d, 31-G-d, 33-St-d, 33-Co-d, 35-Co-p, 37-R-d, 43-M-p, 43-St-d, 45-H-p
Bellanger - 27-B-p
Bellavance - 23-H-p
Belleau - 41-G-p
Bellefeuille - 37-H-p, 39-H-p, 43-H-p
Bellefleur - 37-H-d, 39-H-d, 41-H-d
Bellemare - 41-H-p
Bellemore - 23-H-p
Bellerose - 23-H-p, 33-M-p, 45-G-d
Belleveau - 37-M-p
Bellinger - 41-H-p, 43-Su-p, 45-Su-p
Bellisle - 29-H-p
Belliveau - 23-H-p
Bellofatto - 35-H-d
Bellows - 31-H-p, 33-H-p
Belluscio - 33-Su-d, 41-Ch-p
Belmont - 37-H-p, 41-R-d
Belmonte - 43-R-p, 45-R-p
Belos - 33-H-p
Belrose - 37-H-d
Beltso - 27-H-p
Belvasky - 29-H-p
Belville - 39-Co-d
Bemis - 23-Su-p, 41-H-d
Benedetto - 41-R-p
Benedick - 37-H-d
Benjamin - 29-H-p
Benner - 33-St-d, 45-Su-p

Bennett - 23-H-p, 23-H-d, 29-B-p, 29-M-d, 31-B-p, 31-H-p, 35-G-p, 35-H-d, 37-M-d, 37-Co-d, 41-G-p, 41-Co-p, 43-St-p, 43-H-p, 43-R-p, 43-R-d, 45-H-p, 45-G-p, 45-St-d
Benning - 43-M-p
Benoit - 29-Co-p, 43-B-p
Benson - 33-Su-d, 41-H-p
Bent - 29-H-d, 37-M-p
Benton - 35-Ch-p, 41-M-p
Beott - 41-R-p
Bergeron - 27-St-p, 29-Ch-p, 29-H-p, 31-R-p, 31-H-d, 33-Ch-d, 33-Co-p, 35-H-p, 37-H-d, 41-Ch-p, 41-R-p, 43-H-p, 43-St-p, 43-Su-p, 45-H-p, 45-H-d
Bergh - 37-G-p
Bergholtz - 27-H-p
Bergland - 31-Su-p
Bergstrom - 37-M-p, 43-Ch-p
Berle - 45-H-p
Berlin - 45-R-d
Berman - 45-Ch-d
Bermis - 35-Co-d
Bernaiche - 37-H-p
Bernard - 33-H-p, 35-H-p, 39-H-p, 41-R-p, 41-H-p
Bernay - 43-Co-p, 45-Co-p
Bernd - 43-M-p
Bernheimer - 43-Co-p, 45-Co-p
Bernier - 37-Ch-d, 39-St-p, 43-St-p
Berry - 27-R-d, 29-G-d, 31-R-p, 33-M-d, 35-Co-d, 37-R-p, 37-B-d, 39-R-p, 41-G-p, 41-H-d, 43-H-p, 45-H-p, 45-St-p, 45-R-p, 45-M-p
Berthiaume - 23-R-d, 39-Ch-p, 43-Ch-p
Bertrand - 45-M-p
Berube - 23-Co-p, 37-H-p, 43-H-p, 45-H-p
Besakiriski - 35-G-p
Besse - 45-M-d
Bessette - 25-M-p, 37-M-p
Bessey - 31-H-p
Beston - 31-G-d
Bethune - 33-M-p
Betlej - 41-H-p, 43-H-p
Betley - 41-H-p, 43-H-p
Betz - 41-Ch-p, 45-Co-p
Beveridge - 43-Ch-p
Beverly - 35-Ch-p
Bewley - 35-St-d
Biadacz - 39-R-p
Biagiotti - 27-Su-d
Biancki - 25-R-d
Bibbey - 43-R-p
Bickford - 23-St-p, 23-H-p, 25-St-p, 27-B-p, 31-H-d, 33-St-p, 35-St-d, 37-B-p, 39-B-p, 41-St-p, 41-Ca-p, 43-Ca-d, 45-M-p, 45-Co-p
Biel - 41-G-p
Bielschowsky - 41-G-p
Bienvenue - 31-H-p, 41-H-d, 43-H-p
Biester - 39-R-d
Bilat - 23-R-p
Bilbao - 43-R-d
Billings - 39-M-p
Billman - 39-H-d
Billy - 45-H-p
Bilodeau - 27-H-d, 39-H-p, 39-G-p, 41-H-p, 43-H-p

Binette - 39-H-p, 45-H-p
Bingham - 23-M-d, 45-Ch-p
Bird - 25-M-p
Biron - 37-H-p, 45-H-p, 45-H-d
Birtwell - 43-R-p
Bishop - 23-M-d, 25-M-d, 27-M-p, 29-H-p, 29-G-d, 31-B-p, 35-H-d, 41-R-p, 43-Ca-p, 45-H-p, 45-M-p, 45-Co-p
Bishopric - 43-M-p
Bisonette - 45-Ch-p
Bissell - 37-G-p, 45-Ch-p
Bisson - 31-Co-p, 33-Co-p, 37-B-p, 37-H-d, 41-G-p, 43-St-p, 45-H-p, 45-G-p
Bissonette - 45-Ch-p
Bitos - 25-H-p
Bitters - 45-Ch-p
Bixby - 25-Ch-p, 45-M-p
Bizzoachi - 43-R-p
Bjorkland - 33-R-p
Bjurling - 39-H-p
Black - 25-M-p, 31-B-p, 35-B-p, 41-Ch-p, 41-St-p, 43-Su-p
Blacker - 25-Su-d
Blackey - 35-B-d, 41-B-p, 43-H-p, 45-B-p
Blackman - 45-M-p
Blackwell - 39-M-p
Blackwood - 41-Ca-d
Blain - 35-Ch-p
Blaine - 35-Su-p, 43-Su-p
Blair - 23-Ch-d, 25-R-d, 27-H-d, 29-Ch-p, 35-St-d, 37-R-d, 39-Co-p, 41-Ch-d
Blais - 27-Co-p, 27-Co-d, 41-M-d, 43-G-p, 43-H-d, 45-H-p

Blaisdell - 27-R-d, 27-M-d, 29-St-p, 37-M-p, 41-H-p, 43-H-p, 43-M-p
Blaise - 37-H-d
Blake - 25-H-p, 25-H-d, 29-H-p, 31-R-p, 31-B-p, 31-M-d, 37-H-p, 41-R-p, 41-G-p, 41-R-d, 41-Co-d, 43-B-p, 43-Co-p, 45-G-d, 45-H-d
Blakeley - 33-H-p, 39-M-p, 41-H-d
Blakitis - 35-H-p
Blanch - 37-H-p
Blanchard - 23-Ch-d, 25-H-p, 31-M-d, 33-Su-d, 35-G-d, 41-Ch-p, 43-Su-p, 43-Ca-p, 43-B-p
Blanchet - 41-St-p
Blanchette - 27-H-p, 29-H-p, 33-H-p, 35-H-d, 41-H-p
Bland - 45-Ch-p
Blandin - 31-M-d, 37-M-p
Blasland - 29-Co-p
Blaylock - 45-St-p
Blazejewicz - 39-H-p
Blazo - 25-Ch-p
Blekitis - 41-H-d
Blevens - 31-M-d, 35-M-p
Blidberg - 27-R-p, 39-H-p
Blinn - 45-R-p
Bliss - 27-Su-p, 35-G-d, 45-R-d
Blixt - 39-H-p
Blizzard - 33-R-d
Blodgett - 27-H-p, 39-M-d, 41-Co-p, 41-G-d, 43-Co-p, 43-G-p
Blood - 29-H-p, 29-M-d, 31-M-d, 33-R-d, 35-H-p, 39-H-p, 45-Ch-p

Bloom - 41-Ch-p
Blow - 35-H-d
Blue - 45-Su-p
Blumberg - 45-H-p
Boardman - 23-H-d, 27-G-p, 31-H-d, 33-H-p
Bocon - 41-H-p
Bodge - 25-Ca-p, 43-H-p
Bodware - 37-Ch-d
Bodwell - 35-Ch-d
Boebel - 27-Ch-p
Boemig - 29-G-p, 45-Su-p
Boeshaar - 41-St-p
Bogan - 43-R-p
Bogdan - 43-H-p
Bogle - 37-Ca-p
Bogumiloff - 41-Ch-p
Bohan - 43-H-p
Boilard - 33-H-p, 39-H-p
Boily - 45-H-p
Boire - 43-H-p
Boisclair - 23-H-p
Boisoneau - 41-Su-p
Boisseau - 31-H-d, 35-H-d, 41-H-p
Boissoneault - 37-B-p
Boisvert - 25-Co-p, 25-H-p, 27-H-d, 29-H-d, 31-B-p, 31-H-d, 33-B-p, 37-H-d, 39-H-p, 41-Su-p, 41-G-p, 45-H-d
Boivin - 33-Co-p, 37-H-d, 43-H-d
Boldini - 37-H-d
Bolduc - 27-B-p, 33-Ca-d, 39-H-p, 43-R-p, 43-B-p, 45-H-p
Bolkis - 39-M-p
Bolleyn - 27-H-d, 29-H-p
Bolos - 45-H-p
Bolt - 27-Ch-d

Bomhower - 37-G-d
Bond - 27-R-d, 37-H-d, 45-Su-p, 45-R-d, 45-Ca-d
Bonette - 29-M-p. 41-M-p
Bonfilio - 43-G-d
Bonin - 25-M-p, 35-H-p
Bonner - 45-M-d
Bonneville - 31-H-p
Bonney - 39-R-d, 41-H-d
Bonnin - 27-M-p
Boomhower - 43-M-d
Boone - 41-H-p
Booth - 37-H-p, 39-Co-p, 41-R-p
Boothby - 29-St-d
Borciak - 29-H-p
Borden - 27-B-d, 31-H-d
Borras - 37-M-p
Borry - 45-G-p
Bortas - 39-H-p
Bosen - 43-R-p
Bosiniss - 43-R-p
Bosley - 33-H-p
Boss - 41-G-p
Bosse - 43-H-p
Boubouikas - 45-H-p
Bouboulica - 45-H-p
Bouchard - 27-H-d, 35-Co-p, 39-Su-p, 41-H-p, 41-Co-d, 43-Co-p
Bouchea - 43-H-p
Boucher - 23-Su-d, 27-G-d, 39-B-p, 41-St-p, 43-St-p, 43-Co-p, 45-H-d
Boudle - 43-Co-p
Boudreau - 39-M-p, 43-H-p
Boudreault - 41-H-p
Boudrieau - 45-Ch-p
Bouffard - 41-M-p, 45-Ch-p
Boufford - 23-Ch-p
Bough - 37-St-p

Boulanger - 29-St-d, 37-St-d, 39-H-p, 43-H-p, 43-St-d, 45-H-p
Boulay - 37-M-p, 39-H-p, 41-R-p, 41-M-d, 43-M-p, 45-M-p
Boulerice - 33-Su-d
Boulet - 33-St-p
Bouley - 23-B-d, 45-H-p
Boulia - 29-Ch-p
Boulton - 25-H-p
Bourassa - 37-Co-p
Bourbeau - 43-M-p
Bourcier - 35-H-p
Bourdage - 41-St-d
Bourgeois - 31-H-p, 41-H-p, 41-St-p
Bourinot - 33-R-p
Bourk - 43-R-p
Bourke - 31-M-d
Bourque - 41-H-p, 43-R-p, 43-H-p, 45-H-p
Bourrassa - 23-H-d
Bourzikas - 37-H-d
Boushey - 35-G-p
Bousquet - 35-B-p
Bousquette - 39-B-d
Bousquin - 41-St-p
Boutelle - 31-M-p, 35-M-p, 37-M-p, 39-R-p
Boutin - 43-Co-p
Boutwell - 23-Co-p, 27-H-p
Bouvier - 39-Ch-p
Bouwman - 31-M-d
Boviard - 43-Ca-p
Bowden - 33-B-p, 35-H-p, 37-St-p, 43-R-p, 45-M-p
Bowen - 23-Ca-p, 25-Ch-p, 31-Ch-p
Bower - 41-R-d
Bowerfind - 39-R-p
Bowers - 27-G-d, 37-G-p
Bowhay - 37-Ch-p
Bowin - 39-Co-p
Bowker - 43-Co-p, 45-Su-p
Bowlan - 31-M-p
Bowlby - 23-B-p, 25-B-p, 35-B-p
Bowlen - 33-G-p
Bowler - 37-H-d, 45-H-p
Bowles - 25-G-p, 37-Su-p, 45-Ca-p, 45-G-p, 45-St-d
Bowman - 35-H-p, 39-G-d, 41-St-d
Boy - 35-H-p
Boyan - 23-G-p
Boyce - 25-Co-p, 31-Su-d, 41-M-p, 45-M-p
Boyd - 29-G-p, 31-H-p, 35-R-p, 37-R-p, 39-G-d, 41-St-p, 43-M-p
Boyden - 31-H-p
Boyea - 43-Ch-d
Boyer - 33-H-p, 35-H-p, 37-H-p, 43-Ch-p, 45-M-p
Boynton - 27-H-p, 33-H-p, 33-Ch-p, 39-H-p, 43-G-p, 45-H-p
Bozek - 39-H-p
Brackett - 25-G-p, 41-Ca-p, 43-M-p, 45-B-p
Bracy - 41-B-d
Bradbury - 41-St-p, 45-Ch-p
Bradfield - 45-St-p
Bradford - 23-G-d, 37-H-p
Bradis - 39-H-p
Bradley - 29-R-p, 33-Ca-d, 33-G-d, 41-R-p, 45-M-p
Bradshaw - 33-H-d
Brady - 25-Ch-d, 37-St-p
Braga - 31-H-p, 39-St-d
Bragdon - 43-St-p

Bragg - 33-B-p, 35-G-p, 41-B-p, 41-Ca-p, 45-M-p
Brailey - 25-H-p, 41-Su-p
Braley - 37-Su-d
Branch - 35-H-d
Brandt - 23-H-p
Brandt-Erichsen - 45-Ch-p
Brannock - 23-Ch-d
Brantley - 29-Ca-d
Brasier - 31-Ch-p
Brassard - 25-R-p
Brassaw - 39-Su-p, 39-St-d
Braudis - 23-St-p
Brault - 45-Ch-p
Braum - 41-R-p
Braverman - 45-Ch-p
Brayman - 43-Ch-p
Braynard - 23-G-d
Brayton - 41-R-d
Brazeau - 45-B-p
Brazelton - 45-H-d
Brazer - 41-Ch-d
Brazier - 23-M-d
Brazis - 45-St-p
Brean - 23-St-d
Breault - 29-H-d
Breck - 37-B-p
Breckney - 45-M-d
Breed - 39-H-p, 43-Su-p
Breen - 39-M-d
Brenner - 45-H-p
Brent - 45-M-d
Bresette - 31-G-p
Breslin - 45-M-p
Bresnahan - 27-H-d, 43-G-p
Bresse - 39-H-p
Bressette - 35-G-d
Breton - 41-H-p, 41-Co-p, 45-B-p, 45-H-p
Bretschneider - 23-R-d
Brew - 33-M-d
Brewer - 37-Ca-p
Brewster - 35-R-p, 35-R-d, 45-R-p
Breynaert - 27-H-p
Brianas - 33-H-d
Briand - 41-H-p, 45-H-p
Bricault - 31-H-p
Brickley - 37-H-p
Brideau - 37-M-p, 39-M-p
Bridges - 41-St-d, 43-St-p
Bridgess - 39-H-d
Brien - 31-H-d
Briggs - 23-Co-p, 27-H-p, 31-G-p, 31-R-d, 33-Su-d, 37-G-p, 37-Ch-d, 39-H-p, 43-H-p, 45-Ch-d
Brigham - 41-R-p, 43-Co-p, 45-Co-p
Brill - 25-M-d, 31-M-p, 43-Co-p
Brine - 29-R-p
Brinkman - 37-Co-d
Brisbois - 33-G-p
Brisebois - 29-R-p
Brissette - 41-M-p
Brisson - 43-R-p
Bristol - 35-M-p
Brite - 45-R-d
Britt - 33-R-d
Britton - 23-St-d, 39-Ch-p, 45-Ch-p
Broadhurst - 37-M-d
Brochu - 33-H-p, 37-H-p
Brock - 41-St-p, 43-Ch-p
Brockman - 41-M-p
Brockway - 25-M-d, 29-Ch-p, 29-Ch-d
Broderick - 33-H-p, 39-R-p
Brodeur - 41-H-p
Broes - 41-R-d
Bromley - 39-G-p

Bronson - 27-St-p, 39-G-p, 43-B-p
Brooker - 39-G-d
Brooks - 23-R-d, 25-B-d, 27-Ch-p, 29-Ch-d, 29-Su-d, 31-Ch-p, 31-Su-p, 33-Ch-p, 33-R-p, 35-R-p, 35-G-p, 35-Ch-d, 37-Ca-d, 37-H-d, 39-Su-p, 41-H-p, 41-G-p, 43-H-p, 45-B-p, 45-St-p
Broomfield - 35-R-p
Brosius - 29-Co-p
Brosseau - 37-B-p
Brouillett - 45-G-d
Brousso - 35-H-p
Brown - 23-H-p, 23-B-p, 23-Co-p, 25-R-p, 25-St-p, 25-M-p, 25-Ch-p, 25-G-p, 25-H-d, 27-B-p, 27-Ch-p, 27-M-p, 27-Su-p, 27-H-p, 27-R-d, 29-Su-p, 29-R-p, 29-H-p, 29-St-p, 29-M-d, 29-B-d, 29-H-d, 29-St-d, 31-Co-p, 31-Ch-p, 31-G-p, 31-H-d, 31-Ch-d, 33-Su-p, 33-M-p, 33-St-d, 33-R-d, 33-H-d, 35-R-p, 35-H-p, 35-H-d, 37-G-p, 37-R-p, 37-M-p, 37-H-p, 37-G-d, 39-H-p, 39-M-p, 39-St-p, 39-H-d, 41-R-p, 41-H-p, 41-M-p, 41-Ca-p, 41-Ch-p, 41-Ca-d, 41-Su-p, 43-Ca-p, 43-Su-p, 43-M-p, 43-B-p, 43-St-p, 43-R-p, 43-Ch-p, 43-G-p, 43-G-d, 43-H-d, 45-H-p, 45-St-p, 45-G-p, 45-Su-p, 45-Co-p, 45-G-d, 45-R-d, 45-H-d, 45-St-d
Brownell - 25-St-d, 45-Su-p
Browning - 39-M-d
Brownrigg - 37-Ca-p
Brozeau - 39-M-d
Bruce - 23-H-d, 29-Su-p, 29-H-d, 35-B-p, 37-G-d, 39-Su-d, 41-H-p, 41-St-p, 43-R-p, 43-G-p, 45-B-p
Bruneau - 27-B-p, 43-H-p
Brunell - 35-G-p, 37-Su-p
Brunelle - 31-St-d
Brunkard - 43-St-p
Bruno - 25-H-d, 33-H-d, 45-H-d
Brusoe - 33-G-p
Bryan - 25-Co-p, 27-R-p, 31-Co-p, 39-Co-d
Bryant - 27-St-p, 29-B-d, 29-St-d, 35-Su-p, 39-Ch-p, 41-R-p, 45-B-d
Bryer - 39-H-p
Bryson - 25-St-p
Buber - 35-Co-p
Buch - 29-H-d
Buchanan - 25-M-d, 29-G-p, 31-H-d, 37-B-p, 41-H-p, 43-H-p, 43-Ca-p
Buchanen - 41-B-p
Bucheri - 41-Ch-d
Buckley - 23-Co-p, 27-H-p, 41-Co-p, 41-Ch-d, 45-R-d
Bucklin - 23-M-d
Buckman - 31-R-p
Buckminster - 33-H-d
Bucloveci - 45-H-p
Bucy - 43-H-p
Budd - 31-Su-p
Budnitz - 31-Su-p

Buffelli - 43-H-p
Buffington - 25-B-d
Buffum - 45-Ch-p
Bugbee - 29-G-p, 45-H-p
Buholz - 39-H-p
Bujnievicz - 43-M-p
Bukata - 39-R-d, 41-R-p, 41-R-d
Buker - 45-St-p
Bullard - 31-M-d, 41-G-p, 43-H-p
Bullen - 31-H-p
Bump - 41-G-d
Bunce - 33-Ch-p, 35-M-p, 35-Su-p, 37-G-p
Bundy - 25-G-p, 39-M-p
Bunker - 23-Ch-p, 27-R-p, 33-Su-p, 37-Su-p, 43-Ca-p, 43-St-p
Bunnell - 35-Co-p, 35-Co-d
Bunton - 23-H-p, 25-H-p, 39-H-d
Buoniconti - 41-Co-d
Bura - 43-H-p
Burbank - 37-M-d, 41-Co-p, 45-H-d
Burbee - 23-Ch-p, 43-Su-d
Burbridge - 27-H-d
Burch - 41-Su-p
Burden - 43-H-p
Burdette - 25-H-d
Burdg - 41-R-p
Burdick - 41-B-p, 45-M-d
Bureau - 41-St-d, 43-M-p, 43-St-d, 45-H-p
Burelle - 37-H-d
Burgess - 35-H-p, 37-St-p, 45-R-p
Burgoyne - 37-Ch-p, 41-Co-p
Burke - 23-H-p, 29-R-p, 33-St-d, 35-G-p, 35-H-p, 35-Su-p, 45-H-d
Burkhardt - 25-R-p
Burklund - 33-R-p
Burleigh - 29-St-d, 29-G-d, 31-H-d, 31-St-d, 35-B-d, 37-St-p, 45-St-p
Burley - 25-St-p, 41-B-d, 41-R-d
Burling - 39-H-p
Burlingame - 35-St-p
Burlock - 43-G-p
Burnell - 27-G-p
Burnett - 23-R-d
Burnham - 23-H-p, 27-R-p, 33-B-d, 35-G-d, 41-Ch-p, 43-H-p, 45-H-p, 45-G-d
Burnor - 25-G-d
Burns - 27-Ch-p, 29-M-p, 31-M-d, 33-Co-p, 33-M-d, 39-Su-d, 43-H-p, 43-R-p, 45-H-p, 45-Ch-d
Burpee - 23-H-p, 23-Ch-p, 25-G-p, 29-H-p, 43-H-p, 45-H-d
Burrell - 45-Ch-p
Burres - 43-B-d
Burrill - 27-Su-d, 41-Co-p
Burroughs - 29-B-p, 39-G-p, 43-St-p
Burrowes - 37-R-d
Burrows - 37-St-d, 41-St-d, 45-St-d
Burt - 29-M-p, 29-G-d, 39-Ch-p
Burton - 29-H-d, 31-G-p
Bush - 37-G-d, 43-H-p, 45-H-p, 45-B-d
Bushey - 25-Ch-d, 39-M-d, 41-Ch-p, 43-R-d

Bushia - 41-Ch-p
Bushman - 31-H-p, 37-Ca-p
Bushnell - 25-Co-d
Bushway - 27-Co-d, 31-Co-d, 33-H-p, 37-Ch-p, 41-St-p, 41-Ch-p, 45-M-p
Bushy - 41-R-p
Buslovich - 45-H-p
Bussiere - 25-H-d, 41-Ch-p
Buswell - 23-Ch-p, 27-B-p, 37-St-p
Butcher - 23-R-p
Butler - 25-Ch-d, 27-Ch-p, 27-R-p, 27-R-d, 29-G-p, 35-R-d, 41-St-p, 43-H-p, 43-Ch-p, 45-H-p, 45-St-p
Butman - 35-G-d, 43-G-d
Butterfield - 31-B-p, 33-Ch-p, 33-G-d, 37-St-p, 43-Ch-d
Butters - 35-St-p
Buttman - 41-B-p, 43-B-p
Button - 43-St-p
Buxton - 45-H-p, 45-H-d
Buzzell - 25-Su-d, 31-St-p, 35-St-p, 35-H-p, 39-M-d, 39-St-d, 39-R-d, 43-M-p, 43-Co-d
Buzzelle - 23-R-d
Byam - 37-H-p, 39-H-p
Byerly - 43-St-p
Byrd - 29-Co-d
Byrne - 35-H-p
Byrns - 41-R-p
Byron - 25-G-d, 27-G-d, 31-R-p, 33-H-d, 35-G-p, 39-R-p
Bythrow - 39-Su-p

Cabral - 43-Su-p
Cadieux - 41-H-p
Cadotte - 43-R-p

Cady - 37-G-p
Cahill - 33-Ch-p
Cain - 31-Su-d, 35-H-p
Cains - 39-M-p
Caird - 25-Co-d, 35-Co-d
Cairns - 43-Su-d
Calamargetou - 43-H-p
Caldara - 23-H-d
Calderwood - 45-H-p
Caldwell - 37-St-p, 37-M-d, 39-St-p, 39-Ch-p, 43-H-p
Calef - 23-G-p, 41-Ch-p, 45-Ch-p
Calhoune - 39-H-p
Calkins - 39-Ch-p, 39-Su-d, 45-Ch-d
Call - 31-St-p, 33-Su-d, 41-R-p, 5-R-p
Callahan - 39-H-d, 41-Ch-d, 43-R-d
Callan - 37-Co-d
Calleso - 35-M-p
Calley - 23-M-p
Calnan - 39-M-p
Calvert - 23-M-p, 29-H-p
Camann - 41-H-p
Camelbeek - 39-H-d
Cameron - 25-H-p, 39-M-p, 41-Co-p, 43-St-p
Cammett - 35-R-p, 43-R-p
Camp - 41-H-d
Campas - 43-H-p
Campbell - 23-G-p, 23-Co-d, 25-Ch-p, 25-H-d, 27-H-p, 27-M-p, 27-G-d, 35-H-d, 35-B-d, 39-R-p, 41-B-p, 41-M-p, 41-H-p, 43-Ch-d, 45-M-d
Campobasso - 33-H-d
Canane - 39-H-p
Canavan - 45-Ch-d

Canfield - 29-G-p, 31-B-p, 39-M-p
Cann - 43-St-p
Canney - 25-St-d, 39-St-p
Canning - 27-H-p, 29-H-d
Cannon - 43-H-p, 43-M-p
Cantin - 23-Co-p, 31-B-p, 41-B-p
Cantrell - 33-H-d
Capen - 39-G-p, 39-Ch-d
Caplan - 29-G-d
Capri - 45-Ca-d
Carano - 39-R-d
Caraphil - 37-H-p
Caraphilakis - 37-H-p
Carbee - 27-G-d
Card - 29-H-d
Carden - 39-St-p, 41-R-p
Carder - 45-H-d
Cardial - 45-B-p
Cardin - 41-H-p
Cardinal - 31-G-p, 39-H-p, 43-Ch-d, 45-B-p
Carelli - 41-H-d
Carette - 41-H-d
Carey - 37-Ch-d, 41-H-p, 41-R-p, 41-Ch-d, 43-G-p, 43-Su-d, 45-M-p, 45-Ch-p
Carignan - 33-H-p, 45-H-p, 45-St-p, 45-St-d
Caris - 45-H-p
Carisiti - 31-B-p
Carkin - 23-M-d, 35-R-d
Carkins - 43-St-p
Carle - 27-H-p, 45-G-p
Carleton - 27-H-p, 31-H-p
Carley - 23-Su-p, 41-Su-p, 43-H-p
Carlin - 41-G-p
Carlisle - 29-R-p

Carlson - 23-H-d, 33-H-p, 37-R-p
Carlton - 23-H-p, 35-R-d
Carnes - 29-R-d, 35-B-p, 35-H-d
Caroll - 33-Co-p
Caron - 23-H-p, 35-H-p, 35-Co-p, 37-H-p, 39-H-p, 39-Su-p, 41-H-p, 41-Ch-p, 43-H-p, 43-Co-p, 45-H-p, 45-Co-p, 45-Su-p
Carpenter - 23-Co-p, 27-St-d, 29-Ch-p, 33-H-p, 35-Co-p, 37-St-p, 39-H-p, 39-Ca-p, 43-Ch-p
Carr - 23-Co-p, 25-R-d, 27-B-p, 31-B-p, 35-H-d, 37-G-p, 39-R-p, 39-G-p, 41-Su-p, 43-G-p, 45-B-p, 45-R-p
Carras - 23-St-d
Carrick - 39-H-d
Carrier - 25-H-p, 27-M-d, 39-R-p, 39-H-p, 39-H-d, 41-H-d
Carriere - 29-H-p
Carrigan - 35-H-p
Carrion - 39-H-p
Carroll - 23-G-p, 29-R-p, 29-M-p, 33-R-p, 33-H-p, 33-Su-d, 35-B-d, 45-Su-p
Carros - 41-H-p
Carson - 43-G-p, 43-R-p, 43-H-p
Carswell - 29-H-p
Cartee - 41-St-p
Carter - 23-H-p, 25-R-p, 25-Co-p, 27-H-d, 33-G-d, 35-G-d, 37-Ch-p, 37-G-p, 39-M-p, 39-Ch-p, 39-Ch-d, 41-H-p, 43-R-p,

Carter - 43-H-p, 43-M-d, 45-M-p, 45-H-p, 45-R-p
Cartlidge - 31-H-d
Cary - 45-St-d
Casbe - 41-H-p
Casboris - 31-St-p
Case - 27-R-d, 41-Su-d, 43-H-p, 45-H-p, 45-Ch-p
Casey - 33-R-p, 37-B-p, 41-St-d
Cash - 41-R-p
Cass - 27-M-p, 29-H-p, 37-B-p, 43-M-p, 43-G-p, 45-M-d
Cassarino - 43-H-d
Cassavaugh - 39-Su-d
Cassell - 37-St-p, 41-R-p
Cassidy - 23-H-p, 35-H-d, 39-H-d
Cassista - 37-H-p
Castagnini - 27-H-p
Castaw - 41-Ch-p, 45-Ch-p
Casteels - 25-G-p
Castonguay - 37-H-p
Castor - 27-Ch-p, 41-Ch-p
Castricone - 31-St-p
Castro - 45-H-p
Caswell - 25-R-p, 39-St-p, 39-R-p, 41-R-p, 41-St-d, 43-R-p
Cataldi - 33-Ca-p
Cate - 25-R-p, 29-M-p, 33-R-d, 33-St-d, 43-B-d
Cater - 39-St-p
Cateras - 27-H-p
Catudal - 31-H-p
Caughey - 41-M-p
Caveney - 43-M-p
Caverhill - 27-G-p
Caverly - 23-Ca-d, 25-M-p, 35-St-d, 43-H-p, 43-St-d, 45-St-p
Cayer - 41-H-p
Cayes - 27-G-p
Caza - 43-H-p
Cazzot - 43-H-p
Cecchetti - 33-H-p
Cecchini - 25-H-d
Celarius - 37-Su-p
Celen - 43-H-d
Celey - 35-G-p
Celi - 41-H-d
Center - 29-H-d, 33-M-p, 35-M-p
Cerier - 43-H-p
Cerutti - 43-R-p
Cesarini - 29-H-d
Chabot - 23-H-d, 41-H-p, 45-H-p
Chadbourne - 43-R-p
Chadburn - 29-Co-p
Chadwick - 25-Ch-p, 43-B-p
Chaffee - 27-Co-d
Chaffin - 37-B-d
Chagnon - 25-H-p, 43-M-p, 43-H-p
Chailly - 27-H-d
Chaisson - 43-R-p
Chakalos - 27-Ch-p
Chakolos - 27-Ch-p
Chalmers - 23-G-d
Chamberlain - 25-Su-d, 31-B-p, 35-Co-d, 39-B-p, 41-St-p, 41-B-p
Chamberlin - 23-G-p, 31-B-p, 33-G-d, 41-G-p, 45-M-p, 45-Ch-p
Chambers - 29-M-p, 29-Su-d, 41-R-p, 41-Ca-p, 43-Ch-p

Champagne - 27-G-d, 29-G-d, 35-H-p, 41-H-p, 41-R-p, 45-H-p, 45-Su-p, 45-St-d
Champion - 29-M-p
Champney - 39-Ch-d, 43-G-p, 45-Ch-d
Champoux - 27-H-d, 43-H-p
Chance - 43-R-p
Chandler - 25-H-d, 27-H-p, 27-R-p, 33-M-p, 39-Ca-p, 41-M-p, 45-H-p
Chandronait - 35-M-p
Channell - 31-Ch-p, 35-Ca-d
Chant - 35-Ch-p
Chapdelaine - 25-R-p
Chapley - 41-Co-p
Chaplin - 41-Ch-p
Chapman - 23-R-d, 25-Co-p, 25-G-d, 27-R-p, 29-Su-p, 31-M-p, 35-M-p, 37-Su-p, 37-H-p, 39-Su-d, 41-R-p, 41-M-d, 45-Su-p, 45-St-d
Chappell - 37-R-p, 43-H-p, 43-Co-d, 45-H-p
Chaput - 35-H-p, 39-M-d, 41-H-p
Charait - 37-H-d
Chard - 39-St-p, 39-R-p
Charette - 37-St-d, 39-M-p, 45-St-d
Charious - 45-R-d
Charkis - 45-H-p
Charland - 37-H-p
Charles - 35-St-d, 37-Ca-p, 37-M-p, 39-Ca-p, 41-Su-d
Charnock - 43-M-p
Charois - 31-H-p, 43-H-p
Charpentier - 41-H-p

Charpentier - 23-H-p, 31-H-d
Charrette - 37-St-p
Charrois - 31-H-p
Charron - 23-R-d, 43-H-d
Charter - 37-H-p
Chartier - 27-H-p, 39-H-d
Chartrand - 37-H-d
Charuk - 27-R-d, 43-R-p
Chase - 23-H-d, 23-R-d, 25-H-p, 25-B-p, 25-R-d, 25-Ch-d, 25-Su-d, 27-M-p, 29-M-p, 29-R-d, 29-H-d, 31-R-p, 33-H-p, 33-Co-p, 33-Ch-d, 33-B-d, 35-H-d, 37-Ca-p, 39-H-p, 39-G-p, 41-R-p, 41-Ch-p, 41-G-p, 41-Su-d, 43-H-p, 43-St-p, 45-H-p, 45-M-p
Chasse - 27-H-p, 41-St-d, 43-St-p
Chatel - 33-H-d
Chatrai - 37-H-p
Chatsey - 35-Su-d
Chauncey - 37-H-d
Chenette - 37-M-p
Chenevert - 27-R-p
Cheney - 23-H-d, 25-M-p, 27-St-d, 35-M-p, 35-H-p, 37-Ca-d, 39-H-p, 41-Ch-d, 43-G-p, 45-M-d
Chensky - 39-Ch-p
Cherkas - 45-H-p
Cherry - 43-M-d, 45-H-d
Chesley - 27-St-p, 35-G-d, 45-St-p
Chesnulevich - 37-H-d
Chevrette - 23-H-p
Chevrier - 29-Co-p
Chiasson - 33-H-p
Chick - 33-St-p
Chiesinski - 23-H-d

Chigres - 23-St-p
Childs - 31-Su-p, 45-Co-p
Chilton - 27-R-d, 35-H-d, 41-M-p
Chimiklis - 35-St-p
Chipman - 41-H-p
Chisholm - 35-Su-p, 43-M-p
Chiuszcz - 45-H-p
Chlorianopoulos - 43-H-p
Chloros - 43-R-p, 43-H-p
Chocquette - 23-H-p
Cholette - 45-H-p
Chommard - 41-H-p
Chouinard - 31-H-p, 31-St-d, 37-M-p, 41-St-p, 43-H-p, 45-H-d
Chretien - 41-H-p
Chrisantheas - 41-H-p
Christensen - 45-Su-p
Christian - 39-Ch-p
Christidis - 29-H-d
Christie - 37-St-p, 39-R-p
Christopher - 37-H-d
Christophil - 33-H-p
Christopoulos - 25-St-p
Christou - 27-H-p
Christy - 41-H-p, 43-R-p
Chrusz - 45-H-p
Church - 25-Ch-p, 25-G-d
Churchill - 23-St-d, 29-R-p, 33-H-p, 41-R-d
Ciarla - 45-M-p
Ciechon - 41-H-d
Cilley - 29-St-p, 29-M-d, 41-St-p, 41-M-d, 43-G-d
Cimone - 37-Ch-d
Ciufo - 27-Su-d
Claflin - 37-H-p, 43-B-p
Clair - 23-H-p
Clairmont - 37-B-p, 45-St-d
Clancy - 41-H-p, 45-Ca-p

Clapp - 43-R-p
Clark - 23-Ch-p, 23-H-d, 25-Ch-p, 25-G-p, 27-G-p, 27-H-p, 29-Su-p, 29-R-p, 29-M-d, 31-Su-p, 31-H-p, 33-St-p, 33-H-d, 33-M-d, 35-B-p, 35-R-p, 35-Ch-p, 35-Su-d, 37-M-p, 37-M-d, 37-R-d, 39-M-p, 39-R-p, 39-Ch-p, 39-G-p, 41-G-p, 41-H-p, 41-H-d, 41-Su-d, 43-St-p, 43-H-p, 43-R-p, 43-M-d, 43-R-d, 45-H-p, 45-G-p, 45-H-d, 45-St-d, 45-B-d
Clarke - 25-M-p, 29-M-p, 29-Su-d, 35-H-d, 41-Ch-p, 45-H-p, 45-Su-p
Clarkson - 43-Co-p
Class - 29-H-d, 33-H-p, 43-Ch-p
Classe - 33-H-p
Claveau - 41-H-p
Claxton - 45-H-p
Clay - 41-Ch-p
Claywood - 31-Ch-d
Cleary - 23-St-p, 23-St-p, 41-Ch-p
Cleaves - 23-St-p, 33-St-d
Cleeves - 37-R-d
Cleghorn - 37-Ch-d
Clement - 23-H-p, 23-Su-p, 23-G-d, 25-M-d, 27-H-p, 27-Co-p, 27-H-d, 29-M-p, 37-Su-d, 39-St-d, 43-St-p
Clements - 43-Su-d
Clemons - 27-H-p, 27-G-d, 35-R-p, 41-M-p
Clermont - 33-H-d, 41-H-p

Cleveland - 25-H-p, 27-G-p, 29-R-p, 43-Su-p, 45-G-d
Clevenson - 39-B-p, 43-G-p
Cliche - 43-M-p
Clifford - 23-M-d, 29-G-p, 31-G-p, 41-H-p, 41-H-d, 43-B-p, 43-H-p, 45-H-d
Clock - 37-R-d
Clogston - 41-Co-p
Clough - 23-Ca-p, 23-M-d, 25-B-d, 29-M-p, 33-R-d, 35-M-p, 35-H-d, 35-St-d, 37-Ch-p, 37-M-d, 41-Ca-p, 41-B-p, 41-St-p, 43-Ca-p, 43-H-p, 43-Su-p, 45-G-p
Clouthier - 43-B-p
Cloutier - 25-M-d, 25-Ch-d, 27-R-d, 35-H-p, 37-H-p, 39-H-p, 41-Co-p
Clow - 27-Ca-p, 41-R-p, 43-Su-p, 45-Su-p
Coady - 41-H-p
Cobb - 27-Ch-d, 37-H-d, 41-G-p
Coburn - 25-B-d, 35-M-p, 35-H-p, 45-M-p
Cochran - 25-H-p, 29-H-d, 41-H-p
Coco - 35-H-p
Codere - 43-M-p
Coderre - 45-M-p
Cody - 37-Ca-d, 45-H-p
Coe - 45-Co-p
Coelho - 37-R-p
Coffin - 23-Ch-p, 25-B-p, 45-H-p
Cofran - 27-M-p
Coghlan - 37-G-d

Cohen - 23-H-p, 39-M-p, 41-R-p, 43-R-p, 43-H-d, 45-H-p
Colantonio - 45-Ch-p
Colasacco - 37-H-p, 41-H-p
Colbath - 31-Ca-p
Colbert - 39-Ca-p
Colbroth - 43-St-p
Colburn - 23-Ch-p, 31-R-p, 35-M-d, 35-H-d, 37-H-d, 41-M-d, 43-G-p
Colby - 23-Su-p, 25-M-d, 27-M-d, 29-Co-p, 31-Su-d, 35-M-d, 35-St-d, 37-Su-p, 37-B-p, 37-H-d, 39-R-d, 41-B-p, 41-M-p, 41-M-d, 43-M-p, 43-M-d, 45-M-p, 45-H-p, 45-Su-p
Colcord - 31-Su-d
Coldwell - 37-H-p, 37-H-d, 37-R-d
Cole - 23-Co-p, 23-M-d, 23-Ch-d, 25-R-d, 29-Co-p, 31-H-p, 31-Ca-d, 31-St-d, 39-Ch-p, 39-M-d, 41-St-p, 43-M-p, 43-Co-p, 45-Ch-p, 45-R-d
Colell - 23-St-d
Coleman - 25-R-p, 25-R-d, 27-R-d, 39-H-p, 41-R-p, 41-M-p, 43-R-p
Coles - 45-Su-p
Coletti - 23-H-p
Colle - 41-M-p
Collerette - 41-M-p
Collette - 35-H-p, 43-H-p, 43-H-d
Colley - 37-G-p
Collier - 29-Su-d, 31-H-p, 33-H-p, 39-Ch-p, 41-R-p, 45-H-p

186

Collins - 23-Ch-p, 23-M-d, 27-Co-p, 27-Ch-d, 29-G-p, 35-R-p, 35-Co-p, 37-H-p, 43-H-p, 45-St-p, 45-H-p, 45-M-p, 45-Su-p, 45-Ch-p
Colliston - 29-R-p
Collum - 33-R-p
Colman - 41-Co-d
Colnalcante - 29-St-p
Colombo - 41-R-d
Columb - 43-St-p, 45-Ch-p
Comeau - 43-R-p
Comolli - 37-M-p
Comstock - 39-H-p
Conant - 39-Ch-d
Condoninas - 35-R-d
Cone - 23-B-p, 41-B-p, 41-M-p
Conely - 29-R-d
Conery - 23-H-d, 37-G-p, 41-G-p, 43-G-p
Coney - 45-H-d
Conley - 27-Co-p, 33-R-p, 39-B-p, 39-H-d
Conliff - 41-Ca-d
Conlin - 35-G-d
Conlon - 41-R-p
Connary - 45-Co-p
Connell - 29-St-d, 39-H-p
Connelley - 45-Su-p
Connelly - 39-H-p, 45-Co-p
Conner - 43-St-p, 43-G-p
Conners - 35-Ca-p
Connery - 35-G-d
Connolly - 29-St-d, 37-Co-p, 43-Su-p
Connor - 25-H-p, 27-M-d, 29-M-p, 29-Ch-p, 39-Ch-d, 41-M-p, 41-H-p, 43-H-p, 45-St-p, 45-H-p
Connors - 23-R-p, 35-R-d, 41-B-p, 41-H-d
Conolly - 31-H-p
Conrad - 37-R-p, 43-G-d, 45-H-p
Conrey - 29-H-p, 45-H-p
Constantine - 23-Co-p, 27-B-d
Constantopoulos - 43-St-p, 45-St-d
Constine - 23-H-p
Contos - 41-B-p
Contri - 43-Ch-p
Converse - 45-G-p, 45-Su-p
Conway - 41-St-p, 45-Ch-d
Cook - 23-Su-p, 23-R-d, 27-R-p, 31-Ca-p, 31-Co-d, 33-G-p, 33-St-d, 33-B-d, 35-M-d, 37-St-p, 37-St-d, 39-Ch-p, 39-G-p, 39-B-p, 39-R-p, 39-St-d, 41-R-p, 41-M-p, 41-G-p, 43-R-p, 43-Ch-p, 43-St-p
Cooke - 27-St-d
Cookson - 37-R-p
Cooley - 25-R-d
Coolidge - 31-Ca-p
Coombs - 35-Ch-p
Coon - 31-G-p
Cooney - 37-R-d, 39-B-d, 43-G-p, 45-G-p
Coons - 37-H-p, 43-H-p
Cooper - 41-St-p, 43-R-p
Coots - 43-Su-d
Copadis - 37-H-p
Copeland - 29-R-p
Copp - 41-St-d, 43-M-p
Coppez - 39-H-p
Corbeau - 31-H-d
Corbett - 29-Co-p, 33-M-p, 33-B-d, 41-St-p

Corbin - 27-H-p, 37-M-p, 45-H-p
Corcoran - 39-R-p, 41-R-p
Cordatos - 43-H-p
Cordon - 25-G-p
Corey - 25-G-p, 27-B-d, 35-Su-d, 37-Ch-p, 39-M-d, 41-G-p, 41-Ch-p, 43-G-p, 43-G-d, 45-Co-p
Corliss - 31-B-d, 41-M-p, 41-H-p, 43-St-d
Cormier - 37-B-d, 39-H-p, 45-St-p, 45-H-p
Cornell - 29-H-d
Corning - 29-H-d, 39-R-p
Cornish - 23-R-d, 43-B-p
Corno - 25-B-p
Cornwell - 39-Ch-p
Coronis - 41-H-p
Corosa - 39-H-p
Corrigan - 45-H-p
Corriveau - 25-M-p, 35-H-d, 41-B-p, 41-H-p
Corriveay - 39-M-d
Corrow - 45-Ca-p
Corry - 35-St-d
Corser - 31-M-d, 33-M-d, 39-M-p
Corson - 23-St-d, 25-M-p, 29-R-p, 37-M-p, 37-Ca-d, 43-St-p, 43-R-p
Corthell - 25-R-p
Cory - 45-Co-p
Coskoran - 23-St-d
Cossar - 23-G-p
Cossette - 45-H-p
Cossitt - 33-Su-d
Costa - 39-H-p, 45-H-p
Costantino - 37-H-p
Costello - 23-Su-p, 43-R-p
Costoras - 39-St-d

Cota - 23-M-d, 29-G-p
Cote - 23-H-p, 27-H-d, 29-H-p, 29-H-d, 31-H-p, 35-H-d, 37-H-p, 41-R-p, 41-H-p, 41-Su-p, 43-H-p, 43-St-p, 45-St-p, 45-H-p, 45-Co-p
Coteneau - 27-H-p
Cotnoir - 25-Co-p, 39-G-d, 45-R-d
Cotter - 41-R-p
Cotton - 23-B-p, 45-Ca-p, 45-M-p, 45-B-d
Cottrell - 25-H-p
Coty - 37-Su-p, 37-G-p
Couch - 43-R-p
Couffman - 39-M-p
Coughlin - 33-H-d, 43-Ch-p, 45-Ch-p
Couillard - 41-Ch-d, 43-St-p
Coulson - 33-M-p, 41-M-p
Coulter - 41-G-d
Courage - 37-G-p, 43-R-p
Courser - 35-Co-d, 37-R-p, 41-R-p
Court - 29-St-d, 43-St-p
Courtamarthe - 41-Su-p
Courteau - 41-H-p
Courtemanche - 31-H-p, 35-H-p, 41-Su-p, 43-H-p
Courture - 31-St-p
Courure - 41-Ch-p
Cousins - 41-H-p, 41-H-d
Coustas - 25-H-p
Coutermarsh - 35-Su-p
Couture - 23-H-p, 25-H-p, 31-St-d, 33-H-p, 33-Co-p, 39-St-p, 41-Co-p, 41-Co-d, 43-H-p, 43-B-p, 43-Co-p, 45-St-p, 45-Su-p, 45-H-d

Couturier - 37-M-p, 41-Co-p, 41-M-p, 43-St-p, 43-M-p, 43-H-p
Covell - 31-G-p
Covill - 39-H-p
Covio - 43-Co-p
Cowles - 29-G-p
Cox - 27-H-p, 31-B-p, 33-H-p, 35-B-d, 39-H-p, 41-Su-p, 41-M-p, 43-Ch-p, 43-R-d, 43-H-d, 45-G-p, 45-R-d
Coyer - 45-Su-p
Coyne - 43-St-d
Cozzi - 45-Co-p
Crabb - 23-G-d
Craft - 41-R-d
Crafts - 25-Ch-p
Craig - 25-Su-d, 29-R-d, 41-M-p, 45-B-p
Craigie - 43-R-p
Cram - 39-G-d
Cramer - 35-B-p
Crandall - 37-Ch-p
Crane - 25-M-d, 27-M-p
Cranshaw - 45-G-p
Cranston - 39-B-p
Craven - 41-R-p
Crawford - 29-H-p, 37-St-p, 41-M-p, 43-Co-d, 45-M-p, 45-M-d
Crecco - 45-Ch-p
Creeden - 31-H-p
Creel - 35-H-p
Crennan - 39-St-d
Cressy - 35-M-p
Crisp - 43-H-p
Critchley - 37-R-p
Crocker - 29-G-p
Crockett - 25-Co-p, 29-M-p, 31-H-d, 45-H-p, 45-B-d

Croft - 35-Ch-d, 37-M-p, 37-St-p, 37-R-p
Crommett - 39-M-p
Crompton - 35-R-p
Cronin - 25-H-p, 41-B-p
Cronshaw - 23-H-p
Crosbie - 43-R-p
Crosby - 23-H-d, 25-H-p, 27-Ch-p, 29-G-p, 33-H-d, 39-B-d, 43-H-d, 45-M-p
Croshere - 37-Su-p
Cross - 25-B-p, 25-H-p, 25-M-p, 27-H-p, 29-Su-p, 29-M-p, 29-M-d, 33-Co-d, 35-Ca-p, 39-G-p, 39-St-p, 41-M-d, 43-H-p
Crossett - 27-Su-d
Crossley - 23-Ch-d
Crossman - 41-Ch-p, 41-Ch-d
Croteau - 31-H-d, 31-Ch-d, 35-Ch-p, 39-Ch-p, 39-St-p, 39-St-d, 41-H-p, 41-St-n, 43-Ch-p, 43-H-p, 45-B-p, 45-Ch-p
Crouse - 31-H-p, 41-Ch-p, 43-Ch-p
Crow - 33-R-p
Crowell - 25-H-d, 29-Ca-p, 33-H-d
Crowley - 25-Co-p, 33-Ch-d, 39-H-p, 39-M-d, 41-R-p, 43-G-p
Cruikshank - 33-M-p
Cuddihee - 41-H-p
Culberson - 43-M-p
Cullen - 39-St-p, 41-St-p
Cullinan - 33-H-d, 45-St-p, 45-H-d
Cullinane - 43-Ch-p

Cummings - 23-B-p, 25-M-d, 31-G-p, 41-R-p, 45-H-p, 45-R-p
Cummiskey - 45-St-p
Cunningham - 25-Ch-p, 27-Ch-p, 31-Su-p, 35-M-d
Curran - 27-Ch-p, 33-G-d, 41-H-p, 45-St-p
Currie - 23-H-p, 27-R-d, 27-Co-d, 29-H-p
Currier -
Currier - 23-H-p, 25-R-p, 25-M-p, 31-H-p, 31-H-d, 33-St-p, 33-Ca-d, 33-Ch-d, 33-R-d, 35-R-d, 39-G-p, 39-R-p, 41-M-p, 41-St-d, 43-St-p, 43-Ch-p, 45-Su-p
Curry - 33-M-p
Curtin - 39-Ch-p, 41-Ca-d
Curtis - 25-Ch-p, 29-G-d, 31-Ch-p, 35-H-d, 37-Co-p, 41-Ch-d
Cushing - 33-St-d, 39-H-d, 45-H-p, 45-St-p
Cushman - 41-H-d, 43-M-p
Cushmon - 29-Su-d
Cusson - 45-M-p
Cuthbert - 37-Su-d
Cutler - 25-Co-d, 33-M-p, 39-G-d
Cutter - 31-H-d, 39-H-p, 39-Ch-p, 45-Ch-d
Cutting - 23-G-d, 25-R-p, 41-B-p, 45-H-d
Cutts - 41-H-p
Cyr - 33-M-p, 37-Ch-p, 39-Ch-p, 41-Ch-p, 43-H-p, 43-B-p
Czarnosz - 43-H-p
Czerkis - 45-H-p

D'Amante - 37-Su-d
D'Amours - 37-H-p
Daeris - 43-St-p
Dagenais - 33-Su-d
Daggett - 39-St-d
Dahar - 23-H-p
Dahms - 45-Su-p
Daigle - 29-Su-d, 45-H-p
Daigneau - 41-B-d, 43-B-d
Dailey - 45-Ch-p
Dale - 23-Co-p, 39-Co-p
Daley - 23-H-p, 25-Co-d, 39-M-d, 43-Co-p
Dallaire - 37-H-p
Dalpra - 45-H-p
Dalton - 39-B-p, 41-H-d, 45-M-p
Dambrino - 41-R-d
Dame - 23-B-p, 29-St-d, 37-R-p, 37-G-d, 39-M-p, 41-St-p, 43-St-d
Damon - 23-Ch-d, 35-Su-p
Dana - 39-Ch-p, 41-H-p
Danahy - 31-St-d
Dandeneau - 45-Co-p
Dandley - 43-H-p
Dane - 25-H-d, 35-B-d, 39-Su-d, 39-H-d, 41-H-d
Daneault - 41-H-d, 45-H-d
Danforth - 31-H-d, 33-G-p, 33-Ca-p
Daniel - 29-H-d
Daniell - 25-M-p
Daniels - 25-G-p, 27-H-p, 39-H-p, 41-M-p, 41-Co-p, 43-G-d, 45-H-p, 45-Ch-p
Danley - 41-R-d
Dansevich - 45-H-p
Dantos - 31-B-p
Daoust - 27-H-d, 31-B-p
Darling - 39-B-p, 45-B-p

Darracott - 33-H-p
Darrah - 33-M-d, 41-H-p, 45-H-p
Daskalopulos - 37-H-p
Dastous - 41-H-p
Daukas - 35-H-d, 45-H-p
Dauphinais - 45-Co-p
Dauphney - 45-Co-p
Daurie - 39-Ca-p
Davenport - 29-M-p, 37-H-p, 39-R-p, 45-St-p, 45-R-p
Daverio - 37-St-d
Davey - 27-H-p
Davian - 43-M-p
David - 39-St-d, 41-R-p, 41-H-p, 41-St-p
Davidson - 25-R-d, 31-Ch-d, 41-B-p, 41-Su-p
Davio - 25-Su-d, 37-G-p, 45-G-d
Davis - 23-Su-p, 23-G-d, 23-B-d, 25-H-p, 25-Su-d, 27-Ca-p, 27-St-p, 27-M-d, 29-Co-p, 29-Ch-p, 29-G-p, 31-R-p, 31-B-p, 31-H-p, 31-Ch-p, 31-G-d, 31-R-d, 31-Su-d, 33-R-p, 33-Ch-p, 33-H-p, 33-M-p, 33-Ch-d, 33-Su-d, 33-M-d, 35-St-p, 35-H-p, 35-Ch-p, 35-R-d, 37-Ch-p, 37-Ca-p, 37-R-p, 37-R-d, 39-St-p, 39-M-p, 39-Ca-p, 39-H-d, 41-R-p, 41-M-p, 41-H-p, 41-Ch-p, 41-St-p, 41-B-p, 41-Ca-p, 41-Ch-d, 41-H-d, 43-M-p, 43-R-p, 43-Ch-p, 43-Ca-p, 43-H-p, 43-H-d, 45-H-p, 45-B-p, 45-Ch-p, 45-R-d, 45-G-d
Davison - 31-G-p, 37-R-d, 41-M-p, 43-R-p
Dawson - 45-H-p
Day - 23-M-p, 23-G-p, 23-R-d, 25-Co-d, 27-H-d, 31-St-p, 31-H-p, 31-G-d, 35-H-p, 39-M-p, 43-G-p, 43-Co-p
de Francoeur - 35-H-p
de l'Etoile - 43-St-p
Deaette - 35-H-p
Deakoum - 41-R-p
Deakoumakes - 41-R-p
Deal - 35-R-d, 37-Co-d, 39-St-d
Dean - 33-Ch-p, 35-H-p, 35-Ch-p, 41-M-p, 43-Ch-p
Deane - 27-Ch-d
DeAngelis - 43-M-p
Dearborn - 23-St-d, 25-M-p, 31-Co-p, 33-Ca-p, 33-M-d, 35-St-d, 39-R-p, 39-Su-p
Dearborne - 23-Ca-d
Deardorff - 35-Ca-p
Dearth - 23-G-p
Debelis - 41-H-p, 45-H-p
DeBelis - 45-H-p
DeBlois - 37-B-p, 45-Co-p
Debusschere - 25-H-d
DeCarlo - 31-R-p
Decato - 35-B-p, 41-M-p
DeChamplain - 41-Co-d
Decosse - 39-H-p
DeCota - 33-M-p
Decrow - 39-M-d
Dedo - 41-Ch-p, 43-Ch-p
Dedomenico - 43-Ch-p
Dee - 35-H-d
Deeb - 41-H-p
Deeg - 37-H-d

DeForge - 33-M-d, 35-B-p
Defosses - 27-Co-p
DeFreitas - 43-H-d
Degasis - 35-H-p, 41-H-p
Degrace - 43-St-p
DeGrandpre - 33-H-p
DeGree - 33-Su-p
DeGross - 37-H-p
DeHart - 35-B-d
deLahunta - 37-M-p
Delaney - 23-H-p, 23-G-d
Delangis - 29-Su-p
Delano - 39-Co-p
Delehanty - 37-H-d
Delisle - 41-H-p, 43-Ch-p
Delorme - 29-H-d
DeLorme - 31-M-p, 45-H-p
Delory - 39-Ch-p
Delsanter - 39-G-d
Delude - 35-H-p
Demanche - 41-H-p
DeMar - 41-B-d, 43-B-d
Demars - 39-M-p, 43-Su-p
DeMars - 41-Ch-p
Demarski - 25-R-p
Demasky - 41-R-p
Demeres - 29-R-d
Demeritt - 31-B-p, 33-St-d, 35-St-d, 41-M-p, 41-Ca-d
Demers - 23-H-p, 25-Co-p, 33-H-p, 39-M-p, 39-Ca-p, 41-G-p, 41-H-p, 41-St-d, 43-H-p, 43-St-p, 43-R-p, 43-H-d, 45-M-p, 45-St-p
Demerse - 29-H-p, 45-Ch-d
Demeule - 41-H-d
DeMontigny - 25-H-p
Demos - 45-H-p
DeMosh - 45-G-d
Dempelis - 45-H-p

Dempsey - 45-H-d
Denancourt - 33-H-p
Denault - 27-R-p
DeNazzi - 41-St-p
Denico - 41-Ch-d, 43-Ch-p
Denis - 45-M-p
Denison - 37-H-d
Dennerly - 25-M-p
Dennett - 23-St-d, 33-St-d
Dennis - 23-B-p, 27-M-p, 27-Co-d, 29-H-d, 37-H-p, 39-H-p, 39-Co-p, 41-R-p
Dennison - 35-B-p, 37-R-p
Denno - 37-H-d
Denoit - 33-H-p
Denoncour - 41-H-p
Denoncourt - 39-H-d
Densmore - 23-Su-p, 25-B-p
Denton - 35-H-d, 39-M-d
Denyou - 41-R-p
DePalma - 43-M-p
Der Hovhanesian - 41-H-p
Derby - 23-H-p, 27-M-p, 27-Ch-p, 29-Ch-p, 37-B-p, 39-Ch-p
Derbyshire - 33-H-p
DeRobertis - 45-Su-p
Deroche - 33-G-d, 45-H-d
deRochemont - 43-R-d
DeRome - 37-H-d
DeRosia - 33-Co-p
Derosier - 31-Co-p, 37-M-p, 43-Ch-p
Deroucher - 39-R-d
Derr - 41-H-p
Derrington - 33-G-p
Deruisseau - 39-Ch-p
Dery - 45-H-p
des Santos - 45-H-p
Desautel - 35-St-d
Desbiens - 29-H-d

Deschamps - 43-H-p
Deschants - 37-St-p
Deschenes - 43-St-p
DeSchuiteneer - 37-H-p
Desclaux - 33-H-d
Desclos - 29-H-p
Descoteau - 45-Su-p
Desfosses - 43-Su-p
Desgranges - 37-Ch-p
Desgroseilliers - 45-St-p
DesGroseilliers - 37-H-p
Desiderio - 45-Su-p
Desilets - 41-H-p, 43-St-p
Desjardins - 39-H-d, 45-St-p
Deskowicz - 31-H-p
Deslandes - 37-B-p
Deslaurier - 43-H-d
Deslauriers - 23-Co-p
Desmarais - 23-St-d, 27-H-p, 27-H-d, 39-Ch-d
Desmesmeules - 45-H-p
Desmond - 41-M-p, 45-Su-p
Desotell - 29-H-d
Despres - 43-H-d
Desroche - 31-H-p
Desrochers - 37-H-d, 41-Ch-p
DesRochers - 41-H-d, 43-H-p
DesRoches - 39-G-p
Desrosiers - 31-H-d, 39-M-p, 39-Ch-p, 39-H-p, 41-H-p, 43-H-p, 45-Ch-p
DesRosiers - 23-R-p
Desruisseau - 39-H-p
Deters - 43-Ch-p
Deveau - 37-St-p
DeVeau - 25-R-d
Devine - 23-H-p, 29-H-p
Devino - 23-G-d
DeVlaminck - 23-H-d
Devoe - 39-G-p
Devoid - 45-M-p, 45-St-p

Devolites - 45-H-p
Devoll - 23-H-d
DeWaele - 27-H-d, 41-H-d, 45-H-d
Dewey - 25-H-p, 35-Su-d, 45-Su-p
Dewing - 31-G-p
Dewitt - 29-Ch-d
DeWitt - 33-G-d
DeWolfe - 29-St-d
Dexter - 43-R-p, 45-H-p, 45-G-d
Dextras - 45-H-p
Deyo - 45-Ch-d
Diamond - 39-St-n, 43-H-p
Diamondis - 39-St-n
DiAngelis - 45-R-d
DiBernardo - 43-Ch-p
Dicey - 41-G-p, 45-Ch-p
Dichard - 41-H-p, 45-H-d
Dick - 41-R-p
Dickerman - 29-Ch-d, 45-H-p
Dickerson - 27-M-p
Dickey - 25-Co-d, 43-M-p, 45-Co-p
Dickie - 37-St-d, 41-H-d
Dickinson - 31-H-p, 31-G-p, 31-Ch-p, 33-H-p, 35-St-d, 45-G-d
Dickson - 39-B-d
Didomenico - 41-Ch-p
Diemond - 33-H-p
Diener - 29-R-p, 39-R-p
Dietlein - 33-H-d
Dietrich - 41-R-p
Dignard - 41-H-p
Dillon - 45-M-p
DiMaria - 37-Co-p
diMercier - 23-B-p
Dimick - 25-G-p, 45-H-p
Dimitri - 43-Ch-p

Dimmick - 41-H-p
Dinagan - 43-Ch-d
Dingman - 41-Ch-p
Dinkowski - 29-R-p
Dinwoodie - 23-H-d, 31-H-d
Dion - 23-H-p, 25-H-d, 29-H-d, 37-H-d, 41-H-p, 41-B-p, 43-H-p, 45-B-d, 45-R-d
Dionne - 23-H-p, 27-H-p, 29-H-p, 31-H-d, 33-H-p, 35-Co-p, 43-H-p, 43-H-d, 45-H-p, 45-Co-p
DiProspero - 45-Co-p
Dipucchio - 39-Co-p
Discoe - 41-M-p
Diselets - 41-Co-p
Ditmore - 45-H-p
Diversi - 33-M-d, 35-M-d
Dixon - 39-G-p, 41-R-p, 41-R-d, 43-R-p, 43-Ch-d
Dobbins - 45-St-p
Dobson - 45-R-p
Dockey - 41-M-p
Dockham - 29-R-p, 37-R-p
Docks - 29-H-d
Docos - 29-H-p
Dodge - 25-G-p, 27-St-d, 31-B-p, 31-Co-p, 31-St-d, 35-Ch-p, 35-G-p, 35-St-d, 35-H-d, 39-H-d, 41-Ca-p, 43-Ch-p, 45-B-d
Doe - 45-Ch-p
Doeg - 39-St-p
Doherty - 27-Co-p, 29-H-p, 37-R-d, 45-H-p
Doilliver - 27-St-p
Dole - 39-Su-p
Doll - 39-G-d
Dollard - 37-R-d, 41-R-p

Dolloff - 35-B-p, 35-M-d, 41-R-p
Dolph - 37-St-p
Dolton - 39-R-d
Dolzko - 43-H-p
Dombrowski - 45-Ch-p
Donah - 23-H-d
Donahue - 41-H-p, 41-H-d, 45-St-p
Donaldson - 27-R-d
Donelan - 39-H-p
Donezan - 29-R-d
Donlon - 37-St-p
Donnelly - 35-Co-d, 45-H-p, 45-Ch-p
Donovan - 29-St-d, 33-H-p, 33-H-p, 33-R-d
Doody - 43-Ch-p, 45-H-p
Doolittle - 23-Su-p, 33-H-p, 35-H-p
Doonar - 35-H-p
Doplace - 33-H-d
Dorais - 45-Ch-p
Doran - 43-Ch-p, 45-Ch-p
Dore - 41-R-p
Doremus - 35-G-p
Dorey - 39-R-p
Dorman - 23-Co-p, 43-R-p
Dorney - 45-H-p
Dorothy - 33-H-p
Dorr - 25-St-p, 39-Co-p, 41-Co-d
Dorris - 39-H-p
Dorsett - 45-H-d
Dorsey - 27-Co-d
Dorson - 33-H-p
Dorval - 23-M-d, 25-M-d, 35-H-d
Doschavich - 33-H-p
Dostie - 41-H-d, 45-M-p
Dostilio - 45-Ch-d

Doty - 45-H-p
Doubleday - 37-G-p
Doucette - 27-R-d, 35-Ch-p, 41-R-p, 43-Su-p, 45-St-p
Dougherty - 25-Su-d
Doughty - 39-M-p
Douglas - 39-St-p
Douglass - 31-H-d, 43-St-p, 43-H-p, 45-G-p
Douklia - 43-H-d
Douphinett - 45-M-p
Douse - 37-Co-p
Douville - 45-H-d
Dow - 23-H-p, 25-M-d, 33-Ca-p, 33-H-d, 35-Co-d, 37-M-p, 39-G-d, 39-Ca-p, 39-H-p, 41-Ch-p, 41-G-p, 41-B-p, 43-R-p, 43-B-p, 43-Co-p, 43-R-d, 45-B-p, 45-R-p, 45-G-d
Dowaliby - 39-St-p
Dowe - 45-R-p
Dowling - 25-H-p, 37-St-p
Downer - 27-G-p, 45-G-p
Downes - 27-R-p, 31-G-d, 35-G-p, 35-H-p
Downey - 35-H-p
Downing - 23-H-p, 23-G-p, 27-St-d, 27-G-d, 29-B-p, 29-Su-p, 29-G-p, 29-R-d, 31-G-d, 33-G-p, 35-G-p, 35-M-p, 37-G-p, 39-B-p, 41-R-p, 41-G-p, 41-M-p, 45-R-p, 45-R-d
Downs - 27-R-p, 29-Co-p, 41-St-p, 41-M-p
Dowse - 33-Co-d
Doyle - 29-Ca-p, 33-H-p, 33-Ch-d, 37-H-p, 37-H-d, 41-Ch-p, 41-G-p, 41-Ch-d, 43-Ch-p, 45-H-p

Doyon - 37-St-d, 41-Co-p
Drabinski - 45-H-d
Dragon - 41-M-p
Drake - 35-M-p, 41-R-p
Drapeau - 33-Co-p, 41-St-d
Drayton - 43-R-p
Drazkowska - 33-H-p
Dresser - 33-Co-d, 41-Co-p
Drew - 25-H-d, 27-H-p, 27-M-d, 31-M-p, 33-St-d, 35-Ca-p, 35-Ca-d, 39-Ca-p, 41-Ca-p, 43-M-p, 45-B-p
Driscoll - 25-St-p, 33-H-p, 41-Ch-p
Drobisewski - 43-R-p
Drobisewskia - 43-R-p
Drolet - 33-H-p, 41-H-p
Droskin - 29-Co-p
Drouin - 37-St-p, 37-St-d, 39-B-d
Drouse - 41-H-p, 43-M-p
Drown - 43-Co-p
Drowns - 45-B-d
Drozdoff - 41-H-p
Drugg - 37-Ch-p
Drury - 35-R-d, 39-B-d, 45-B-p
Dubal - 43-Ch-p
Dube - 35-H-p, 41-H-p, 43-H-p, 45-H-p
Dubey - 25-H-d
Dublow - 27-H-p
Dubois - 23-H-p, 25-H-d, 33-B-p, 35-M-p, 37-St-p, 39-St-p, 39-H-p, 41-H-p, 45-H-p
DuBois - 33-H-p, 39-St-p, 45-St-p
Dubowsky - 27-H-p
Dubreuil - 43-Su-d, 45-Su-p
Dubriske - 45-Ch-p

Dubuc - 33-H-p, 35-H-p
Duby - 29-Ch-p
Ducharme - 41-Su-p, 43-G-p
Duclos - 39-M-p, 45-M-p, 45-H-d
Duda - 43-H-p
Duddy - 39-H-d
Dudley - 31-G-p, 35-G-d, 41-Su-d, 45-H-p
Dudzenski - 27-Ch-p
Duerbitz - 45-H-p
Duff - 39-M-p
Dufferin - 39-Su-p
Duffy - 25-H-p, 39-H-p
Dufield - 43-B-p
Dufort - 37-H-p
Dufour - 31-St-d, 41-H-p, 43-H-p, 45-B-d, 45-H-d
Dufresne - 45-H-p
Dugan - 31-H-p
Dugas - 31-H-d, 41-H-d, 45-H-p
Duggan - 41-St-p
Dugre - 31-H-p
Duguay - 33-Su-p, 37-Ch-p, 45-H-p
Duguie - 41-Su-p
Duhamel - 37-H-p
Duke - 23-Ca-p, 23-H-p, 25-R-p, 31-H-d, 33-H-p, 43-St-p
Dukette - 41-M-p
Dulac - 41-B-p
Dumais - 27-B-p, 35-R-p, 43-Co-p
Dumas - 41-H-p, 41-Co-p, 43-B-p
Dummaskowski - 41-R-p
Dunbar - 23-Su-d, 25-H-p, 27-M-p, 33-Su-p, 43-H-p, 45-M-p

Duncan - 23-H-d, 25-H-p, 33-R-d, 39-H-p, 43-H-d
Dunham - 23-G-d, 27-Ch-p, 39-R-p, 39-G-d, 45-G-p
Dunican - 45-H-d
Dunkerton - 43-G-d
Dunlap - 31-G-p, 33-Ca-p, 33-G-p, 37-St-p, 43-R-p, 43-St-d, 45-Ch-p
Dunleavy - 43-G-d
Dunn - 23-Co-p, 33-G-p, 39-Ch-p, 41-R-p, 41-Ch-p, 43-H-p, 45-B-p, 45-Su-p
Dunne - 39-H-p
Dunphy - 39-R-d
Dunsford - 27-M-p, 31-M-d
Dunton - 37-R-d
Duperron - 23-H-p, 45-H-p
Duplessis - 27-H-p, 37-G-d, 41-H-p
Dupont - 33-H-p
Dupre - 45-H-p
Dupree - 41-Ch-p
Dupuis - 25-H-p, 29-M-p, 33-St-p, 37-B-p, 43-R-p, 45-B-p
Duquette - 35-H-p, 35-B-d, 41-St-p, 43-H-d
Durand - 39-H-d
Durant - 41-H-p, 43-Ch-d
Durepo - 33-M-d
Durette - 25-R-p
Durgan - 35-H-d
Durgin - 29-H-d, 29-B-d, 41-M-p, 43-B-p
Durkee - 29-H-d
Durost - 37-M-p
Dussault - 25-Co-p, 43-R-d
Dustin - 23-Ch-p, 25-G-p, 31-M-p, 43-M-p, 43-Su-p, 45-Su-p

Dutilly - 41-St-n
Dutton - 25-Co-p, 45-Ch-p
Duval - 23-H-p, 25-Ch-d, 33-H-p, 37-Ch-d, 39-M-d, 41-Ch-p, 43-Ch-p, 45-H-p, 45-Ch-p
Duvall - 43-Ch-p
DuVarney - 27-Ch-p
Duvernay - 25-M-p
Dvareckas - 45-H-p
Dwinell - 45-H-p
Dwire - 35-St-d, 39-Su-p, 41-St-d
Dwyer - 37-R-p, 41-St-d
Dyer - 41-H-p, 45-H-p, 45-G-d
Dykeman - 45-M-d
Dyment - 45-M-p
Dynkowski - 23-R-d
Dyrkacz - 41-H-p
Dzengelewski - 37-G-p
Dziadosz - 37-H-p

Eafrate - 31-H-p
Easter - 31-H-d
Easterberg - 35-H-p
Eastman - 25-R-p, 25-Ca-p, 25-M-p, 25-B-p, 25-Co-d, 27-H-p, 29-G-p, 31-G-p, 33-H-p, 33-Su-d, 33-Co-d, 35-Co-p, 37-H-p, 37-St-d, 39-Ch-p, 39-St-p, 39-M-p, 39-St-d, 41-G-p, 41-M-p, 41-H-d, 43-G-d, 45-Su-p, 45-G-d, 45-St-d
Eastwood - 23-Ch-d
Eaton - 23-R-d, 25-H-p, 25-Co-d, 27-H-d, 27-H-p, 29-M-p, 29-H-d, 31-G-p, 37-Ca-p, 41-M-p, 41-H-p, 41-R-d, 43-M-p, 43-R-p, 43-H-p

Eckerman - 39-Su-p
Economides - 29-H-p
Economu - 29-Su-p, 45-Ch-p
Edberg - 43-Co-p
Edgerly - 27-St-d, 35-St-p, 35-St-d, 39-St-d, 45-Ca-p
Edison - 37-H-d
Edminster - 41-Su-p
Edmondson - 31-H-p
Edmunds - 25-M-p, 27-M-p, 35-M-d, 37-Ch-p
Edoff - 45-Ch-p
Edwards - 39-H-p, 41-Ch-d, 45-R-d
Egan - 35-Ch-p, 37-Co-d, 43-H-p, 43-Co-p
Eichorn - 33-H-d
Eickman - 43-H-d
Eidler - 43-R-p
Eidlow - 43-R-p
Eivers - 27-H-p, 31-H-p
Ekdahl - 41-H-p, 43-H-p
Eklund - 29-H-p
Ekman - 39-Su-p
Elder - 23-Su-p
Eldredge - 43-R-p
Eldridge - 35-Ca-p, 41-R-p, 41-Ca-p, 41-St-p, 45-B-p
Elgart - 41-H-p
Eli - 27-B-p
Elkins - 27-B-p, 29-M-p, 35-St-p
Ellingsworth - 25-H-p
Ellinwood - 29-Ch-p
Elliot - 35-R-d
Elliott - 27-G-p, 27-H-d, 39-G-p, 41-H-p, 41-R-p, 41-G-p, 41-M-p, 43-H-p, 43-M-p, 45-Ca-p, 45-M-p, 45-B-p, 45-H-p, 45-Ch-p, 45-St-d

Ellis - 27-St-p, 29-B-p, 31-H-p, 33-M-d, 37-G-p, 37-St-p, - 37-G-p, 39-B-p, 39-St-p, 39-G-p, 39-M-d, 41-M-p, 41-St-d, 43-Ch-p, 43-M-p, 43-M-d, 45-St-p, 45-B-p, 45-G-p
Ellison - 43-St-p
Ellor - 25-Ch-d
Ells - 23-Ch-d
Elmes - 31-H-d
Elmora - 43-G-d
Elms - 41-R-p
Elwell - 35-Ch-p
Elwood - 41-G-p
Emerson - 23-M-p, 23-G-d, 23-R-d, 27-Co-p, 27-M-d, 29-M-p, 29-R-p, 29-B-p, 33-M-d, 35-H-p, 35-M-p, 37-R-d, 37-H-d, 39-Ca-p, 39-Ca-d, 39-M-d, 41-B-p, 41-R-p, 41-H-p, 41-H-d, 41-Ca-d
Emerton - 45-G-p
Emery - 23-R-d, 31-G-p, 33-R-d, 35-Ch-p, 35-G-p, 37-R-d, 45-M-p, 45-R-d
Emmes - 39-Ch-p
Emmons - 23-St-p, 31-Ca-p, 39-H-p, 45-H-p
Emond - 23-St-p, 27-H-p
Emory - 23-H-p
Emperor - 27-Ca-p
Empey - 23-Su-d
England - 43-R-p
English - 35-H-p, 45-H-d
Enire - 25-R-d
Ennis - 33-H-p
Eno - 43-Ch-p
Enos - 39-G-d
Enright - 43-Ch-p

Entwistle - 43-R-d
Enwright - 45-B-p
Eola - 25-Ch-p
Erickson - 25-R-d, 33-Co-p, 41-Ch-p, 45-Co-p, 45-Su-p, 45-R-d
Ericson - 27-B-p
Eriksson - 45-R-d
Ermalavich - 35-H-p
Ermalovich - 45-H-d
Erskine - 39-Su-p, 41-H-d, 45-H-d
Ervine - 37-Ca-p
Erwin - 27-M-p
Eryou - 25-B-p, 41-B-p, 43-B-p
Esmail - 41-St-n
Estabrook - 27-G-p, 39-R-p
Estes - 25-H-p, 25-Ca-d, 29-G-p, 33-Co-p, 37-St-p, 37-R-d, 41-R-p, 41-H-d
Estey - 37-B-p, 39-Ch-d
Etheridge - 43-R-d
Evans - 25-Co-p, 27-H-p, 33-R-p, 35-St-d, 37-Ca-p, 37-Co-d, 39-St-p, 45-G-d
Everet - 23-G-d
Everhart - 37-H-p
Evirs - 29-B-p
Ewen - 25-G-p
Ewer - 37-R-p
Ewins - 33-Ch-p

Faery - 37-Ch-p
Fagan - 29-M-d
Fagnant - 35-H-p, 43-H-p
Fahey - 41-H-p
Fair - 45-Ch-d
Fairbanks - 23-Ch-p, 37-Ca-p, 41-Ch-p, 45-Su-p
Fairchild - 43-R-d

Fairfield - 33-Ch-p, 39-H-d
Falconer - 33-Su-p
Fales - 41-G-d
Falin - 45-H-p
Fallgren - 41-H-p
Falmer - 45-M-p
Faneras - 35-R-p
Fannie - 45-St-p, 45-M-p
Fanny - 39-M-p, 43-M-p
Farcas - 45-R-p
Farewell - 43-Su-p
Farinoli - 45-Ch-p
Faris - 31-M-p
Farland - 35-H-p, 39-H-p
Farley - 37-St-d
Farmer - 27-R-d, 43-H-p, 43-M-p
Farnham - 31-G-d, 33-G-p, 35-B-d
Farnsworth - 25-M-d, 31-H-p, 35-Su-d, 37-Su-d
Farnum - 35-M-p, 45-M-d
Faro - 45-H-p
Farr - 39-G-d
Farra - 41-B-p, 43-B-p
Farrar - 25-H-d, 39-R-p
Farrell - 23-H-p, 25-H-p, 25-G-d
Farrington - 29-G-p, 33-Ch-p, 41-R-p, 45-H-p
Farris - 35-H-d
Farwell - 27-M-d
Faucher - 23-H-d, 33-R-p
Faulkingham - 45-H-p
Fay - 39-Ch-p
Fearer - 39-R-d
Feather - 27-B-p
Fecteau - 27-St-d, 29-G-d, 45-H-p
Fedelski - 45-Su-p
Federick - 45-R-d

Feinauer - 31-R-p
Felch - 41-H-d, 45-R-p, 45-R-d, 45-H-d
Felix - 41-Ch-d
Fellows - 25-G-p, 27-R-p, 35-H-p, 41-G-d, 43-H-p
Felming - 31-Co-d
Fennessy - 45-Ch-p
Fenoff - 27-G-d, 29-G-d
Ferguson - 23-B-p, 25-H-p, 35-G-p, 37-Ch-d, 41-H-d
Feris - 23-St-p
Ferland - 29-M-p, 37-H-p, 39-St-n, 45-St-p, 45-R-p
Fernandez - 41-Ca-p
Ferrari - 31-Co-p, 43-Co-p
Ferrera - 41-H-p
Ferrigan - 43-St-p
Ferrin - 31-G-p, 33-M-d
Feuerstein - 41-H-p, 43-H-p
Feurstein - 41-B-p, 43-H-p, 43-B-p, 45-H-p
Fickett - 37-M-p, 41-R-d
Field - 29-M-p, 33-Ch-p, 35-H-p, 43-R-p, 43-H-p
Fielding - 43-M-p
Fields - 25-B-p, 37-B-p, 37-St-p, 41-G-p, 43-G-p, 45-M-p, 45-G-p
Fifield - 29-B-p, 41-G-d
Figerle - 43-R-p
Files - 31-St-d, 37-M-p
Filion - 35-H-p, 39-M-d
Fillion - 25-G-p, 39-G-p
Filspatore - 29-M-d
Filteau - 39-Co-p, 43-H-d
Finan - 41-M-p, 43-G-p
Fineblit - 27-H-p
Finnin - 39-St-p
Firestone - 41-H-p, 43-H-p, 43-B-p, 45-H-p, 45-H-d

Fischer - 33-H-p, 39-St-p
Fisette - 45-Su-p
Fish - 39-G-p, 43-Ch-p
Fisher - 23-G-p, 25-H-p, 27-G-d, 29-Ch-p, 29-H-p, 29-St-d, 35-M-p, 37-St-p, 39-M-p, 39-H-d, 41-H-p, 41-M-d, 43-G-d, 45-H-p, 45-B-p, 45-R-p
Fisk - 35-St-p, 37-H-p, 45-Co-p
Fiske - 37-H-d, 39-H-d
Fitch - 23-H-d, 25-H-d
Fitts - 27-R-p, 33-H-p, 37-R-p, 37-H-d, 39-Su-p, 43-M-p
Fitzgerald - 23-H-p, 23-H-d, 25-M-p, 27-Ch-p, 27-M-d, 29-G-p, 29-H-d, 31-Ch-d, 35-H-p, 41-St-n, 45-H-p
Fitzherbert - 43-St-p
Fitzpatrick - 27-H-p, 31-H-p, 41-H-p
Fitzsimmons - 27-M-p
Fix - 39-R-p
Fizette - 31-G-p
Flack - 31-B-p
Flagg - 25-H-p, 39-Ch-p, 39-H-d, 41-G-p, 45-Ch-p
Flaherty - 37-H-p
Flanders - 23-H-p, 23-G-p, 31-H-p, 39-G-p, 39-H-p, 39-R-d, 39-H-d, 41-H-p, 41-M-p, 43-Ca-d, 45-H-p, 45-Ch-p, 45-B-d
Flannigan - 35-H-p
Fleming - 27-H-p, 39-R-d
Fletcher - 25-H-p, 29-R-d, 31-H-p, 37-M-d, 39-H-p, 45-G-p

Fleury - 33-M-p, 45-M-d, 45-H-d
Flint - 25-M-d, 39-M-p, 43-St-d
Flioras - 43-H-p
Flis - 35-H-d
Floberg - 23-H-p
Flodin - 25-G-p, 43-H-p
Flooyd - 41-R-p
Florand - 35-R-p
Floras - 43-H-p
Florence - 39-M-p, 41-R-d, 43-R-p
Floros - 43-B-p
Flower - 37-H-p, 39-H-p, 43-Co-p
Floyd - 37-Ca-p, 41-Ca-d
Fluck - 43-R-p
Flynn - 29-H-p, 31-Ch-p, 39-M-p, 41-St-p, 43-H-p, 43-R-d, 45-Co-p
Fober - 41-H-d
Fogerty - 29-Su-p
Fogg - 23-B-p, 23-R-d, 25-B-p, 37-M-p, 37-B-p, 39-R-p, 39-Ch-p, 41-Co-p, 41-R-d
Foisie - 29-M-p, 29-H-p
Foisy - 37-Su-p, 43-Su-d
Foley - 27-Ch-p, 33-H-p, 39-B-p, 43-Ch-p, 45-H-p, 45-Ch-p
Folis - 41-H-p
Folsom - 29-M-d, 33-M-p, 33-H-p, 37-St-d, 41-G-p
Fontaine - 25-H-p, 41-Su-p
Fontana - 33-Ca-d
Fontenot - 37-R-d
Foote - 29-R-p, 39-Ch-p, 39-M-p, 41-M-p, 41-R-p

Forbes - 27-B-p, 27-Ch-d, 29-B-p, 33-St-p, 37-St-d, 39-G-p, 43-R-p
Forbush - 31-Co-p, 31-Co-d, 33-H-p
Forcier - 29-Ch-p, 43-Ch-d, 45-H-p, 45-St-d
Ford - 23-M-p, 25-B-p, 29-M-p, 31-H-p, 37-H-d, 37-G-d, 41-H-p, 41-Ch-p, 43-H-p, 45-M-p
Forger - 39-M-p
Forgues - 37-St-d
Forrest - 33-St-d, 37-B-d, 39-H-p
Forster - 35-Ca-d
Forsyth - 41-B-p, 41-Ch-d, 45-Ch-p
Fortier - 25-Co-d, 27-H-p, 27-H-p, 31-G-p, 31-H-p, 41-H-d, 43-B-d, 43-Ch-d
Fortin - 25-H-p, 41-H-p, 45-M-p, 45-B-d
Fortune - 39-Su-p, 41-M-p
Fosberg - 25-M-p
Fosburgh - 23-Ch-p
Fosdick - 33-Ch-p
Fosher - 31-H-p
Fosie - 35-G-d
Foskett - 25-M-p, 39-H-p
Foss - 23-H-d, 23-St-d, 25-St-d, 27-St-d, 31-St-d, 35-St-d, 39-St-p
Fossett - 41-R-p
Foster - 25-B-p, 27-R-p, 29-Co-d, 29-H-d, 31-Ca-p, 31-M-p, 33-H-p, 33-Co-d, 35-H-p, 35-M-d, 37-G-p, 37-Ch-p, 39-H-p, 39-Co-d, 41-H-p, 41-B-p, 43-M-p, 45-H-p, 45-St-p

Fottler - 37-H-p, 39-H-p
Fountain - 23-B-p, 31-H-d, 45-Su-p
Fournier - 23-R-p, 25-H-p, 25-G-p, 27-Co-p, 29-H-p, 29-H-d, 31-H-p, 31-H-d, 33-H-d, 37-H-p, 43-G-p, 45-B-p, 45-H-p
Fowle - 41-H-p
Fowler - 25-M-p, 27-H-p, 29-Su-d, 37-R-p, 39-M-p, 41-R-d, 41-Ch-d, 45-R-p, 45-B-p, 45-H-p
Fox - 23-H-p, 25-B-d, 25-H-d, 25-G-d, 33-G-d, 37-H-p, 41-R-p, 41-H-p, 41-St-p, 41-Ca-p, 43-Ca-p, 43-R-p
Frabee - 45-Co-p
Fragopulos - 45-Su-p
Fragoyanes - 27-H-p
Francis - 27-H-p, 37-Su-p, 43-H-p, 43-R-d
Franco - 25-Su-p
Francoeur - 29-H-p, 37-H-p, 39-H-p, 43-H-p, 43-Co-p, 45-H-d
Frandaca - 41-R-p
Franggos - 43-H-p
Frangos - 33-H-d
Frank - 39-G-p, 45-H-p
Franklin - 27-H-d, 43-H-p, 45-Su-p, 45-G-d
Frantz - 41-R-p
Franz - 43-R-p
Frary - 25-M-d
Fraser - 33-R-p, 41-M-p, 45-H-d
Fratus - 43-Ca-p, 45-M-p
Frazee - 43-Su-p
Frear - 41-H-d

201

Frechette - 29-Co-p, 45-Co-p
Frederick - 23-Ch-p
Fredette - 25-G-d, 31-M-p, 41-St-p
Freeland - 45-Su-p
Freeman - 29-M-p, 33-Ch-p, 33-H-d, 35-H-p, 35-Ch-p, 35-H-d, 37-H-d, 39-H-p, 43-H-d, 45-Ch-p, 45-Su-p
Freese - 45-H-p
Freitas - 37-M-d
French - 25-M-d, 25-G-d, 27-B-d, 31-G-d, 33-M-p, 33-H-p, 33-H-d, 35-M-p, 35-Ch-p, 41-H-p, 41-Co-p, 41-M-p, 41-R-p, 43-Ca-p, 43-M-p, 43-H-p, 45-H-p, 45-G-p, 45-H-d, 45-M-d
Frenette - 33-Su-p, 41-M-p, 45-H-d
Frenier - 27-H-d
Fretwell - 39-M-p
Frick - 41-M-p
Fridell - 45-M-p
Friese - 37-H-d
Frink - 45-R-d
Frizzell - 25-Co-d
Frost - 27-Ca-p, 29-Ca-p, 35-R-p, 37-H-p, 39-H-p, 41-St-p, 45-M-p, 45-R-d
Froton - 43-H-p
Frye - 31-St-p, 31-G-p, 45-H-p
Fudge - 33-R-p, 41-R-d
Fugere - 31-B-p, 45-B-p
Fullam - 43-Ch-p
Fuller - 29-R-d, 33-M-d, 35-H-p, 37-G-p, 37-Ch-p, 41-R-p, 45-Ch-p, 45-G-d, 45-Ch-d, 45-Co-p
Fulton - 39-Ch-p, 43-H-p, 45-H-p
Funkhouser - 39-G-p
Furman - 35-R-p, 37-H-d, 41-H-p
Fusco - 45-St-p
Futyra - 23-H-d
Fyffe - 45-H-d

Gabriel - 25-H-p, 37-H-p, 41-St-p, 45-H-d
Gackowski - 43-H-p
Gadbois - 37-H-p, 41-H-p
Gade - 39-Co-p
Gadis - 35-R-d
Gadoury - 41-St-p
Gadwah - 23-Co-p
Gaffney - 37-St-p
Gage - 29-H-p, 31-R-p, 39-St-p, 39-H-p, 41-St-p, 43-M-p, 45-H-p
Gagne - 27-H-d, 29-H-p, 31-H-p, 37-B-d, 39-St-p, 39-St-d, 41-Ca-p, 41-H-p, 43-B-p, 45-St-p, 45-Co-p, 45-St-d, 45-H-d
Gagner - 45-Su-p
Gagnon - 23-G-d, 27-H-d, 29-H-d, 31-H-p, 33-H-d, 35-Co-p, 37-H-p, 37-St-p, 39-H-p, 39-Co-p, 41-H-p, 41-H-d, 43-B-p, 43-H-p, 43-Su-p, 45-H-p, 45-M-p, 45-B-d
Gaidis - 27-R-d
Gailey - 45-St-p
Gaillardetz - 45-M-d
Gainor - 33-Co-p

Gale - 25-Co-p, 41-Ch-d, 41-Co-d
Galecki - 33-H-p
Galinsky - 43-R-d
Galipeau - 25-H-d
Gall - 25-Co-p
Gallacher - 23-R-p
Gallagher - 25-M-p, 29-H-d, 31-H-p, 39-G-p, 43-B-d, 45-H-p, 45-H-d
Gallant - 33-Co-d
Gallo - 45-H-d
Galloupe - 31-B-p, 35-B-d
Galloway - 37-St-p, 41-G-p
Gallup - 25-Su-d, 31-H-p, 45-H-p
Galt - 35-R-p
Gamache - 35-H-p, 41-H-p, 43-H-p, 45-G-p
Gamble - 35-H-p
Gamelin - 39-H-p
Gammon - 45-R-p, 45-R-d
Ganitos - 45-R-p
Gannett - 43-R-p
Gannon - 23-Ch-d
Gantz - 45-M-p
Garabedian - 45-H-d
Garand - 45-H-p
Garant - 27-M-p, 43-R-d
Garbarine - 33-H-p
Garceau - 31-H-p
Gardiner - 35-G-p
Gardner - 25-G-d, 29-G-d, 33-Su-p, 33-R-d, 33-St-d, 35-Su-p, 37-G-d, 41-H-p, 41-St-p, 43-H-p, 45-St-p
Garfield - 33-Ch-p, 43-Ch-p
Garland - 27-St-d, 31-Ca-p, 31-M-p, 33-St-d, 37-Ca-p, 37-H-d, 39-St-p, 41-R-p, 41-M-p, 41-G-p, 43-Ch-p, 43-St-d
Garneau - 27-B-d, 29-Co-p, 41-St-n, 45-B-p
Garon - 39-Co-p, 41-Co-p
Garrigan - 29-B-p
Garside - 31-St-d, 33-R-p
Gartner - 23-H-p
Garvin - 41-St-p
Gaskell - 31-M-d, 39-M-p
Gaskin - 39-H-d
Gatchell - 29-R-p
Gately - 45-R-d
Gates - 23-Ch-d, 37-Ch-p, 41-H-p, 43-M-p
Gatto - 41-H-p, 45-H-p
Gaudet - 33-Co-p
Gaudette - 27-H-p, 33-H-p, 37-H-p
Gaudreau - 35-H-p
Gault - 31-H-p, 35-St-p, 35-G-d, 45-G-p
Gaumond - 41-R-p
Gaura - 43-H-p
Gauthier - 37-R-d, 39-Ch-d, 39-H-d, 41-St-p, 41-Ch-p, 43-Ch-p, 45-H-p, 45-H-d
Gauthrie - 23-H-p
Gavel - 37-G-p
Gaw - 39-R-p
Gawel - 45-H-p
Gay - 37-G-p, 45-B-p
Gaynor - 33-Co-d, 41-M-d
Gazley - 33-G-p, 41-G-p
Geary - 29-Ca-p, 37-St-p, 41-M-p
Gebo - 45-H-p
Gecim - 41-St-n
Geddis - 39-B-d, 41-St-p
Gedenberg - 39-H-d

Geeb - 45-G-p
Geiger - 35-Ch-p
Geisler - 27-H-p
Gelardi - 45-H-p
Gelb - 43-H-d
Gelinas - 23-H-d, 29-H-p, 29-M-p, 41-H-p, 45-H-p
Gendron - 27-B-p, 29-H-p, 41-R-d, 45-M-p, 45-H-p, 45-Su-p
Genest - 31-B-p, 39-M-p, 43-H-p
Genna - 33-G-d
Gento - 45-R-p
Geoghegan - 33-Ch-d
George - 23-H-d, 23-Su-d, 25-R-d, 27-H-p, 29-H-d, 31-H-d, 33-H-d, 39-H-d, 39-St-n, 41-G-d, 43-H-p, 45-H-p, 45-St-p, 45-St-d
Georgina - 35-Ch-p, 41-M-p
Georgion - 23-St-p
Gerald - 29-M-p, 41-M-d
Gerard - 25-Ch-d
Gerew - 41-H-p
Germain - 27-H-p, 45-H-p
Germanos - 31-Ch-p
Germas - 37-H-p
Gero - 37-H-p
Gerow - 31-H-p
Gerrish - 25-H-p
Gerry - 23-H-d, 27-St-d
Gervais - 31-H-p, 37-H-p
Gervaise - 43-H-p
Gessner - 23-Co-p
Gianakos - 37-H-d
Gibbons - 39-H-p, 43-H-p
Gibbs - 33-G-d, 35-M-p, 39-G-d, 41-St-d
Giberson - 29-Co-d, 41-St-p

Gibson - 33-H-p, 39-B-p, 43-Ca-p, 45-G-p
Gielarowski - 41-M-p
Gifford - 27-St-d
Gignac - 43-M-p, 45-M-p
Giguere - 23-G-d, 41-Ch-d
Gilbert - 29-H-p, 33-R-p, 39-St-p, 39-Ch-p, 41-M-p, 41-H-p, 43-St-p, 43-R-d, 45-M-p, 45-Co-p, 45-H-d
Gilchrest - 41-R-d
Gilchrist - 29-G-d, 43-R-p
Gile - 41-M-p, 45-M-p, 45-G-p
Giles - 29-H-d, 37-H-d, 41-M-p, 43-M-p, 43-Ca-p, 45-Ch-p
Gilford - 31-R-d
Gilinsky - 41-H-p
Gilkey - 39-R-p
Gill - 33-H-d, 35-Ch-p, 41-H-p, 43-R-p
Gillan - 29-H-p
Gillespie - 23-M-d, 25-M-d, 43-H-p, 45-R-p
Gillett - 33-R-p
Gillette - 33-H-d
Gillies - 31-M-p
Gillingham - 33-M-p, 35-Su-p
Gillon - 39-G-p
Gilman - 23-R-p, 23-Ca-p, 23-St-d, 27-H-p, 29-M-d, 33-M-p, 39-G-p, 39-R-p, 45-H-p
Gilmore - 29-R-p, 41-M-p
Gilpatric - 23-B-p, 25-G-p, 43-G-p
Gilpatrick - 23-St-p, 41-M-p
Gilson - 35-Su-d, 37-M-p, 39-St-d
Ginalski - 45-R-d

Gingras - 33-G-p, 41-R-p, 41-H-p, 43-H-p
Ginniss - 39-M-p, 41-M-p
Girard - 29-Co-p, 33-H-d, 43-H-p, 45-H-p, 45-St-d
Girdley - 33-M-p
Girndt - 37-G-d
Girouard - 31-M-p, 39-H-d, 43-Ch-d
Giroux - 27-H-p, 35-M-p, 45-Co-p
Gitchell - 23-G-p
Givetz - 41-R-p
Gladding - 23-R-p
Glancy - 43-H-p
Glannon - 43-H-p
Glass - 35-St-p, 39-St-d
Glassburn - 45-St-p
Glaude - 43-H-d
Glazier - 39-G-p
Gleason - 25-R-p, 25-B-d, 31-H-d, 43-R-p, 45-B-d
Glendenning - 33-Ch-p
Glidden - 29-Ca-p, 33-St-d, 33-B-d, 39-Co-p, 45-St-p
Glines - 29-H-d, 37-H-p, 39-H-p, 41-Co-d
Gloddy - 27-H-p
Glode - 41-G-p
Glover - 23-R-d, 35-Ch-p, 35-G-d, 41-H-d
Glynn - 43-Su-p
Goad - 25-R-p
Gobbi - 41-R-p
Gobeil - 43-Ch-p
Gober - 23-G-d
Gobin - 27-H-p, 43-H-p
Godbout - 37-H-p, 45-H-p
Goddard - 29-M-p, 31-Co-p, 37-M-p
Godfrey - 33-Su-p, 43-Su-p
Godin - 41-G-p, 43-H-p, 45-St-p
Goethnee - 23-H-p, 35-H-p
Gogas - 23-H-p, 25-H-p
Goings - 33-H-p
Gold - 39-Su-p
Goldbaum - 43-St-p
Goldman - 41-M-d
Goldstein - 39-B-p
Golfinos - 43-H-d
Golofsky - 39-Su-p
Golter - 35-R-d
Gomez - 31-G-p
Gonin - 29-R-d
Gonsalves - 43-H-p, 45-Su-p
Gonthier - 33-H-p, 43-H-p
Gonyea - 25-Su-p
Gonyer - 39-B-p
Good - 45-Ch-p
Goodale - 27-H-p
Goodall - 45-H-p
Goodell - 43-R-d, 43-G-d, 45-Ch-d
Goodfellow - 35-H-p, 41-M-p
Goodhue - 23-H-p, 31-G-d, 37-H-d
Goodman - 33-H-p
Goodrich - 23-Ch-p, 25-R-d, 37-G-d, 43-Ca-d
Goodrow - 41-Su-p
Goodrum - 45-Ch-d
Goodsell - 29-G-p
Goodson - 37-Ca-p
Goodwin - 25-H-p, 25-M-d, 29-H-d, 31-G-d, 33-G-d, 33-H-d, 35-B-p, 35-Su-d, 39-G-p, 39-St-p, 39-H-p 39-G-d, 41-St-p, 41-H-d, 43-St-p, 43-G-p, 45-St-p, 45-R-d
Googins - 29-St-p

Gooley - 35-Ch-p
Goonan - 37-H-p, 41-H-p
Gorczyca - 35-H-d
Gordan - 25-Su-p, 25-R-d, 27-M-p
Gordon - 23-Co-d, 25-H-p, 29-M-p, 31-B-p, 31-M-p, 33-H-p, 37-M-d, 37-R-d, 37-Ch-d, 39-R-d, 41-G-p, 43-R-p, 43-R-d, 45-H-p, 45-M-p
Gorenstein - 45-H-p
Gorey - 43-H-d
Gorman - 37-R-p, 43-R-p, 43-Ca-p, 45-H-p, 45-Su-p
Gormley - 35-H-d
Gorton - 43-R-p
Goss - 29-B-p, 29-G-d, 33-G-p, 37-G-p, 41-R-p, 41-H-p, 43-M-p
Gosselin - 27-H-p, 29-H-p, 35-R-p, 37-M-p, 45-St-p
Gosseline - 41-H-p
Gossler - 45-H-p
Gotts - 23-St-d
Gotz - 41-R-p
Goudreau - 27-H-d, 41-H-p
Gough - 37-R-p
Gouin - 23-Ca-p, 43-St-p, 45-H-d
Gould - 25-G-d, 27-M-d, 29-M-p, 31-B-p, 33-H-p, 33-Co-d, 35-H-p, 35-Co-d, 37-G-p, 37-G-d, 39-H-p, 39-B-d, 41-H-p, 43-St-p, 45-M-p, 45-St-d
Goulet - 23-H-p, 35-H-p, 37-H-p, 41-St-p, 45-H-p
Goulette - 39-R-p
Goulson - 41-H-p
Goumalatsos - 41-St-n

Goupil - 45-St-d
Gourd - 41-H-p
Gourdeau - 39-H-d
Gouzoules - 41-R-p
Gove - 25-R-d, 31-R-p, 39-H-p, 39-R-d, 45-Co-p
Gowan - 43-R-p
Gowans - 23-H-p
Gowing - 31-H-p
Goyette - 29-G-p, 43-B-p, 45-Su-p
Goyner - 33-B-p
Grabowski - 43-B-p
Grace - 33-G-d, 37-R-p
Gracie - 27-Ch-d
Grady - 39-Co-p
Graeher - 43-R-p
Graff - 23-H-d
Graham - 27-M-p, 27-B-d, 31-R-d, 33-Ch-d, 35-H-p, 37-H-p, 41-R-p, 41-R-d, 43-B-p, 43-Ca-d, 43-R-d
Grammont - 33-M-d, 35-R-p
Granger - 39-B-d
Grant - 23-M-p, 23-H-p, 25-H-p, 25-M-p, 25-B-p, 25-Su-d, 27-H-p, 27-G-d, 29-M-d, 31-H-p, 33-H-p, 33-St-p, 33-St-d, 35-M-d, 39-St-p, 41-H-p, 43-H-p, 43-R-p, 45-H-p, 45-H-d
Granz - 29-H-d, 45-H-d
Grapes - 39-G-d
Grass - 33-St-p
Grasset - 33-H-p
Grassi - 25-H-d
Graton - 35-Ch-p
Gratton - 41-R-p, 43-R-p
Grauer - 45-H-d
Grave - 37-R-p
Gravel - 27-H-d, 39-St-n

Graves - 27-H-p, 41-Ch-p, 45-St-p
Gravett - 41-G-p
Gray - 23-Co-p, 23-G-p, 27-H-p, 27-R-d, 29-R-p, 29-Co-d, 31-St-d, 33-R-p, 33-Ca-p, 35-M-p, 35-Ch-p, 35-M-d, 37-St-p, 37-G-d, 37-Co-d, 39-M-p, 39-Co-p, 41-B-p, 43-St-p, 43-H-p, 43-Su-p, 43-St-d, 43-G-d, 45-St-p, 45-B-p, 45-H-p, 45-G-p, 45-R-d
Grealish - 29-H-p
Greeley - 25-H-p, 41-H-p, 41-H-d
Greemore - 45-B-p
Green -
Green - 29-M-p
Green - 29-Ch-p, 29-Ch-d, 35-H-p, 37-M-p, 41-Su-p, 41-Ch-p, 43-H-p, 45-H-p
Greenan - 35-G-d
Greenblatt - 41-H-p
Greene - 23-G-d, 23-H-d, 25-H-p, 37-Ch-p, 41-B-d, 43-M-p, 43-B-d, 45-H-p
Greenhalgh - 23-H-p, 35-G-d
Greenia - 43-G-d
Greenlaw - 29-Su-d, 45-H-p
Greenman - 31-R-p
Greenough - 43-H-p
Greenwood - 23-R-p, 29-Ch-p, 29-H-d, 31-B-p, 33-Su-d, 41-Su-p, 41-R-p, 45-H-p, 45-B-d
Gregg - 31-H-p
Gregoire - 23-St-p, 25-St-p, 35-H-p, 41-St-p, 41-M-p, 41-H-d, 45-H-p

Gregory - 33-Su-d, 35-M-p, 37-Ch-p
Greig - 31-R-d
Grelish - 29-R-p
Grenache - 39-Su-p
Grenier - 29-G-d, 35-H-p, 35-H-d, 37-G-p, 41-H-p, 41-St-d, 45-St-p
Gresty - 33-St-d
Grevior - 39-H-p
Grew - 41-H-p
Grey - 27-H-d
Grieg - 45-St-p
Grieves - 27-B-d
Griffeth - 45-Co-p
Griffin - 23-G-d, 27-R-p, 27-M-p, 27-H-d, 35-G-p, 37-H-p, 43-H-p, 43-B-p
Griffith - 25-H-p
Grigas - 41-H-p, 43-H-p
Grigg - 41-St-p
Griggs - 41-G-d, 45-M-p
Grimaldi - 29-M-p
Grimard - 45-H-p
Grimes - 25-H-p, 41-Su-p, 45-M-p
Grimoutes - 25-H-p
Grimstone - 39-B-p
Griswold - 41-Ch-p
Groder - 45-R-d
Groetz - 33-R-p
Grogan - 43-H-p
Grondin - 27-St-p, 29-St-p, 33-St-p, 35-G-p, 39-St-p, 43-St-p, 45-H-p, 45-St-p
Gross - 31-M-p, 33-H-d, 37-Su-p
Grostein - 43-Ch-p
Grotty - 45-St-p
Grout - 29-G-d, 33-Ch-p

Grover - 27-R-d, 29-St-d, 31-R-p, 37-St-d, 41-H-p, 43-M-p, 43-R-d, 45-Co-p, 45-M-d
Grube - 29-Ch-p
Grugnale - 45-H-p
Grzymski - 43-H-p
Guarino - 41-R-d
Guay - 27-B-p, 27-H-p, 39-M-p, 41-G-p, 41-H-p, 45-B-p
Guerette - 35-H-p
Guerin - 27-R-p
Guernsey - 39-G-d
Guerriero - 37-H-d
Guerski - 43-H-p
Guertin - 37-M-p, 43-H-p
Guess - 33-H-p
Guest - 37-Su-d
Guevin - 25-M-p
Guguy - 37-Ch-p
Guichard - 41-H-p, 45-H-d
Guiffrida - 37-R-d
Guiley - 41-R-p
Guillemette - 29-H-p, 39-H-p
Guillot - 29-H-p
Guillow - 43-Ch-p
Guilmain - 45-H-p
Guilmette - 39-Co-p, 39-H-p
Guilmette - 27-H-p, 33-H-p, 41-Co-d
Guimond - 35-H-p, 45-M-p
Guimont - 39-H-p
Gulley - 31-M-p, 33-M-p, 41-B-d, 43-B-d
Gulubicky - 45-St-p
Gunn - 45-Su-p
Gunnion - 25-M-p
Guptill - 37-M-p, 41-R-p, 43-H-p, 45-St-p
Gurganus - 43-R-p

Gurkowski - 33-H-p
Gurney - 33-G-d, 37-B-p
Gurska - 37-H-d, 43-H-p
Gustafson - 43-M-p
Gustitus - 45-H-p
Gutterson - 31-H-p
Guy - 45-St-p
Guyer - 23-Su-p, 25-G-p, 43-G-p
Guyett - 29-M-p
Guyette - 23-G-p, 25-Su-d, 29-R-d, 33-Ch-p
Guymond - 23-M-p
Guynn - 43-H-p
Guzman - 41-H-d
Gwong - 45-H-p
Gwynn - 43-G-p
Gynan - 41-R-d
Gzywacz - 41-R-p

Haas - 41-R-p, 43-H-p
Haase - 43-H-d
Habel - 45-St-d
Hackett - 27-Ch-p, 45-H-p
Hackler - 37-Ch-p, 43-Ch-p
Haddad - 33-Ch-p
Haddock - 39-B-p
Hadley - 29-Ch-p, 33-H-p, 33-H-d, 35-Ch-d, 41-R-p, 43-G-p
Haedt - 39-St-p
Hafford - 39-Co-d
Hagar - 27-M-p, 37-Ca-p
Haggert - 41-M-p
Haggerty - 27-R-p, 29-M-d, 31-M-d, 35-G-d, 39-R-p, 41-M-p
Haight - 35-H-p
Haigney - 39-Ch-p
Haines - 25-M-p
Haisen - 39-Co-p

Haisen - 41-Co-p
Hajicostas - 41-H-p
Hakala - 37-Ch-p
Hakansson - 43-H-p
Hakola - 43-Ch-p
Halainen - 37-Su-p
Halcombe - 41-M-p
Haldane - 39-G-p
Halden - 43-M-p
Hale - 23-R-d, 35-Ch-p, 39-Ca-p, 41-Ch-d, 43-R-p, 43-H-d
Haley - 35-R-p, 39-Co-p, 41-R-p, 43-H-p, 45-G-p
Hall - 23-St-p, 25-Co-d, 25-H-d, 25-R-d, 27-R-p, 29-M-p, 29-H-p, 31-St-p, 31-Ch-p, 31-M-d, 33-Ch-p, 35-H-p, 35-H-d, 39-M-p, 39-R-p, 39-St-p, 39-B-d, 39-H-d, 39-St-d, 41-St-p, 41-H-p, 41-R-d, 43-H-p, 43-Su-p, 43-M-p, 43-H-p, 43-St-p, 43-G-p, 43-R-d, 45-M-p, 45-St-p, 45-H-p, 45-Ch-p, 45-G-p, 45-St-d
Hallett - 31-H-p
Halley - 33-H-p
Hallin - 41-Su-p
Hallinan - 37-R-d, 39-R-p
Hallisey - 31-H-p
Halloway - 25-Co-p
Hallstrom - 39-H-p
Halme - 35-M-p
Halpert - 37-St-p
Halprin - 43-R-d
Ham - 23-G-p, 23-R-d, 25-R-p, 25-St-p, 27-R-d, 29-R-d, 35-St-p, 39-H-d
Hamblett - 23-M-p, 25-R-p, 25-H-d, 29-R-d, 37-R-d

Hamblin - 45-H-p
Hamburger - 33-Ch-p
Hamby - 41-M-p
Hamel - 25-Su-p, 25-Co-p, 27-H-d, 29-R-d, 35-H-p, 37-Co-p, 39-B-d, 41-St-p, 41-St-d, 43-St-p, 43-B-p, 45-Su-p, 45-B-d
Hamilton - 25-Co-p, 29-Co-p, 33-Ch-p, 33-H-d, 37-M-d, 39-St-p, 41-B-p, 41-St-p, 41-R-d, 43-H-p, 43-R-p
Hamlin - 29-M-d
Hamm - 23-H-p, 43-R-d
Hammond - 27-H-p, 33-M-p, 35-R-p, 35-Co-p, 39-H-p, 41-R-p, 43-Ca-p, 43-Ch-p, 45-M-p, 45-G-d
Hamp - 27-M-d
Hampton - 43-H-p
Hamson - 45-H-p
Hanaford - 27-G-p
Hanchett - 33-H-p
Hancock - 35-H-p
Handly - 31-Su-p
Handy - 41-Ch-p
Hanes - 23-Co-p
Haney - 27-Co-p, 27-Ca-p, 41-M-d
Hankins - 43-R-d
Hanley - 39-Su-d, 41-H-d, 45-H-d
Hanna - 45-Ch-p
Hannett - 45-G-p
Hannington - 29-M-p
Hansen - 31-Co-p, 33-R-p, 33-R-d, 41-Su-p, 43-H-d, 45-Ca-p, 45-G-d
Hanson - 23-Su-d, 25-G-d, 27-H-p, 27-R-d, 29-Co-p,

Hanson - 31-H-d, 33-B-p, 39-St-d, 41-Ch-p, 41-H-p, 45-B-p
Hapchis - 43-R-p
Hapgood - 41-Co-p
Happny - 27-M-p
Hapsis - 43-R-p
Harb - 23-St-d
Harding - 27-G-d, 39-G-p, 41-Su-p, 45-H-p
Hardman - 39-H-d
Hardy - 23-Ch-p, 23-R-p, 25-H-p, 33-H-p, 37-R-d, 39-H-p
Harisiadaes - 43-H-d
Harlow - 29-M-p, 41-G-p
Harmon - 45-B-d, 45-St-d
Harness - 23-R-d
Harnish - 35-Ca-p, 43-G-p
Harnowski - 43-R-d
Harold - 43-M-p
Harper - 23-G-p, 25-G-d, 41-Ch-p
Harrell - 25-St-p, 41-H-p
Harrigan - 37-R-p
Harriman - 29-M-d, 37-Ca-p, 43-H-p, 43-Co-p, 45-H-d, 45-G-d
Harrington - 25-Ch-p, 29-M-p, 39-H-d, 43-R-p, 45-H-p
Harris - 25-Ch-p, 27-B-p, 29-H-d, 33-M-p, 33-St-p, 35-Ca-p, 39-G-p, 43-St-p, 43-H-p, 45-H-p, 45-St-p, 45-G-d
Harrises - 43-H-p
Harrison - 23-H-d, 37-R-d, 43-H-p, 43-G-p, 43-H-d
Harrower - 35-G-d

Hart - 39-M-p, 41-Co-p, 43-R-p, 45-H-p, 45-Su-p, 45-G-p
Harte - 39-H-p
Hartfiel - 41-St-p
Hartford - 25-R-p, 25-R-d, 37-H-p, 37-R-p, 37-R-d, 41-R-d, 45-Co-p
Hartman - 37-M-p
Hartofelis - 43-H-p
Hartshorn - 45-H-p, 45-H-d
Hartt - 33-M-d
Hartwell - 43-G-p, 43-G-d, 45-H-p
Harvey - 23-G-p, 25-H-p, 31-R-p, 33-R-d, 43-M-p, 43-B-d, 45-B-p, 45-H-p, 45-G-d, 45-R-d
Harwood - 37-H-p
Haseltine - 33-Ca-p
Haselton - 23-H-p, 25-H-p, 35-H-p
Hashem - 39-St-n, 41-St-p, 41-St-n, 43-St-p
Hashim - 25-R-p
Haskell - 25-B-p, 39-St-p, 41-B-p, 41-M-p, 45-G-p
Haskins - 45-G-p
Hasler - 45-M-p
Hassan - 41-Co-p
Hassett - 29-G-p, 41-M-d
Hastedt - 39-H-p
Hastings - 29-Ch-p, 29-Su-d, 31-Su-p, 33-Ch-p, 35-B-p, 41-Ch-d, 43-Su-d
Haswell - 43-Su-d
Hatch - 23-H-p, 25-Su-d, 29-Ch-d, 33-R-d, 39-H-d, 41-Su-p, 41-R-p, 41-M-p, 43-St-p
Hathaway - 31-H-p

Hathorne - 43-G-d
Hatt - 39-Co-p
Hatzekelekas - 41-B-p
Hatzes - 35-H-p, 41-B-p
Hatzgioga - 25-H-p
Hatzigogas - 23-H-p
Hatzilelikas - 35-H-p
Haughn - 41-G-p
Hautenan - 33-Ch-p
Hautsch - 45-H-p
Haven - 41-B-p
Havey - 39-H-d
Hawco - 41-R-p
Hawes - 35-G-p, 41-Co-p
Hawkins - 25-H-p, 43-R-p, 43-St-p, 43-Su-p
Hawksworth - 31-H-p
Hawley - 31-Su-p, 33-H-d
Hawthorne - 39-R-p, 45-M-p
Hay - 33-G-p
Haycock - 45-St-p
Hayden - 27-H-p, 41-H-p
Hayes - 23-H-d, 23-St-d, 25-Ch-p, 25-Co-p, 25-M-d, 27-St-p, 29-H-p, 29-M-d, 33-H-p, 33-R-d, 35-G-d, 35-M-d, 37-St-p, 37-Ch-d, 39-Ca-p, 39-St-p, 39-St-d, 41-St-p, 41-M-p, 43-St-p, 43-R-p, 43-M-p, 45-St-p, 45-Co-p, 45-H-d
Hayford - 33-H-d
Haynes - 25-Co-p, 31-St-d, 45-M-p, 45-G-p
Hays - 39-H-p
Hayward - 23-Su-p, 25-B-d, 29-M-p
Haywood - 33-H-p, 33-G-d, 45-St-d
Hazard - 43-H-p
Hazeltine - 43-Ch-p, 43-G-d

Hazelton - 25-M-p, 33-M-p
Hazleton - 43-Ch-d
Heacock - 23-H-p, 45-R-d
Heald - 37-Ch-p
Healey - 27-M-p, 27-Ch-p, 29-H-d, 41-R-p, 43-M-p
Healy - 33-H-p, 39-Co-p, 39-H-d, 41-G-p
Heard - 25-Ch-p
Hearrin - 41-R-d
Heartz - 25-M-p, 29-M-p
Heath - 27-M-p, 29-M-p, 29-B-p, 29-M-d, 31-St-p, 31-M-p, 31-Su-d, 33-Su-p, 33-H-p, 33-Co-p, 35-R-p, 37-M-p, 39-R-p, 41-B-p, 43-M-p, 43-H-p, 45-B-p, 45-R-p
Hebert - 23-H-p, 33-H-p, 35-Ch-d, 39-St-p, 41-R-p, 43-B-d, 45-St-p, 45-St-d
Heckbert - 29-St-d
Heckelton - 33-R-d
Hecker - 41-H-p
Hedgepeth - 43-R-p
Hedrick - 45-H-p
Hee - 45-H-p
Heeney - 35-R-p
Heffler - 39-R-p
Heflin - 41-M-p
Heger - 41-R-d, 45-R-d
Heiden - 29-H-p
Heikkila - 45-H-p
Heil - 43-Ch-p, 45-Ch-d
Heimis - 41-B-p
Heinis - 41-B-p
Heino - 41-H-d
Heinonen - 43-Ch-d
Heinrich - 35-G-d
Helm - 41-G-p

Hemeon - 31-R-p, 43-M-p, 45-Ch-d
Hemm - 43-R-d
Hemphill - 39-Su-d
Henault - 39-G-p
Henchey - 41-Ch-p
Henderson - 25-R-d, 25-Co-d, 29-G-p, 31-R-p, 43-H-p, 45-H-p
Hendrickson - 41-Su-p, 41-Ch-p
Heney - 35-M-p
Hennessey - 27-H-p
Henson - 39-R-d, 41-St-p
Hentschel - 45-Su-p
Hepill - 31-H-d
Hepworth - 25-R-d
Herbert - 23-St-d, 27-R-p, 27-St-d, 33-G-p, 35-Ca-p, 39-G-p, 41-Su-p, 41-Ca-d, 43-R-p
Herbut - 43-H-p
Hermann - 23-Co-p
Hermanson - 43-M-d
Hermsdorf - 37-H-p
Hernon - 25-G-d
Heron - 37-Ch-p, 43-H-p, 43-H-d
Herregodts - 27-H-p
Herrick - 37-Ca-p
Hersey - 25-R-d, 37-R-d, 41-R-p, 45-B-p, 45-H-d
Hersom - 27-R-d, 43-R-p, 43-Co-d
Heselton - 29-H-p, 29-R-p, 33-H-d, 41-H-p
Heskett - 45-R-d
Hester - 29-St-d
Heureux - 41-R-p
Hewes - 27-H-p
Hewey - 41-M-p, 43-Su-p

Hewitt - 43-H-p
Heyl - 23-H-d
Heywood - 43-R-d
Hiatt - 37-H-p
Hibbert - 41-M-p
Hicken - 33-M-p
Hickey - 39-Co-p, 41-Co-p
Hickley - 29-H-d
Hickman - 29-H-d, 37-H-p
Hicks - 27-B-p, 29-Co-p, 41-Co-p
Hicksenhytzer - 41-R-p
Hidden - 37-H-p
Higgins - 23-R-d, 25-Ch-d, 37-Su-p, 37-Ca-d, 37-Ch-d, 41-M-p, 41-B-d, 43-Ch-p, 45-G-d
Hilchey - 41-H-d
Hildreth - 33-R-p, 39-St-d
Hill - 23-G-p, 23-Ca-p, 25-M-p, 25-G-d, 27-M-p, 27-R-d, 29-Ch-p, 29-R-p, 29-H-p, 29-H-d, 31-R-d, 33-St-p, 33-M-p, 33-H-d, 33-Co-d, 35-R-p, 35-St-p, 35-M-p, 35-H-p, 37-M-p, 37-H-p, 37-St-d, 37-Su-d, 39-M-p, 39-G-p, 41-R-p, 41-G-p, 43-R-p, 43-M-d, 43-G-d, 45-G-p
Hilliard - 25-Co-p, 29-Co-p, 37-Ca-p
Hills - 23-Co-p, 41-St-p, 43-H-p
Hillsgrove - 41-M-p
Hillyard - 39-R-p
Hilson - 41-H-p
Hilton - 41-H-d
Hilty - 43-Su-p
Himes - 43-M-p
Hinckley - 39-R-d

Hinds - 39-Ch-d
Hines - 45-H-d
Hinman - 37-Co-p
Hinnen - 37-G-d
Hinson - 41-St-d
Hipsher - 45-H-p
Hird - 35-R-p
Hirsch - 41-Su-p
Hirschman - 43-H-d
Hirtle - 43-M-p
Hissen - 41-Co-p
Hitchcock - 27-H-d, 29-H-p, 45-M-p
Hoadley - 23-B-p, 31-M-d
Hoag - 25-Ca-d
Hoagland - 33-B-d
Hoague - 35-Su-p, 35-H-d
Hoague-Onley - 35-Su-p
Hobart - 37-G-p, 39-B-p
Hobbs - 37-G-d, 43-St-p
Hobson - 43-Ch-p
Hock - 25-H-p
Hodder - 45-Su-p
Hodgdon - 23-M-d, 29-St-p, 37-H-p, 37-R-d, 39-Ca-p, 41-St-p, 43-St-p, 43-R-d
Hodge - 29-H-p, 37-M-d
Hodgman - 25-H-p, 33-M-p
Hodgson - 29-St-p, 31-B-p, 39-B-p, 45-B-p
Hodsdon - 37-G-d, 43-Ca-p
Hodson - 43-R-p, 45-R-p
Hoffman - 39-Ch-d
Hoit - 27-M-d, 41-M-d, 45-M-p
Hoitt - 37-H-d
Holbitter - 41-Su-p
Holbrook - 23-Ch-d, 33-Ch-p, 39-Ch-p, 43-M-p
Holcomb - 25-Ch-p
Holden - 43-M-p, 43-B-p, 45-H-p

Holdsworth - 33-M-p
Holinbrook - 39-G-p, 41-G-p
Holland - 29-St-d, 43-H-p, 45-St-d
Hollander - 29-R-d
Hollins - 41-H-p
Holloway - 29-H-p
Holman - 31-G-p, 45-Co-p
Holmes - 25-M-p, 27-R-p, 31-St-p, 33-Co-d, 33-St-d, 35-Ch-p, 35-H-p, 35-St-d, 37-M-p, 41-B-p, 41-H-d, 45-B-p, 45-M-p
Holmgren - 23-R-d
Holt - 23-G-p, 25-H-d, 27-R-p, 29-G-p, 33-H-p, 33-G-p, 41-Ch-p, 41-R-d, 43-M-p, 43-G-p, 45-R-d, 45-Ch-p, 45-Ch-d
Homan - 23-G-p
Homoleski - 37-H-p
Hondrogen - 41-H-p
Hondrogiannia - 41-H-p
Honey - 45-M-p
Honkamaki - 37-Ch-p
Honny - 39-Su-d
Hood - 23-H-p, 33-H-p, 37-M-d, 43-H-p
Hook - 29-Co-p, 31-Su-p, 45-H-p
Hoolock - 25-R-d
Hooper - 27-Ch-p, 33-H-p, 43-R-p
Hopf - 41-B-p
Hopkins - 25-Su-d, 27-M-p, 35-G-d, 37-B-p, 37-H-d
Hopps - 43-Co-d, 45-St-p
Horam - 29-G-p
Hornberger - 41-M-p
Horne - 23-B-d, 31-St-d, 43-H-p

Hornig - 37-Ch-p
Horr - 41-St-p, 45-St-p
Horrocks - 43-G-d
Horton - 25-R-d, 45-Ch-p, 45-H-d, 45-R-d
Hosking - 45-H-p
Houde - 25-R-d, 33-Su-d
Hough - 41-St-p
Houghton - 37-G-p, 39-G-d
Houle - 25-M-d, 27-H-p, 29-H-p, 29-R-p, 31-R-p, 33-H-p, 33-H-d, 37-St-p, 37-M-d, 41-R-p, 41-H-p, 41-H-d, 45-H-p, 45-Co-p
Houley - 45-Co-p
Houlihan - 35-R-d
Housman - 45-M-p
Houston - 39-H-p, 41-R-p
Hovaness - 45-Ch-p
Hovey - 25-Co-d
Howard - 29-R-p, 29-St-p, 31-R-p, 31-St-d, 33-R-d, 33-G-d, 33-Ch-d, 37-G-p, 39-H-p, 39-H-d, 41-M-p, 41-Su-p, 41-R-d, 43-Ca-p, 43-Ch-p, 43-Su-p, 43-G-d, 43-R-d, 45-R-p, 45-St-p, 45-Su-p, 45-R-d, 45-Ch-d, 45-G-d
Howe - 23-R-d, 25-Su-p, 33-G-d, 35-Ch-p, 35-Co-d, 41-M-p, 45-M-p, 45-Su-p
Howell - 43-R-p
Howes - 25-M-d
Howland - 25-G-p, 31-H-p, 31-Co-p, 35-M-p, 35-G-d, 37-St-p, 39-M-p, 41-Co-d, 45-H-p, 45-St-p, 45-Ch-p, 45-Ch-d
Howser - 41-B-d, 43-B-d, 45-Su-p

Hoyt - 29-Su-d, 35-Ch-p, 35-R-d, 37-M-p, 39-Ca-p, 39-H-d, 39-G-d, 41-G-p, 45-M-p, 45-R-d
Hrisantheas - 41-H-p
Hroniack - 31-H-p
Huard - 33-H-p
Hubbard - 31-Ch-p, 37-H-d, 39-B-p, 41-Ch-p, 43-Ch-p, 45-Ch-p, 45-R-d
Hubel - 27-H-p
Hubley - 33-R-p
Huckins - 23-B-p, 29-B-p, 37-H-p, 39-B-p
Huddell - 25-R-p
Huddleston - 27-H-d, 45-H-p
Hudson - 35-St-d, 35-Ch-d, 39-Ch-p
Hueftline - 41-M-p
Huff - 29-Ca-p, 33-B-d
Huffman - 23-H-p
Hughes - 29-M-p, 31-Co-p, 33-Ch-d, 33-H-d, 35-B-d, 41-St-p, 43-St-p, 43-H-p, 43-G-p, 45-Ca-p, 45-St-p
Hull - 29-G-p
Hulslander - 43-Ch-p
Humphrey - 25-H-p, 29-H-p, 45-G-p
Humphreys - 43-St-p
Hunt - 23-Ch-p, 25-Su-d, 29-Ch-p, 35-H-p, 39-M-p, 39-Ch-p, 39-H-d, 41-R-p, 41-M-p, 43-H-p, 45-M-p
Hunter - 27-H-p, 37-H-p, 39-Co-d, 43-R-p, 45-Co-p
Hunting - 41-H-p
Huntington - 37-B-p, 45-M-p, 45-H-p
Hunton - 31-R-p

Huntoon - 23-H-p, 23-M-d, 37-R-d, 39-Co-p, 41-R-p
Huntsman - 37-St-p
Huot - 45-H-p
Hurd - 23-St-p, 23-St-d, 31-Ca-p, 31-R-p, 31-St-p, 33-M-p, 39-St-p, 39-Co-d, 41-M-p, 41-H-p, 43-St-p, 45-H-p
Hurlbert - 45-Co-p
Hurlburt - 43-H-p
Hurley - 23-Ch-d, 33-G-p, 43-R-d
Hurst - 29-R-p
Husband - 43-B-p
Huse - 31-Ch-p, 39-M-p, 41-Ch-p
Huseby - 45-R-d
Huskie - 45-H-d
Hussey - 25-R-p, 35-R-d, 35-St-d, 45-St-p
Huston - 33-M-p, 37-B-p, 45-Su-p
Hutchings - 35-R-p, 43-R-d
Hutchins - 29-R-p, 41-R-p, 41-G-p, 43-Ca-p, 43-R-p, 43-Su-p, 45-St-d
Hutchinson - 33-H-d, 35-H-p, 39-Su-p, 45-G-d
Hutson - 45-H-p
Hutt - 31-Ca-p
Hyde - 35-St-p
Hyllman - 45-St-d
Hyman - 45-Su-p
Hynes - 25-Co-p
Hyrk - 27-Ch-d

Iacoboni - 25-Co-d
Iamele - 35-R-p
Ide - 25-H-p
Igel - 29-B-d

Ihalainen - 37-Su-p, 41-Su-p
Ikan - 29-R-p
Imm - 31-Ch-d
Ingalls - 27-Ch-p, 35-B-p, 35-G-d, 37-R-d, 41-Ch-p, 43-G-p, 43-Ch-d, 45-R-d
Ingeborg - 43-H-p
Ingell - 23-Ch-p
Ingelstrom - 33-H-p
Ingersoll - 35-M-p
Ingerson - 27-Co-d
Inglis - 41-Ch-p
Ingraham - 29-R-p, 35-H-d
Ingram - 23-Ch-p, 25-B-d, 29-G-d, 39-R-p, 41-R-p
Inman - 41-R-p
Innes - 35-H-p
Innie - 43-H-p
Insogna - 43-H-p
Ioshpa - 39-H-p
Ireland - 23-H-p, 37-M-p, 45-H-p
Irish - 23-Ca-d, 27-Ca-d, 43-Ca-d
Irmalowicz - 43-H-p
Irvin - 27-R-p
Irvine - 43-R-p
Irwin - 33-H-p
Isaacson - 33-St-d
Isabelle - 29-Ch-d, 45-H-d
Israel - 27-H-d
Israelian - 45-B-p, 45-B-d
Italion - 43-St-p
Ivanow - 41-H-p
Ivarnoff - 41-H-p
Ives - 37-B-p
Ivon - 37-H-d
Iwanicki - 31-R-p

Jaastad - 43-M-p
Jackman - 29-H-p

Jackson - 23-G-p, 31-H-p, 33-R-p, 33-St-d, 37-R-p, 39-R-p, 39-Ca-p, 39-H-p, 41-M-p, 41-R-d, 43-St-p, 43-H-p, 43-G-d, 45-H-p, 45-G-p, 45-St-d
Jacob - 45-H-d
Jacobs - 23-Ca-d, 27-R-p, 29-R-d, 29-Su-d, 31-R-p, 33-R-p, 33-M-d, 37-St-d
Jacobson - 41-Su-d, 45-H-d
Jacques - 23-H-p, 31-H-p, 35-H-d, 35-R-d, 37-R-p, 43-B-p
Jadosz - 37-H-p
Jaffarian - 43-St-p
Jaffas - 31-Ch-p
Jainkowsky - 41-R-p
Jalbert - 45-Co-p
Jalmar - 43-Su-p
James - 25-Ch-p, 33-R-d, 37-Ch-p, 37-G-p, 39-M-p, 41-St-p, 41-St-d, 43-H-p, 43-B-p, 45-H-p
Jameson - 39-R-p, 41-R-p, 43-H-p
Janelle - 43-H-p, 45-H-p
Janes - 39-St-d
Janieszewska - 35-H-d
Janko - 29-H-p
Jankousky - 41-R-p
Janssen - 39-B-d
Januzewski - 45-H-p
Jaques - 27-G-p
Jaquith - 23-Ch-p, 27-G-p
Jarest - 31-H-p
Jarowsky - 39-R-p
Jarvi - 43-M-p
Jarvis - 33-R-p, 37-Ch-d, 43-H-p, 43-Ch-d
Jasiewicz - 35-Su-p

Jassop - 39-Co-p, 41-Co-p
Jauron - 45-H-p
Jazel - 45-H-d
Jean - 45-Ch-p
Jeannotte - 27-H-p, 33-H-p
Jebb - 27-G-d
Jeeves - 41-R-p
Jefferson - 41-M-p, 41-B-d, 43-B-d
Jelley - 25-Ch-p, 35-H-p
Jeneau - 39-St-d
Jenkaites - 33-R-p
Jenkerson - 39-Su-p
Jenkins - 23-R-d, 27-M-p, 29-R-d, 33-B-d, 39-G-p, 41-Su-p, 43-H-p, 45-H-p
Jenne - 43-R-p
Jenness - 23-St-d, 25-G-p, 33-Ca-d, 37-St-p, 41-M-p
Jennings - 25-H-p, 33-R-p, 43-M-p
Jennison - 39-Su-p
Jenovese - 41-M-p
Jensen - 39-H-d, 41-H-p
Jenson - 35-B-p
Jenvey - 37-M-p
Jerard - 27-Su-d
Jermuziah - 23-M-p
Jervah - 37-H-d, 45-M-p
Jesseman - 37-G-p
Jessup - 25-B-p
Jestude - 43-St-p
Jette - 39-Ca-p, 43-G-p
Jewell - 23-St-p, 23-G-p, 29-M-p, 31-G-d, 33-R-p, 37-M-p, 45-R-d
Jewett - 35-St-d, 37-M-p
Jimerson - 45-St-d
Jobin - 23-G-p
Jodoin - 41-B-p
Jodrie - 41-Co-p

Johansen - 41-H-p
Johansson - 27-H-p
John - 25-M-p
Johndeo - 43-B-p
Johnson - 23-Ch-p, 23-H-p, 23-Su-p, 23-G-p, 23-R-d, 23-H-d, 23-G-d, 25-M-p, 25-Ch-p, 25-G-d, 25-R-d, 27-St-p, 27-Ca-p, 27-Co-p, 27-H-p, 27-M-p, 27-H-d, 29-G-p, 29-R-p, 29-Co-p, 29-M-p, 29-H-p, 29-G-d, 29-Su-d, 31-Ca-p, 31-M-p, 31-H-p, 31-Co-p, 31-G-d, 33-R-p, 33-Su-p, 33-Co-p, 33-Ch-d, 35-R-p, 35-Su-p, 35-G-p, 35-H-p, 35-Co-p, 35-R-d, 35-Su-d, 35-G-d, 35-St-d, 37-Su-p, 37-Co-p, 37-B-p, 37-Su-d, 39-R-p, 39-Ch-p, 39-B-p, 41-Ch-p, 41-H-p, 41-Ca-p, 41-M-p, 41-R-p, 41-Co-p, 41-St-p, 41-M-d, 41-R-d, 41-St-d, 43-Ch-p, 43-Su-p, 43-H-p, 43-R-p, 43-Co-p, 43-R-d, 43-H-d, 45-H-p, 45-B-p, 45-Su-p, 45-Co-p, 45-G-p, 45-B-d, 45-M-d, 45-H-d
Johnston - 23-H-d, 31-R-p, 39-R-p
Johnstone - 45-St-d
Jolly - 41-St-p
Jonaitis - 33-Ch-d
Jondreau - 45-M-p
Jondro - 43-Su-d
Jones - 23-R-p, 23-H-d, 25-Su-d, 25-M-d, 27-B-p, 29-M-p, 31-Ch-p, 31-H-p, 33-H-p, 37-M-p, 39-Ca-p, 43-B-p, 43-Ch-p, 43-H-p, 43-St-d, 45-B-p, 45-H-p, 45-M-p, 45-R-d
Jordan - 23-R-d, 23-Ch-d, 25-G-p, 29-M-p, 29-H-p, 31-Su-p, 35-H-p, 39-H-p, 39-R-d, 39-B-d, 41-R-p, 41-Co-p, 41-H-p, 43-Su-p, 43-G-d, 45-G-p
Jordon - 25-G-p, 41-B-p, 43-G-d
Joron - 27-H-p
Joscelyn - 39-G-p
Joseph - 31-H-p, 39-St-n, 43-G-p
Jositas - 41-H-p
Joslin - 27-H-p
Joslyn - 27-Ch-p, 39-R-p, 43-R-p
Joudrey - 41-Ch-p
Joudry - 23-B-p
Jowders - 33-H-p
Joy - 23-St-d, 31-St-p, 31-St-d, 39-M-p, 43-Su-p, 45-H-p
Joyal - 41-H-p, 43-St-d
Joyce - 27-Co-d, 37-M-p, 41-Ch-p, 43-H-p, 45-B-p
Jozaitis - 39-H-d, 41-H-p
Judd - 33-St-d, 39-St-p, 39-Su-p
Judkins - 35-H-p, 43-H-p
Juneau - 25-H-p
Juringius - 39-M-p
Jurva - 43-Ch-d
Jussila - 45-St-p
Jutras - 27-B-p, 41-H-p

Kachadoorian - 37-M-p

Kaczanowski - 41-R-p
Kahill - 43-R-p
Kahn - 23-H-p
Kajzy - 45-H-p
Kalens - 25-R-p, 33-R-p, 41-R-p
Kaline - 43-H-p
Kalinsky - 25-R-p, 33-R-p
Kalmonowith - 41-H-p
Kanada - 43-R-p
Kane - 23-Co-p, 31-R-p, 37-M-p, 43-H-p, 45-M-p, 45-H-p
Kanerva - 43-Su-d
Kangas - 43-H-p
Kankaanpaa - 43-H-p
Kankolander - 41-Su-p
Kanpp - 45-Ch-p
Kansala - 27-Ch-d
Kapela - 37-H-d
Kaperonis - 23-H-d
Karahalios - 45-H-p
Karamaplas - 45-R-p
Karamitopoulos - 41-H-p
Karanikas - 37-H-p
Karatsanos - 41-B-p
Karey - 35-Ch-p
Karins - 43-Su-p
Karipi - 43-R-p
Karippey - 43-R-p
Karkunis - 33-H-p
Karpuk - 31-G-p
Karr - 41-Ch-p
Karson - 45-Ch-p
Karstok - 45-H-p
Kart - 43-M-p
Kartaczewicz - 43-M-p
Karwocki - 45-M-p
Kasper - 33-H-p
Kassraras - 25-H-p
Kat - 35-H-p
Kate - 35-H-p
Kathan - 27-H-d, 41-Ch-p
Katsalis - 29-H-d
Katsanos - 45-R-p
Katulak - 45-H-d
Katz - 29-H-d
Kauffman - 39-M-p
Kauffmann - 33-Ch-p
Kaufman - 37-H-p
Kaukolander - 39-Su-p
Kawzowicz - 45-Su-p
Kay - 29-St-d, 31-R-p, 37-H-p, 41-Ch-p, 41-H-p, 45-R-p
Kazanas - 37-Ch-p
Kazanowich - 41-Su-p
Kazlaris - 27-H-d
Keach - 45-Co-p
Kean - 43-B-p
Kearns - 37-H-p
Keating - 37-B-d, 41-Co-p
Keays - 35-St-d, 45-St-p
Kebalka - 45-Su-p
Kebrich - 29-Su-d, 37-G-d, 39-G-d
Kecy - 41-H-p
Keddie - 29-M-d, 39-Ch-p
Keddy - 33-H-p
Keefe - 23-Ca-p, 23-H-d, 31-H-p, 35-H-p, 39-H-d, 41-H-p, 45-H-d
Keen - 39-R-p, 43-R-d
Keenan - 27-Co-d, 33-H-p, 45-Ch-p
Keene - 33-R-p, 41-St-p
Keezer - 43-R-p
Keir - 39-Co-p, 45-Co-p
Keirstead - 29-H-d
Keith - 27-G-d, 29-H-p
Keko - 25-H-d
Kellam - 27-G-d
Kelleher - 35-R-p

Keller - 37-R-p, 37-St-p
Kelley - 23-B-p, 23-M-p, 27-M-d, 27-G-d, 29-G-d, 35-B-p, 37-R-p, 37-St-d, 37-H-d, 39-H-p, 39-R-p, 39-M-p, 39-B-d, 39-H-d, 41-H-p, 43-St-p, 45-St-p, 45-Ch-p, 45-R-d
Kelliher - 23-H-d
Kellock - 45-B-d
Kellom - 45-Ch-p
Kelly - 23-B-p, 23-M-d, 27-R-p, 25-M-d, 27-H-d, 41-G-p, 43-H-p, 45-G-p, 45-St-d
Kelsea - 33-G-d
Kelsey - 43-St-p
Kem - 45-H-p
Kempton - 31-Ch-d
Kendall - 23-H-d, 35-G-d, 39-Su-d, 45-M-p
Kendrick - 31-Ca-d, 33-Su-d
Kendrigan - 43-H-p
Kenerson - 31-St-d
Keneson - 43-Su-p
Kenick - 45-H-p
Keniskman - 41-Ch-p
Keniston - 27-M-p, 31-G-d, 35-M-d, 37-G-p, 41-G-p, 45-B-p, 45-G-d
Kennard - 43-H-p, 45-H-p
Kennedy - 23-M-d, 29-St-d, 33-M-d, 35-H-p, 39-M-d, 41-St-n, 43-H-p, 45-Ch-p, 45-H-d
Kennett - 27-Ca-p, 43-Ca-p, 45-R-p
Kenney - 23-Ch-p, 29-H-d, 35-Ch-p, 39-St-p, 43-R-p, 45-M-p, 45-G-d
Kennick - 33-R-d

Kennison - 45-Su-p
Kenniston - 43-M-p
Kennon - 27-Ca-d
Kenny - 39-G-d
Kent - 39-St-d, 45-Ch-d
Kenyon - 27-Ch-p, 29-Ch-p, 29-H-d, 33-Su-p, 45-H-p
Keough - 25-Co-p, 43-Ch-p, 45-R-d
Kerby - 25-H-p
Kercewich - 33-Ch-p
Kereazopoulous - 33-Su-p
Keroack - 29-Co-p
Kerrick - 35-M-p
Kershaw - 33-Ch-p
Kerslake - 23-M-p
Kesterson - 45-H-p
Ketchen - 33-St-d
Kettelle - 31-H-p
Keyser - 29-H-p
Keyza - 45-H-p
Kibbie - 25-Ch-d, 29-Su-p
Kidder - 25-H-p, 27-H-p, 27-G-d, 35-Su-d, 45-St-p
Kier - 43-Co-p
Kierstead - 45-H-p
Kieve - 37-R-d
Kilburn - 31-M-p, 35-Ca-p
Kiley - 43-H-p
Kilgore - 31-Ca-p
Kilkis - 45-M-p
Killam - 25-G-p
Killeen - 37-Ch-d
Killmer - 33-R-d
Kilroy - 33-H-p
Kilton - 27-M-p, 41-H-d
Kimball - 23-R-p, 23-Ch-d, 23-G-d, 25-R-d, 27-B-p, 27-M-p, 27-Co-p, 31-G-p, 33-B-p, 33-R-p, 35-R-p, 35-B-d, 37-R-p,

Kimball - 37-B-d, 39-G-p, 39-H-p, 41-St-p, 41-M-d, 41-H-d, 41-Ca-d, 43-R-p, 45-Su-p, 45-M-d
Kimerling - 43-R-p
Kincaid - 35-H-p
Kinduris - 27-H-p
King - 25-G-p, 25-B-p, 25-H-d, 27-M-p, 27-Co-d, 27-G-d, 29-M-p, 29-R-p, 31-G-p, 33-St-p, 33-Co-p, 33-M-p, 35-Ca-p, 37-G-d, 37-H-d, 39-Co-p, 39-B-p, 39-St-p, 39-Su-p, 41-R-p, 41-Ch-p, 41-M-p, 41-St-p, 41-G-p, 41-Ch-d, 43-M-p, 43-R-d, 45-M-p, 45-St-p, 45-Ch-p, 45-Su-p, 45-Ch-d, 45-R-d
Kingsbury - 23-Su-p, 27-Ch-p, 27-R-d, 39-Ch-p, 45-H-p
Kingsley - 43-R-p
Kingsman - 41-Ch-p
Kingston - 45-Co-p
Kiniry - 29-Ch-p, 43-Ch-p
Kinne - 23-G-d, 41-G-p
Kinney - 45-Su-p
Kinnie - 35-B-p
Kinsley - 27-St-p, 29-St-p, 33-St-p
Kinsman - 29-Ch-p
Kiritsis - 43-H-p
Kirk - 43-H-p
Kirkpatrick - 35-M-p
Kirnsky - 27-St-p
Kirouac - 45-St-p
Kirsch - 41-H-p
Kiser - 33-Co-p
Kisiolek - 45-H-p
Kitchen - 43-B-p

Kittredge - 29-M-p
Kittridge - 43-St-p
Klardie - 37-H-p, 43-H-p
Klauberg - 39-R-p
Klenke - 35-M-d, 41-R-p
Kliewinski - 45-R-p
Klug - 43-Ca-p
Knapp - 25-M-p, 25-Co-p, 25-G-d, 37-St-p, 39-H-p, 39-B-d, 41-Co-p, 45-Ch-p
Kneeland - 43-St-p
Kneiper - 33-St-d
Knight - 23-H-d, 29-H-p, 29-H-d, 35-G-d, 37-Ch-p, 39-G-p, 41-St-d, 43-Su-p, 43-M-p, 43-R-p, 45-St-p, 45-H-p, 45-Su-p, 45-Ca-d
Knighton - 29-G-p
Knights - 35-G-d, 39-R-p, 43-R-p
Knoetzsch - 39-M-p
Knopel - 23-H-p
Knowles - 31-Ca-p, 31-H-p, 41-H-p, 41-R-d, 43-R-p, 43-Ch-p, 43-R-d, 45-R-p
Knowlton - 25-M-p, 45-H-p, 45-B-p
Knox - 35-M-d, 39-St-d, 41-Ca-p, 41-Ch-p, 41-Co-d
Knudsen - 41-H-p, 45-H-p
Koch - 31-H-d
Koehler - 45-H-p
Koenig - 37-H-p
Kofer - 45-H-d
Koivista - 45-Su-p
Koivisto - 43-Su-p, 45-Su-p
Kokoszka - 33-H-p
Kokulis - 41-H-p
Kolano - 23-H-p
Kolinsky - 45-G-p

Kolioburdas - 45-M-p
Kolvig - 33-R-p
Konigs - 45-H-p
Kontinos - 45-Ch-p
Koopman - 43-M-p
Koozanovich - 37-Su-p
Kopac - 39-St-p
Kopecki - 35-R-p
Korkovelos - 37-H-d
Kosch - 39-R-d
Koski - 37-Ch-p, 41-Ch-p
Kosky - 41-R-p
Kosowicz - 43-H-p, 45-H-p
Kostas - 41-H-p, 43-Ch-p
Kostopoulos - 35-Ch-p, 43-Ch-p
Kott - 37-H-p
Koufopoulas - 43-H-p
Koukos - 27-H-p
Kourevesis - 35-Ch-p
Koutsonikas - 25-H-p
Kovach - 45-H-p
Kowalewski - 29-H-p
Kowzan - 37-Su-p, 41-Su-p
Kozacki - 45-H-d
Kozlowski - 45-R-d
Kozminski - 45-St-p
Krajewski - 43-H-p
Kramer - 41-Ca-p, 45-G-d
Kreger - 27-R-p
Kreps - 45-H-p
Kreshpani - 25-M-p
Kreuzer - 33-R-p
Krewski - 45-H-p
Krieger - 23-R-d
Krinsky - 29-St-p, 33-St-p
Krisiak - 43-St-d
Kristof - 39-Ch-p, 41-Ch-p, 43-Ch-p
Kristoff - 43-H-p, 45-H-p
Kropp - 41-M-d

Kruczek - 41-H-p
Krukowski - 39-R-p, 41-R-p
Krupa - 43-H-d
Kruse - 39-St-p
Krym - 37-H-p, 41-H-p
Krystapowicz - 43-H-p
Krystofowiez - 43-Ch-p
Krystoic - 43-R-p
Krystopowicz - 39-Ch-p, 41-Ch-p, 43-H-p, 45-H-p
Kryzanowski - 41-H-p
Krzewski - 45-H-p
Kubiak - 23-R-p
Kubiszyn - 25-H-p
Kubosky - 39-Ch-p
Kucharczyk - 39-R-p, 39-H-p, 41-R-p
Kuchinsky - 31-R-p, 33-R-d
Kudolis - 37-H-d
Kudzma - 33-H-p
Kujeska - 45-R-p
Kujeske - 37-R-d
Kukolander - 37-Su-p
Kukurabas - 25-H-d
Kunes - 31-R-p
Kungulus - 33-Su-p
Kuntz - 37-R-p, 45-R-p
Kuriger - 37-H-d
Kuronen - 31-B-p
Kurylak - 43-H-p
Kurylock - 43-H-p
Kusiak - 45-H-p
Kuszewski - 23-G-p
Kuusisto - 43-H-p
Kvaraceis - 39-H-p
Kwiatek - 37-H-p
Kyle - 35-R-p
Kyne - 29-Su-p
Kyriakakis - 27-H-p
Kyriax - 27-H-p

L'Heureux - 43-H-p
L'Homme - 37-H-p, 45-H-p
L'Italien - 41-H-p
Labarge - 31-H-p
Labarre - 29-H-p
Labbe - 33-Co-p, 39-R-p, 41-St-d
LaBell - 39-Co-p
LaBelle - 25-G-p, 31-H-d, 35-G-d, 37-Su-d, 45-Ch-d
Laben - 45-H-p
Laber - 35-Su-p
LaBier - 25-Ch-d
Labnon - 45-Co-p
LaBombard - 31-M-p, 31-G-d, 33-G-d, 39-Ch-d, 39-G-d
Labombarde - 45-H-p
Labonte - 35-H-p, 35-St-p, 39-M-p, 43-St-d, 45-St-d
LaBonte - 33-H-p, 33-Co-d, 45-H-p, 45-G-p
Labore - 33-H-p
Labossiere - 41-St-p
Labounty - 41-H-p
LaBounty - 39-H-p
LaBranche - 41-H-p, 45-H-p
Labrecque - 25-M-p, 27-H-d
LaBrecque - 27-G-d
LaBree - 27-St-d
LaBrie - 33-St-d, 41-M-p
LaBuke - 41-M-p
Labunsky - 45-H-p
Lacasse - 27-G-d, 29-Co-p, 35-Su-p, 41-St-d, 45-St-p
Lachance - 29-H-p, 41-H-p
Lachat - 23-G-d
Lackey - 35-M-d, 45-G-p
LaClair - 31-H-p
LaClair - 31-M-p, 37-M-p, 39-Co-p, 45-Su-p

LaClaire - 27-B-p
Lacock - 29-H-p
LaCoille - 41-Ch-p
LaCoss - 43-R-p
Lacosse - 31-H-p
Lacourse - 27-B-p
LaCourse - 23-B-p, 35-G-d
Lacroix - 33-B-p, 41-B-p, 41-Co-d
Lacross - 41-R-p
LaCross - 41-B-p
Lacy - 33-H-d, 45-St-p
Ladam - 41-Ch-p
Ladd - 23-M-p, 29-R-p, 31-R-p, 43-H-p, 43-Ch-p
Ladeau - 37-G-d
Ladin - 45-St-p
LaDuca - 37-Ch-d
LaDuke - 43-Co-p, 45-M-p
LaFarr - 45-Ch-p
LaFay - 45-St-p
Lafazanis - 29-H-d
LaFerte - 45-M-d
Lafferty - 43-M-p
Laflamme - 41-H-p
LaFlamme - 45-G-p
Lafleur - 37-Ch-p
LaFleur - 41-H-p, 43-St-d
Laflotte - 25-H-p
Lafoe - 35-G-d
Lafond - 41-H-p
Lafontaine - 37-H-p, 43-H-p
LaFontaine - 43-H-p
LaForge - 29-M-p
LaFountain - 37-H-d
Lafountaine - 45-Su-p
Lafrance - 35-R-p
LaFrance - 29-Su-d, 37-St-p, 41-H-d
Lafreniere - 31-H-p
Laganiere - 29-H-p

Lagasse - 37-St-d, 39-H-p, 45-H-p
Lagerquist - 35-H-p
Lagotte - 41-St-p
LaHaise - 33-B-p
Lahart - 41-R-p
Lahaye - 25-G-d
Laird - 33-M-d, 35-M-d
Lajoie - 39-H-d, 41-H-p, 45-Co-p, 45-H-d
LaJoie - 41-H-p
Lakeman - 43-H-p
Lakin - 37-Co-d
Lakr - 43-H-p
Lalerle - 23-Co-p
Laliberte - 23-H-p, 41-H-p
LaLiberte - 29-G-p
Lalibertee - 39-Su-d
Lally - 45-H-p
Lalmond - 35-H-p
Lalonde - 29-G-d
Lamarche - 29-H-p
LaMarche - 41-H-p
Lamare - 25-Su-p
LaMarre - 37-G-d
LaMay - 27-B-p
Lamb - 33-H-p, 39-Ch-p
Lamber - 35-Ch-d
Lambert - 23-Ch-p, 23-H-d, 23-Su-d, 25-Co-p, 29-M-p, 39-Ch-p, 41-Ch-p, 43-H-p, 45-St-p, 45-H-p, 45-H-d
Lambi - 23-H-p
Lamere - 43-B-p
Lamontagne - 41-H-p, 45-H-p, 45-St-p
LaMontagne - 37-Co-p, 41-R-p
Lamontague - 27-Ca-p
Lamontte - 31-St-d

Lamora - 37-H-p, 39-M-p
LaMora - 35-M-p, 37-M-p
Lamoreux - 33-H-p, 35-M-p
Lamothe - 39-H-p, 43-H-p, 45-H-d
LaMott - 43-G-p
LaMotte - 43-H-p
LaMountain - 23-H-d
Lamoureux - 35-R-p, 37-M-p, 45-Ch-d
Lamphrey - 31-St-d
Lampinen - 39-Ch-p
Lampman - 41-B-p, 45-Ch-d
Lamprey - 27-B-d
Lamprinakas - 37-H-d
Lampro - 29-G-d
Lampron - 45-H-p
Lamson - 45-M-p
Lamy - 23-H-d, 39-H-p, 43-H-p
Lancaster - 45-B-d
Lancey - 27-Ch-d, 37-M-p
Lancisi - 25-M-p, 37-M-p
Landers - 31-H-p
Landis - 37-H-p
Landry - 23-B-p, 23-B-d, 25-H-p, 27-St-d, 31-H-p, 33-H-p, 35-B-d, 35-Co-d, 45-St-p, 45-G-p, 45-Co-p
Lane - 23-H-p, 23-Ca-d, 27-B-p, 27-G-d, 29-Ch-p, 29-G-d, 31-R-p, 33-St-p, 33-R-d, 33-H-d, 35-H-p, 35-M-d, 37-R-p, 39-Ch-d, 41-Su-p, 43-Su-p, 45-Ch-d
Lang - 29-R-p, 39-Co-p, 41-Ch-p, 43-B-p, 43-R-p
Langas - 35-H-p
Langdon - 35-Ch-p
Lange - 31-H-p

Langevin - 41-M-d
Langford - 35-St-p
Langley - 27-Ca-p, 39-R-d, 41-R-p
Langlitz - 29-M-p
Langlois - 41-R-p, 43-Co-p
Langmaid - 27-St-d, 29-St-d, 45-G-p
Lank - 41-B-p, 41-R-p, 43-B-p
Lankoysky - 41-R-p
Lanning - 41-G-p
Lannon - 43-R-p, 45-R-p
Lanoie - 43-H-p
Lanoix - 29-G-d
LaPage - 25-Ch-p
Laperle - 29-Co-p, 33-Co-p
Lapete - 45-St-p
Lapierre - 33-M-d, 35-B-p, 35-M-p, 37-B-d, 41-Ch-p, 43-H-d
LaPierre - 41-Su-p, 43-B-p, 45-H-p
Lapin - 43-H-p
Lapitre - 41-B-d
LaPlant - 31-Co-d
Laplante - 43-H-d, 45-B-d
LaPlante - 23-H-p, 37-Co-p, 41-Su-p, 41-Ch-d, 43-H-p, 43-H-d
Lapoint - 23-R-p, 29-Su-d
LaPoint - 39-G-p
Lapointe - 23-H-d, 35-R-p
LaPointe - 29-M-p, 29-Ch-d, 37-Ch-d, 43-H-d, 45-H-p
Laporte - 27-M-p, 31-H-p
LaPorte - 41-R-p
Lappas - 43-H-p
Laprise - 37-Su-p
Laraba - 27-H-p
Laramie - 29-G-d, 35-M-p, 43-M-p, 43-R-p, 45-B-p

Laramy - 33-H-d
Lareau - 23-H-p
Larion - 37-H-p
Lariviere - 25-H-d, 35-St-p, 39-H-p, 41-G-p, 41-H-p
Larkin - 33-Co-d, 39-Co-p
Larkinson - 43-H-p
Larlee - 31-Ca-p
Larmy - 25-H-p
Larner - 23-Ch-d
Laro - 39-M-p, 43-H-p
Laroche - 23-H-p, 41-B-p, 45-H-p
Larochelle - 29-H-p, 31-H-d, 37-H-p, 43-H-p
LaRochelle - 37-M-p
Larose - 25-H-d
Larouche - 39-H-d
LaRouche - 43-Su-p
Larrabee - 39-Ch-p
Larrivee - 33-H-p, 45-Co-p
Larsen - 29-Co-p, 39-R-p
Larson - 27-H-d
Laschkowsky - 29-H-d
Lasher - 45-R-d
Lasheway - 41-B-p, 43-B-p
Lashua - 25-M-p, 41-B-p, 45-H-p
Laski - 43-H-p
Latham - 45-M-p
Lathrop - 31-Ch-p, 31-H-p
Latour - 31-H-p
LaTour - 33-Su-p
LaTourette - 41-H-p
Latuch - 37-H-p
LaTulippe - 41-Su-p
Latvala - 43-Su-p
Laughton - 43-R-p, 43-St-p
Laurent - 35-H-p
Laurier - 27-H-p
Lauste - 43-Su-p

224

Laustee - 43-Su-p
Lauzier - 41-M-p
Lavallee - 33-H-p, 37-H-p, 39-H-p, 41-H-p, 45-H-p
LaValley - 41-Ch-p
Lavarnway - 43-H-p
Lavely - 41-Ca-p
Lavender - 23-Ch-p
Laventure - 35-H-d
Laverdiere - 39-St-d, 45-H-p
Lavery - 37-H-d
Lavigne - 27-H-p, 33-H-p, 35-H-p, 39-H-p, 41-H-p, 41-H-d, 43-H-p, 45-St-p, 45-Ch-p, 45-Ch-d
LaVoice - 41-G-p
Lavoie - 23-H-d, 25-Co-d, 27-M-p, 29-H-p, 33-H-p, 37-H-p, 43-H-p, 45-H-p
Law - 35-H-p
Laware - 29-G-p, 41-G-p, 41-Ch-p
Lawless - 37-Su-p
Lawrence - 27-H-d, 27-G-p, 29-H-p, 29-H-d, 31-G-p, 33-H-d, 37-R-p, 37-Ch-p, 39-H-p, 39-Ch-d, 41-H-p, 43-H-p, 43-Co-d
Lawson - 37-H-p
Lawton - 27-R-d
Layfield - 45-H-p
Layman - 25-H-p
Laythe - 45-G-d
Lazotte - 45-H-p
Lea - 39-St-p
Leach - 25-G-p, 33-Co-p, 33-G-d, 35-Su-p, 41-M-p, 45-Co-p, 45-G-p
Leacock - 27-R-p
Leahy - 23-Ch-p
Learmouth - 39-Su-p

Learnard - 35-R-p
Learned - 45-B-p
Leary - 45-H-p
Leavitt - 25-H-p, 31-St-d, 41-R-p, 41-M-p, 41-G-p, 41-M-d, 43-M-p, 45-H-p, 45-G-p
Leazott - 39-H-p
Lebeaux - 45-G-d
Lebel - 25-H-p
LeBel - 31-Co-p
Lebelle - 23-Co-p
Leblanc - 25-M-d, 27-H-p, 33-H-p, 33-H-d, 33-Co-d, 37-M-p
LeBlanc - 25-H-d, 35-M-p, 41-M-p, 41-R-p, 41-Su-p, 41-H-d, 43-M-d, 43-St-p
Lebnon - 45-Co-p
LeBorgne - 43-H-p
LeBracque - 41-Ch-p
Lebrecht - 41-St-p
Lebrun - 43-Co-p
LeBrun - 43-Co-p
Leclair - 39-H-p
LeClair - 31-R-p, 33-H-p, 35-H-p, 35-Ch-d, 37-H-d, 39-St-p, 41-R-p, 43-Su-p
LeClaire - 41-H-p
Leclare - 33-M-p
Leclerc - 41-H-p, 45-Co-p
LeClerc - 41-G-p
LeClercq - 35-B-p
LeComte - 41-H-d
Lecour - 45-B-p
Lecuyer - 41-Ch-p, 43-Ch-d
Ledger - 43-Co-p
Ledoux - 23-G-p, 27-H-p, 33-H-p, 39-H-d, 45-H-p
Leduc - 43-St-p

Lee - 33-H-p, 37-Ch-d, 39-G-p, 39-G-d, 43-H-p, 45-H-p
Leemon - 29-M-p
Lees - 29-Su-d, 43-M-p, 45-M-p
Leete - 39-H-p
Lefebvre - 23-H-d, 37-St-p, 39-St-p, 39-H-p, 41-M-p, 41-Co-d, 43-H-p
LeFrancois - 27-B-p
LeGanger - 35-Su-p
Legault - 45-H-d
Legendre - 33-H-p, 43-H-p
Leger - 43-R-p
Lehmann - 39-H-p
Lehoullier - 35-H-p
Leighton - 33-R-p, 33-Co-d, 39-M-d, 41-Co-p, 43-St-p
Leistner - 23-H-p
Leitch - 23-Ch-p
Lemay - 23-R-p, 27-H-d, 29-M-p, 33-H-p, 39-H-p, 39-H-d, 41-G-p, 43-H-p, 45-M-p
LeMay - 41-H-p
Lemelin - 35-H-p, 37-H-p, 43-H-p, 45-H-p
Lemere - 37-Su-p
Lemery - 45-H-p
Lemieux - 41-Co-p
Lemire - 27-H-p, 39-H-p, 43-H-p
Lemiux - 45-B-p
Lemorn - 37-Ca-p
Lenane - 45-R-d
Lenchte - 33-R-p
Lenfest - 41-St-d
Lenneville - 43-R-p
Lent - 31-M-p
Lenz - 25-H-p, 41-R-p

Lenzi - 35-St-p
Leo - 39-M-p
Leonard - 27-Ch-p, 27-Ch-d, 31-G-d, 35-G-p, 35-M-p, 41-Ch-d, 41-M-d, 43-St-p, 45-H-p, 45-G-p
Lepa - 43-G-p
Lepage - 25-H-d, 45-Co-p
LePage - 39-Co-d, 41-H-p, 43-H-p
Lepetre - 43-H-p
Lepicier - 37-Su-d, 41-Su-p
Lepitre - 41-Ch-p, 43-B-d
Lepore - 41-R-p
Leroux - 25-M-p, 35-Co-p
LeRoux - 45-H-p
Lescord - 43-Ch-p
Lesieur - 39-H-p
Leslie - 35-Ch-p
Lesmerises - 43-M-p
Lesniak - 29-H-p
Lesperance - 29-Su-d, 41-St-p
Lessard - 23-H-d, 25-B-p, 25-M-p, 31-Co-p, 35-Ch-p, 39-St-p, 41-St-p, 43-B-d, 45-H-p, 45-Ch-p, 45-H-d
Lester - 29-G-d, 41-H-p
Letalien - 29-R-p
Letarte - 41-St-p
Letendre - 41-H-p, 43-H-p, 45-M-p
Letourneau - 41-Ch-p, 41-H-d
Letourneux - 39-H-p
Letzkus - 45-H-p
Levasseur - 31-B-p, 39-H-p
Leveck - 41-H-p
Leveillee - 31-Co-p
Lever - 39-St-p
Levere - 31-R-p
Leverich - 45-Ch-p

Levesque - 25-R-p, 25-Co-p, 27-H-p, 35-H-p, 39-St-n, 41-H-p, 41-M-p, 43-H-p, 43-R-p, 45-Co-p, 45-H-d
Levi - 41-H-p
Levia - 27-R-p
Levine - 35-H-p, 39-H-p
LeVine - 27-R-p
Levis - 43-R-p
Levoy - 33-B-p, 33-B-d
LeVoy - 43-G-d
Levy - 35-St-p
Lewis - 23-Su-p, 25-Ch-p, 29-R-p, 31-G-p, 33-Su-p, 35-Ca-p, 35-M-p, 37-M-p, 37-G-p, 39-Ch-p, 39-St-p, 39-M-p, 39-R-p, 41-B-p, 41-Su-p, 41-St-d, 43-Ca-p, 43-M-p, 43-St-p, 45-R-p, 45-Su-p, 45-Co-p, 45-St-d
Lexner - 23-R-p, 41-H-p
Leyden - 29-R-p
Libbarres - 37-Ch-p
Libbey - 39-Ca-d
Libby - 23-Su-p, 27-Ca-p, 27-St-d, 35-B-p, 37-Co-d, 43-R-p
Liberty - 41-H-p, 43-M-p, 45-M-p, 45-R-d
Lidstone - 25-Co-p
Lieach - 37-St-d
Liebermann - 27-Co-p
Light - 39-Su-d
Lightbody - 43-R-p
Liimatainen - 25-H-p
Liliopoulos - 35-H-p
Lilley - 41-St-p
Lilly - 31-H-p, 41-H-p
Limbourg - 39-H-p
Lincoln - 25-Ch-d, 45-St-d

Lind - 33-Su-p
Lindbom - 45-St-p
Lindemulder - 39-M-d
Lindgren - 41-Co-p
Lindquist - 41-Su-d
Lindsay - 23-G-p, 29-Su-p, 31-G-p, 39-St-p, 41-Ch-p
Lindsey - 37-M-p
Lindstrom - 33-Su-p
Linehan - 37-H-p, 41-H-p
Linen - 41-M-p
Lingley - 33-G-p
Linnell - 39-Co-p
Linscott - 25-H-p, 31-R-p
Linscott -
Linscott -
Linscott - 41-R-p, 43-R-p, 45-M-p
Lintott - 25-H-d, 29-H-d
Lioliopoulos - 37-H-p, 45-H-p
Liptzer - 39-St-p
Lirette - 41-St-p
Lisherness - 27-H-p
Litheland - 27-Ch-p
Little - 25-H-p, 35-M-p, 39-Ch-d, 43-M-p, 45-H-p
Littlefield - 31-R-p, 35-B-p, 41-Ch-p, 41-St-p, 41-R-d, 43-B-p, 45-M-p
Littlehale - 41-Co-p
Lively - 33-M-p
Livingston - 27-H-d, 29-Ch-p, 37-Co-d
Livingstone - 41-H-p
Lizotte - 41-H-p, 43-H-p
Lloyd - 45-H-d
Locicero - 37-H-d
Locke - 25-St-p, 27-St-p, 29-R-p, 31-R-d, 33-H-p, 33-M-p, 35-R-p, 37-R-p, 39-

Locke - M-p, 39-B-p, 43-R-p, 45-St-p
Lockwood - 27-B-p, 27-Su-p, 33-M-p, 45-M-p
Lodge - 41-M-d
Loehn - 35-R-p
Loftus - 23-R-d
Logan - 45-G-d
Loiselle - 29-Ch-p, 37-H-p, 39-H-p
Lombard - 27-Ch-p
Londa - 43-Ca-d
Londo - 37-St-p
London - 25-B-p
Lonergan - 23-H-p, 35-H-p
Lones - 35-H-p, 45-H-p
Long - 33-H-p, 41-R-p, 41-Co-p, 41-R-d, 43-Co-p
Longchamps - 39-G-p
Longeran - 37-H-p
Longever - 41-Ch-d
Longley - 23-R-p, 35-St-d, 41-M-p
Longstaff - 37-Co-p
Lonie - 43-Ch-p
Lonsdale - 45-Co-p
Looney - 27-H-p, 31-H-p
Lopez - 27-St-d
Lord - 31-St-d, 37-M-p, 39-H-d, 39-Su-d, 41-H-p
Lorden - 29-M-p, 33-G-p
Loring - 27-Ch-p, 33-St-d
Lougee - 25-R-d, 35-St-p, 39-St-p, 41-B-p, 43-Ca-p, 45-M-p
Lough - 29-St-d
Loughlin - 33-R-p, 37-H-p, 41-R-d
Lougis - 41-G-d
Louiselle - 35-Su-p
Loukedes - 33-H-p

Louks - 35-Ch-p, 37-Co-d
Loukx - 27-R-d
Lounder - 39-Ch-d
Louthian - 43-M-p
Lovci - 31-H-p
Love - 27-H-p
Lovejoy - 27-H-p, 31-H-p
Lovelle - 27-B-d
Lovely - 43-B-p, 45-G-p, 45-St-p
Loveren - 23-H-p
Loverin - 27-Co-p
Lovering - 33-H-d, 35-Ch-d, 39-H-p
Lovesey - 31-H-p
Lovett - 29-H-p
Loville - 41-Ca-p
Lowe - 27-St-p, 41-Co-p
Lowell - 27-H-p, 29-M-p, 31-G-p, 31-H-p, 41-G-p, 43-H-d, 45-R-p
Lower - 33-Ch-d, 35-G-p, 35-Ch-d, 37-Su-d, 45-G-p
Lozo - 39-Su-p
Lubin - 37-H-p
Lucas - 37-H-p, 39-H-p, 45-G-d
Lucca - 27-Ca-d
Lucchetti - 33-Co-d, 35-Co-p
Luce - 29-Ch-p, 41-Ch-d, 41-H-p, 45-Ch-p, 45-R-d
Luchinsky - 39-R-p
Lucia - 23-G-p, 27-G-p, 41-M-p
Lucien - 39-H-d
Lucier - 25-M-d, 35-H-p, 41-H-p, 41-M-d, 43-H-p, 45-H-d
Lucille - 35-Co-p
Lucinski - 39-R-p
Luckers - 41-H-p

Luckury - 41-H-p, 43-H-p
Luckwryz - 43-H-p
Luczkewicz - 41-H-p
Luczkewycz - 41-H-p
Luczkiewicz - 41-H-p
Ludgate - 45-G-p
Lufkin - 29-H-d
Lugliani - 43-B-p
Lugsch - 37-M-p
Lula - 25-H-d, 33-H-p
Luman - 33-Su-d
Lund - 31-M-d
Lundeen - 37-M-d
Lunderville - 41-Su-p
Lunt - 45-M-p
Lupien - 41-H-p
Lupiers - 23-Co-p
Lurvey - 35-Ch-p
Lusier - 39-Su-p
Lussier - 29-H-d, 29-G-d, 31-Su-p, 39-Su-p, 45-H-p, 45-H-d
Lydon - 45-R-d
Lyford - 41-M-p
Lyle - 43-R-p
Lylis - 35-H-p, 37-H-p, 45-H-p
Lyman - 25-B-p, 43-B-p
Lynaugh - 25-Co-p, 27-Co-d
Lynbourg - 39-H-p
Lynch - 27-M-p, 31-G-p, 31-M-p, 31-R-p, 33-H-p, 35-Su-p, 41-R-d
Lynde - 45-G-d
Lyon - 23-H-p, 25-H-p, 45-H-d
Lyons - 45-H-d

Maban - 41-B-p
Mabry - 39-H-p
MacAdams - 23-Su-p
MacArthur - 39-H-p
MacCann - 37-H-d

MacCormack - 39-H-d
MacCowan - 45-M-d
MacDonald - 23-G-p, 23-R-p, 23-H-d, 29-G-p, 31-H-p, 33-B-p, 33-Co-d, 37-M-p, 39-St-d, 41-Ch-d, 43-H-p, 45-B-p, 45-Ch-d, 45-H-d
MacDougall - 39-H-p
MacDuffie - 27-H-p
MacEachran - 41-M-p
Macenas - 43-H-p
MacGillivray - 23-H-p
Mach - 45-H-p
Macia - 23-R-d
MacInnis - 43-H-p
MacIntosh - 25-B-p, 37-B-d
MacIntyre - 39-Su-d
MacIsaac - 37-H-p
Mack - 23-R-d, 31-H-p, 33-M-p, 39-B-p, 39-Ch-p, 43-H-p, 45-Su-p
Mackay - 25-M-p
MacKenzie - 45-Ch-p, 45-St-d, 45-G-d
Mackey - 37-Ch-p, 37-St-p, 39-M-p, 43-Ch-p, 43-Su-p
MacKinley - 29-R-d
Mackly - 31-G-p
MacLaughlin - 27-M-p
MacLean - 23-Ch-p, 25-Ch-p, 25-G-d, 45-R-d
Macloon - 37-Co-p
MacNaught - 29-M-p
MacNeil - 23-St-p
MacQuarrie - 37-B-p
Macri - 37-H-p
Macropal - 41-G-p
Macuilevicious - 43-H-p
Macy - 43-G-p

Madigan - 41-R-p
Madison - 23-H-p, 25-M-d, 41-H-p
Madore - 37-Su-p, 43-G-p
Madsen - 41-H-p
Magee - 23-H-d, 23-M-d, 33-Su-d
Magny - 31-G-p
Magoon - 23-G-p, 41-M-p
Magunson - 23-H-p
Mahan - 41-St-p, 45-Co-p
Maher - 27-Ch-p, 45-H-p
Mahmot - 45-M-p
Mahomet - 45-M-p
Mahoney - 25-H-d, 41-R-p, 41-H-p, 43-M-p
Mahony - 35-H-p
Maier - 35-Ch-p
Mailhiot - 45-St-p
Mailhot - 43-St-p, 43-H-d
Mailot - 43-St-p
Maine - 31-B-p, 45-St-d
Majer - 33-Ch-p
Majkowski - 25-H-d
Makarias - 43-H-p
Maker - 23-H-d, 43-Co-p
Maki - 27-M-p, 37-Ch-p, 39-Ch-p, 41-H-p, 43-Ch-p, 45-H-p
Maksymiec - 45-H-p
Malas - 43-Co-p
Malasky - 43-Co-p
Malenfant - 45-H-p
Malhoit - 37-H-p
Malik - 41-H-p
Malin - 45-St-p
Malinoski - 43-H-p
Malinowski - 43-H-p
Malinowsky - 43-H-p
Mallard - 43-G-p
Mallek - 43-H-d
Mallila - 39-Ch-p
Mallinoski - 43-H-p
Malloy - 43-R-p
Malonay - 23-H-p
Malone - 45-R-p
Maloney - 27-R-d, 31-H-p, 39-H-p, 39-St-d, 43-H-p, 43-Su-p, 45-Co-p
Malony - 37-Su-p
Malouf - 25-H-p
Malouin - 37-B-d, 41-B-d
Maltais - 29-B-p, 39-M-d
Maltby - 25-R-p
Manchester - 31-H-p, 31-G-d, 35-G-d
Mandigo - 43-R-p, 45-R-p
Manis - 25-H-p
Manissadjian - 25-H-p
Manley - 31-G-p, 41-Ca-p
Mann - 27-St-d, 45-R-p
Mannell - 41-R-p
Manninen - 45-H-p
Manning - 25-R-p, 25-H-p, 29-M-p, 29-M-d, 31-M-p, 35-H-p, 37-Ch-p, 37-H-p, 39-R-d, 45-M-p, 45-H-p, 45-B-p, 45-Su-p
Mannion - 35-M-d
Manoleros - 41-H-p
Manolesco - 39-H-d
Manouras - 25-H-p
Mansfield - 23-Ch-d, 25-Co-p, 41-M-d, 45-H-p
Mansour - 43-St-p
Mantia - 45-Su-p
Mantyla - 37-Ch-p
Manuel - 23-Ch-p
Maple - 45-H-p
Maranda - 33-H-p
Marble - 45-St-p
Marceau - 41-H-p

Marchand - 27-B-d, 45-M-p, 45-Ch-d
Marchetti - 41-H-p, 45-G-d
Marchion - 41-H-p
Marcott - 45-Ch-p
Marcotte - 23-G-d, 25-St-d, 25-Ch-d, 27-H-p, 33-Su-p, 35-St-d, 39-M-p, 41-St-p, 43-St-p, 45-H-p, 45-G-p
Marcouex - 45-B-d
Marcoux - 29-H-d, 45-H-p, 45-St-p
Marcovicy - 31-H-p
Marcroft - 25-G-p
Marcuri - 35-R-d, 45-R-d
Marcus - 33-H-d, 39-G-d, 45-H-p
Marden - 23-G-d, 31-G-p, 33-Ch-p, 35-M-p, 37-M-p, 39-R-p, 39-B-p, 41-H-p, 41-R-p
Mardin - 39-Su-p
Mardorcheo - 43-R-d
Margaritis - 41-H-p
Margeson - 45-Su-p
Margetou - 43-H-p
Marinelli - 37-M-p
Marines - 43-H-p
Marino - 43-H-p
Marinopoulos - 37-R-p
Marinopoulus - 45-R-p
Marinos - 37-R-p, 45-R-p
Marion - 43-H-p
Markarian - 45-H-p
Marker - 45-H-p
Markey - 29-H-p, 39-R-d
Marks - 31-H-p, 41-R-d
Marlowe - 31-H-p
Marnell - 39-Ch-d

Marquis - 41-H-p, 45-H-p, 45-St-p, 45-H-d
Marro - 31-Su-d, 39-Su-p
Marrone - 45-G-p
Marrs - 27-Co-p
Marsh - 23-St-p, 23-B-p, 23-G-d, 25-H-p, 33-Ch-p, 33-H-p, 35-M-p, 35-Su-p, 41-R-d, 43-Ca-p, 45-H-p
Marshall - 25-Su-d, 29-H-p, 29-M-p, 31-Ch-p, 33-H-p, 33-St-p, 37-H-p, 37-R-d, 39-R-d, 41-H-p, 41-R-p, 43-H-p, 43-R-p, 43-Ch-p, 45-M-p, 45-St-p
Marson - 27-H-d
Marston - 27-B-p, 31-H-p, 33-M-p, 35-R-p, 35-H-p, 35-G-d, 37-G-p, 41-R-p, 41-B-d, 43-H-p, 43-B-d
Martel - 35-St-d, 37-R-d, 37-M-d, 41-Co-p, 41-Su-d, 43-R-p, 43-Co-p
Martell - 43-R-p
Martin - 23-Ca-p, 23-M-p, 25-Su-p, 27-H-d, 27-M-d, 29-R-p, 29-G-p, 29-Ch-d, 29-H-d, 31-R-p, 33-Su-p, 33-B-p, 35-Co-p, 35-R-d, 35-M-d, 37-H-p, 37-H-d, 37-Su-d, 39-H-p, 39-Ch-p, 41-H-p, 41-Ch-p, 41-Co-p, 43-H-p, 43-M-d, 45-Ca-p, 45-H-p, 45-G-p, 45-Co-p
Martineau - 33-H-p, 37-St-d, 41-H-p, 43-St-p
Martinetz - 43-B-p
Martinez - 45-G-p
Martinuk - 31-R-p
Martyn - 43-G-p

Marvin - 33-Ch-p
Marvin-Kaufmann - 33-Ch-p
Marvrellis - 43-H-p
Mascari - 35-G-p
Masellis - 41-R-p
Masialis - 41-R-p
Maskell - 45-Su-p
Maskwa - 45-R-p
Mason - 25-R-d, 27-M-p, 27-Ch-p, 29-H-d, 33-H-p, 33-M-p, 37-Co-d, 39-H-d, 41-R-p, 41-Ch-p, 41-H-d, 43-H-p, 45-R-p, 45-Su-p, 45-G-d
Massa - 41-R-p
Massey - 23-R-p, 41-Ca-p, 45-Co-p
Massie - 29-H-d
Masslick - 39-G-p
Masson - 45-M-p
Masters - 29-H-p, 39-Co-p
Masury - 41-St-d, 45-St-d
Masztal - 43-H-p
Mates - 27-R-p
Matevier - 43-G-d
Mather - 25-G-d
Mathers - 43-Ca-p
Matheson - 27-R-d
Mathews - 39-Ch-d, 41-St-p, 43-H-d, 43-R-d
Mathieu - 27-H-d
Matott - 45-M-p
Matsen - 41-H-p
Matsis - 27-H-p, 45-H-p
Matson - 39-Su-d, 43-Ch-p, 43-M-p
Matsopoulos - 45-H-p
Matte - 35-M-p
Matthewes - 37-R-d
Matthews - 33-Co-d, 35-Su-p, 41-Ch-p, 45-B-d, 45-H-d

Mattice - 37-Co-p, 39-M-d
Mattson - 45-Ch-p
Maure - 41-Co-p
Maurice - 43-St-p
Mavrogeorge - 45-H-p
Max - 43-R-p
Maxfield - 27-St-d, 39-Su-d, 43-St-p
Maxson - 35-M-p
Maxwell - 23-Ch-p, 23-H-d, 35-Ch-p, 45-B-p
May - 29-B-p, 43-H-p
Maybay - 39-H-d
Mayette - 31-G-p
Mayhew - 25-M-d, 29-H-d, 31-Ch-p, 37-M-d, 41-H-p, 41-M-p
Maynard - 23-H-p, 23-R-d, 27-Co-p, 35-H-p, 37-H-p, 37-H-d, 39-B-d, 41-M-p, 41-H-p, 43-H-p, 45-St-p, 45-G-p
Mayo - 37-Su-p, 41-M-p, 41-B-p
Mayott - 37-Ca-p, 39-St-d
Mayou - 27-H-d, 35-H-p, 45-H-d
Mazur - 39-H-d
Mazza - 23-H-p
McAdoo - 31-H-d
McAfee - 43-H-p
McAlister - 29-H-p, 31-St-d
McAllister - 37-H-d, 43-St-p
McArthur - 27-Ch-d
McAuliffe - 37-H-p, 45-G-p
McBride - 27-R-p, 27-H-d, 41-Ca-p
McCabe - 23-H-p, 25-H-d, 27-St-d, 35-Su-p, 39-G-p, 43-H-p, 45-St-d
McCain - 43-R-p

McCann - 23-H-d, 29-Ch-p, 33-Ca-p, 35-Ca-p, 43-H-p
McCarron - 27-St-d, 31-St-d
McCarthy - 23-St-d, 25-Co-p, 25-G-d 27-H-p, 29-H-p, 27-Co-d, 39-H-p, 41-H-p, 41-H-d, 43-R-p, 45-G-d
McCartney - 27-R-p
McCarty - 23-H-p, 27-H-p
McCauley - 31-St-p
McClarty - 35-H-p, 41-H-p, 43-B-d
McClary - 29-M-p
McClellan - 33-R-p, 43-Ca-p
McClintock - 25-M-p, 35-Co-d
McClure - 45-H-p
McCollester - 45-Ch-p
McCollum - 41-R-p, 45-G-p
McCombe - 39-St-p
McConnell - 27-H-d
McCormack - 45-St-p, 45-H-p
McCormick - 29-Su-d, 33-R-p, 39-Ch-p, 45-M-p, 45-Ca-p
McCoy - 25-Ch-p
McCray - 41-Ch-p
McCready - 41-Co-p
McCrillis - 39-St-p, 41-Ca-p
McCrink - 45-H-p
McCue - 39-G-d
McCullough - 41-R-p
McCullum - 31-R-p
McCuskie - 39-H-p
McCutcheon - 31-H-p
McDaniel - 43-St-p
McDonald - 29-Ca-p, 31-R-p, 33-M-p, 41-H-p, 45-M-p
McDonough - 23-B-p, 25-R-p, 45-St-d
McDougle - 33-B-d

McDowell - 27-Ca-p
McDuffee - 27-H-p, 31-R-p
McDuffey - 31-G-d
McElreavy - 25-Su-d
McElroy - 41-St-d
McEnnis - 43-St-p
McEwan - 31-St-d
McFarland - 27-Co-p, 43-G-d
McGaffigan - 43-M-p
McGall - 35-H-p
McGarey - 45-M-d
McGarr - 23-R-d
McGee - 31-Co-p, 37-Co-p, 43-St-p, 45-Co-p
McGennis - 37-Co-d
McGettigan - 43-H-p
McGettrick - 23-Co-p
McGill - 33-M-d
McGillivary - 37-Co-d
McGilvray - 43-M-p
McGinnis - 29-H-p, 45-Co-p
McGoff - 29-Co-p
McGovern - 45-H-p
McGowan - 25-H-d, 45-H-p
McGown - 41-M-d
McGrane - 29-Su-d
McGrath - 25-M-d, 33-Ch-p, 35-M-p, 41-H-p
McGraw - 43-Ca-p
McGuigan - 35-H-p, 37-H-p, 37-Ch-d, 37-H-d, 43-M-p
McGuire - 39-Su-p, 43-H-d
McHugh - 41-H-d
McInnis - 29-M-p, 43-H-p
McIntire - 25-St-p, 29-G-d, 33-Ca-d
McIntosh - 27-M-p, 33-R-d, 37-H-p, 39-M-p
McIntyre - 23-B-p, 27-H-p, 27-G-d
McKay - 31-Su-d, 37-St-p

233

McKeage - 41-Co-p
McKean - 27-B-p, 43-M-p
McKee - 43-Co-p, 45-H-p
McKeen - 35-G-p
McKelvey - 39-H-d
McKenna - 39-H-p, 39-Co-d, 41-St-d
McKenne - 35-Su-d
McKenney - 33-St-d, 45-St-p
McKenzie - 33-H-p, 33-Su-p, 43-M-d
McKinnon - 41-R-d
McKone - 43-St-p
McKuskie - 39-H-p
McLachlan - 23-R-p
McLachlin - 35-G-d
McLane - 25-B-p, 45-R-d
McLaughlin - 27-M-p, 29-H-p, 33-M-p, 33-Co-d, 35-M-p, 35-H-d, 37-H-d, 41-Co-p, 43-H-p, 45-M-p, 45-H-p
McLean - 31-R-p, 31-R-d, 39-R-p
McLellan - 37-Ca-p, 37-G-p, 43-Ca-p
McLeod - 25-G-d, 27-G-d, 29-G-d, 43-M-p
McLin - 29-R-d
McLouth - 31-M-d
McMahon - 43-G-p
McManus - 23-G-p
McMaster - 29-Ch-p
McMillan - 23-St-d, 23-H-d
McNabb - 33-R-d
McNally - 25-H-d
McNeely - 29-R-d
McNeil - 27-H-d, 29-H-p, 37-St-p, 41-G-p, 43-H-p, 45-St-p
McNichols - 41-H-p

McNicol - 41-H-p
McNulty - 39-M-p
McPhee - 45-Su-p
McPheters - 33-Co-d
McQuade - 43-H-p
McQuarrie - 45-R-d
McQuesten - 25-H-p
McQuillan - 37-H-d
McRae - 23-St-d, 35-Ca-p, 39-H-p, 41-Ch-p, 45-Co-p
McRell - 29-H-p
McShane - 27-H-p
McSorley - 35-St-d, 45-St-p
McSweeney - 23-H-d
McWilliams - 41-B-d, 43-B-d
Meachem - 41-B-p
Mead - 23-M-p, 35-H-p
Meader - 27-M-p, 35-H-d, 35-R-d, 37-St-d, 37-H-d, 39-Ca-p, 45-St-p, 45-Ch-p
Meagher - 29-M-p
Means - 45-Co-p
Meatty - 43-R-p
Meczelski - 37-Su-p
Medoff - 31-Ch-p, 37-Ch-p
Medvidofsky - 31-Ch-p, 37-Ch-p
Mee - 43-R-d
Meehan - 41-R-p
Meeker - 45-M-p
Meeks - 23-R-p, 45-M-d
Meersman - 25-H-d
Meiklen - 23-H-p
Melancon - 45-H-p
Melanson - 23-Ca-p, 33-H-p
Melbury - 29-Co-p
Melcher - 39-H-d, 45-Su-p
Meldrum - 41-Ca-p
Melendy - 23-Su-d
Melenkwich - 23-H-d

Melin - 45-H-d
Mellen - 41-R-d
Mellott - 41-St-p
Melonous - 39-St-n
Meloon - 29-H-d, 41-R-d
Meltzer - 27-H-p
Melville - 31-Co-p
Menard - 27-H-d, 29-B-d, 37-H-p, 43-H-p, 45-H-p
Menczywor - 35-H-p
Menter - 25-H-p, 45-H-p
Merchant - 29-R-p, 31-G-p, 41-G-p, 41-B-d, 43-H-p, 43-M-d, 43-B-d
Mercier - 39-M-d, 43-St-p, 43-H-p
Merlin - 23-H-d
Mermingis - 43-H-p
Merola - 39-R-d
Merrick - 43-G-p, 43-Co-p
Merrifield - 39-Ch-p
Merrill - 23-H-p, 23-G-p, 23-Ca-d, 25-Ca-p, 25-H-p, 25-Ch-p, 27-H-p, 31-H-p, 33-H-p, 35-H-p, 35-H-d, 37-B-d, 37-B-p, 39-B-p, 39-Co-p, 39-St-p, 39-Su-p, 41-R-p, 41-M-p, 41-St-d, 41-R-d, 43-H-p, 43-B-d, 45-M-p, 45-G-p, 45-B-d
Merritt - 43-Co-d
Merrow - 31-Ca-p, 39-Co-p, 45-Co-p
Merry - 41-Ch-p
Merton - 43-Su-p, 45-H-p, 45-Su-p
Mesaelis - 43-H-p
Meserve - 29-Ca-p, 29-R-p, 33-H-p, 41-St-p
Messer - 25-M-d
Messier - 33-H-d
Metcalf - 25-M-p, 27-M-p, 29-M-p
Metivier - 33-Ch-d, 37-M-p
Metrakas - 41-H-p
Metres - 41-B-p
Metropolis - 39-H-d
Mettlach - 31-R-p
Metz - 37-Ch-p
Meyer - 23-H-p
Meyers - 31-G-p, 41-G-p
Micaroni - 45-Ch-p
Michaud - 27-M-p, 27-Ch-p, 29-H-p, 31-H-d, 37-H-p, 37-H-d, 41-H-p, 43-G-p, 45-B-p, 45-Co-p, 45-St-d
Michel - 43-H-p
Michie - 39-R-d, 43-H-p
Mickelboro - 39-G-d
Mickielevich - 41-H-p
Micocci - 39-St-p
Middaugh - 43-B-p
Middleton - 41-R-p
Mientkievicz - 27-Ch-p
Mignault - 45-Su-p
Migneault - 33-H-p
Mikowski - 23-G-d
Milas - 39-H-p
Milasiewicz - 39-H-p
Milbury - 39-Co-p
Miles - 31-Su-d, 37-Ch-p, 39-St-d, 43-Ch-p, 43-H-p, 45-H-p, 45-Ch-p
Milette - 41-R-p
Milewski - 41-H-p
Miliauskas - 39-H-p
Milios - 45-Su-p
Miller - 23-G-d, 25-H-p, 25-Co-p, 25-Su-p, 25-Su-d, 27-M-d, 29-H-p, 31-H-d, 33-Ca-p, 35-Ch-p,

Miller - 35-H-p, 35-H-d, 35-Ch-d, 39-H-p, 39-St-p, 41-R-p, 41-H-p, 43-H-p, 43-R-d, 45-G-p, 45-Su-p, 45-M-d, 45-Ch-d
Millett - 27-H-p
Millette - 25-St-p
Milliard - 37-H-d
Milligan - 39-M-d
Millinuski - 43-H-p
Millis - 33-M-d
Mills - 35-R-d, 39-H-p, 39-St-d, 41-H-p, 41-Ca-d, 43-H-p, 45-St-p, 45-Ch-p, 45-Co-p
Milosl - 43-H-p
Miloszek - 43-H-p
Mims - 41-M-p
Minah - 29-Co-p
Minasian - 43-H-p
Miner - 25-H-d, 27-H-p, 37-M-p, 39-Ch-d, 41-Co-p
Minichiello - 27-St-p, 41-St-p
Minkiewicz - 45-Ch-p
Minnion - 29-M-p
Minnon - 39-M-p
Minor - 41-Ch-p
Minott - 45-H-d
Minturn - 35-H-p
Mirmingis - 43-H-p
Misiak - 25-H-d
Mitchell - 23-H-p, 25-H-p, 27-St-p, 27-H-p, 27-M-p, 29-St-p, 29-H-p, 29-M-p, 31-R-p, 31-H-d, 33-R-d, 33-Ch-p, 37-Su-p, 37-H-d, 39-Su-p, 41-R-p, 41-M-p, 41-B-p, 41-St-p, 41-H-p, 43-Ch-p, 43-St-p, 43-St-d, 45-R-p, 45-M-p, 45-H-d
Miti - 43-Ch-p
Mitten - 35-H-p
Mitton - 25-G-p
Mixer - 43-R-p
Mizo - 39-H-p
Mlecezko - 37-Ch-d
Mock - 43-R-d
Moeckel - 43-R-d
Moffett - 45-H-p
Moffette - 33-H-d
Moffitt - 41-H-p
Mohammed - 41-St-p
Moir - 23-H-d, 25-H-d, 31-H-p
Moison - 41-St-p
Moline - 33-Ch-p
Moller - 35-H-p
Mollor - 29-H-d
Molte - 45-R-p
Monaco - 39-H-p
Monahan - 33-Co-p, 35-Co-p, 37-Ca-d, 41-Co-p, 43-Su-p
Monast - 31-H-d
Mondoux - 43-St-p
Monette - 27-H-p
Monica - 33-G-d
Monroe - 23-R-p, 45-H-p
Montambeault - 41-Co-p
Montayne - 41-R-d
Montgomery - 35-Ch-d, 39-Ch-p
Montsie - 29-G-p
Montville - 43-R-p
Moody - 23-St-p, 25-Ca-p, 25-R-d, 29-G-p, 33-Ca-d, 37-R-d, 39-H-p, 41-R-p, 41-M-p, 41-H-p, 41-R-d, 43-B-p, 45-M-p
Moon - 31-Ch-p

Mooney - 33-G-d, 37-H-d, 41-B-p, 41-G-p, 45-M-p, 45-B-p
Moore - 23-R-p, 27-B-p, 27-Ca-p, 29-R-p, 29-R-p, 31-St-d, 33-St-d, 35-B-p, 35-M-d, 37-Ch-p, 39-G-p, 39-M-p, 39-Ca-p 39-H-d, 41-Ca-p, 41-St-p, 41-R-d, 43-H-p, 43-St-p, 45-H-d, 45-Su-p
Mooreside - 41-St-p
Moran - 23-H-p, 31-Su-d, 33-H-p, 35-R-d, 39-G-d, 41-Su-p, 43-St-p, 43-B-d
Morang - 39-St-p
Moreau - 29-H-d, 41-St-d, 43-R-p, 43-H-d, 43-R-d
Morel - 43-Co-p, 45-Co-p
Morell - 31-M-p
Morenghi - 43-H-p
Moreno - 43-H-p
Morey - 45-H-d
Morgan - 29-R-d, 31-M-d, 35-R-p, 35-St-p, 37-Su-p, 43-M-d, 45-R-p
Moriarty - 27-H-p, 37-Ca-d
Morin - 27-H-p, 29-B-p, 31-B-p, 33-Co-p, 35-Co-p, 35-H-p, 35-G-d, 37-B-p, 41-H-p, 41-B-p, 43-R-p, 43-B-p, 45-M-p, 45-B-p
Morisette - 39-H-p
Morison - 23-H-d
Morissette - 31-Co-p, 45-H-p
Moritts - 25-H-p
Morley - 39-Ch-p
Morra - 35-H-p
Morrell - 41-H-d, 45-H-d
Morrill - 25-St-d, 29-R-d, 31-H-p, 31-St-d, 37-R-p, 39-M-p, 41-H-d, 43-H-p, 45-Ch-d
Morris - 25-R-d, 25-Su-d, 27-H-d, 29-Ch-d, 41-Ch-d, 41-M-d, 45-G-p
Morrisette - 29-Co-p
Morrison - 27-R-p, 29-St-p, 29-G-p, 33-M-p, 33-M-d, 33-St-d, 35-B-d, 39-H-p, 41-M-p, 41-H-p, 45-B-p, 45-St-p
Morrissette - 35-Co-p, 37-G-d, 41-H-p, 45-H-p
Morrissey - 31-R-p
Morse - 23-M-p, 23-H-d, 27-G-p, 27-Ch-p, 29-M-d, 31-G-p, 33-G-p, 33-R-d, 37-St-p, 37-B-p, 37-R-d, 37-Su-d, 39-Su-p, 39-Su-d, 41-H-p, 41-B-p, 41-Co-p, 43-M-p, 43-B-p, 45-St-p, 45-H-p, 45-Ch-p, 45-Co-p
Mortenson - 45-Co-p
Morton - 23-H-p, 23-G-d, 25-H-p, 39-R-p, 41-R-p, 43-H-p
Moscardini - 39-B-p
Moseley - 35-H-p
Mosely - 37-St-d
Moses - 29-M-d, 31-M-d, 41-H-p, 43-B-p, 45-G-d
Mosher - 39-Co-p, 41-R-d
Mosier - 37-M-p
Mosney - 43-R-p
Moss - 37-Co-d
Mossey - 33-Ch-p
Mougamian - 43-H-p
Moulaert - 23-H-d
Moulton - 27-Ca-p, 33-Su-d, 35-R-d, 37-St-p, 39-G-p,

Moulton - 39-M-p, 39-R-d, 41-R-d, 41-B-p, 41-G-d, 43-G-p, 43-R-d, 45-B-p, 45-H-d
Mountford - 45-St-p
Mourad - 41-St-n
Mousseau - 45-H-p
Moustakas - 31-H-p
Mowatt - 41-R-p
Mowers - 39-G-p
Moylan - 45-Su-p
Moynahan - 41-Ch-p
Moynihan - 41-R-p
Mozitis - 41-H-d
Mozroll - 25-M-p, 41-B-p
Muchmore - 31-G-d, 41-G-p
Muckuskie - 39-H-p
Mudge - 43-H-p
Mudgett - 31-B-p
Muhlenbein - 43-Ch-p
Muir - 45-G-p
Mulherin - 45-G-p
Muller - 35-R-d, 37-H-p, 39-H-p
Mulligan - 25-St-d
Mullikin - 39-H-d, 43-R-p
Mullins - 41-R-p, 45-St-p
Mumford - 41-H-p
Mundell - 29-Ch-p, 35-Ch-p
Mundy - 37-M-p
Munroe - 45-G-d
Munsey - 27-G-p, 41-St-d, 45-M-p
Munson - 31-H-d
Murdock - 33-B-d, 39-St-p, 43-Ch-p
Murdough - 25-H-d
Murgatroy - 43-Su-p
Murphy - 23-G-p, 25-M-p, 25-H-d, 35-B-p, 35-G-p, 35-H-p, 35-H-d, 37-M-p, 39-G-p, 39-H-d, 41-H-p, 43-Ch-p, 43-H-p, 43-Co-p, 43-G-d, 45-H-p, 45-Co-p, 45-Su-p, 45-H-d
Murray - 23-St-d, 25-Ch-p, 27-Co-p, 27-Ch-d, 27-St-d, 29-H-d, 29-Su-d, 31-St-p, 33-Ch-p, 39-H-p, 41-Ca-p, 41-H-d, 43-Ch-p
Mushlin - 33-H-d
Musk - 33-H-p, 35-H-p
Mussey - 45-M-d
Mutney - 35-Su-p
Muzzey - 33-H-p, 35-H-p, 45-M-p
Myers - 33-Su-p, 41-R-p, 43-Co-d
Myhaver - 25-H-d
Myllymaki - 41-H-p
Myott - 29-G-p
Myrh - 23-St-p
Myrick - 41-M-p

Naczas - 45-H-p
Nadeau - 29-H-p, 29-G-p, 31-H-p, 31-St-d, 31-Ch-d, 33-B-d, 37-M-p, 39-St-p, 41-Co-p, 41-B-d, 43-Co-p, 43-B-d, 45-H-p, 45-Co-p
Nagle - 37-Su-d
Nahil - 39-H-p
Naismith - 45-H-p
Nalette - 41-H-p
Nalewski - 41-R-p
Nallett - 41-Ch-p
Nangle - 39-St-p
Nantel - 33-H-p
Napert - 39-Co-p, 41-Co-p, 45-Co-p

Napsey - 39-G-p
Nardini - 27-M-d, 45-M-p
Naro - 45-H-d
Naromore - 39-Ch-d
Nash - 23-G-p, 33-Ch-d
Nasman - 43-St-p
Nason - 23-Ch-p, 25-St-p, 31-H-d, 37-Ca-p, 41-H-p, 41-Ch-p, 43-Ca-p, 45-H-p
Natches - 45-H-p
Nau - 43-R-p
Naughton - 43-M-d
Nault - 35-B-p, 41-Co-d, 45-St-d
Navelski - 41-R-p
Navish - 35-Ch-p, 45-Ch-d
Naylor - 39-R-d
Neal - 35-R-p, 37-R-p
Nealley - 31-H-p
Neary - 43-M-p
Neaves - 41-Ch-p
Nebrydoski - 45-Su-p
Negus - 29-Su-d
Neil - 23-G-p
Neilsen - 45-H-p
Neitz - 39-G-d
Nelson - 23-R-p, 25-M-p, 27-R-p, 27-G-d, 29-M-p, 35-R-p, 35-Ch-p, 35-G-d, 41-H-p, 41-G-p, 41-St-p, 41-Ch-p, 41-R-d, 41-G-d, 43-Ch-p, 43-M-p, 45-Ca-p, 45-R-d, 45-M-d
Nerbonne - 41-H-p, 41-R-p
Nerden - 31-M-p
Nerenberg - 43-Su-p
Nesbit - 23-H-p
Nesman - 43-St-p
Ness - 41-B-d
Nessen - 45-H-p
Neubert - 27-H-p
Neudeck - 43-H-d
Nevers - 41-St-d
Nevins - 41-Co-d
Newbury - 37-St-p, 41-St-p, 43-R-p
Newcomb - 35-H-d
Newcombe - 39-H-p
Newell - 25-R-p, 39-M-p, 39-G-p, 39-G-d, 41-G-p, 45-Ch-p
Newhall - 39-R-d, 43-Ca-p
Newman - 23-H-p, 33-Co-d
Newton - 23-H-d, 27-Su-d, 27-M-d, 29-H-p, 33-Ca-p, 39-M-p
Nichol - 33-G-p
Nicholas - 41-Ch-p, 41-H-p
Nichols - 23-R-p, 25-Su-d, 27-M-d, 27-H-d, 29-H-d, 31-H-p, 35-H-p, 35-G-p, 35-St-d, 35-H-d, 39-H-p, 41-H-p, 41-St-d, 43-St-p, 43-H-p, 43-Co-p, 43-M-d, 45-St-p, 45-M-p, 45-Su-p, 45-Co-p, 45-R-d
Nicholson - 37-R-d, 41-R-p, 43-Co-p, 45-H-d
Nickel - 33-G-p
Nickerson - 31-B-p, 33-H-p, 37-M-d, 37-Ca-d, 41-Ca-d, 43-St-p, 43-R-p, 43-H-p, 43-Ca-d
Nicolas - 41-Ch-p
Nicoll - 43-M-p
Niebrzydoski - 45-Su-p
Nielsen - 37-St-p
Niemi - 45-Co-p
Niescier - 37-R-d
Niles - 37-Su-d, 41-Su-p, 41-B-p, 43-Su-p, 43-Su-d

Niquette - 45-H-d
Nisonger - 45-St-p
Nixon - 45-B-p
Niziankowicz - 29-H-p, 43-H-p
Noakes - 41-Su-p
Nobert - 41-St-p
Noble - 45-R-d
Nocky - 33-Co-p
Noel - 37-R-d, 37-H-d, 43-H-p, 43-St-p
Noels - 43-H-p
Nokes - 25-M-p
Nolan - 27-M-d, 35-Su-d
Nolet - 45-Co-p
Nordine - 39-St-p
Nordstrom - 31-B-p
Noreen - 35-Ca-p
Norman - 41-St-n, 45-Ch-p
Normand - 37-H-p, 37-H-d, 43-St-p, 43-H-d
Normandeau - 41-H-p
Normandin - 41-Su-p
Norris - 39-St-p, 39-H-p
North - 33-St-p
Northrup - 25-H-p, 41-Ch-d
Norton - 35-G-d, 39-R-p, 41-St-d, 41-B-d, 45-Ch-d, 45-St-d
Norwood - 29-H-p, 31-St-d, 41-H-p
Noto - 41-R-p
Nottage - 45-Su-p
Notvig - 29-Co-p
Nourse - 31-Co-d, 41-Co-p
Noury - 41-M-p
Novak - 45-R-d
Novelle - 45-R-d
Novia - 41-B-p
Novick - 39-H-p
Nowakowski - 41-H-d

Noyes - 25-R-p, 31-Co-d, 35-H-p, 35-Co-d, 37-H-p, 37-G-p, 37-Co-d, 41-H-p, 41-M-d, 43-R-p
Nudd - 25-R-d, 33-M-p, 39-M-p, 41-R-p, 43-M-p, 43-R-p
Nugent - 31-Co-p
Nunes - 45-M-d
Nusenoff - 45-H-p
Nutbrown - 33-H-d, 45-St-p
Nute - 41-R-p
Nutt - 41-St-p
Nutter - 25-St-p, 27-G-p, 43-M-p
Nutting - 29-R-p, 39-Su-p, 45-Su-p
Nye - 41-M-p
Nyman - 45-M-p

O'Blenis - 33-H-p
O'Brien - 23-H-p, 27-M-p, 27-H-d, 29-R-p, 35-R-p, 39-R-p, 41-H-p, 43-H-p, 43-R-p, 45-R-p, 45-H-d
O'Connell - 27-M-p, 29-H-p, 37-M-p
O'Conner - 39-St-p
O'Connor - 25-G-p, 25-R-d, 35-G-p, 37-R-p, 45-Su-p
O'Dare - 39-R-p
O'Donnell - 43-St-d
O'Gara - 27-H-p, 33-H-p
O'Grady - 43-H-p
O'Hara - 33-R-p, 41-H-p
O'Hare - 29-H-p
O'Hearn - 35-St-p, 35-Co-p
O'Leary - 23-St-p, 31-H-p, 35-R-p, 37-R-d, 39-R-p, 39-M-d, 41-R-p, 43-H-p, 45-R-d

O'Malley - 29-St-d
O'Neil - 27-Ch-p, 29-Ch-p, 33-St-p, 33-H-p, 45-Co-p
O'Neill - 27-H-p, 33-H-p
O'Reilly - 43-H-d
O'Rourke - 45-H-p, 45-Su-p
O'Shaughnessy - 35-M-p
O'Shea - 41-B-d
O'Sullivan - 45-H-p
Oakes - 33-G-p, 33-Co-p, 45-M-d
Oakleaf - 27-H-p
Ober - 27-M-p, 29-M-p
Oberg - 41-St-p
Oberstebrink - 27-M-p, 29-M-p
Obin - 41-H-p
Ochs - 45-St-p
Oday - 37-M-d
Odekirk - 45-H-d
Odell - 41-M-p, 41-Su-p
Oden - 43-R-d
Odiorne - 23-R-p, 43-R-d
Ogden - 41-R-d, 45-Su-p
Ohliger - 33-R-d
Oikari - 41-Su-p
Oikelmus - 43-H-p
Oja - 43-Ch-d
Ojala - 31-Ch-p
Oksanen - 41-Ch-p
Olden - 43-R-p
Olena - 39-H-d
Oleson - 29-Co-p, 35-H-p, 39-Co-p
Olinsky - 45-Ch-p
Olive - 43-H-p
Oliver - 23-Ch-p, 23-R-d, 23-Ch-d, 31-R-p, 35-B-d, 37-M-p, 41-H-p
Olkkonan - 27-M-p
Olko - 39-St-d

Olkonen - 39-M-p
Olmstead - 23-Ch-d, 33-M-d
Olsen - 25-B-d, 31-M-p, 37-G-d, 43-H-p, 45-H-p, 45-G-p
Olson - 25-R-p, 43-H-d
Olsson - 37-G-p
Oltman - 43-R-p
Oman - 41-Ch-p
Orcutt - 33-Ca-p
Ordeen - 27-M-d
Ordway - 25-M-p, 33-Su-p, 35-Su-d, 41-G-p
Orens - 43-B-p
Orkins - 37-Ch-d
Orr - 31-St-p, 39-St-p, 39-M-d
Orton - 27-G-p
Orvin - 23-H-p
Osborn - 25-R-p, 45-St-p
Osborne - 23-H-p, 23-Su-p, 25-St-p, 35-H-p, 41-H-p, 45-M-p, 45-H-p
Oscar - 39-Co-p
Osgood - 23-R-d, 25-M-p, 27-Su-p, 33-M-d, 39-G-p, 39-St-p, 39-R-p, 41-M-p, 43-M-p
Osinski - 41-B-p
Osmer - 37-G-p, 41-H-p
Osterman - 27-St-d
Ostler - 37-St-p
Othot - 37-H-p
Otis - 25-R-p, 25-H-p, 31-St-d, 35-B-p, 35-St-d, 39-H-p, 41-H-p, 43-H-p, 45-St-d
Otterson - 39-Su-p
Otto - 37-M-p
Ouelette - 37-Ch-p, 39-H-p, 39-St-p
Ouellet - 43-St-p

Ouellette - 23-H-d, 25-H-d, 27-H-p, 31-H-p, 35-H-p, 39-H-p, 41-H-d, 43-H-p, 43-St-p, 45-H-p, 45-M-p, 45-H-d
Ouimet - 41-M-p
Oullet - 45-H-p
Overs - 43-M-p
Owen - 25-Co-d, 31-M-d, 39-H-p, 41-St-p, 45-R-p
Owens - 25-H-p, 41-St-p
Owsink - 45-H-p
Owsiuk - 43-H-p
Owsley - 41-St-p
Oxley - 39-H-p

Paakkari - 39-M-p
Pace - 31-Co-p
Pachajakis - 41-H-p
Packard - 43-R-p, 43-R-d
Packer - 43-H-p
Paddock - 23-Ch-p
Padelinetti - 23-H-p
Padell - 23-H-p
Page - 23-Su-p, 23-G-p, 29-R-p, 31-H-p, 31-H-d, 35-G-p, 39-R-p, 39-Su-p, 39-R-d, 41-Su-p, 41-B-p, 41-H-p, 41-M-p, 43-M-p, 43-Ch-p, 45-B-p, 45-St-p, 45-Co-p, 45-G-p, 45-Su-p
Pahutsky - 45-R-p
Paige - 25-G-p, 25-G-d, 35-Co-d, 39-Ca-p, 39-M-p, 43-St-p, 43-R-d
Pailloucq - 39-H-p
Paine - 39-G-p, 41-B-p, 41-H-p, 43-B-p, 45-H-p
Pair - 33-Ch-p, 43-Ch-p
Paire - 43-Ch-p

Paisley - 45-St-p
Palardy - 25-St-p
Palathiotis - 45-B-p
Palenska - 41-H-d
Palfrey - 33-R-d, 35-R-d
Palisoul - 33-H-d
Pallas - 37-Su-p, 45-B-p
Palm - 23-H-p, 25-St-p, 39-B-p
Palmer - 23-G-p, 23-Co-p, 27-Ca-p, 37-Co-p, 39-Ch-p, 41-Su-p, 43-Su-p, 43-G-p, 45-R-p
Palnaire - 45-H-p
Palreiro - 43-H-p, 45-H-p
Pano - 25-M-p
Papacostas - 45-H-p
Papademas - 31-H-p
Papadoplos - 33-H-p, 43-H-p
Papadopoulos - 45-St-p
Papageorge - 23-St-p, 25-St-p, 43-St-p
Papagianis - 29-H-p
Papagianopoulos - 27-H-p
Papagien - 43-H-p
Papalevizopoulos - 37-H-p
Papalevizos - 37-H-p
Papalevizou - 37-H-p
Papamastasiou - 31-H-p
Papanastasiou - 41-H-p
Papasodero - 39-R-p
Papchristos - 31-H-p
Papineau - 41-Ch-p
Papp - 33-H-p, 37-H-p, 43-H-p
Pappachristos - 31-H-p
Pappacostas - 39-H-p
Pappalardo - 43-R-d
Pappanickola - 43-M-p

Pappas - 25-St-p, 33-H-p, 35-R-d, 41-H-p, 41-G-d, 43-H-p, 43-R-d, 45-St-p
Papsotero - 37-R-p
Paquet - 29-Co-p
Paquett - 25-G-p
Paquette - 25-H-d, 27-H-p, 27-H-d, 31-Co-p, 31-H-d, 33-R-p, 35-H-p, 37-H-p, 39-H-p, 39-H-d, 41-H-d, 41-G-d, 43-H-p, 43-G-p, 45-Ch-p
Paquin - 29-H-p, 43-B-p
Paradee - 43-B-p
Paradie - 23-H-p
Paradis - 29-B-p, 29-Co-d, 41-H-p, 43-H-d
Paradise - 41-Ch-d
Pare - 41-St-p, 45-G-p
Parent - 25-G-p, 27-R-d, 29-B-p, 35-R-p, 35-H-p, 39-Co-p, 39-St-p, 41-B-p, 43-St-p, 43-G-p, 45-H-p
Paris - 29-H-p, 29-H-d, 41-H-p, 43-H-p, 43-Su-p, 45-H-p
Pariseau - 33-Su-p, 35-Su-p, 37-Su-p, 39-Su-d, 41-Su-p
Parizo - 33-Su-p, 33-Ch-d, 35-Su-p, 37-Su-p, 41-Su-p, 45-Ch-d
Park - 29-H-p, 45-M-p
Parker - 23-H-p, 25-Ch-p, 25-G-d, 27-Ch-p, 29-H-p, 29-Su-d, 31-H-p, 31-G-p, 33-H-p, 35-H-d, 37-H-p, 37-Ch-p, 39-Co-p, 41-R-p, 41-G-p, 41-Ch-p, 41-H-p, 43-M-p, 43-G-p, 43-Su-d, 45-R-p, 45-Co-p, 45-R-d, 45-H-d
Parkey - 31-B-p, 31-G-p
Parkhurst - 27-H-p, 31-Co-d, 39-Ch-p, 41-H-d, 43-Ch-p, 43-H-d
Parkinson - 33-H-d
Parks - 35-Co-p, 41-Ch-p, 43-H-p, 45-Ch-p, 45-R-d
Parlon - 43-H-p
Parmelee - 37-Su-p
Parmenter - 45-H-p
Paro - 25-G-p, 45-G-p
Parry - 43-Ch-p
Parshley - 25-M-d, 29-M-p, 29-M-d, 31-St-p, 33-St-p, 35-Co-d
Parson - 43-H-p
Parsons - 23-Co-p, 23-M-d, 25-M-d, 31-H-p, 37-B-p, 37-Ch-d, 41-Ch-d
Partlow - 35-Su-d
Partridge - 39-M-p, 41-H-p
Parttinaa - 25-Ch-p
Parzych - 45-H-p
Pascal - 35-St-d
Pascoe - 43-Ca-d
Paselt - 43-G-p
Paskevich - 41-H-p
Paskiwicz - 41-H-p
Pasno - 23-Ch-p, 25-Ch-p, 27-Ch-p
Pastedenos - 39-St-n
Pastene - 39-St-n, 41-St-p, 41-St-d
Pasthedenos - 41-St-p
Patch - 25-H-p, 27-Ca-p, 31-St-p, 33-Co-p, 39-R-d, 41-R-p, 43-H-p, 43-M-d
Patenaude - 39-H-p, 41-G-p, 41-Ch-p

Pateneaude - 41-Ch-p
Paterson - 33-R-d
Patkus - 45-H-p
Patmaude - 29-R-d
Patnaude - 43-H-d
Patno - 23-Ch-d
Patnode - 27-Ch-p, 39-Ch-p, 45-Ch-p
Patoine - 39-M-p
Paton - 23-H-d
Patrick - 45-Co-p
Pattee - 37-G-p
Patten - 25-Su-d, 29-H-p, 33-H-p, 35-H-p, 39-M-p
Patterson - 37-R-p, 41-H-p, 43-R-d, 45-St-p, 45-Ch-p
Patton - 41-H-p
Paul - 33-R-p, 41-M-p, 41-R-d, 43-M-p, 45-H-p, 45-St-p, 45-H-d, 45-R-d
Paulding - 29-R-p
Paules - 27-R-d, 45-R-p
Paulette - 41-Su-p
Paveglio - 39-M-p, 41-M-d
Pavey - 29-R-d
Payant - 35-H-p
Payeski - 43-Ch-p
Payeur - 31-H-p
Payn - 41-R-p
Payne - 37-Ch-p, 43-M-p
Pazychuck - 35-H-d
Peabody - 27-H-p, 39-H-d, 41-B-d, 45-G-p
Peach - 25-H-p
Peacor - 43-Su-p
Peak - 33-Ch-d
Peal - 23-R-p
Peare - 27-Ca-p
Pearl - 23-R-p, 41-B-p, 43-M-d
Pearlstein - 41-Co-p

Pearson - 23-St-p, 39-R-p, 39-H-d, 41-Ch-p, 43-G-d, 45-St-p, 45-Ca-d
Peary - 45-B-d
Pease - 27-B-p, 31-R-d
Peaslee - 23-H-p
Peavey - 41-B-p, 43-B-p, 43-St-d
Peck - 23-R-d, 37-St-p, 41-B-p, 45-H-p
Pecker - 23-H-p, 45-R-p
Peckham - 31-R-p, 31-R-d, 41-G-p
Pecunias - 29-R-d
Pecunies - 41-Ca-p
Pederson - 45-Su-p
Peecha - 41-H-p
Peek - 37-R-p
Peel - 33-Ch-d
Peet - 27-Ca-d
Peightell - 33-G-p
Peirce - 23-R-p
Pelchat - 31-Co-p, 41-Co-d, 43-Co-p, 45-Co-p
Pelissier - 43-H-d
Pelkey - 41-Ch-p
Pellegrino - 37-R-d
Pellerin - 41-Ch-p, 43-Ch-d
Pelletier - 23-H-d, 23-H-d, 29-H-p, 29-Ch-p, 31-Co-p, 35-Su-p, 37-Ch-p, 39-M-p, 41-H-p, 43-H-p, 43-R-p, 43-Co-p, 43-H-d, 45-M-p, 45-H-p, 45-R-p, 45-Ch-p, 45-H-d
Peloquin - 39-St-p, 43-R-p
Pelotte - 45-B-p
Pelton - 35-G-p, 39-Ch-p, 45-Su-p
Peltonen - 37-Su-p
Pender - 39-R-p

Pendergast - 27-Ca-p, 33-R-p
Pendleton - 45-H-p
Peneault - 23-R-p
Penn - 41-H-p
Pennewaert - 41-R-d, 43-R-d
Penney - 41-R-p
Pennington - 45-H-p
Pennock - 37-G-p
Pentland - 25-H-p
Penttila - 37-Su-p
Peon - 41-R-p
Pepin - 27-H-p, 31-H-p, 37-H-p, 39-St-n, 41-H-p
Peppin - 45-H-d
Peppler - 41-M-p
Percival - 35-St-p
Percot - 39-Ca-p
Percy - 41-St-p
Perdue - 37-H-p, 39-H-d
Pereia - 39-St-n
Perfect - 37-R-d
Perham - 23-H-p
Perkins - 23-H-p, 23-Co-p, 23-H-d, 23-G-d, 25-R-p, 25-St-p, 27-R-d, 29-Su-d, 31-R-p, 31-St-p, 33-Ca-d, 33-St-d, 35-B-p, 35-Su-p, 39-R-p, 39-B-p, 39-M-p, 41-M-d, 43-St-p, 43-R-p, 45-R-d
Pero - 29-M-d, 37-M-p
Peroskas - 23-Ch-d
Perras - 39-H-p, 43-H-p
Perrault - 23-H-p, 25-H-d, 41-Ch-p
Perreault - 25-Co-p, 35-H-p, 45-M-p
Perrino - 45-H-p
Perron - 35-Ch-d, 41-M-p, 43-R-d, 45-G-d
Perry - 27-Co-p, 29-Co-p, 37-B-p, 37-H-d, 39-Su-p, 39-H-p, 39-St-n, 41-R-p, 41-B-p, 41-M-p, 43-R-p, 43-G-d, 45-B-p, 45-Ca-p, 45-St-p
Person - 41-Ch-p
Pertyczkowicz - 45-H-p
Pervere - 33-Co-d
Pesola - 41-Su-p
Peter - 25-B-p
Peters - 29-M-p, 33-H-p, 41-St-p, 41-M-p, 43-H-p, 45-H-p
Peterson -
Peterson - 25-Ch-p, 29-R-p, 29-M-d, 31-H-p, 31-M-d, 33-R-d, 35-H-p, 37-R-p, 39-Co-p, 39-Su-p, 39-H-p, 41-Co-p, 41-M-p, 41-B-p, 43-R-p
Pethick - 23-M-d, 43-H-p, 45-H-p
Petit - 41-H-p
Petitt - 43-Ch-p
Petrin - 45-Su-p
Petriw - 43-H-p
Petro - 45-R-d
Petry - 45-H-p
Petryczkowycz - 45-H-p
Petrykoz - 45-H-p
Pettee - 35-M-p
Pettengill - 39-Su-d
Pettigrew - 29-B-d
Pettingill - 41-Co-p
Pevear - 25-R-d
Peverly - 29-M-p
Pfefferkorn - 39-H-p
Pfeiffer - 23-H-p
Pfleiderer - 37-Su-d

Phelps - 25-Su-d, 41-R-d, 41-B-d, 43-B-d, 45-Ch-d, 45-G-d
Philbert - 43-H-p
Philbrick - 27-R-p, 29-Ca-p, 31-R-p, 35-Ca-p, 35-R-d, 43-R-p, 43-R-p, 43-R-d
Philbrook - 41-H-d, 43-Su-p
Philippe - 37-Ca-d
Philips - 27-Co-p
Phillips - 27-St-d, 29-G-d, 33-St-d, 35-G-d, 35-St-d, 41-R-d, 43-M-p, 43-B-d, 45-R-p, 45-Ch-d
Phinney - 29-Ca-d, 41-H-p, 43-R-p
Pialtos - 43-H-d
Piaseczny - 45-H-p
Piatkewicz - 29-B-p
Pichette - 23-M-p, 41-M-p, 45-St-p
Pickard - 27-R-p, 39-H-p
Pickering - 23-R-d, 23-G-d, 37-St-p, 37-G-d, 43-St-p, 43-Ch-p, 43-B-p, 43-R-d
Pickett - 23-M-p, 35-Ch-p, 41-H-p
Pickford - 41-Co-d, 45-Ch-p
Pickup - 45-St-d
Picozzi - 45-G-p
Piecuch - 39-St-n, 45-H-d
Pierce - 23-B-p, 23-G-d, 27-G-p, 31-M-p, 31-M-d, 39-H-d, 43-R-d, 45-M-p, 45-H-d
Piercy - 43-St-p
Pieritz - 31-H-p
Pieroni - 41-R-p, 45-M-p
Pierson - 43-G-p, 45-Ch-p
Piertrantoni - 33-H-p
Pietrantoni - 33-H-d

Pigeon - 45-H-p
Pike - 25-R-p, 27-H-d, 29-Ch-p, 29-St-p, 31-Ca-p, 31-M-p, 33-R-d, 43-R-p
Pikielnez - 45-Su-p
Pilarczyk - 23-R-p
Pilkowicz - 45-H-p
Pillsbury - 23-Ch-p, 37-St-p, 39-M-p, 41-G-p, 41-Co-d
Pilote - 45-B-p
Pilotte - 29-B-p, 33-G-d
Pinard - 25-Su-d, 39-H-p, 45-G-d
Pineo - 35-St-d
Pinet - 41-H-p, 45-H-p
Pinette - 27-Co-p, 33-H-p
Pingree - 27-R-p
Pinker - 41-M-p
Pinkham - 27-H-d, 31-R-d, 37-St-d
Pinney - 41-Ch-p
Piotrowski - 41-H-p
Piper - 25-St-p, 25-M-d, 27-Ch-p, 29-H-p, 29-H-d, 35-Ch-p, 39-R-d, 43-H-p, 45-H-p, 45-B-p
Pippin - 43-Ca-p
Pis - 45-R-p
Pistolas - 41-H-p
Pitarys - 45-H-p
Pitcher - 39-H-d, 43-H-p
Pitkin - 35-Su-d
Pitt - 29-Ch-p, 33-Ch-p
Piwonski - 43-M-p
Piwowarczyk - 45-H-p
Pizz - 45-R-p
Place - 23-B-p, 23-G-p, 25-M-p, 43-M-d, 43-G-d
Plaisted - 45-M-p
Plancon - 33-B-d

Plant - 25-G-d, 27-Ca-p, 31-G-d, 41-B-p, 41-G-p
Plante - 27-H-p, 29-M-p, 37-St-d, 39-B-p, 41-H-p, 43-M-d, 43-R-d
Plantier - 39-H-p
Plastridge - 29-M-p, 31-M-p
Platts - 27-R-d
Plaurd - 45-H-p
Pleatsekas - 41-H-p
Pleatsikas - 41-H-p, 43-H-p
Plechekos - 43-H-p
Plentzas - 43-H-p
Plessas - 35-St-d
Pliakos - 31-H-p
Ploch - 43-H-p
Plocharcyk - 43-H-p
Plouff - 35-B-p
Plouffe - 41-R-p, 43-R-p, 45-R-p
Plourde - 43-H-p, 45-M-p
Plowright - 39-H-p
Pluff - 41-R-p, 43-R-p
Plummer - 31-M-d, 33-M-p, 37-Su-p, 41-M-p, 45-Ca-p, 45-G-d
Plunkett - 41-Su-d
Pockell - 45-H-p
Poehlman - 23-H-d, 35-H-p, 39-H-p, 43-H-d
Poire - 35-B-p, 39-M-p, 41-B-p, 45-B-p
Poirier - 27-H-p, 43-H-p
Poisson - 33-H-p, 37-St-p, 43-Co-p, 45-St-p, 45-H-p, 45-Ch-p
Poitopoulos - 25-R-p
Pokultinis - 45-H-p
Poland - 35-R-p
Polar - 41-H-d
Polaski - 39-G-p
Polchlopek - 23-R-d, 45-H-p
Polewik - 41-Ch-p
Polidori - 27-H-p
Poliquin - 25-M-p, 41-St-p
Polk - 43-H-p, 45-H-p
Pollack - 35-Ch-p, 37-Ch-d, 37-G-d, 39-Ch-p, 41-Ch-d, 43-R-p, 43-R-d, 43-H-d, 45-H-p
Polson - 31-G-p
Pomeroy - 23-Ch-p, 45-Su-p
Pontbriand - 29-H-p
Poole - 31-H-d, 33-B-d, 43-H-p
Pooler - 41-B-p
Poore - 33-H-d, 37-H-d
Poplawski - 43-H-p
Popoff - 41-R-d
Popp - 41-H-p
Popple - 39-H-d
Portas - 35-Ch-p
Porter - 23-G-p, 23-H-p, 25-M-p, 27-M-p, 27-Ca-d, 29-M-p, 37-H-p, 41-R-p, 41-M-p, 41-St-d, 45-H-p, 45-Ch-p
Portigue - 43-Co-d
Posey - 41-Su-p
Potter - 29-B-p, 31-H-p, 35-B-p, 35-Ca-d, 39-M-p, 41-Ca-p, 45-B-d, 45-St-d
Potvin - 43-H-p
Poulas - 43-H-p
Poulin - 41-B-p, 43-St-d
Pouliot - 45-H-d
Poulis - 37-St-d
Pouloit - 43-St-p
Pounder - 39-G-d
Powell - 25-Co-p, 35-R-p, 35-H-p, 39-R-p, 39-G-p, 45-Su-p

Powers - 25-R-p, 25-Co-p, 31-G-p, 31-H-d, 33-H-d, 35-H-p, 35-R-d, 37-R-d
Prairio - 43-Ch-p
Prakapas - 41-B-p
Prantilla - 41-M-p
Prassler - 43-H-d
Pratt - 23-St-d, 25-R-p, 25-H-p, 27-St-d, 39-R-d, 41-Ch-p, 41-Su-p, 45-Ca-p, 45-G-p
Pratte - 45-H-p
Pratz - 43-M-p
Pray - 31-H-d, 41-B-p, 43-St-d
Prech - 41-G-p
Predoehl - 35-Co-d
Predue - 23-G-p
Pregent - 43-Ch-p
Presby - 31-G-p, 41-M-d, 43-H-p
Prescott - 23-R-d, 25-Ch-p, 25-H-d, 31-H-p, 31-H-d, 35-M-p, 35-Ca-d, 37-R-p, 39-St-p, 39-M-d, 41-G-p
Preston - 25-H-d, 27-M-p, 35-R-p, 39-St-p, 39-R-p, 43-Ch-p
Prevost - 29-H-p, 39-Co-p 41-Ch-p, 41-Ch-d, 45-H-p
Price - 25-R-p, 31-St-d, 33-G-d, 43-R-p, 43-Su-p, 45-M-p
Prichard - 45-H-p
Pride - 23-G-d, 45-Su-p
Priest - 37-R-p
Primeau - 43-Ch-p
Prince - 25-M-p, 37-B-p, 41-B-d, 45-H-p, 45-H-d
Printy - 39-St-p
Prior - 39-H-p
Prisby - 37-H-p
Pritchard - 31-H-p, 45-H-d
Prive - 29-H-p
Procter - 29-R-p, 33-R-p
Proctor - 23-G-d, 29-H-d, 35-R-p, 41-Ch-d, 43-M-p, 45-M-p
Prokop - 41-B-p
Prolman - 29-R-p
Proof - 23-Co-d
Proud - 41-M-p
Proulx - 35-H-d, 39-H-p, 45-H-p, 45-St-d
Prouty - 33-H-d
Provencal - 35-B-d, 41-Su-p, 45-B-d
Provencher - 33-H-p, 35-H-p, 41-M-d, 43-H-p, 43-G-p, 45-Co-p
Provost - 33-H-p, 43-H-d
Prowell - 25-Co-d
Prowse - 45-M-d
Prud'homme - 25-H-p
Prudden - 45-H-p
Prue - 25-Su-d
Prutsalis - 23-H-p, 41-H-p
Przybyla - 37-H-p, 45-H-p
Psaltis - 39-H-p
Ptno - 41-B-p
Publicover - 31-M-d
Puckett - 45-H-d
Puffer - 35-Ca-p
Pullos - 25-R-p
Puras - 41-H-p
Purdie - 35-H-p
Purdy - 41-R-d
Purington - 29-R-p, 33-H-d
Purrell - 41-M-p
Purtell - 39-M-p
Purull - 41-M-p
Pushard - 31-Su-d

Pushee - 23-Co-p
Puslecki - 35-H-p
Putnam - 23-Su-d, 37-Su-d, 39-H-d, 43-H-d, 45-G-p, 45-H-d
Putt - 45-St-d

Quackenbush - 23-H-p
Qualters - 37-Ch-p
Queor - 37-Co-p, 41-R-p
Quigley - 23-G-p, 37-R-p
Quimby - 25-M-p, 27-St-d, 35-R-p, 41-M-p, 43-R-p, 45-St-d
Quinlan - 39-B-p, 41-R-p
Quinn - 23-Ch-d, 31-Ch-p, 35-M-p, 41-H-p
Quint - 33-St-p, 43-Ch-p
Quintiliani - 41-M-d
Quintillio - 25-Ch-p
Quirk - 43-R-p

Raatikainen - 43-Ch-d
Rabadeau - 43-H-d
Raby - 33-H-p, 43-H-p
Racette - 23-H-p, 25-H-d
Raczka - 43-G-p
Raczki - 41-H-p
Radford - 27-R-d
Radigan 23-R-p
Radsky - 41-Co-d
Rae - 29-H-p, 39-B-p
Ragna - 31-Ca-p
Rahmanop - 43-H-d, 45-H-d
Rainaud - 33-St-p
Rainer - 39-G-p
Rainey - 35-R-d, 45-G-d
Rainville - 29-H-d, 37-R-d, 41-Co-p, 43-R-d, 45-H-d
Raitanen - 43-H-p
Raitt - 45-R-d

Rajotte - 43-H-d
Ralph - 45-H-d
Ramesdell - 23-R-d
Ramsay - 31-M-p
Ramsdell - 37-H-p
Ramsey - 35-H-p, 39-St-p
Ranalli - 39-H-p
Rancour - 31-G-d
Rancourt - 31-H-d, 41-H-d
Rand - 29-R-p, 33-R-p, 33-R-d, 39-G-p, 41-R-p, 43-M-p
Randall - 23-H-p, 25-M-p, 27-Ch-p, 29-R-d, 33-Ca-d, 35-St-p, 35-M-p, 35-St-d, 39-Ch-p, 45-St-p
Randell - 29-B-p
Randlet - 31-H-p
Randlett - 27-M-d, 31-G-p
Rando - 41-R-d
Ranger - 37-H-p
Rankin - 27-M-p, 45-G-p
Rapsis - 45-H-p
Rathburn - 35-G-d
Ratner - 45-Su-p
Ratta - 39-B-p, 41-R-p, 43-R-d
Rau - 35-H-p
Rausch - 23-H-d, 45-B-d
Ray - 25-R-d, 27-M-p, 37-G-p, 45-Su-p
Raymond - 25-M-p, 27-H-p, 29-H-p, 31-H-d, 33-Su-d, 35-H-p, 35-G-d, 37-H-p, 43-R-p, 43-G-p, 45-H-p
Raynes - 29-Ch-p, 37-R-p
Rayno - 25-Su-d, 45-H-p
Raza - 37-H-p, 41-H-p
Rea - 43-R-p

Read - 27-Co-p, 35-H-p, 37-Ca-p, 39-H-p, 43-R-p, 45-Ch-d
Reagan - 41-M-p, 41-R-p, 43-H-p, 45-H-p
Reardon - 23-H-d, 31-H-p, 35-M-d, 37-B-p, 39-M-d, 41-H-p
Reason - 45-Ch-p
Record - 23-G-p, 39-Ch-p, 41-Ch-p
Rector - 45-Ca-d
Redden - 33-H-p
Redington - 41-Ch-p
Redlon - 23-R-d
Redman - 27-R-p, 39-B-p
Redstone - 27-Ch-p
Reed - 23-H-d, 25-H-d, 27-R-p, 29-H-p, 31-Su-p, 31-H-d, 33-R-p, 33-H-p, 35-H-p, 35-Co-d, 37-M-p, 37-G-p, 39-Ch-p, 41-H-p, 43-Co-p, 45-H-p, 45-B-d
Regan - 33-H-p, 35-H-p, 43-H-d
Rego - 35-M-d
Reid - 25-Ca-d, 41-R-p, 45-Su-p, 45-M-d
Reidy - 35-H-p
Reilly - 31-H-p, 41-H-p, 41-H-d
Reimer - 41-H-d
Reiter - 27-G-d
Rell - 43-M-p
Remick - 27-St-d, 29-St-d, 33-H-p, 35-Co-p
Remillard - 35-H-p, 45-Co-p
Remington - 27-H-p, 35-B-p, 41-M-p
Renaud - 35-H-p, 37-H-p, 41-H-p, 41-H-d
Renee - 41-M-p
Reney - 33-H-p
Renihan - 37-G-d
Rennie - 31-M-d
Renouf - 35-Ch-d
Reschke - 43-R-d
Resse - 31-M-d
Ressler - 43-R-p
Retter - 35-M-p
Revoir - 41-G-p, 43-G-p
Reynolds - 35-H-d, 37-Su-d, 43-R-p
Rezenders - 27-H-p
Rheault - 41-H-p
Rheaume - 33-H-p, 43-H-p
Rhines - 27-Ca-p
Rhoades - 25-H-p, 27-Ch-p, 43-Ch-p, 43-Su-p, 45-Su-p
Rhodes - 41-M-p
Ricard - 29-St-d, 33-H-p, 43-H-p, 45-H-d
Rice - 23-H-d, 25-R-p, 29-H-p, 31-H-d, 33-St-d, 43-Ch-p, 45-M-p, 45-Su-p, 45-Co-p, 45-R-d
Rich - 23-Ch-p, 29-Su-p, 29-Co-p, 31-Co-d, 41-H-p, 41-H-d, 43-R-p, 45-B-p
Richard - 23-H-p, 25-Co-p, 31-H-p, 35-Ch-p, 39-St-p, 41-H-p, 43-H-p
Richards - 23-R-p, 25-Co-d, 27-Ch-p, 29-H-p, 29-Ch-p, 31-H-p, 33-H-p, 33-H-d, 35-G-p, 39-H-p, 41-R-p, 43-Co-p, 45-Ch-p, 45-Su-p
Richardson - 25-Ch-p, 27-G-d, 29-Su-p, 33-G-d, 35-G-d, 37-Su-p, 37-Ch-p,

Richardson - 37-G-p, 37-Su-d, 39-St-d, 41-G-p, 41-Ch-d, 45-B-p
Richer - 37-H-p, 39-Ch-p
Richmond - 23-H-d, 29-H-d
Richotte - 33-M-p
Richter - 43-Ch-p
Ricker - 23-Co-p, 27-B-p, 29-R-d, 33-Co-p, 41-Co-p
Riddel - 41-H-p
Rideout - 45-Su-p
Ridgewell - 41-Co-p
Ridgway - 33-R-d
Ridlon - 33-Ca-p, 41-R-p
Riel - 25-M-p, 39-M-p, 41-H-d, 45-B-p
Riley - 29-H-p, 33-H-p, 33-St-d, 35-G-d, 37-B-d, 41-R-p, 43-B-p, 45-St-d
Rinalducci - 27-R-d, 43-R-d
Rines - 39-M-d, 41-Ca-p, 41-M-d
Ring - 39-Ch-p, 41-M-p, 41-H-p
Ringer - 43-B-p
Rioux - 23-H-p, 27-H-p, 35-H-p, 39-H-p, 43-H-p, 45-R-d
Ripley - 31-R-p, 35-M-p
Rippy - 39-R-d
Ritchie - 33-Ca-p
Rivard - 35-H-p, 37-H-d, 39-H-p, 41-H-p, 43-H-p
Rivers - 33-G-p, 45-H-p
Rix - 31-Co-p
Roach - 23-R-p, 31-M-p, 39-Su-p
Robb - 39-Ch-d
Robbins - 25-R-d, 27-H-d, 29-Ch-p, 31-Su-d, 37-H-d, 39-H-p, 41-St-p, 41-G-p, 41-Ch-p, 41-H-p, 43-H-p, 45-H-p, 45-Ch-p, 45-St-d
Roberge - 23-H-p, 35-H-p, 37-B-d, 41-H-p, 43-H-p
Robert - 31-H-p, 39-Co-d, 43-M-p, 45-H-p
Roberts - 23-H-p, 23-B-d, 23-H-d, 25-St-p, 25-Co-p, 25-B-d, 27-Ca-p, 27-R-d, 29-M-p, 29-H-d, 31-St-p, 33-Ch-p, 37-Ch-p, 37-M-p, 37-R-p 37-St-d, 39-G-p, 39-St-d, 39-Su-d, 41-H-p, 41-M-d, 43-H-p, 43-M-p, 45-H-p, 45-G-p
Robertson - 23-R-p, 25-M-d, 27-Ca-p, 27-H-d, 29-Co-d, 31-Su-p, 33-R-p, 41-Ch-p, 41-St-d, 43-Ch-p, 45-H-p
Robichaud - 27-H-p, 35-H-p, 39-H-p
Robidas - 41-H-p
Robie - 35-Ca-p, 39-G-d
Robin - 23-H-p
Robinovitz - 39-H-p
Robinowitz - 41-H-p
Robins - 39-G-p
Robinson - 25-St-p, 25-Ch-d, 25-R-d, 27-Ca-p, 29-H-p, 29-R-d, 29-H-d, 31-B-p, 31-Ch-p, 35-H-p, 35-B-d, 35-H-d, 39-B-d, 41-R-p, 41-B-p, 43-Ch-p, 43-R-p, 43-M-p, 43-Co-p, 45-B-p, 45-Ca-p, 45-M-p, 45-St-p
Roby - 41-R-p, 43-M-p
Roche - 39-R-d
Rochfort - 41-H-p
Rochon - 39-St-p
Rochou - 41-M-p

Rock - 37-H-p, 43-G-p, 45-H-p
Rocker - 37-R-p
Rockus - 31-H-p
Rockwell - 25-M-p, 33-H-d
Rodd - 35-Ca-p
Rodger - 31-Su-p, 37-H-d
Rodier - 35-H-p, 43-H-p
Rodis - 41-St-n
Roditis - 41-St-n
Rodney - 45-St-p
Rodonis - 45-H-p
Roelse - 43-G-d
Rogers - 23-Ca-p, 23-St-d, 27-H-p, 27-Ca-p, 27-St-p, 27-M-p, 33-B-p, 33-H-p, 33-H-d, 35-H-p, 35-M-d, 37-St-p, 37-H-p, 37-R-p, 37-St-d, 37-R-d, 41-R-p, 41-St-p, 41-M-p, 41-M-d, 43-H-p, 43-M-p, 43-R-p, 43-St-p, 45-H-p, 45-Ca-p, 45-H-d, 45-M-d
Rogier - 41-H-p
Rogler - 39-H-p
Rohner - 27-H-p
Rohr - 45-R-p
Roi - 35-Su-p
Roland - 43-H-p
Roll - 33-H-d
Rolland - 23-H-p
Rollins - 23-B-p, 23-H-p, 23-St-d, 27-H-d, 27-St-d, 31-Co-d, 31-H-d, 35-B-p, 35-M-p, 35-Su-p, 37-H-p, 39-Su-p, 41-B-p, 41-M-p, 41-B-d, 43-R-p, 45-Su-p, 45-B-d
Rollinson - 25-Ch-p
Rolstein - 29-G-d
Roma - 35-H-p

Romani - 43-H-p
Romberg - 41-H-p
Romprey - 41-G-p
Ronan - 41-H-p
Rondeau - 45-M-p
Rood - 27-H-p, 35-H-p
Roody - 39-M-p
Rookey - 39-St-p
Rooney - 31-H-d
Root - 39-R-p
Rosa - 37-R-p, 39-R-p, 41-R-p, 43-R-d
Rose - 25-H-p, 37-Ch-p, 43-H-d
Rosen - 39-R-p, 39-Ch-p, 43-H-p
Rosenberg - 35-St-p, 45-Co-p
Rosenstiel - 27-St-d
Rosenthal - 31-Su-p
Rosi - 37-Co-d
Ross - 25-R-d, 27-Co-p, 29-H-p, 31-G-p, 35-R-p, 35-Co-p, 35-Co-d, 43-R-p, 43-St-p, 43-R-d, 45-Ca-p, 45-R-d
Rossiter - 23-St-d
Rothwell - 37-St-d
Rotkiewicz - 45-H-p
Roubo - 41-B-p, 43-B-p
Rouckey - 23-St-p
Rouleau - 35-H-p, 39-H-p, 39-St-p, 39-B-p, 41-H-d, 43-H-p, 45-H-p
Roulx - 45-H-p
Rounds - 43-M-p
Roundy - 23-Ch-p
Rouner - 37-R-p
Rouselle - 35-G-p
Rousseau - 27-Ca-p, 37-H-d, 39-Su-p, 41-M-p, 41-H-p

Routhier - 39-St-p, 41-H-p, 43-St-d, 45-Co-p, 45-St-d
Roux - 35-H-d, 41-H-p, 43-H-p, 45-St-p
Rowe - 23-St-p, 25-St-p, 25-B-p, 33-G-d, 37-R-d, 39-R-d, 41-R-d, 41-M-p, 45-R-d
Rowell - 25-H-p, 33-B-d, 39-H-p, 41-Co-p, 41-Su-d, 45-B-p, 45-Co-p
Rowland - 45-G-d
Rowley - 27-Co-d
Rowman - 45-H-p
Roxbee - 23-St-p, 23-St-d
Roy - 23-H-p, 23-M-d, 23-H-d, 23-Ch-d, 25-M-d, 27-Co-p, 29-H-p, 31-H-p, 31-G-p, 33-St-p, 33-H-d, 35-St-p, 35-Su-p, 35-Co-p, 37-B-d, 39-Ch-p, 41-R-p, 41-M-p, 41-H-p, 41-St-p, 43-M-p, 43-Ch-p, 43-H-p, 43-Su-p, 43-St-d, 45-M-p, 45-R-p, 45-H-d, 45-G-d
Royal - 27-H-p, 45-B-d
Royce - 23-Ch-d, 25-Su-p, 43-Ch-p
Royer - 41-H-d
Roys - 25-Su-p
Roystan - 35-H-d
Rucz - 45-H-p
Ruddy - 41-St-p
Rudisill - 45-H-d
Rudolf - 33-Ch-d, 43-Ch-d
Rudynski - 43-B-p
Rudzinski - 41-B-p
Rue - 39-Ch-d
Ruel - 23-St-d

Ruest - 45-H-p
Ruez - 45-H-p
Ruffini - 33-Ch-p
Ruggiero - 37-St-p
Ruggles - 29-Su-p, 33-Ch-d, 35-G-d
Rule - 39-Su-p
Rumrill - 43-R-d
Rundlett - 25-M-d
Runnells - 41-B-p
Runnels - 41-Ca-d
Rupley - 45-Ch-p
Rush - 41-M-p, 43-H-p, 45-M-p
Rushton - 29-H-p, 31-G-p
Russ - 41-G-p
Russell - 23-G-p, 25-H-p, 27-H-p, 27-H-p, 27-G-d, 37-M-p, 39-R-p, 39-Ch-p, 39-Co-p, 41-Su-p, 41-H-p, 43-H-p, 43-M-d, 45-Ch-d
Russillo - 31-B-p
Rutta - 39-B-p
Ruuskanen - 39-Su-d
Ryan - 25-R-d, 29-R-d, 33-M-p, 33-Ch-p, 35-H-p, 41-H-p, 41-Su-p, 43-H-p, 43-Co-p, 43-Ch-d, 45-H-p, 45-St-p
Ryder - 27-H-p, 37-Ch-p
Rylander - 39-R-d
Ryll - 45-H-p
Rzenikiewicz - 29-H-p
Rzeznikiewicz - 39-H-p, 39-H-d, 43-H-p

Saad - 37-H-p
Saari - 45-G-p
Sabatini - 45-Ch-p
Sabin - 41-M-p, 45-M-p

Sabins - 43-R-d
Sadauskas - 43-H-p
Sados - 41-R-p
Sadowski - 45-H-p
Saffell - 39-R-p
Sage - 45-H-p
Saida - 25-H-d
Saidel - 45-H-p
Saj - 45-H-p
Sakellarides - 45-H-p
Sakellariou - 45-H-p
Sakowich - 39-H-p, 39-Su-p
Salatas - 45-Ch-p
Salinsky - 33-Su-p
Saliskey - 39-Ch-p
Salitski - 39-Ch-p
Salls - 33-G-d
Salmela - 43-Su-p
Salo - 45-H-p
Salter - 41-H-p
Saltmarsh - 29-M-p, 41-M-p
Salvadori - 27-Ca-d
Salvail - 43-H-p
Salvas - 45-H-p
Samaha - 37-G-p
Samalis - 29-H-p
Sammis - 27-M-d
Sampson - 31-B-p, 37-B-p
Samson - 43-Co-p, 45-B-p, 45-H-p
San Antonio - 39-M-p
San Soussi - 45-M-p
Sanborn - 23-M-p, 23-R-d, 25-B-p, 25-M-p, 25-Co-d, 27-B-p, 29-M-p, 29-G-d, 31-St-p, 31-G-p, 31-St-d, 33-M-p, 37-M-p, 39-St-p, 41-M-p, 41-G-p, 41-Ca-p, 43-H-p, 43-St-p, 43-Su-p, 45-H-p, 45-Su-p, 45-M-d

Sandelin - 41-Co-p
Sanders - 23-B-p, 25-M-d, 31-M-p, 33-B-d, 35-H-p, 35-Ch-d, 39-H-p, 39-St-p, 41-M-d, 43-H-p, 45-B-p, 45-G-p
Sanderson - 27-R-p, 27-M-p, 37-H-p, 37-M-p, 43-M-p, 45-H-p
Sandwell - 43-H-p
Sanford - 45-Su-p
Sanger - 41-H-p
Sansouci - 35-H-p
SanSouci - 41-M-d
Sansoucie - 25-H-d, 35-H-p
Sanstock - 45-Ch-d
Santos - 45-H-p
Santucci - 23-H-p
Santy - 41-G-p
Sanville - 23-G-d
Sapurka - 25-H-d
Sargent - 23-G-p, 23-M-d, 27-H-p, 29-M-p, 31-B-p, 31-H-p, 31-H-d, 33-M-d, 35-G-p, 35-H-p, 35-H-d, 37-G-p, 37-G-d, 39-B-p, 41-R-p, 41-B-p, 41-M-p, 43-Co-p, 45-R-p, 45-Ch-p, 45-G-d, 45-H-d
Sario - 33-H-d
Sarkise - 25-R-p
Sarpi - 43-H-p
Sartwell - 27-B-d
Satin - 33-Su-p
Satinski - 33-Su-p
Satowitz - 41-R-p
Saulnier - 39-G-d
Saunders - 35-Ch-p, 37-G-p, 39-H-p
Savage - 41-H-p, 41-M-p, 43-G-p, 43-Co-p, 45-B-d

Savageau - 41-H-d, 43-H-p, 45-H-p
Savard - 29-H-p
Savoie - 45-H-d
Savoy - 31-M-d, 33-M-d, 37-H-p
Sawtell - 41-Ch-d
Sawtelle - 23-Ch-p
Sawyer - 23-Ch-p, 27-G-p, 31-H-p, 31-M-p, 33-B-d, 39-R-p, 39-H-p, 39-Co-d, 41-R-p, 41-M-p, 41-H-p
Saxon - 43-H-p
Saxton - 41-H-p
Sayers - 35-Ch-p
Saylor - 25-R-p, 33-St-d
Scalion - 25-Co-d
Scamporino - 41-R-d
Scanlan - 33-St-d
Scanlin - 39-M-p
Scanlon - 37-H-p
Scannell - 37-H-p
Scarboro - 43-B-p
Scarborough - 37-R-d, 41-R-d, 45-B-d
Scarponi - 35-R-d, 43-M-p
Schadt - 45-H-d
Schakowski - 33-R-p
Schambier - 41-H-p
Schelin - 39-B-d
Schellenger - 27-H-p, 31-H-p, 33-H-p, 45-H-p
Schellinger - 25-H-p
Schirnack - 25-H-d
Schlichting - 41-Ch-d
Schloth - 29-H-d, 45-H-p
Schlottmann - 41-H-p
Schmalfuss - 41-R-p
Schmidtchen - 41-H-p
Schmohl - 37-G-p
Schmuck - 45-R-p

Schneider - 29-R-p, 39-H-p, 39-G-p
Schneiderheinz - 27-H-p
Schneiderheinze - 35-H-d
Schoch - 39-M-d
Schoff - 23-Co-p
Schofield - 41-G-p
Schoolcraft - 29-M-p
Schoonmaker - 37-St-d
Schott - 39-M-d
Schrafft - 39-G-d
Schricker - 43-H-p
Schriver - 39-M-p
Schroeder - 25-H-p, 35-H-p, 37-Su-d
Schubert - 37-R-p, 43-H-p, 43-M-p
Schuck - 39-G-d
Schuerfeld - 41-B-p
Schuessler - 45-H-p
Schultz - 25-R-p
Schunemann - 23-H-p
Schurman - 35-Ch-p
Scofield - 41-H-p
Scott - 25-H-p, 25-St-p, 27-St-p, 27-St-d, 29-Ch-p, 29-Su-p, 29-H-p, 35-Ch-p, 37-M-p, 37-B-p, 37-R-p, 39-Ch-p, 41-Ch-p
Scribner - 31-H-d, 41-M-p
Scrosati - 39-St-n
Seace - 41-G-p
Seaman - 31-G-p
Seamans - 33-R-d, 45-G-p
Sears - 25-G-d, 27-H-p, 43-Ch-p
Seaver - 23-B-p, 25-H-p
Seavey - 35-R-d, 37-H-p, 37-R-p, 39-B-p, 41-St-p, 43-R-p
Seaward - 25-M-d, 35-B-p

Sebastian - 41-R-d
Secord - 39-St-p
Sedlewich - 43-H-p, 45-H-p
Sedlewicz - 35-H-p, 39-H-p
Seeley - 23-B-p, 29-G-p, 41-Ca-p, 45-B-p
Sefton - 23-M-d
Segal - 43-H-d
Seger - 37-H-p
Segole - 41-B-p
Seibaha - 37-H-p
Seifert - 31-H-d
Seldon - 45-M-p
Selig - 43-H-d
Seliga - 41-R-p
Seligson - 45-M-p
Seliskey - 39-Ch-p
Selmi - 39-Su-p
Semons - 45-G-p
Semple - 45-R-d
Seneca - 45-St-d
Senechal - 33-H-p, 43-H-d
Senise - 39-M-p
Senneville - 29-R-p, 31-H-p, 43-M-d
Sensinig - 41-G-p
Senter - 39-R-p, 41-St-p, 45-R-d
Serbian - 39-Su-p
Serin - 33-M-p
Serues - 27-H-p
Servas - 41-St-p
Serviss - 43-Su-p
Seymore - 23-R-d
Severance - 25-R-d, 27-Ca-p, 33-M-p, 41-M-p
Severy - 45-Ca-p
Sevigny - 35-St-d, 37-H-p
Sewall - 39-St-p, 43-St-p
Seymour - 35-Ch-d, 45-H-d
Shackelford - 41-B-p

Shackette - 23-Ch-p
Shackleford - 31-B-p
Shae - 29-M-p
Shamoun - 41-St-p
Shaner - 43-R-p
Shannon - 29-G-p, 45-H-p
Shapleigh - 41-R-p, 41-R-d, 43-R-d
Sharby - 41-H-d
Sharkey - 27-Ch-p, 27-Ch-d, 43-M-p, 43-Ch-p, 45-Ch-d
Sharon - 31-G-d
Sharp - 41-G-p
Sharpe - 45-H-p
Sharrock - 41-St-p
Sharron - 23-R-d
Shatford - 41-St-n
Shattuck - 23-St-d, 43-St-p, 43-M-d
Shaw - 25-St-p, 25-H-d, 27-H-d, 29-M-p, 31-B-p, 31-M-p, 33-B-d, 35-R-p, 35-Ca-p, 37-H-p, 37-R-d, 41-St-p, 41-R-d, 43-Co-p, 45-H-p, 45-St-d, 45-H-d
Shea - 25-H-p, 29-Ch-p, 31-H-d, 35-Ch-p, 35-Co-p, 35-St-d, 35-H-d, 37-Su-d, 41-R-p, 43-H-p, 45-H-p
Sheaff - 43-R-p
Sheard - 39-M-p
Sheburne - 23-B-p
Shedd - 31-Ch-p, 41-H-d
Sheehan - 25-H-p, 45-Su-p
Sheehy - 39-Co-p
Sheldon - 25-H-p, 37-H-p, 37-Su-d, 37-B-d, 41-St-p
Shelley - 25-Ch-p

Shelton - 23-R-p, 39-R-p
Sheltry - 43-St-p
Shepard - 25-B-p, 27-Ch-p, 27-G-d 29-G-d, 35-M-p, 39-R-p, 45-Ch-p
Sheppard - 39-Ch-p
Sherburne - 25-R-p, 39-H-d
Sheridan - 43-G-p, 43-Co-p, 43-H-p
Sherman - 35-Ch-p, 41-R-p, 45-M-p
Sherrad - 43-Ch-p
Sherry - 43-Ch-p
Sherwin - 45-H-p
Sherwood - 39-G-p
Sheska - 41-H-p
Shields - 41-G-p
Shilale - 41-R-p
Shina - 41-R-p, 45-R-d
Shine - 45-Ch-d
Shirley - 29-B-p, 31-R-d, 35-Ca-p, 43-H-d
Shirra - 37-H-d
Shivel - 39-St-n
Shoff - 45-Co-p
Shomsky - 45-H-p
Shonyo - 43-M-p
Shores - 41-Co-p
Short - 39-Su-d
Shortt - 45-G-d
Shoulders - 37-R-d
Shoults - 33-H-d
Shover - 41-Ch-p
Shrague - 41-R-p
Shubert - 43-M-p
Shuck - 31-G-p
Shufelt - 25-Ch-p, 31-Co-d
Shulenberger - 37-Ch-p, 43-Ch-p
Shulins - 23-Su-p, 33-Su-p, 43-Su-p, 45-Su-p

Shulinsky - 23-Su-p
Shulman - 41-M-p
Shultis - 33-M-d
Shum - 41-St-p
Shumway - 25-St-d
Shupe - 25-St-p
Shurbert - 43-B-p
Shute - 43-Co-p
Shuttleworth - 23-R-d
Shynott - 33-H-d
Sibley - 35-Ch-p
Sibulkin - 29-H-p, 29-H-d, 37-H-d
Sidebottom - 25-R-p
Sidelinger - 31-Co-d
Siedlewicz - 39-H-p, 41-H-p
Sieradski - 35-H-p
Sievers - 41-H-p
Signor - 35-H-d, 37-H-p, 41-H-p, 45-H-p
Sikorsky - 45-B-p
Sillery - 41-R-p
Silsby - 37-G-d
Silton - 27-St-p
Silva - 31-H-p, 37-H-p, 41-R-p
Silver - 25-G-p, 43-M-p, 45-Su-p
Silveria - 41-R-p
Silverman - 25-Su-d, 41-G-p
Silverstein - 27-St-p, 43-G-d
Silvia - 43-R-p
Simano - 23-Su-d
Simard - 27-H-p, 41-H-p
Simes - 43-R-p
Simkovetz - 43-Ch-p
Simmons - 29-Su-d
Simon - 23-R-d, 25-H-p
Simonds - 27-Co-p, 35-G-d, 39-Ch-p, 41-M-p, 43-Ch-p

Simoneau - 27-B-p, 27-M-d, 33-H-p, 33-H-p, 37-H-p, 41-H-p
Simonella - 39-M-p
Simonelli - 25-R-d
Simons - 45-H-d, 45-Ch-d
Simpanen - 33-Ch-p
Simpson - 23-Co-p, 25-B-p, 25-G-d, 27-B-p, 29-R-p, 31-R-d, 31-Co-d, 33-M-p, 41-Su-d, 43-R-p, 43-M-d, 43-G-d, 45-H-p
Sims - 45-M-d
Sinclair - 27-H-d, 33-Ca-d, 37-R-d
Sinkervitch - 43-H-p
Siomas - 25-H-p
Sippell - 43-G-d, 45-G-d
Sisco - 33-Co-p
Sisk - 23-M-d
Sisko - 41-H-p
Sivula - 33-Ch-p
Sizemore - 45-Ch-d
Skelly - 41-St-p, 41-R-d
Skibb - 41-R-p
Skibniowski - 41-R-p
Skibnoski - 41-R-p
Skiffington - 45-Ch-p
Skillings - 39-St-p
Skinner - 25-B-p, 31-R-p, 35-M-p, 37-G-p, 45-B-p
Sklar - 41-H-p
Sklarsk - 41-H-p
Skopecki - 35-R-p
Skwara - 45-H-p
Skwarzynski - 45-H-p
Slack - 23-Ch-p
Slate - 41-H-d
Slattery - 41-H-p, 43-Su-p
Slayback - 29-H-d

Slayton - 29-G-p
Sleeper - 23-B-p, 23-G-p, 33-St-d, 39-Ch-p, 41-G-p, 45-M-p, 45-Ca-d
Sloane - 35-Co-d
Slowinas - 41-R-p
Small - 25-Co-p, 29-M-d, 31-M-p, 31-M-d, 33-M-d, 37-St-p, 37-M-d, 41-H-p, 41-Su-d, 43-Su-p, 43-R-d, 45-Su-p
Smart - 23-R-d, 35-H-d, 37-St-p, 39-Ch-d, 39-H-d
Smas - 41-H-p
Smeitami - 37-H-p
Smietana - 37-H-p, 41-H-p
Smiley - 29-St-p
Smith - 23-H-p, 23-B-p, 23-Co-p, 23-R-p, 23-H-p, 23-G-p, 23-G-d, 25-M-p, 25-B-p, 25-G-p, 25-Su-d, 25-M-d, 25-H-d, 27-H-p, 27-Co-p, 27-B-p, 27-H-d, 27-R-d, 29-M-p, 29-H-p, 29-Ca-d, 29-H-d, 31-R-p, 31-B-p, 31-H-p, 31-Su-p, 31-M-p, 31-R-d, 33-B-p, 33-M-p, 33-H-p, 33-B-d, 33-H-d, 33-Co-d, 33-Ch-d, 33-M-d, 33-St-d, 35-R-p, 35-H-p, 35-Su-p, 35-M-p, 35-B-p, 35-St-d, 35-B-d, 35-G-d, 35-H-d, 37-H-p, 37-M-p, 37-G-p, 39-Ch-p, 39-B-p, 39-G-p, 39-Ca-p, 39-Su-p, 39-Co-p, 39-St-p, 39-H-p, 39-R-d, 39-M-d, 41-H-p, 41-Ca-p, 41-R-p, 41-M-p, 41-B-p, 41-Su-p, 43-R-p, 43-St-p, 43-H-p,

Smith - 43-M-p, 43-G-p, 43-H-d, 43-St-d, 43-M-d, 43-R-d, 45-B-p, 45-M-p, 45-St-p, 45-Ca-p, 45-Co-p, 45-Ch-p, 45-G-p, 45-Su-p, 45-St-d, 45-R-d, 45-B-d
Snarski - 37-H-d
Snell - 45-St-p
Snipes - 41-St-p
Snow - 25-B-p, 43-H-p
Snowman - 45-H-p
Snyder - 29-R-d, 39-R-d
Soderholm - 35-Ch-p
Sofatzis - 37-H-d
Solari - 23-Ch-p
Solberg - 35-G-d
Solomon - 45-Ch-d
Somers - 27-G-d, 29-H-d, 29-G-d, 39-G-d, 45-H-d
Somerville - 33-H-p
Somes - 43-G-p
Soper - 23-H-d, 39-H-d, 45-G-d
Soraghan - 33-H-p
Sornberger - 45-H-p
Sorrell - 45-B-p
Sosnowski - 45-H-p
Soter - 39-H-d
Soteros - 41-R-d
Souci - 41-M-p
Soucise - 45-Ch-p
Soucy - 25-H-p, 31-H-d, 39-H-d, 41-M-p, 41-H-p
Soulakiotis - 25-H-p
Soule - 29-H-d
Sourides - 37-H-p
Sousa - 27-G-d
Spackman - 39-R-d
Spafford - 41-G-p
Spatz - 37-Su-p

Spaulding - 23-Co-p, 27-R-d, 29-M-p, 31-H-d, 45-G-p
Speco - 45-St-d
Spellman - 23-St-d
Spence - 41-G-d, 43-H-d
Spencer - 37-Ch-p, 43-Co-p, 45-Co-p
Speney - 23-H-p
Spillane - 31-H-p
Spinelli - 41-Ch-p, 43-Ch-p, 45-H-p, 45-R-d
Spinks - 39-H-d
Spinney - 23-St-p, 23-Co-d, 25-R-d, 27-St-p, 41-St-p, 41-R-p
Spiracos - 41-H-p, 43-H-p
Spiretos - 37-H-p, 41-H-p
Spiriden - 41-St-p
Spiridondes - 39-St-d, 41-St-p
Splude - 45-G-p
Spofford - 39-M-p, 41-M-p
Spokesfield - 29-G-d
Spoon - 27-Ch-d
Spoone - 45-Su-p
Spooner - 23-G-d, 33-Ca-d, 37-Su-p, 41-Su-p, 43-M-p, 45-B-d
Sposito - 33-Su-d
Sprague - 33-M-p, 33-H-d, 39-R-p, 39-Ch-d, 45-M-d, 45-H-d
Spreadbury - 41-Co-p
Springer - 25-Co-d, 27-H-d, 43-Ch-p
Springfield - 39-H-p
Sproul - 43-Co-p
Spydell - 37-Ch-d
Squire - 43-R-p
St. Armand - 43-M-d
St. Clair - 25-R-d, 37-Su-p
St. Cyr - 41-H-p, 43-H-p

259

St. Denis - 31-H-p, 35-H-p
St. Francis - 43-G-p
St. Francois - 45-H-p
St. Germain - 43-G-p
St. Germaine - 25-H-d, 43-Ch-p
St. Hilaire - 41-H-p
St. Jean - 41-H-p, 41-St-p, 43-H-p
St. John - 41-H-p, 41-R-d
St. Laurent - 35-H-p, 43-St-p, 45-H-p
St. Lawrence - 31-G-p, 39-G-d, 43-St-p, 45-G-p
St. Onge - 41-H-p
St. Peter - 25-St-d
St. Pierre - 37-H-d, 39-St-p, 41-H-p, 43-H-p, 43-H-d, 45-G-d
Stack - 23-R-p, 39-R-p, 39-H-p
Stackpole - 27-M-p, 31-Ch-p, 31-St-p
Stacy - 23-H-d, 29-Ch-p, 33-R-p, 43-R-d, 45-St-p
Stafford - 25-H-d, 41-R-p, 45-R-d
Stahl - 23-G-p, 25-Co-d, 35-Co-d
Staite - 45-H-p
Stalbird - 43-Ch-p
Stamelos - 45-H-p
Stamopoulas - 39-Ch-p
Stamos - 43-Ch-p
Stamps - 35-R-p
Stanard - 37-H-d
Stancisco - 43-R-p
Stancisko - 43-R-p
Stanczak - 41-H-d
Stanford - 43-Co-p, 43-G-p
Staniszewski - 43-H-p
Stankiewicz - 39-G-p, 41-R-p
Stanley - 25-St-d, 27-M-p, 29-G-d, 35-Co-p, 37-Ch-p, 43-M-p, 43-H-p, 45-Ca-d
Stanskouskis - 41-H-p
Stantial - 35-H-d, 45-H-d
Stanton - 35-Ca-p
Stanyan - 31-R-p
Stapanon - 45-H-p
Staples - 25-H-p, 27-Ca-p, 27-H-p, 35-H-d, 37-B-d, 41-R-p, 41-St-d, 43-R-d, 45-Ch-p
Starita - 43-H-p, 45-H-p
Stark - 45-H-d
Starkweather - 39-H-p
Starr - 23-B-p, 37-Su-p, 39-Su-p, 41-Su-p
Starrett - 25-H-p, 37-Ca-p
Starumpski - 43-H-p
Stauffer - 43-Co-p
Stavrou - 41-H-p
Steadman - 43-St-p
Steady - 39-R-p, 41-H-p
Stearns - 27-Ch-p, 41-H-p, 43-Ch-p
Stebbins - 37-Ch-p, 37-Su-d
Steckewicz - 45-H-p
Steckute - 27-H-p
Steele - 23-R-d, 33-B-d, 35-M-p, 37-H-p
Steere - 43-H-d
Stefen - 45-H-p
Stefonowicz - 45-H-p
Steger - 41-H-p
Stein - 45-R-p
Steinbruch - 41-Co-p
Steman - 43-Ch-d
Stendor - 41-Ch-p
Stepanionis - 43-H-p, 45-H-p
Stepanon - 43-H-p, 45-H-p

Stephens - 41-B-p
Steponovitch - 45-H-p
Sterling - 25-St-p, 41-H-p
Stetson - 25-Ca-p, 37-B-p, 43-G-d
Stetton - 31-H-p
Steuart - 29-H-p
Steuerwald - 31-H-p, 33-H-p
Stevens - 25-M-d, 25-R-d, 27-Co-p, 27-R-d, 29-R-p, 29-G-p, 29-Su-p, 29-G-d, 29-St-d, 31-Ca-p, 33-Co-p, 35-H-p, 35-R-p, 35-M-p, 35-H-d, 35-Co-d, 37-R-p, 37-Ch-d, 37-G-d, 39-R-p, 39-G-p, 39-G-d, 41-R-p, 41-St-p, 41-Co-p, 41-H-p, 41-G-p, 41-Su-p, 41-Ch-p, 41-R-d, 41-St-d, 41-Ch-d, 43-R-p, 43-Ca-p, 45-H-p, 45-R-p, 45-G-p, 45-R-d, 45-H-d
Stevenson - 35-R-p, 37-G-p
Steves - 39-Ca-p
Stewart - 23-M-d, 31-Co-d, 33-M-d, 33-G-d, 35-R-p, 35-H-p, 35-Ch-d, 37-M-d, 39-B-p, 41-R-p, 41-M-p, 43-M-p, 43-H-p, 45-M-p, 45-M-d
Stickeny - 25-R-p
Stickis - 27-H-p
Stickle - 29-B-d
Stickler - 29-H-d
Stickles - 41-R-p
Stickles - 33-M-d
Stickney - 23-G-p, 25-St-p, 45-H-p
Stiko - 43-H-p

Stiles - 39-G-p, 41-Co-p, 41-H-d
Stillings - 31-Ca-p, 45-Ca-d
Stilson - 39-Su-p
Stimmell - 41-M-d
Stimson - 41-H-p, 43-M-p
Stinson - 35-Ch-p
Stitzgerald - 45-H-p
Stockholm - 45-Su-p
Stockley - 41-H-p
Stockman - 41-R-p
Stockwell - 29-M-p, 33-B-p, 33-Su-d
Stoddard - 35-B-d
Stokel - 43-H-p
Stokes - 43-St-p, 45-M-p
Stoklosa - 43-H-d
Stolovsky - 23-G-p
Stone - 23-H-p, 23-H-p, 25-Ch-p, 25-Co-d, 27-Su-d, 29-H-d, 29-Ch-d, 31-H-p, 31-St-d, 31-G-d, 33-H-p, 33-Ch-d, 33-Co-d, 35-B-p, 37-Ch-p, 41-Ch-p, 41-H-p, 41-B-p, 41-B-d, 43-H-p, 43-Ch-p, 45-H-p, 45-B-p, 45-H-d
Stoneham - 41-M-p
Stoodley - 45-Ch-p
Storer - 29-R-p, 35-H-p
Storrs - 31-M-p, 43-B-p, 43-M-p
Stover - 45-M-d
Stovish - 29-H-p
Stowell - 41-M-p
Strachan - 37-St-d
Strandberg - 43-H-d
Strandell - 45-R-p
Stratton - 25-H-p, 27-Ch-p
Strauss - 43-St-p

Straw - 25-Su-d, 29-Co-d, 31-M-p, 31-Co-p, 33-G-p, 35-H-p, 37-G-d, 41-M-p
Streeter - 29-G-d, 31-H-p, 35-St-d, 37-Su-d, 39-G-p, 39-Su-p, 43-Co-p
Stribling - 27-H-p, 31-H-p
Strickland - 25-R-p
Strobridge - 43-M-p
Strong - 25-H-p, 29-H-d, 31-Co-p, 35-G-p
Strout - 29-Co-p, 41-R-p
Strugis - 45-Su-p
Stuard - 35-H-p
Stuart - 23-G-p, 41-H-d, 45-G-p
Stubbs - 41-R-d
Study - 33-H-p
Stulginskas - 43-H-p
Stulgis - 43-H-p
Sturtevant - 23-H-p, 29-Su-p, 29-H-d, 31-H-p, 33-H-d, 39-Ca-d, 45-R-d
Styles - 43-Su-p
Sudosky - 43-H-p
Suffill - 45-Co-p
Sullivan - 23-St-d, 27-H-p, 27-G-p, 27-Co-d, 29-H-p, 29-Ch-d, 29-M-d, 31-H-p, 31-Ch-p, 31-M-d, 33-H-p, 35-Ch-p, 35-Ch-p, 39-H-p, 41-H-p, 41-M-p, 41-H-d, 43-H-p, 43-H-d, 45-B-p, 45-M-p, 45-H-p, 45-G-d, 45-H-d
Sullos - 41-R-d
Sulloway - 25-G-p, 33-G-d, 41-Co-d
Sumner - 45-H-p
Supko - 45-Su-p
Suprise - 45-H-p

Surpine - 41-B-p
Susmann - 45-St-p
Sutcliffe - 31-G-d
Sutherland - 43-H-p
Sutton - 43-M-d
Swain - 25-Su-d, 37-Ch-d, 39-B-p, 41-M-d, 43-G-p
Swan - 23-Su-p, 31-Ch-d, 43-Su-p
Swanson - 45-H-p
Swaracki - 45-H-p
Swart - 25-H-p, 31-H-p, 45-H-p
Swatzer - 29-Ch-p
Sweatt - 29-Co-p
Sweeney - 25-Ch-p, 29-Ch-p, 33-H-p, 33-H-d, 33-M-d, 39-M-p, 43-R-p
Sweet - 25-M-d, 37-G-p, 37-G-d, 39-G-d
Swensiski - 41-St-n
Swenson - 41-H-p
Swetnam - 31-M-p
Swett - 25-H-d, 35-Ca-p, 45-G-d
Swienton - 31-R-p
Swiesz - 39-H-p
Swietuk - 23-H-d
Swift - 41-Co-d, 43-Co-p
Swinnerton - 33-G-d
Swiss - 39-H-p
Sycamore - 35-G-p, 39-G-p
Sydeman - 45-M-p
Sydserff - 45-H-p
Sykes - 27-H-d
Sylce - 41-G-p
Sylvain - 27-St-d
Sylvester - 29-St-d, 33-G-p, 41-H-p, 41-St-d
Sylvia - 35-B-p
Symonds - 35-Ch-p

Syrek - 43-H-p
Syrios - 41-R-d
Syx - 27-H-p
Szabo - 43-R-p, 45-St-p
Szaine - 41-R-p
Szalajeski - 43-B-p
Szalucka - 45-Su-p
Szemela - 35-H-d, 45-H-d
Szewczyk - 39-H-p
Szewczyszyn - 39-H-p
Szostakiewicz - 45-H-p
Sztucinski - 41-B-p
Tabachnick - 45-H-p
Taber - 29-B-p
Tabor - 29-B-p, 33-G-p, 39-R-p
Taboske - 41-H-p
Tack - 45-H-p
Tagalakis - 43-H-p
Taggart - 45-Su-p
Taimi - 39-Su-d, 45-Su-p
Taintor - 29-H-p
Takesian - 37-Ca-p
Talbert - 31-G-d
Talbot - 25-G-d, 45-H-d
Talent - 37-H-p
Tallman - 45-Su-p
Talmers - 39-M-p, 41-M-p
Tambakiss - 41-H-d
Tamposi - 27-H-p
Tamulonis - 43-H-d
Tanczos - 45-H-d
Tanguay - 35-H-p
Tankard - 35-Co-d
Tanner - 33-St-d, 45-M-p
Tansey - 43-H-p
Tappan - 35-Ca-p, 35-Ca-d, 37-St-p
Tarbox - 29-G-p

Tardiff - 39-B-d, 41-Co-p, 41-H-p
Tarlton - 31-R-p
Tarmey - 45-St-p
Tarr - 29-H-d, 45-G-p
Tarrant - 29-H-d
Tarrien - 31-Su-p
Tartaglia - 37-Ch-p
Tartalis - 35-R-p
Tarullo - 39-H-p
Tashro - 43-Su-d
Task - 29-R-p, 29-R-d, 35-R-d
Tasker - 27-St-d, 33-H-d, 45-M-p
Tasoulas - 45-Ch-p
Tassinari - 41-B-p, 41-H-d
Tatakes - 45-B-p
Tate - 43-H-p
Tatham - 43-R-d
Tatro - 23-G-p, 35-R-p, 43-H-p
Tattrie - 37-Su-p
Taube - 41-H-p
Tayloff - 39-H-p
Taylor - 25-M-p, 29-R-p, 31-M-p, 31-Ch-d, 33-St-d, 35-Ca-p, 35-Co-d, 37-H-p, 37-Ca-p, 37-Ch-d, 39-M-d, 39-Ch-d, 39-B-d, 39-R-d, 41-R-p, 41-B-p, 41-Ch-p, 41-Ca-p, 41-St-p, 41-Su-d, 43-M-p, 43-H-p, 43-Ch-p, 43-St-p, 43-G-p, 43-Ch-d, 43-M-d, 43-Co-d, 43-Su-d, 45-M-p, 45-H-p, 45-G-d
Teaberg - 39-St-p
Tebbetts - 41-St-d, 45-St-p
Tebo - 35-M-d
Tedford - 43-Ch-d, 45-Ch-p

Tedoff - 27-M-p
Tedovsky - 27-M-p
Teel - 23-G-p
Teft - 41-B-d
Teger - 35-Ch-p
Tegoutsios - 27-H-p
Telicza - 39-H-p
Tellia - 41-Ch-p
Tellier - 35-H-p, 41-Ch-p, 43-H-p
Tempeli - 45-H-p
Tempelis - 37-H-p
Temple - 37-Co-d, 41-M-d, 41-Co-d, 45-Co-p
Tenerowicz - 27-H-p
Tenney - 25-Ch-d, 27-B-p, 27-Co-p, 45-Su-p
Tenofsky - 45-Ch-d
Tergis - 23-H-d
Terrell - 41-M-p
Terrill - 25-B-p, 27-Co-d, 35-M-p, 39-Co-p
Terwoert - 29-H-d
Tessicini - 45-R-d
Tetreault - 29-R-p, 45-Su-p
Teuber - 39-H-d
Tewksbury - 29-R-d, 31-G-p
Thalasinos - 45-Su-p
Thaoharis - 25-H-d
Thayer - 31-Ch-p, 37-M-p, 41-St-p, 41-Ch-p, 41-H-p, 43-Ch-p, 45-Ch-p, 45-St-d
Theberge - 29-H-p, 41-B-p
Theg - 23-R-p
Theodora - 31-St-p
Theodoropoulos - 41-H-p
Theriault - 43-H-p, 43-Co-p, 45-H-p, 45-Co-p, 45-H-d
Theros - 41-H-p
Therreault - 27-H-d
Therrian - 25-B-p
Therriault - 37-Su-d
Therrien - 25-St-p, 33-G-p, 35-H-p, 37-St-p, 39-G-p, 43-St-p, 43-Co-d
Thibault - 29-H-p
Thibeault - 37-R-p, 43-Co-d
Thibedeau - 23-G-p
Thibodeau - 27-G-p, 27-Co-p, 29-H-p, 31-Su-p, 31-Co-p, 37-H-p, 43-Co-d, 45-G-p, 45-Su-p
Thiboutot - 27-H-p
Thifault - 35-H-p
Thivierge - 45-St-p
Thomas - 23-B-p, 23-G-p, 23-G-d, 25-Co-p, 25-H-d, 27-H-p, 27-R-p, 29-Su-d, 29-H-d, 33-Co-d, 43-H-p, 45-M-p, 45-R-p
Thompson - 23-H-p, 23-Su-p, 23-St-d, 23-H-d, 25-Ca-d, 27-St-p, 27-R-d, 29-R-p, 29-H-d, 31-R-p, 31-Ca-p, 31-M-p, 31-R-d, 33-M-p, 33-St-d, 33-M-d, 35-R-p, 35-H-p, 35-Ca-d, 37-Ca-p, 37-R-d, 37-M-d, 39-M-p, 39-Co-p, 39-H-d, 41-Ca-p, 41-B-p, 41-H-p, 41-St-p, 41-Ch-p, 41-Ch-d, 41-M-d, 43-Ch-p, 43-B-p, 43-R-d, 43-G-d, 43-St-d, 45-M-p, 45-St-d, 45-G-d
Thorning - 27-Ch-p
Thornton - 43-G-d, 45-M-p
Thorson - 27-M-p
Thrasher - 23-Su-d, 45-H-p
Thurber - 37-M-p, 41-Su-p
Thurlo - 35-St-p

Thurlow - 33-G-d, 35-St-p, 41-Co-p, 41-H-p, 43-Co-p
Thurston - 25-Ca-p, 29-Ca-p, 29-Ca-d, 43-G-p, 43-M-d, 45-B-p
Thwing - 27-H-d
Thyng - 43-R-p
Tibbets - 25-R-d
Tibbetts - 23-R-p, 25-M-p, 29-B-p, 37-M-d, 39-H-p, 39-St-p
Tieger - 35-Ch-p
Tielinen - 43-Ch-p, 45-Ch-p
Tierney - 41-H-p
Tierny - 41-R-d
Tillman - 41-Ch-p
Tilton - 23-Ca-p, 35-G-p, 35-R-d, 37-M-p, 37-H-d, 43-Co-d
Timbas - 43-H-p
Timmons - 45-St-p
Timmony - 41-Co-p
Tinker - 35-R-p, 41-St-d
Tinkham - 31-M-d
Tippett - 23-G-d, 33-M-d
Tirrell - 31-B-p, 33-St-d, 35-H-d, 41-H-p, 45-H-p
Titus - 33-H-d, 43-Ca-p, 43-H-d
Tivey - 37-R-d
Tjampiris - 27-H-p
Tjimaki - 45-Ch-p
Tkacz - 29-H-d
Tkagut - 41-G-d
Tobias - 35-H-p
Tobin - 35-G-d, 43-H-p
Tobine - 33-Su-p, 41-G-p
Tobyne - 39-R-p
Todd - 27-Ch-p, 43-R-d
Todt - 45-H-p

Tolman - 41-Ch-p, 43-Ch-p
Tomaselli - 29-H-p
Tomashevski - 45-H-p
Tomaszewska - 45-R-d
Tondreau - 35-H-p, 35-Co-d
Tong - 43-H-p, 45-H-p, 45-B-p
Tonkin - 33-St-d, 35-St-p
Toomey - 27-Ch-p, 37-St-d, 43-Ch-d
Torrey - 37-B-p
Tortorelli - 43-G-p
Toscano - 45-H-d
Tosuignant - 39-B-p
Totte - 41-H-p
Totten - 29-H-d
Totton - 23-H-p
Touchette - 23-Su-d
Toumbas - 31-H-d
Toupin - 23-H-p
Tourtellott - 25-Ch-d
Tousignant - 23-H-p, 41-M-p
Tousner - 41-M-p
Toussaint - 29-H-p, 31-Ch-p, 39-Ch-p, 45-M-p
Towle - 23-Co-d, 29-M-d, 31-H-p, 33-H-p, 39-B-d, 41-Ca-p, 41-St-p, 41-H-p, 45-M-d
Towne - 25-H-p, 29-H-p, 35-H-d, 39-G-d
Towns - 45-B-d
Townsend - 29-Su-d, 41-Ch-p, 43-M-p, 45-H-p
Towsley - 45-Ch-p
Tracy - 41-H-p
Trafton - 33-R-p, 35-St-d, 41-R-p, 41-R-d, 45-R-d
Trahan - 37-St-p, 43-H-p
Trainer - 25-Co-d
Trainor - 41-M-d, 43-St-d

265

Tranfaglan - 37-H-p
Tranfalia - 37-H-p
Trask - 25-Co-p, 29-Ch-d
Travers - 41-H-p
Travini - 37-H-p
Treahey - 43-St-p
Trecartin - 23-R-p
Tredo - 39-Ch-p
Trefethen - 35-R-p, 41-R-d, 43-R-d, 45-R-d
Tremaine - 45-Co-p
Tremblay - 23-R-p, 35-H-p, 37-H-p, 39-H-p, 43-H-p
Trembly - 23-B-p
Trepanier - 31-H-d, 45-Su-p
Trevena - 33-R-p
Trew - 27-R-d
Trider - 41-R-p
Triggs - 29-H-p
Triller - 45-G-p
Trimble - 41-H-p
Triplett - 37-R-d
Tripp - 23-Co-d, 37-H-p, 37-St-d, 43-M-p
Trojano - 41-B-p
Trongeau - 45-St-p
Trosky - 45-R-p
Trott - 41-St-d
Trottier - 35-M-p, 45-H-p
Troutman - 43-R-p
Trow - 31-H-d, 33-Su-d
Trowbridge - 25-B-p, 35-B-p
Trowridge - 23-B-p
Truchon - 35-H-p
Trudeau - 39-H-p, 41-B-d, 43-B-d, 45-H-d
Trudo - 27-Ch-p
Trueman - 29-R-p, 35-R-d
Truman - 39-St-p
Trumbull - 33-H-p, 33-G-d, 37-G-p, 45-B-d

Tsaridis - 41-M-d
Tseckares - 41-M-p
Tsekares - 39-M-p
Tsitsos - 45-H-p
Tsourides - 37-H-p, 45-H-p
Tubinis - 31-H-p
Tuck - 23-R-p
Tucker - 23-R-p, 23-G-p, 27-M-p, 29-H-d, 39-R-d, 41-R-p, 41-M-p, 41-M-d, 41-H-d, 43-M-p, 43-H-p, 45-M-d
Tuckerman - 31-Ca-p
Tuffts - 41-B-p
Tufts - 23-H-p, 41-R-p
Tulin - 35-H-d, 39-Su-d
Tully - 33-Co-p
Tumblin - 43-H-d
Tuomi - 43-Ch-p
Tupper - 25-G-d
Turcotte - 23-Ch-p, 29-H-p, 29-B-p, 41-H-d, 43-R-p, 45-B-p, 45-Ch-p, 45-H-d
Turgeon - 25-B-p
Turley - 39-B-p
Turlis - 45-B-p
Turnbull - 43-H-p
Turner - 23-G-p, 27-H-p, 35-Ca-p, 41-Ch-p, 41-Ca-p, 41-St-d, 43-R-p, 43-H-d
Turney - 43-R-d
Turrekens - 29-H-d
Tutt - 37-Ca-p, 39-Ca-p
Tuttle - 25-M-p, 27-Co-p, 29-Su-p, 31-St-d, 33-St-p, 35-M-p, 39-St-p, 43-R-p, 45-H-p, 45-R-p, 45-H-d
Tuxbury - 29-G-p
Tuzik - 23-G-p
Twiss - 29-H-d

Twitchell - 31-Co-p, 45-Ch-p, 45-Co-p
Twombly - 25-St-p, 31-B-p, 31-H-p, 41-R-p, 43-St-p
Tyler - 29-B-p, 33-St-d, 37-Ch-p, 39-G-p
Tyo - 25-Ch-p, 45-Ch-d
Tyrrel - 33-M-p, 41-M-p
Tyrrell - 23-Co-p
Tytus - 27-R-p
Tzrinska - 43-R-d

Uhlig - 37-R-d
Ulman - 45-M-p
Underhill - 33-H-d, 37-R-d, 41-R-p
Underwood - 33-G-d, 39-Ch-d, 43-H-p
Unglaub - 37-St-p
Unwin - 29-H-p
Upham - 43-H-d
Upton - 35-M-p
Urgelevicz - 45-H-p
Ustin - 43-H-p
Uzarek - 31-R-p
Uzdavinis - 43-H-p

Vaccarest - 35-H-p
Vachon - 31-Co-p, 37-H-p, 39-St-p, 41-St-p, 43-St-p, 43-St-d, 45-H-d
Vadeboncoeur - 35-R-d, 43-H-p
Vadney - 25-M-p, 31-Su-p, 39-M-d
Vaillancourt - 33-Ch-p, 43-H-p, 45-H-p
Vaillant - 43-Ch-p
Valcourt - 27-H-p, 45-H-p
Valenti - 33-Ch-p, 37-Su-p
Valentukievicz - 45-H-p
Valia - 25-G-p
Vallas - 43-H-d, 45-H-p
Vallee - 43-Co-p
Valles - 37-H-d
Valley - 31-Ch-d, 31-H-d, 39-G-d, 41-St-p, 41-Ch-p, 41-H-p, 45-St-p
Vallia - 45-B-p
Vallier - 45-R-p
Valliere - 35-M-p, 39-B-p, 39-H-d, 43-H-p, 45-B-p
Vallis - 29-Co-d
Valopulus - 43-H-p
Van - 45-Su-p
Van Buskirk - 39-St-d
Van Curen - 29-G-d
Van De Velde - 29-H-p
Van Denburgh - 45-M-d
Van Dusen - 45-Su-p
Van Duyne - 39-H-p
Van Housen - 29-G-d
Van Neel - 29-M-p
Van Tassel - 27-Ca-p
Van Tetley - 35-H-p
Van Voast - 27-H-d
Vanasse - 33-H-p, 41-H-p, 45-M-p
Vandegrift - 45-Su-p
Vanden Molen - 39-R-d
Vanderberghe - 27-H-d
Vanderhoof - 31-B-p
Vanni - 41-Ch-d
Vantine - 37-H-p
Vargas - 35-Ch-p
Varger - 41-H-p
Varnerin - 33-R-p
Varney - 27-St-p, 31-G-p, 33-St-d, 35-B-p, 37-Ca-d, 39-B-p, 41-M-p, 41-St-p, 41-G-p, 45-B-p
Varnum - 37-H-d

Varrell - 23-R-p, 37-B-p, 45-B-p
Varville - 33-Ch-p
Vasiliou - 35-H-p, 37-H-p
Vasselian - 39-R-p
Vassil - 41-H-p
Vasyabedient - 41-H-p
Vaughan - 35-Ch-d
Vaughn - 37-Ch-p, 39-G-d, 45-Ca-d
Veilleux - 41-Co-p, 43-R-p, 43-Co-p, 43-H-d
Velmont - 33-B-p
Venable - 35-Ch-p
Venette - 25-M-p
Venn - 33-Ch-d
Vennard - 39-St-p
Venne - 29-H-p, 33-M-d
Vennott - 33-H-p
Veno - 27-M-d
Verge - 39-H-p
Verheyen - 39-H-p
Vermette - 33-H-d
Veroneau - 39-H-p
Verrill - 27-Ch-d
Verville - 45-St-p
Vetters - 27-G-d
Vezeau - 37-St-p
Vezina - 27-H-d, 31-B-p
Vickarey - 41-Su-p
Vieira - 43-H-d
Vien - 31-G-p
Vigneault - 45-Ch-d
Vigue - 43-H-p
Vigurs - 27-G-d
Villeneuve - 35-G-d
Vincent - 33-H-p, 39-St-p, 45-H-p, 45-Co-p
Virgin - 41-M-d
Vittum - 41-B-p, 41-Ca-p
Vlahopoulos - 39-H-p, 43-H-p

Vocha - 41-St-p
Voge - 45-St-p
Voinonatix - 33-St-d
von der Marwitz - 35-Ch-d
von Schmiterlow - 45-H-p
Von Iderstine - 45-H-d
Vondal - 39-R-d
Vondell - 43-M-p
Voth - 45-H-p
Vrakatitsis - 39-Ch-p
Vrettas - 41-R-p
Waas - 43-R-p
Wade - 25-R-p, 25-H-d, 27-Ca-p, 41-St-p, 41-M-p
Wadsworth - 45-Ch-p
Wagner - 29-H-p, 39-H-p, 45-H-p, 45-R-d
Wahamaki - 39-M-p
Wahlen - 37-Ch-p
Waillancourt - 41-H-p
Wainwright - 37-H-p
Waite - 45-Ch-p
Waitt - 33-G-d
Wajda - 43-H-p
Wakefield - 29-B-p, 37-B-d, 41-B-d, 45-St-d
Walbridge - 33-H-p, 35-H-p, 45-St-p
Walden - 41-M-p
Waldo - 41-M-p, 45-B-p
Waldron - 31-Su-p, 31-H-d
Walenkrikenic - 45-H-p
Walent - 39-H-p, 41-H-p, 45-H-p
Walentukvicz - 39-H-p
Walentutuawicius - 41-H-p
Walerstein - 43-M-p
Waleryszak - 41-R-p, 43-R-p
Walker - 27-B-p, 27-G-p, 29-Ch-p, 29-Su-p, 31-Su-d,

Walker - 33-H-p, 33-R-d, 35-H-p, 35-Su-p, 35-Co-p, 35-St-d, 37-Ch-p, 37-H-p, 39-G-p, 39-H-p, 41-H-p, 41-H-d, 43-B-p, 43-H-p, 45-H-p, 45-Su-p, 45-G-d
Wallace - 23-H-p, 23-G-p, 23-R-d, 23-St-d, 25-Su-p, 25-M-d, 27-H-p, 27-St-d, 29-R-d, 29-Ch-d, 31-H-d, 33-Ch-p, 35-Su-d, 37-H-p, 37-B-p, 41-B-p, 41-R-p, 41-Ch-d, 43-H-p, 43-G-p
Wallett - 25-B-d
Wallingford - 41-St-p, 43-St-p, 45-St-d
Wallis - 39-St-p
Walsh - 37-H-p, 39-H-p, 39-St-d, 41-H-p, 43-H-p, 43-H-d, 45-H-d
Walter - 43-M-p
Walters - 45-H-p, 45-M-p
Walton - 25-St-d, 29-R-p, 31-R-p, 33-R-d, 35-B-p
Walukinas - 39-R-p
Wamester - 37-H-d
Waning - 43-R-p
Warburton - 29-R-p, 29-H-p
Warcholik - 37-H-p, 41-H-p
Warcup - 37-G-p
Ward - 27-Ch-d, 29-Ca-p, 29-Co-d, 39-Ca-p, 39-R-p, 39-G-p, 41-R-p, 41-Ca-p, 45-Ch-p
Warde - 43-H-p
Warden - 25-R-p
Wardner - 41-H-p
Ware - 27-Ch-d, 35-G-p
Wares - 29-H-d, 39-R-p

Warfield - 25-Co-p
Warn - 39-Ch-d
Warner - 25-Ca-p, 25-G-p, 37-Ch-d, 43-R-p, 43-Ch-p
Warren - 25-H-p, 25-H-d, 29-Ca-p, 35-R-p, 35-Ch-p, 37-H-d, 39-M-p, 39-Co-p, 39-H-d, 41-H-p, 41-B-p, 43-M-p, 43-H-p, 45-H-p
Warriner - 45-Ch-d
Warring - 41-H-p
Washburn - 27-Co-p, 29-G-p, 31-G-p, 43-Ca-p
Wason - 31-R-p
Wasson - 37-B-d
Waterhouse - 25-R-p, 37-Su-p
Waterman - 33-G-d
Waters - 39-Co-p, 41-Su-p, 45-H-d
Watkins - 29-H-p, 31-H-d, 41-H-p, 41-H-d, 45-H-d
Watson - 23-Ca-d, 23-G-d, 25-Ch-p, 29-G-p, 31-H-p, 33-G-p, 35-H-p, 43-H-p, 43-Ch-p, 43-Co-p, 45-B-p, 45-Ch-p, 45-St-d
Watt - 23-R-d
Watterson - 39-Ch-p
Watts - 45-R-p, 45-R-d, 45-St-d
Way - 25-G-d
Wayson - 29-H-p
Wazniak - 29-H-p
Weare - 27-St-d
Weatherbee - 41-M-p, 41-H-d, 41-M-d
Weatherly - 39-R-d
Weathers - 41-St-p, 45-St-p

Webb - 23-G-d, 37-H-p, 41-H-p, 41-R-d, 43-R-p, 45-G-p
Webber - 23-St-p, 23-H-d, 39-R-d, 41-Co-p, 43-M-d, 45-R-p, 45-R-d
Weber - 41-R-p, 45-R-p
Webster - 23-R-d, 29-R-p, 29-H-p, 33-B-d, 37-Ch-p, 37-Ch-d, 39-R-p, 39-St-d, 43-H-p, 43-R-d, 45-H-p
Wedge - 27-Co-d
Weed - 25-M-p, 35-St-p, 39-G-p
Weeks - 23-Ch-p, 23-St-d, 31-G-d, 41-Ch-p, 41-Ch-d, 43-St-p, 43-G-p, 45-G-p, 45-Ch-p
Weightman - 29-H-p
Weinberg - 43-Co-p
Weinstein - 45-H-p
Weir - 41-B-p
Welch - 25-R-p, 25-G-p, 27-M-d, 29-Ch-p, 33-R-p, 33-G-d, 33-Ca-d, 35-H-p, 35-H-d, 37-Ca-d, 37-H-d, 39-M-p, 39-H-d, 41-Su-p, 43-M-p, 43-H-d, 45-R-d, 45-Co-p, 45-Ca-d
Welcome - 37-G-d
Weldon - 43-R-p
Weller - 39-G-p
Wellman - 23-H-p
Wells - 23-B-p, 23-G-d, 27-M-d, 29-M-p, 33-G-d, 35-Su-d, 35-Co-d, 41-R-p, 41-H-p, 41-St-p, 43-R-p
Wendell - 45-R-p, 45-R-d
Wender - 27-G-p
Wenhold - 35-R-p

Wentworth - 27-B-d, 29-H-p, 33-R-p, 33-St-d, 37-St-p, 39-M-d, 41-St-p, 43-M-p, 43-M-d, 45-H-p
Wenzel - 27-H-p
Werden - 25-H-d, 43-H-d
Wescom - 35-M-d, 39-M-p
Wescome - 39-Ch-d
Wescott - 29-B-p, 37-G-p, 45-B-p, 45-M-d
West - 33-Ca-d, 37-B-d, 41-H-p, 43-R-p
Westcott - 25-H-d
Westerdahl - 45-H-d
Westerhoff - 45-H-p
Westgate - 45-R-p
Westling - 31-G-d
Westney - 41-B-p
Weston - 33-H-p, 39-R-p
Wetherbee - 23-Ch-p, 31-G-d, 35-H-p, 41-R-p, 41-Ch-d
Wetherell - 37-R-d
Wetmore - 39-R-d
Wexler - 37-R-p
Weyant - 23-Su-d
Whalen - 29-B-p, 45-H-p
Wheatley - 23-H-p
Wheaton - 31-R-p, 39-H-d
Wheeler - 23-H-p, 23-Ch-p, 25-Ch-p, 25-R-p, 27-M-p, 27-H-p, 27-G-d, 31-St-p, 31-M-p, 33-Ch-d, 35-H-d, 35-M-d, 35-G-d, 35-Co-d, 37-B-p, 39-M-p, 39-H-p, 41-R-p, 41-H-p, 41-Co-p, 41-Ch-p, 43-H-p, 43-Co-d, 45-St-p
Wheelock - 29-H-p
Whidden - 29-R-p, 43-H-d

Whipple - 27-Ch-p, 35-Ch-p, 37-M-p, 37-G-d
Whitaker - 23-Ch-p
Whitby - 31-R-d
Whitcher - 25-H-d, 25-Ch-d, 31-G-p
Whitcomb - 29-M-p, 33-Ch-p, 33-Co-p, 35-Ch-d, 35-Co-d, 37-Ch-p, 39-Ch-p, 39-G-p, 39-Ch-d, 41-Ch-p, 45-Ch-p, 45-G-p
White - 23-H-p, 25-R-p, 27-H-p, 27-Ch-p, 27-Su-p, 29-H-p, 29-Ch-d, 31-H-p, 33-H-p, 33-G-p, 33-R-d, 33-H-d, 35-M-p, 35-H-p, 35-Ch-p, 35-Su-p, 35-G-p, 35-St-d, 35-Ca-d, 37-H-p, 37-St-d, 39-H-p, - 39-Ch-p, 39-G-p, 41-R-p, 41-Ca-p, 41-G-p, 41-R-d, 41-St-d, 43-H-p, 43-St-p, 43-G-p, 43-Co-p, 43-R-d, 43-H-d, 43-Su-d, 45-St-p, 45-G-p, 45-Su-p
Whiteaker - 37-R-p
Whitehead - 25-H-p, 31-Ch-p
Whitehouse - 37-St-p, 43-St-p, 45-G-d
Whiteman - 35-B-d
Whitfield - 23-Ca-d
Whities - 43-R-p
Whiting - 25-G-p, 31-H-p, 35-M-p, 37-M-p, 39-M-d, 43-R-p, 43-Ch-p
Whitlock - 23-H-d
Whitman - 35-Ch-p, 37-G-p, 41-Ch-d
Whitney - 23-Su-p, 25-H-p, 25-Ch-d, 29-H-p, 29-G-p, 33-H-p, 35-R-p, 37-Su-d, 39-R-p, 39-B-p, 41-G-p, 41-H-p, 43-H-d, 45-H-p
Whittaker - 43-St-p
Whittemore - 25-Ch-d, 29-H-p, 39-R-d, 41-Su-p, 45-H-p, 45-Ch-p
Whitten - 33-B-p, 35-R-p
Whittet - 43-H-p
Whittey - 45-B-p
Whittier - 23-R-p, 25-R-d, 37-Su-d, 39-R-p, 39-Ca-p
Whittle - 37-H-d
Whittpenn - 41-B-d
Whittum - 43-Co-p
Wiersma - 45-M-p
Wiese - 27-H-d
Wiggin - 25-H-d, 39-R-p, 41-Ca-p, 41-St-d, 45-G-p
Wiggins - 39-H-d, 41-B-p
Wightman - 39-R-p
Wilber - 29-H-p, 41-Ch-p
Wilbur - 39-Ch-d, 41-R-p, 43-R-p
Wilcox - 23-G-p, 23-R-d, 29-R-d, 33-Ch-d, 35-H-p, 35-G-d, 39-Ch-p, 43-R-p, 45-Ch-p
Wilde - 41-R-p
Wilder - 27-H-p, 33-Ch-p, 35-Ch-p, 37-H-p, 41-Ch-p, 45-Ch-p, 45-Ch-d
Wilds - 33-G-p
Wiley - 39-G-p
Wilkaites - 35-H-p
Wilkie - 31-G-p
Wilkins - 29-B-p, 31-St-p, 31-H-d, 33-B-d, 37-G-p, 41-B-d, 43-Su-d
Wilkinson - 41-M-p, 43-St-p, 43-H-p, 45-H-p
Willand - 27-St-d

Willard - 23-Ch-p, 25-M-p, 35-Ch-p, 39-St-p, 39-Ch-p, 41-H-p, 43-H-p, 43-Ch-p, 45-G-p
Willcox - 23-M-d
Willett - 43-B-p
Willette - 39-H-p, 45-R-d
Willey - 25-Ca-d, 27-Ca-p, 31-H-d, 41-Ca-p, 43-G-p, 45-R-p, 45-Co-p
William - 23-H-p
Williams - 23-St-d, 25-G-p, 27-St-p, 27-Su-p, 29-H-d, 31-Ch-p, 33-R-p, 33-R-d, 33-G-d, 35-Ca-p, 35-Co-p, 37-M-p, 37-R-d, 37-Su-d, 39-R-p, 39-Su-p, 39-Co-p, 39-B-d, 41-R-p, 41-Ch-p, 41-Su-p, 41-H-d, 41-Ch-d, 41-Su-d, 43-B-p, 45-M-p, 45-St-p, 45-R-p, 45-Ca-p, 45-M-d, 45-H-d
Williamson - 23-R-d, 41-B-p, 41-R-d, 43-R-d, 43-G-d, 45-G-p, 45-G-d
Williford - 25-R-d
Willis - 25-Co-p, 25-G-p, 25-Su-d, 35-Su-p, 37-Co-d
Willmott - 43-B-p
Willoughby - 41-B-p
Willson - 39-Co-p, 41-G-p, 41-St-p
Wilmarth - 29-Su-d
Wilmot - 41-M-p
Wilson - 23-R-p, 23-H-p, 23-Co-p, 25-R-p, 25-Co-p, 27-G-d, 27-Co-d, 29-H-d, 31-B-p, 31-H-d, 31-Co-d, 33-R-d, 33-B-d, 35-H-d, 37-St-d, 37-M-d, 37-Su-d, 39-Ch-d, 41-R-p, 41-B-p, 41-Ch-p, 41-H-p, 41-R-d, 41-H-d, 41-Ch-d, 41-Su-d, 43-R-p, 43-B-p, 43-B-d, 45-Su-p, 45-Ch-p, 45-H-d
Winchester - 33-R-p
Windemiller - 43-M-p
Wineberg - 37-H-d
Wing - 41-St-p, 41-M-d, 43-B-p, 45-M-d
Winkler - 27-H-p, 39-B-p
Winkley - 27-B-p
Winn - 35-H-p, 35-Ch-d, 37-Ch-d, 41-Ch-p, 43-Ca-p, 45-R-d
Winship - 35-M-p
Winslow - 31-G-p, 39-H-p, 45-M-p, 45-H-p
Winter - 29-B-p, 29-H-p, 41-Su-d, 45-H-p
Winters - 41-H-p
Wirein - 43-Ch-p
Wirta - 39-Su-p
Wirtanen - 43-H-p
Wisell - 33-Ch-p
Wisner - 37-M-p
Wiswell - 29-B-d, 39-Co-d
Witham - 31-Ca-p, 33-R-p, 35-H-d, 35-M-d 35-Ch-d, 35-Co-d, 37-R-d, 43-R-p, 43-H-d
Withers - 27-Co-d
Withey - 37-M-p
Withman - 35-St-p
Withstandley - 39-H-p
Witson - 45-M-p
Witt - 23-G-d
Wittpenn - 43-B-d
Wix - 41-H-d
Wixson - 25-Ch-p

Woddard - 31-G-p
Wojchick - 39-Ch-d
Wolahan - 25-H-d
Wolcowski - 41-H-p
Wolfsohn - 33-M-d, 37-G-p, 39-G-d
Wolkow - 41-H-p
Wolkowski - 41-H-p
Wolski - 43-St-p
Wong - 43-H-p, 45-H-p
Wood - 23-H-p, 25-H-d, 31-G-p, 31-M-d, 37-H-p, 37-Ch-p, 39-St-p, 41-M-p, 41-Ch-p, 41-G-p, 43-M-p, 43-H-p, 43-St-p
Woodard - 25-H-p
Woodburn - 31-R-p
Woodbury - 39-R-p, 39-M-p, 41-St-p, 43-R-p
Woodman - 39-St-p, 39-St-d, 39-G-d
Woodmancy - 35-Ca-d
Woodrow - 37-Co-d
Woodruff - 37-H-p
Woods - 25-M-p, 39-H-p, 39-Ch-p, 41-H-p, 41-H-d, 41-St-d, 43-Ch-p, 45-G-d
Woodward - 23-Ca-p, 25-M-d, 25-G-d, 29-Co-d, 35-Su-p, 37-B-p, 37-Ch-p, 41-G-p, 43-Ch-p, 45-Ch-p, 45-G-p
Woodworth - 35-R-d
Wooldridge - 23-B-p, 43-R-p
Woollacott - 33-H-p
Woolson - 33-G-d
Worcester - 23-Ch-p, 41-H-p, 43-H-p, 45-B-p, 45-Ch-p
Worden - 23-R-d, 43-St-p
Wordios - 45-H-d
Worley - 43-St-p

Wormbrand - 43-M-p
Wormell - 43-Co-p
Wormwood - 41-R-p
Worster - 41-R-p
Worth - 45-H-d
Worthen - 29-M-p, 39-H-d, 41-H-p, 45-G-d
Wright - 23-Su-p, 25-G-p, 25-G-d, 27-G-p, 27-G-d, 29-M-p, 29-G-d, 31-Co-p, 31-R-p, 33-St-p, 33-Su-p, 33-Su-p, 35-St-p, 37-H-d, 41-B-p, 41-G-p, 41-G-d, 43-G-p
Wrisley - 41-B-p
Wuorela - 43-Su-d
Wyatt - 29-Ch-p, 31-Ch-p, 33-H-p, 39-St-d
Wyman - 23-R-p, 23-H-p, 27-M-d, 29-Ch-p, 31-M-p, 35-R-p, 43-R-p, 43-H-d, 45-Ch-p, 45-Ch-d

Yarmolovich - 43-H-p
Yarmotowich - 45-H-p
Yasevitch - 35-Su-p
Yates - 29-H-d
Yeagle - 41-R-p, 43-R-p
Yeaton - 41-H-d, 45-M-p
Yeatter - 29-H-d
Yee - 37-H-p
Yendell - 43-Ch-p
Yeo - 37-M-p
Yergeau - 41-H-p
Yermal - 45-H-p
Yetman - 39-Su-d
Yiacas - 27-H-p
Yianahopolas - 45-H-p
York - 25-H-p, 33-M-p, 37-Su-d, 39-G-d, 41-Su-p,

York - 41-Co-p, 41-H-d, 43-St-p, 43-M-p
Young - 23-B-p, 23-M-p, 23-G-p, 23-R-d, 23-H-d, 25-H-p, 27-St-d, 29-B-p, 29-Su-p, 31-M-p, 31-G-p, 31-Co-p, 31-M-d, 35-St-p, 35-M-p, 35-H-d, 37-H-p, 37-Su-p, 39-Su-p, 39-M-d, 39-G-d, 41-St-p, 41-H-p, 41-G-p, 41-Co-p, 41-H-d, 43-St-p, 43-H-p, 43-Su-p, 43-Co-p, 43-H-d, 45-M-p, 45-B-p, 45-Su-p, 45-G-p, 45-Co-p, 45-H-d, 45-St-d
Zagamy - 45-M-p
Zahn - 45-R-d
Zahos - 41-Ch-p
Zahos - 45-Ch-p
Zajaczkowski - 43-H-p, 45-H-p
Zalanskas - 37-M-p
Zanes - 31-B-p, 35-B-p
Zangari - 43-R-d
Zankowski - 43-H-p, 45-H-p
Zarmarkupis - 43-H-p
Zautra - 45-H-d
Zazofsky - 43-H-p
Zbierski - 39-H-p
Zdeb - 41-R-p
Zdon - 43-H-p
Zecha - 25-Ch-d
Zeeler - 41-H-p, 45-H-p
Zegarowska - 33-H-p
Zeisel - 37-H-p
Zela - 45-H-p
Zemacoupis - 31-H-p
Zeminsky - 41-Ch-p
Zerbinos - 43-H-d

Zeriadki - 25-Su-p
Zertopoulis - 31-G-p
Zertos - 31-G-p
Zervas - 41-St-p
Ziarko - 35-H-d, 41-H-d
Zibolis - 43-H-p
Zielinski - 31-R-p, 43-R-p
Ziemba - 29-H-p, 41-H-p
Zienisz - 45-H-p
Zimmerman - 25-R-p
Zinis - 41-H-p
Zink - 39-H-p
Zirdzin - 31-Su-p
Zissis - 45-H-p
Ziter - 45-G-d
Zmaskie - 41-Ch-p
Zoes - 43-H-p
Zoller - 39-R-p
Zorbas - 45-St-d
Zorn - 37-M-p
Zozofsky - 43-H-p
Zullo - 37-H-d
Zwezila - 41-H-p
Zyla - 45-H-p
Zylak - 45-H-p

Other Heritage Books by the author:

Alton, New Hampshire Vital Records, 1890-1997

Barnstead, New Hampshire Vital Records, 1887-2000

Barrington, New Hampshire Vital Records

Dover, New Hampshire Death Records, 1887-1937

Gilmanton, New Hampshire Vital Records, 1887-2001

Marriage Records of Dover, New Hampshire, 1835-1909

Marriage Records of Dover, New Hampshire, 1910-1937

Milton, New Hampshire Vital Records, 1888-1999

Moultonborough, New Hampshire Vital Records

New Castle, New Hampshire Vital Records, 1891-1997

New Hampshire Name Changes, 1768-1923

New Hampshire Name Changes, 1923-1947

Ossipee, New Hampshire Vital Records, 1887-2001

Rochester, New Hampshire Death Records, 1887-1951

Vital Records of Durham, New Hampshire, 1887-2002

Vital Records of Effingham and Freedom, New Hampshire, 1888-2001

Vital Records of Farmington, New Hampshire, 1887-1938

Vital Records of New Durham and Middleton, New Hampshire, 1887-1998

Vital Records of North Berwick, Maine, 1892-2002

Vital Records of Tamworth and Albany, New Hampshire, 1887-2003

Vital Records of Wakefield, New Hampshire, 1887-1998

Wolfeboro, New Hampshire Vital Records, 1887-1999

www.ingramcontent.com/pod-product-compliance
Lightning Source LLC
Chambersburg PA
CBHW070939230426
43666CB00011B/2488